Co-operative Compliance and the OECD's International Compliance Assurance Programme

EUCOTAX Series on European Taxation

VOLUME 68

Series Editors

Introduction

EUCOTAX (European Universities Cooperating on Taxes) is a network of tax institutes currently consisting of eleven universities: WU (Vienna University of Economics and Business) in Austria, Katholieke Universiteit Leuven in Belgium, Corvinus University of Budapest, Hungary, Université Paris-I Panthéon-Sorbonne in France, Universität Osnabrück in Germany, Libera, Università Internazionale di Studi Sociali in Rome (and Università degli Studi di Bologna for the research part), in Italy, Fiscaal Instituut Tilburg at Tilburg University in the Netherlands, Universidad de Barcelona in Spain, Uppsala University in Sweden, Queen Mary and Westfield College at the University of London in the United Kingdom, and Georgetown University in Washington DC, United States of America. The network aims at initiating and coordinating both comparative education in taxation, through the organization of activities such as winter courses and guest lectures, and comparative research in the field, by means of joint research projects, international conferences and exchange of researchers between various countries.

Contents/Subjects

The EUCOTAX series covers a wide range of topics in European tax law. For example tax treaties, EC case law, tax planning, exchange of information and VAT. The series is well-known for its high-quality research and practical solutions.

Objective

The series aims to provide insights on new developments in European taxation.

Readership

Practitioners and academics dealing with European tax law.

Frequency of Publication

2-3 new volumes published each year.

The titles published in this series are listed at the end of this volume.

Co-operative Compliance and the OECD's International Compliance Assurance Programme

Edited by

Ronald Hein
Ronald Russo

Wolters Kluwer

Published by:
Kluwer Law International B.V.
PO Box 316
2400 AH Alphen aan den Rijn
The Netherlands
E-mail: international-sales@wolterskluwer.com
Website: lrus.wolterskluwer.com

Sold and distributed in North, Central and South America by:
Wolters Kluwer Legal & Regulatory U.S.
7201 McKinney Circle
Frederick, MD 21704
United States of America
Email: customer.service@wolterskluwer.com

Sold and distributed in all other countries by:
Air Business Subscriptions
Rockwood House
Haywards Heath
West Sussex
RH16 3DH
United Kingdom
Email: international-customerservice@wolterskluwer.com

ISBN 978-94-035-1951-7

e-Book: ISBN 978-94-035-1980-7
web-PDF: ISBN 978-94-035-1983-8

Editors

Ronald Hein is a researcher at Tilburg University, the Netherlands. Formerly, he was active as a tax specialist with the Dutch Internal Revenue for 13 years and with Dutch financial institution Rabobank for 19 years, latterly as global head of tax.

Ronald Russo (1963) obtained his Master's in 1986 from the University of Amsterdam and his doctorate from the University of Utrecht in 1992. He started working as a professional in the Netherlands in 1985, first as a tax inspector and later as a tax lawyer. Since 2006 he works mainly for Tilburg University where he is full professor of Tax Law. He is also of counsel Deloitte tax advisors and substitute judge.

Contributors

Achim Pross is the Head of the International Co-operation and Tax Administration division, within the OECD's Centre for Tax Policy and Administration. Prior to joining the OECD, he has worked in the tax department of a large U.S. law firm (Washington D.C., Paris and London), and as an assistant at Munich University's Research Centre for Foreign and International Tax and Financial Law. Mr. Pross is a lawyer and received his legal training at the University of Munich, the London School of Economics and Georgetown Law Centre, Washington D.C. He holds a Ph.D. (Summa cum laude) in international taxation and was the winner of the International Fiscal Association's Carroll B. Mitchell prize in 1997.

Allison Christians is the H. Heward Stikeman Chair in the Law of Taxation at the McGill University Faculty of Law. Her research and teaching focus on national and international tax law and policy issues, with emphasis on the relationship between taxation and economic development and on the role of government and non-government institutions and actors in the creation of tax policy norms.

Andreas Kowallik heads Deloitte GmbH's Tax Management Consulting practice in Germany, focused on tax processes, tax data, tax technology, and tax organization. He has more than twenty-three years of work experience serving international clients from different countries and industries on national and cross-border tax matters. Andreas Kowallik holds a Master of Business Administration and a Ph.D. in International Taxation. He is a German Certified Tax Advisor, a regular lecturer at external conferences and regularly publishes on German taxation both in domestic and international tax journals and publications.

Benedicte Brøgger is a full professor at BI Norwegian Business School. Her present research is on socio-cultural conditions for sustainable economic growth. She teaches cross-cultural management and tutors business interns. In her spare time, she works with several social enterprises.

Celeste M. Black is an Associate Professor at the University of Sydney Law School, Australia, where she teaches and researches in Taxation and Commercial Law, with particular emphasis on tax administration and international tax. She is a member of the Parsons Centre of Commercial, Corporate and Taxation Law, the International Fiscal Association (Australia branch) and the Law Council of Australia. Her Ph.D. considered the domestic and international tax implication of carbon trading transactions.

Dennis de Widt is a Lecturer in Accounting & Finance (Assistant Professor) at Cardiff Business School, U.K., and an Associate Research Fellow with the Tax Administration Research Centre at the University of Exeter Business School, U.K.. His main research interests include tax administration, intergovernmental and local government finances and public sector accounting. Dennis' recent publications have appeared in the *British Tax Review*, *Government Information Quarterly*, *Regional Studies*, and *Public Administration*.

Francesco Cannas is a post-doctoral researcher at the University of Hasselt and Adjunct Professor (professore a contratto) of Tax Law at the University of East Piedmont. He is a qualified Italian lawyer and holds an LL.M. and a Ph.D. in taxation, both awarded by the Vienna University of Economics and Business (WU).

Freek Braken is a Tax Policy Advisor at the Dutch Ministry of Finance. He obtained a Master's in Tax Law from Leiden University. Subsequently, he worked as a tax lawyer at a major Dutch law firm, where he specialized in Dutch and international tax law with a focus on dispute resolution (MAP and arbitration). Freek has published several articles in (international) tax literature.

George Clarke is a partner at Baker McKenzie in Washington, DC and chair of the Firm's North American Tax Dispute Resolution Group. His practice focuses on tax litigation for civil and criminal tax matters, and resolution of governmental investigations. He routinely advises and represents multinational corporations, financial institutions, and high-net-worth individuals on complex international and federal tax matters. He also defends clients in non-tax federal criminal procedures, including allegations of misconduct under the Foreign Corrupt Practices Act and other criminal laws of the United States (U.S.).

Hans Rijsbergen works with the Netherlands Tax and Customs Administration (NTCA)/ Large Business as strategy advisor. He led the NTCA ICAP- team in the first pilot and is member of the ICAP Steering Group. He also led the project for further development of Horizontal Monitoring (Co-operative Compliance) in the Netherlands.

Joy Williamson is a partner at Baker McKenzie in Dallas, TX. Her practice focuses on federal tax controversies, with a significant emphasis on transfer pricing, subpart F, and other international tax issues. She regularly assists clients in the resolution of tax issues through administrative audits and appeals, competent authority processes, and, if necessary, litigation.

J. Carlos Pedrosa López is Assistant Professor of Tax Law at University of Valencia (Spain). He studied his Ph.D. in Law, specialized in International Taxation, at University Carlos III of Madrid (Spain). He holds a Master's in Tax Law and Taxation and a double Bachelor Degree in Law and Economics from the University of Valencia. He is the author of monographs on topics of international tax law, has written chapters of books in different languages and has published scientific articles in prestigious Spanish and foreign journals. He has carried out research stays in European and American Universities and he is a member of the scientific committee of several research projects.

Kiran Aziz is a lawyer with background from law firm, academic, and asset management. She has broad experience from International tax and human rights. She has been a part of the European Union Fairtax project on taxation and researched on responsible tax practices from an investment point of view. In addition, she is a board member of Norwegian Refugee Council and International Commission of Jurists.

Lynne Oats is Professor of Taxation and Accounting and Deputy Director of the Tax Administration Research Centre at the University of Exeter Business School, U.K. Lynne is Managing Editor of the Journal of Tax Administration, Subject Editor (Accounting) of British Tax Review, and Associate Editor of Accounting Forum and has published widely on both contemporary and historical tax issues. She is co-author of Taxation Policy and Practice and Principles of International Taxation and editor of Taxation: A Fieldwork Research Handbook.

Małgorzata Sęk holds a Ph.D. in law (*doktor nauk prawnych*) with specialization in tax law (2016, University of Lodz, Poland) and works as an adjunct (adiunkt) at the Tax Law Department of the Faculty of Law and Administration of the University of Lodz and as a Senior Specialist at the Centre of Tax Documentation and Studies in Lodz; she conducts research and teaching focused on VAT, protection of taxpayer's rights and taxation of new business models (including digital ones).

Mario Grandinetti is a Researcher and Assistant Professor of Tax Law at the University of Turin, and habilitated as an Associate Professorship by the National Scientific Committee. He holds a Ph.D. in Public and European Tax Law from the University of Bergamo (Italy). Visiting researcher at institutions such as the Max Planck Institute in Intellectual Property and Tax Law of Munich (Germany) and the University of Valencia (Spain). He was awarded a scholarship by the Giovanni Goria Foundation. His areas of expertise are domestic company taxation (accounting and taxation), European and International Taxation, value-added tax (VAT) and the Taxation of Groups. As a book editor, he frequently publishes in Italian and International journals.

Mário H. Martini is a Ph.D. candidate at the Fiscal Institute Tilburg, Tilburg University. Qualified lawyer and accountant in Brazil, he has worked for over seven years leading the in-house international tax planning and international tax advisory activities of Brazilian multinational corporations. He holds an M.Sc in Finance, an LL.M in

International and European Tax Law, an MBA in Brazilian Tax Management, a Master's in International Business Law and a degree in Brazilian Tax Law.

Mark Johnson is Co-Head of the Tax Certainty Unit at the Organisation for Economic Co-operation and Development (OECD) Centre for Tax Policy & Administration, with responsibility for the OECD's work on country-by-country reporting and tax dispute prevention, including ICAP. Mark has twenty-five years of experience in corporate and international tax, mainly from working in large advisory firms, in financial institutions and in the HM Revenue & Customs. Since 2011 Mark has been a member of the OECD Secretariat, during which time he has led work on combating tax and financial crime, addressing harmful tax practices and countering aggressive tax planning.

Simon Hofstätter works with the Austrian Tax Administration since 2010. He is currently a tax auditor in the auditing office for large-scale enterprises. He is involved in Austrian Co-operative Compliance initiative as well as in the International Compliance Assurance Programme (ICAP 2.0) project.

Taco Wiertsema has eleven years of experience advising clients on Dutch and Luxembourg tax law as well as transfer pricing. Before joining Atlas Tax Lawyers in April 2020, Taco worked at the offices of Dutch law firm Loyens & Loeff in Rotterdam and Luxembourg and for KPMG Meijburg & Co in Amstelveen. Taco advises companies on various transfer pricing matters, including transfer pricing documentation, model optimization, dispute resolution and mutual agreement procedures.

Tarcísio Diniz Magalhães is a postdoctoral researcher at McGill University Faculty of Law, where he is involved in teaching international taxation and tax policy and researching on tax law, digitalization, and sustainability. He is a former postdoctoral research fellow at IBFD and a member of the Permanent Commission on Review and Simplification of Tax Legislation, Brazil.

Wouter de Ruiter is a member of the CFO Services team at MHP Management and IT Consulting. He has worked as a tax and finance adviser in consulting firms in the Netherlands, United Kingdom (U.K.) and Germany. His special areas of expertise are the optimization and automation of (tax relevant) processes, the development of organizational structures and relevant IT, tax and finance-related topics. Wouter has Bachelors' degrees in Tax Economics and Business Administration as well as a Master's in Accounting & Finance from the Erasmus University Rotterdam.

Yasuyuki Kawabata is Professor of Law, at the Graduate School of International Social Sciences, Yokohama National University. LL.B. (1982), Master of Laws (1985), Master of Commerce (1987). Adjunct Lecturer, Japan National Tax College. Invited Lecturer (Adjunct), Utrecht University School of Law. Invited Lecturer, Malaysian National Tax Academy. Supervisor of Japanese Translation version of condensed version of the OECD Model Tax Convention on Income and on Capital (2010).

Summary of Contents

Table of Contents

Preface

On November 6, 2019, we had the pleasure of hosting a congress at Tilburg University, sponsored by the Deloitte Tax Assurance Fund, around the theme of "Co-operative Compliance and ICAP around the globe". At the conference, tax academics and professionals from many countries related the state of affairs on this theme in their respective jurisdictions. The objectives of the congress were to bring the international knowledge on the subject together, to learn from each other's experience with all the various systems and to take the development of this particular field of taxation one-step further. In view of the many interesting discussions and positive reactions, we are hopeful of having succeeded in these ambitions.

To further the objectives, we asked all contributors to the congress to produce an analytic paper on their respective jurisdictions and this book is the result of their efforts. We think the various chapters paint an inclusive and up-to-date picture and we are proud to be able to present it to you. The book starts with a general introduction on the subject, followed by two perspectives on ICAP: one from the OECD and one from a participating tax administration. These are followed by the country reports in alphabetical order and a chapter on the main issue in international tax disputes, which is transfer pricing. The final chapter briefly reviews the collected contributions and contains some concluding remarks.

We very much enjoyed editing this book and in the process learned a great deal on the congress subject. It has certainly given us many fresh ideas and perspectives and we hope it will do the same for you.

Ronald Russo
Ronald Hein
Tilburg, February 2020

CHAPTER 1

Introduction: An Investigation of Co-operative Compliance Regimes and the ICAP

Mário H. Martini

§1.01 OBJECTIVES OF THE BOOK AND METHODOLOGICAL CONSIDERATIONS

This book investigates the latest developments regarding Co-operative Compliance and the International Compliance Assurance Programme (ICAP) in twelve selected countries,[1] and which connections between Co-operative Compliance and the ICAP can be identified in these countries.

While there are of course many differences between countries, such as differences in culture, legal tradition, economic development, political environment, the primary objective of this book was to determine which similar pillars and procedures were adopted in the Co-operative Compliance approaches investigated. Some of the specific elements reviewed were the following:

- work in the present;
- real-time consultation procedures;
- appeal procedures within the program;
- the possibility to "agree to disagree" and to continue Co-operative Compliance in cases of litigation;
- the regulatory framework of the program (whether it is provided in tax regulations, guidelines or tax administrations' practices);
- whether the participation in the program is mandatory or voluntary;

1. Australia, Austria, Canada, Germany, Italy, Japan, Netherlands, Norway, Poland, Spain, the U.K. and the U.S.

- whether a formal instrument must be executed between the parties;
- the obligation to have a tax control framework (TCF) in place;
- risk assessment of taxpayers;
- criteria to enter the program;
- risk management strategies within tax authorities;
- whether the taxpayer must "clear its past" before it can join the program;
- the range of taxes covered by the program;
- whether the tax audit plan of the tax administration is shared with the taxpayers.

By looking at these specific elements, and whether they were inserted in the Co-operative Compliance approaches of the selected countries, two research questions were formulated:

(1) Which are the specific mechanisms adopted in the Co-operative Compliance approaches of the selected jurisdictions?
(2) Can connections between Co-operative Compliance and the ICAP be identified?

The jurisdictions selected were the eight originally party to the ICAP,[2] i.e., Australia, Canada, Italy, Japan, the Netherlands, Spain, the United Kingdom (U.K.) and the United States (U.S.). In addition, of the eleven new jurisdictions that joined the ICAP 2.0[3] as of March 26, 2019, four were included in the review, i.e., Austria, Germany, Norway, Poland. Of the twelve jurisdictions thus selected, Germany and Poland did not have any Co-operative Compliance approach implemented when they joined the ICAP 2.0. Canada had a risk assessment approach implemented when it joined the ICAP.[4] And all other nine jurisdictions (Australia, Italy, Japan, the Netherlands, Spain, the U.K. and the U.S., at the time of the ICAP; Austria and Norway at the time of the ICAP 2.0) had some sort of Co-operative Compliance approach implemented when they joined.[5]

Country reporters were selected among reputable tax professionals and tax academics who had previous experience with Co-operative Compliance and/or with ICAP. First, they were asked to describe the current status of Co-operative Compliance and the ICAP in their jurisdictions in the form of a country report. Second, to present

2. OECD/FTA (2018). *International Compliance Assurance Programme Pilot Handbook.* Paris: OECD Publishing (Mar. 4, 2019), https://www.oecd.org/tax/forum-on-tax-administration/publications-and-products/international-compliance-assurance-programme-pilot-handbook.pdf.
3. OECD/FTA (2019). *International Compliance Assurance Programme Pilot Handbook 2.0.* Paris: OECD Publishing (Apr. 3, 2019), http://www.oecd.org/tax/forum-on-tax-administration/publications-and-products/international-compliance-assurance-programme-pilot-handbook-2.0.pdf.
4. OECD (2013). *Co-operative Compliance: A Framework—From Enhanced Relationship to Co-operative Compliance.* Paris: OECD Publishing (Mar. 5, 2019), doi:https://dx.doi.org/10.1787/9789264200852-en, pp. 22-23.
5. OECD (2019). *Tax Administration 2019: Comparative Information on OECD and Other Advanced and Emerging Economies.* Paris: OECD Publishing (Nov. 3, 2019), doi:https://doi.org/10.1787/74d162b6-en, Annex A, Table A.150.

their findings in a Conference organized by the Fiscal Institute Tilburg, held on November 6, 2019 at Tilburg University. During the Conference, a representative from the Organisation for Economic Co-operation and Development (OECD) exposed about the lessons learned in the ICAP and the respective improvements implemented in the ICAP 2.0. A representative from the Dutch Tax Administration shared some practical experiences they had with the ICAP and the challenges of acting as a lead country in the program. Further practical experiences were shared by a big four transfer pricing specialist, who discussed the current relevance of double taxation resulting from transfer pricing adjustments and the limitations of the ICAP to solve this problem conclusively. Third, the reporters were asked to incorporate the discussions and inputs from the Conference in their final country reports.

Although the reporters were free to describe their countries' experiences in their own words, they were all asked to address the same questions, structured in the form of a questionnaire (Annex A), so that all the reports would essentially cover the same features of their domestic relationship approaches and the ICAP experiences. The questionnaire contained four groups of questions. In the first group, questions one and two aimed at assessing the tax compliance and tax policy environment in the selected countries. The second group is comprised of questions three and five, adapted from the questions of the OECD 2013 publication[6] but not restricted to formally structured Co-operative Compliance programmes, including any "programs that regulate the relationship between companies and tax authorities." The third group, comprised of question four, investigated the specific elements and mechanisms related with Co-operative Compliance existing in each country. The fourth group, which corresponds to question six, questioned about possible connections between existing national Co-operative Compliance programmes and the ICAP.

§1.02 DELIMITATION OF THE STUDY

Because Co-operative Compliance is a relatively new experience, which started in only a few countries in mid-2000s,[7] it still lacks a uniform understanding of its definition,[8] and a consensus[9] on which specific elements and mechanisms make up Co-operative

6. OECD (2013), *supra* n. 4, pp. 31-35.
7. *Id.*, pp. 21-24.
8. Note that the OECD, in publications from 2008 and 2013, gave its vision on what should be general pillars of Co-operative Compliance, and made important contributions to its promotion and adoption across the world but, because of its political background, the OECD is unable to prescribe specific elements and mechanisms which should be expected from Co-operative Compliance. *See* OECD (2013), *supra* n. 4, p. 3, where the OECD states that "strict parameters and guidance would not be compatible with different cultures of its members."
9. Russo, R. & Martini, M.H. (2019). The International Compliance Assurance Programme Reviewed: The Future of Cooperative Tax Compliance? *Bulletin for International Taxation*, IBFD, 452-463.: "In the 2013 OECD report, in which the members of the Large Business Network responded to a survey representing 21 countries, it was noted that Austria, Canada, Denmark, South Africa and Sweden were jurisdictions in which cooperative compliance regimes were in place in 2012. The 2017 OECD report, in which the survey was replied to by 55 tax administrations, found different conclusions regarding these same countries. It affirmed that none of them had a cooperative compliance programme in place neither in 2014 nor in 2015, and that Austria,

Compliance. At the same time, Co-operative Compliance is necessarily country-specific, which by definition makes it susceptible to cultural, political and economic influences.

For the purposes of the present study, the pillars put forward by the OECD in its 2008[10] and 2013[11] publications[12] were taken as the paradigm to establish whether a given country has truly adopted Co-operative Compliance. Beside these pillars other elements were also observed, such as the abovementioned "work-in-the-present" approach; real-time consultation procedures; possibility to "agree to disagree," i.e., continued Co-operative Compliance even in cases of litigation.

§1.03 THEORETICAL BACKGROUND: FROM AUTHORITY TO CO-OPERATION

During the past decades, theoretical and empirical researches have been conducted to determine what motivates taxpayers to pay taxes. By identifying these factors, it was expected that more effective tax systems could be created.

Tax studies which followed Becker's theory of crime[13] put forward the idea that taxpayers, as utility maximizers, always make a cost-benefit analysis to decide whether or not to pay taxes. Therefore, as demonstrated by Allingham & Sandmo[14] and Srinivasan,[15] the weaker the deterrence mechanisms (audit probability and penalty rate), or the higher the tax rates, the lower the degree of tax compliance is expected to be. Under these assumptions, tax systems will tend to adopt strict and punitive regulations. Tax administrations should make their power noticed and as such, in the relationship with taxpayers, they should adopt a role based on authority and control.

However, a robust body of literature, produced mainly as of the late 1980s, brought up assorted theoretical arguments and empirical evidence demonstrating that there are many other factors besides a mere cost-benefit (or risk-reward) analysis which influence taxpayers' decisions on whether or not to pay taxes.

Denmark and Sweden were only implementing programmes in 2014-2015. Unless those countries abandoned their cooperative compliance programmes between 2012 and 2014-2015, the most likely explanation for the conflicting replies is the lack of a common understanding of a definition of cooperative compliance."

10. OECD (2008). *Study into the Role of Tax Intermediaries*. Paris: OECD Publishing (Mar. 20, 2019), http://www.oecd.org/tax/administration/39882938.pdf.
11. OECD (2013), *supra* n. 4.
12. The OECD, in its 2008 and 2013 publications on Co-operative Compliance, puts forward the following pillars for tax administrations: commercial awareness, impartiality, proportionality, openness through disclosure and transparency, and responsiveness, and the implementations of risk assessment and internal governance mechanisms within the tax administrations' bodies. For taxpayers, it proposes disclosure and transparency, and the implementation of effective tax control framework.
13. Becker, G. S. (1968). Crime and Punishment: An Economic Approach. *Journal of Political Economy*, 72(2), 169-217. (Nov. 20, 2019), doi:https://doi.org/10.1086/259394.
14. Allingham, M. G., & Sandmo, A. (1972). Income Tax Evasion: A Theoretical Analysis. *Journal of Public Economics*, 1(3-4), 323-338.
15. Srinivasan, T. N. (1973). Tax Evasion: A Model. *Journal of Public Economics*, 2(4), 339-346.

To begin with, Smith & Kinsey[16] noted that some non-compliance is actually unintentional, and therefore unlikely to be affected by deterrence mechanisms. Alm, McClelland & Schulze[17] found empirical evidence demonstrating that, different from what common sense might suggests, most individuals actually pay taxes even when it is unlikely that they will be caught and penalized. Cowell & Gordon,[18] Levi[19] and Moore[20] suggested that taxpayers are more willing to pay taxes when they perceive that the Government will provide benefits corresponding to the taxes paid (fiscal exchange theory). Frey[21,22] proposed the existence of intrinsic motivations to pay taxes, known as tax morale. According to Snavely,[23] tax behavior is influenced by the social norms of the group of which the taxpayers are part, i.e., individuals adopt behaviors corresponding with how they believe others from their group will behave (social influence theory). Frey & Feld[24] proposed a psychological contract theory, according to which individuals pay taxes in proportion to their ability to participate in the government: the more directly they participate, the more taxes they are prepared to pay. Wenzel[25] suggested that taxpayers are also influenced by factors such as (their own) reputation, justice and fairness. McKerchar & Evans[26] identified the main motivation to pay taxes in the ideas of justice and equitable treatment (equity theory).

The slippery-slope theory, proposed by Kirchler, Hoelzl & Wahl,[27] integrated the intrinsic and extrinsic motivators to pay taxes. The extrinsic motivator is the individuals' perception of the authority's power (potential to detect and punish tax evasion). The intrinsic motivator derives from the trust in authorities, belief in authorities'

16. Smith, K. W., & Kinsey, K. A. (1987). Understanding Taxpaying Behavior: A Conceptual Framework with Implications for Research. *Law & Society Review*, 639-663. (Nov. 20, 2019), https://www.jstor.org/stable/3053599.
17. Aim, J., McClelland, G. H., & Schulze, W. D. (1992). Why Do People Pay Taxes?. *Journal of Public Economics*, 48(1), 21-38. doi:10.1016/0047-2727(92)90040-M.
18. Cowell, F. A., & Gordon, J. P. (1988). Unwillingness to Pay: Tax Evasion and Public Good Provision. *Journal of Public Economics*, 36(3), 305-321. (Nov. 20, 2019), doi:https://doi.org/10.1016/0047-2727(88)90013-8.
19. Levi, M. (1988). *Of Rule and Revenue*. University of California Press.
20. Moore, M. (2004). Revenues, State Formation, and the Quality of Governance in Developing Countries. *International Political Science Review*, 25(3), 297-319. (Nov. 20, 2019) doi:https://doi.org/10.1177/0192512104043018.
21. Frey, B. S. (1994). How Intrinsic Motivation Is Crowded Out and In. *Rationality and Society*, 6(3), 334-352.
22. Frey, B. S. (1997). *Not Just for the Money: An Economic Theory of Personal Motivation*. Edward Elgar Publishing.
23. Snavely, K. (1990). Governmental Policies to Reduce Tax Evasion: Coerced Behavior Versus Services and Values Development. *Policy Sciences*, 23, 57-72. (Nov. 20, 2019), doi:https://doi.org/10.1007/BF00136992.
24. Frey, B. S., & Feld, L. P. (2002). *Deterrence and Morale in Taxation: An Empirical Analysis*. CESifo Working Paper Series No. 760. (Nov. 20, 2019), https://ssrn.com/abstract=341380.
25. Wenzel, M. (2002). The Impact of Outcome Orientation and Justice Concerns on Tax Compliance: The Role of Taxpayers' Identity. *Journal of Applied Psychology*, 87(4). (Nov. 20, 2019), doi:10.1037/0021-9010.87.4.629.
26. McKerchar, M., & Evans, C. (2009). Sustaining Growth in Developing Economies Through Improved Taxpayer Compliance: Challenges for Policy Makers and Revenue Authorities. *eJournal of Tax Research*, 7(2), 171-201.
27. Kirchler, E., Hoelzl, E., & Wahl, I. (2008). Enforced Versus Voluntary Tax Compliance: The "Slippery Slope" Framework. *Journal of Economic Psychology*, 29(2), 210-225, (Nov. 20, 2019), doi:10.1016/j.joep.2007.05.004.

benevolence, services and engagement. The main point is that taxpayer's perception of the power of the tax authorities and taxpayer's trust in the tax authorities can achieve the same level of tax compliance, but there is an optimal equilibrium to be achieved between power and trust.

It must be noted that significant differences[28] exist between individual and corporate taxpayers, meaning caution is required when applying the conclusions reached for individuals to corporations. A bridge still needs to be built to connect individuals' motivators to pay taxes with corporates' motivators. A suggestion, adopted by the OECD,[29] was to use "tax certainty" for corporates in the place of "tax morale," which is used for individuals.

These theoretical and empirical instances demonstrate that there are situations where deterrence mechanisms (enforcement and control) are not the reason, or not the main reason, why taxpayers pay taxes. It appears that a significant portion of taxpayers will simply pay their taxes[30] irrespective of the existence of power and authority.

By realizing that authority is not the only factor which influences tax compliant behaviors, tax administrations started to conceive new policies and objectives in the design of tax systems. It became clear that tax administrations' limited resources would be more efficiently used if cooperative taxpayers were treated differently from uncooperative and even fraudulent ones. Why should tax administrations devote the same amount of resource to such different groups of taxpayers? Tax reviews, audits and inspections should logically be more intense with regard to taxpayers which pose higher risks of non-compliance. Conversely, taxpayers who have a willingness to comply with tax regulations may not even need to be audited or inspected at all.

§1.04 CO-OPERATIVE COMPLIANCE EVOLUTION AND THE ARRIVAL OF THE ICAP

Recent developments, aligned with the theoretical and empirical background discussed above, indicate that the "cops and robbers" approach, a model which has been

---

28. To name some examples of these differences: the tax calculation of corporate taxpayers is a much more complex process; corporate taxpayers count with the services of very specialized tax intermediaries; corporations usually operate in a much wider geographical reach, creating tax arbitrage opportunities not commonly available to individuals.
29. OECD (2019). *Tax Morale: What Drives People and Businesses to Pay Tax?*. Paris: OECD Publishing (Sep. 27, 2019), https://www.oecd-ilibrary.org/sites/f3d8ea10-en/index.html?itemId=/content/publication/f3d8ea10-en&mimeType=text/html, p. 37: "There is relatively little research and data on business tax morale currently available ... . A recent OECD tax certainty survey of MNEs ... provides a useful proxy to open the debate on business tax morale in developing countries. Simply put, when MNE's perceive low tax certainty they may be less likely to participate actively or positively in the tax system (or at least the parts that are most uncertain). As tax certainty is only a proxy of tax morale, it presents some limitations, thus while the conclusions derived from the analysis point to some policy implications, further research is needed."
30. Alm, McClelland & Schulze (1992), *supra* n. 16.
    The Internal Revenue Service reported in 2019 that, from 2011 to 2013, voluntary compliance in the U.S. was higher than 80%. (Oct. 4, 2019), https://www.irs.gov/pub/irs-pdf/p1415.pdf, p. 9.

governing the interactions between taxpayers and tax administrations for many years, is becoming obsolete. Events such as the increased complexity of tax regulations,[31] higher tax uncertainties,[32] increased transparency,[33] shrinking budgets of tax administrations,[34] civil society and non-governmental organisation's scrutiny over multinational enterprise's (MNE's) tax affairs, are turning the "cops and robbers" approach too inefficient and unattractive both for taxpayers and for tax administrations.

From the taxpayers' standpoint, the "cops and robbers" approach leads to high administrative and tax consulting costs while, at the same time, tax positions remain very uncertain. On the other side, due to the evolving complexity and internationalization of commercial relations,[35] tax administrations need an ever-increasing amount of resources to catch up with the tax affairs of big multinational conglomerates acting on a global scale.

The early 2000s saw a reevaluation of the traditional way that taxpayers and tax administrations have been interacting with each other, consolidating the ideas of more co-operation-based interaction. The first countries to adopt relationship approaches based on trust, collaboration and co-operation, using deterrence as a tool of last resort only, were Australia (2001), South Africa (2004), Ireland (2005), the Netherlands (2005), the U.S. (2005) and the U.K. (2006).[36]

In 2008, the OECD analyzed the experiences of three of these countries[37] and proposed the development of a:

> more collaborative, trust-based relationship ... between revenue bodies and large corporate taxpayers who abide by the law and go beyond statutory obligations to work together co-operatively.[38]

That was called the "enhanced relationship," an approach based on the experiences of Ireland, the Netherlands and the U.S., in which tax administrations should behave with "commercial awareness, impartiality, proportionality, openness through disclosure and transparency, and responsiveness," while the taxpayers should behave by "providing disclosure and transparency." From those behaviors, it was expected that a tax environment with trust and co-operation would be created.[39] In 2013, the

31. The World Bank, Doing Business project (2018). Time to prepare and pay taxes (hours). The World Bank Group. (Apr. 4, 2019), https://data.worldbank.org/indicator/IC.TAX.DURS.
32. IMF & OECD (2019). *Progress Report on Tax Certainty: IMF/OECD Report for the G20 Finance Ministers and Central Bank Governors*. Paris: OECD Publishing (Nov. 20, 2019), http://www.oecd.org/tax/tax-policy/g20-report-on-tax-certainty.htm.
33. McKinsey & Company: McKinsey Global Institute (2016). *Digital Globalization: The New Era of Global Flows*. (May, 27, 2019), https://www.mckinsey.com/~/media/McKinsey/Business%20Functions/McKinsey%20Digital/Our%20Insights/Digital%20globalization%20The%20new%20era%20of%20global%20flows/MGI-Digital-globalization-Full-report.ashx.
34. OECD/FTA (2012). *Working Smarter in Structuring the Administration, in Compliance, and Through Legislation*. Paris: OECD Publishing, p. 7. OECD (2019), *supra* n. 5, p. 121.
35. McKinsey & Company (2016), supra n. 32.
36. OECD (2013), *supra* n. 4, pp. 21-24.
37. Ireland, the Netherlands and the USA.
38. OECD (2008), *supra* n. 10, p. 39.
39. *Id.*, pp. 40; 77-86.

OECD replaced the terminology "enhanced relationship" by "Co-operative Compliance."[40] On the same occasion, the OECD stressed the necessity for taxpayers to implement an effective TCF,[41] and the need for tax administrations to put in place risk assessment and internal governance mechanisms.

Especially after the 2013 OECD publication,[42] the term "Co-operative Compliance" has been widely adopted to refer to any approach which promotes a relationship between taxpayers and tax administrations based on trust, collaboration and co-operation. But because there is not yet a uniform understanding of Co-operative Compliance definition, the pillars and procedures adopted by each country may vary considerably.

The number of countries adopting Co-operative Compliance, which was at least six in 2008[43] and seventeen in 2012,[44] went up to eighteen in 2015[45] and twenty-two in 2017.[46] There were at least eight additional countries implementing Co-operative Compliance in 2017, which could result in around thirty countries with Co-operative Compliance implemented after 2017.

In 2018, a group of eight OECD countries[47] launched the ICAP,[48] a multilateral risk assessment program which puts the pillars of Co-Operative Compliance on an international level.[49] A second pilot[50] followed in 2019 with eleven additional countries.[51]

The ICAP is an international and multilateral risk assessment and assurance program, where taxpayers have the opportunity to present and discuss with multiple tax administrations any risks with an international taxation connection. Its drivers are: (i) better and more standardized information for transfer pricing risk assessment; (ii) a global mutual agreement procedure (MAP) review; (iii) well-established MNE compliance frameworks; (iv) advances in international collaboration; (v) providing a pathway to improved tax certainty for low or medium risk MNE groups; and (vi) capitalizing on the multilateral context to provide greater certainty for MNEs and tax administrations.[52]

---

40. OECD (2013), *supra* n. 4, pp. 16-17.
41. OECD (2016). *Co-operative Tax Compliance: Building Better Tax Control Frameworks.*
42. *Id.*
43. *Id.*, p. 21.
44. *Id.*, pp. 22-24.
45. OECD (2017). *Tax Administration 2017: Comparative Information on OECD and Other Advanced and Emerging Economies.* Paris: OECD Publishing (Jun. 15, 2019), https://read.oecd-ilibrary.org/taxation/tax-administration-2017_tax_admin-2017-en#page148, p. 148.
46. OECD (2019), *supra* n. 5, p. 54.
47. Australia, Canada, Italy, Japan, the Netherlands, Spain, the U.K. and the U.S.
48. OECD/FTA (2018), *supra* n. 2.
49. OECD (2013), *supra* n. 4, p. 88: "Of equal importance is to keep attention focused on opportunities for multilateral co-operative compliance; in an increasingly globalised world in which more countries are adopting co-operative compliance strategies. Increasing cross border transparency, disclosure and early certainty are of vital importance to both revenue bodies and MNEs."
50. OECD/FTA (2019), *supra* n. 3.
51. Austria, Belgium, Denmark, Finland, France, Germany, Ireland, Luxembourg, Norway, Poland and Russia.
52. OECD/FTA (2019), *supra* n. 3, p. 8.

§1.05 CONTROVERSIAL TOPICS CONCERNING CO-OPERATIVE COMPLIANCE

There are some topics of special interest in the current debate about Co-operative Compliance and the ICAP. Why is Co-operative Compliance, in many countries, capable of providing certainty while the ICAP only provides assurance? Should the Co-operative Compliance framework and/or ICAP rely on a psychological or on a regulatory approach? Is Co-operative Compliance and the ICAP a privilege to only a few MNEs? In the current era, with their strong public focus on transparency, how transparent are tax administrations about the conditions, results and facts concerning the Co-operative Compliance and the ICAP?

These questions are presented here not to be answered conclusively but to call the reader's attention to these discussions and to the way they have been addressed in the countries analyzed in the next chapters of the book.

[A] Tax Assurance Versus Tax Certainty

There are two important differences between Co-operative Compliance and the ICAP, which determine whether tax administrations can grant tax certainty or tax assurance.

First, Co-operative Compliance discusses facts and circumstances in the present, sometimes even before they happen, while the ICAP generally looks at facts and circumstances which have already taken place.[53] In Co-operative Compliance, taxpayers are expected to bring to the attention of tax administrations, before tax returns are filed, any transactions that create new risks. As a result, in the case of Co-operative Compliance, tax administrations may provide tax certainty on the analysis of concrete facts and transactions.

As a second difference, because in essence the ICAP is a risk assessment program, its focus should be mainly on the internal controls. More precisely, it zooms in on the TCF of MNEs, with the intention to assure that the output of information is, and will continue to be, free from material misstatements. MNEs participating in the ICAP must resort to tools outside the program, such as advanced pricing agreements, tax rulings, joint audits, MAPs and arbitration, if they want to be granted tax certainty.[54] In Co-operative Compliance, by contrast, there is the possibility to discuss concrete facts and transactions with tax administrations even before they have occurred.

Only the ICAP provides a multilateral channel for simultaneous discussions with up to nineteen tax administrations.[55] That is a unique opportunity for MNEs, which by themselves should already make the ICAP worth their while.

53. One of the suitability criteria to join the ICAP is that the MNE have filed Country by Country (CbC) reporting for the years covered by the program: OECD/FTA (2019), *supra* n. 3, p. 15: "... whether CbC reports are available for fiscal years commencing on or after 1 January 2016."
54. OECD/FTA (2018), *supra* n. 2, p. 7; OECD/FTA (2019), *supra* n. 3, p. 8.
55. OECD/FTA (2019), *supra* n. 3, p. 16: "No limit has been set on the number of covered tax administrations in a particular ICAP risk assessment, and this will be considered by the lead tax

[B] Co-operative Compliance: Regulatory Framework Approaches

Regulating Co-operative Compliance using a too formal approach (hard law-oriented regulation) can induce a "check the box" behavior, where taxpayers would only do the minimum to comply with the regulation requirements,[56] which would contradict the aims of Co-operative Compliance.[57]

A soft law approach, in turn, seems to better support the intrinsic motivators of tax compliance, as taxpayers will not feel compelled to co-operate merely to avoid sanctions that could be imposed by tax administrations.[58]

In practice, the optimal solution in any given jurisdiction seems to depend on culture and national legal traditions.

[C] The Principle of Equality Before the Law in Relation with Co-operative Compliance and the ICAP

The OECD 2008 envisaged that "early disclosure and resolution" of tax issues, provided by Co-operative Compliance, would result in at least two tangible benefits for taxpayers: advance certainty and reduced compliance costs.[59] Any program, or relationship approach, that does not adopt "objective and rational"[60] criteria to choose which taxpayers can access these benefits, will likely be in breach of the equality principle.

As such, at least two considerations must be made regarding Co-operative Compliance in relation with the principle of equality before the law. First, it should be verified who, in abstract, can access Co-operative Compliance in a given jurisdiction,

---

administration and MNE on a case-by-case basis. Experience from the first ICAP pilot suggests that a multilateral risk assessment including between four and eight covered tax administrations is likely to be most effective."

56. That is the case, for example, with the discussions in the Netherlands on whether the TCF should be described in legislation. *See* R. Russo, *Risk Management, Internal Control and Cooperative Compliance in Taxation*, in *The Future of Risk Management*, Volume I: Perspectives on Law, Healthcare, and the Environment pp. 329-350. (P. De Vincentiis, F. Culasso & S.A. Cerrato eds., Palgrave Macmillan 2019), who states that: "The first problem is that all companies are different and the details of a TCF are entity specific. Further more concrete guidance could lead to 'tick the box' behaviour rather than true control."
57. *See* for example the obligation assumed by taxpayers to disclose information beyond the statutory obligations. OECD (2008), *supra* n. 10, p. 41: "Disclosure goes beyond information taxpayers are statutorily obliged to provide. It should include any information necessary for the revenue body to undertake a fully informed risk assessment."
58. It seems that even friendly actions from tax administrations, in an attempt to compel taxpayers to act in a certain way, can result in decreased tax compliance. *See* Gangl, K., Torgler, B., Kirchler, E., & Hofmann, E. (2014). Effects of Supervision on Tax Compliance: Evidence from a Field Experiment in Austria. *Economics Letters*, 123(3), 378-382. (Nov. 20, 2019) doi:https://doi.org/10.1016/j.econlet.2014.03.027, p. 380: "The reported results indicate that supervision can backfire. Rather than increasing tax compliance, even a friendly version of deterrence reduces tax compliance. Thus, supervision seems to crowd out the intrinsic motivation of tax compliance."
59. OECD (2008), *supra* n. 10, p. 41: "... we believe in the longer term there will be a noticeable financial advantage for taxpayers through reduced compliance costs. If revenue bodies are able to succeed in directing more of their resources into high-risk issues and high-risk behaviour by taxpayers, there will be a long-term gain for lower-risk taxpayers."
60. OECD (2013), *supra* n. 4, p. 45.

i.e., the criteria to be accepted to Co-operative Compliance. Is it available only to MNEs? Or is it available only to companies that have implemented a TCF? That makes a significant difference, as in the first scenario the criterion is the size of the company (net income, total assets or any other financial measure), allowing situations where low-risk Small and Medium Enterprises operating in multiple countries would be excluded, while high-risk MNEs could be accepted into Co-operative Compliance. In the second scenario, the criterion is the existence of a TCF, i.e., an objective criterion which allows for an assessment of the risk profile of the taxpayer, and seems to be better aligned with the equality principle. The OECD proposes that for Co-operative Compliance the discrimination criteria should be "the taxpayer's ability and willingness to provide the necessary disclosure and transparency and of the adequacy of the TCF in place."[61] With regard to the ICAP, some of the entry criteria are "volume and materiality of the MNE's covered transactions."[62]

Second, once companies are admitted into Co-operative Compliance, equality between the participating taxpayers must once again be ensured by differentiating, for example, between taxpayers who have an effective TCF in place that allows for a reliable risk assessment of the company, and taxpayers whose TCF is weak or insufficient to assure whether or not the output information is free from material misstatements.

[D] Lack of Transparency of the Programmes

In terms of data about participating companies and results achieved by the ICAP, or by domestic Co-operative Compliance initiatives, not much information is shared with the public. In the ICAP, for example, the number of MNEs joining the program is officially reported neither by the participating jurisdictions nor by the OECD.

This opacity creates important risks to these programmes, as poorly informed media and public opinion could take the view that Co-operative Compliance and the ICAP are tools that grant sweetheart deals to large corporations. If that risk materializes, the costs to reverse unfavorable public opinion will probably be much higher than creating more transparent communication in the present.

§1.06 CONCLUSION

The book provides an unprecedented analysis of practical and theoretical aspects of Co-operative Compliance and the ICAP around the globe.

By comparing various experiences, it is possible to notice, for example, how newcomers to Co-operative Compliance can build up their approaches from the experiences of pioneer countries and from the work of the OECD. At the same time, the current discussions on the pioneer countries seem to indicate that there are still many

61. *Id.*, p. 47.
62. OECD/FTA (2019), *supra* n. 3, p. 15.

challenges to be addressed before Co-operative Compliance and the ICAP are definitively established as reliable tools to enhance the communications and relationship between taxpayers and tax administrations.

ANNEX A OUTLINE FOR THE REPORT ON CO-OPERATIVE COMPLIANCE PER COUNTRY

Introduction

For the congress on November 6, 2019 on co-operative compliance and ICAP we ask representatives from several jurisdictions to report on the state of affairs in their country regarding these topics. To ensure that the reports are easily comparable for the readers we would like the reports to treat the same issues as much as possible, hence this outline. We have worked with questions to be answered, to some extent following the OECD report of 2013 on Co-operative Compliance[63] but adding some more detail. If your country does not have a co-operative compliance regime, please try to describe the system within the format as much as possible. It is hard to exactly define what a co-operative compliance system must have at minimum before it can be regarded as such. We do not want to limit things here with a strict definition. Some points are however strongly connected to co-operative compliance: working in the present and not in the past, emphasis on the internal controls of the company, trust and open contact between company and tax authority (transparency).

Please regard this outline as a suggestion and feel free to add anything you think relevant.

As you know it is our intention to publish the reports in a book.

OUTLINE

1. Taxpayers around the world borne significant administrative costs to calculate and pay taxes.[64] In your country, is administrative compliance burden an issue which would promote co-operative compliance, or any other program?
2. The OECD and the IMF published, in a joint report, the main sources of tax uncertainty as pointed out by taxpayers and tax authorities around the world[65]. In your country, is tax uncertainty an issue which would promote co-operative compliance, or any other program?
3. Please comment on OECD questions[66] below considering not only the OECD "co-operative compliance model", but also any other programs that regulate the relationship between companies and tax authorities in your country:
   - Is the approach established in legal or other regulation?
   - Is the approach open to all taxpayer segments?
   - Is entry into the program upon application or invitation?

63. OECD (2013). *Co-operative Compliance: A Framework—From Enhanced Relationship to Co-operative Compliance*, https://read.oecd-ilibrary.org/taxation/co-operative-compliance-a-framework_9789264200852-en#page31.
64. The World Bank, Time to prepare and pay taxes (2018), https://data.worldbank.org/indicator/IC.TAX.DURS?view=chart&year_high_desc=true.
65. IMF/OECD (2017). *Report for the G20 Finance Ministers*. figure 7, p. 35, https://www.oecd.org/tax/tax-policy/tax-certainty-report-oecd-imf-report-g20-finance-ministers-march-2017.pdf.
66. OECD (2013). *Co-operative Compliance: A Framework—From Enhanced Relationship to Co-operative Compliance*. Paris: OECD Publishing, p. 30, https://read.oecd-ilibrary.org/taxation/co-operative-compliance-a-framework_9789264200852-en#page31.

- What are conditions for acceptance into the program?
- Is disclosure mandatory or voluntary?
- Does Multilateral Co-operative Compliance work?

4. In complement to OECD questions listed above, please comment on the following:
   - Is the program voluntary or mandatory? In case it is mandatory and it is a co-operative compliance model, is it still based on collaboration, trust, openness, transparency (and is no contradiction perceived)?
   - Must the relationship program be formalized in any specific kind of instrument, like a covenant or other form of contract? If so, is there a standard model of such instrument, or is it negotiated on a case-by-case basis? If not, how is it formalized?
   - What is the legal nature of such instrument? For how long is the instrument valid? Is the instrument enforceable by the parties? Are the parties free to opt out at any moment? Does the instrument provide for any specific penalties which may differ from the statutory penalties already provided by the applicable tax regulations?
   - Are there requirements for the risk management, risk appetite and tax strategy and principles? Must the taxpayer have a tax control framework in place as a requirement to join the relationship program? If yes, are the requirements of the TCF provided for by guidelines (issued by the tax authorities or any other administrative body)? Or are the TCF requirements provided by law? Do the tax authorities evaluate the soundness and effectiveness of the TCF before the taxpayer can join the relationship program? If they do, what are the relevant criteria and does the company have the (enforceable) right to appeal the decision? A relevant issue in this matter is whether the information provided by taxpayers within a TCF is audited by third parties. Is this the case in your country?
   - Do the characteristics of the TCF influence how the tax authorities will interact with the taxpayers? Do tax authorities reduce the number or intensity of their audits?
   - Within the relationship program, how easy can the taxpayers contact the tax authorities? Are there clear communication procedures? Must the tax authorities respond in a certain period of time?
   - Does the program provide possibilities for companies or tax authorities to go to a higher level if the relationship is not progressing satisfactorily without ending the program?
   - Is it possible within the program to bring concrete issues to court (agree to disagree) and if so, what are the criteria? If not, how is this reconciled with the rights of the company?
5. Are there any studies or investigations which evaluated the results of the relationship programs which were put in place in your country? Can you please comment, either based on such a study or based on your experience, if the expectations below were achieved? (these expectations were listed by OECD (2013)[67] regarding the co-operative compliance models but feel free to add others)

   For revenue bodies:
   - An enhanced relationship
   - Understanding the business
   - Risk management
   - Certainty in advance

67. *Id.*, p. 34.

For business:

- An enhanced relationship
- Reputation
- Risk management
- The opportunity to highlight problems with the tax code or its administration
- Certainty in advance
- Reduction of administrative burdens

6. How does ICAP relate to the program in your country, both formally and informally? Has ICAP influenced the program and if so, how?

CHAPTER 2

International Compliance Assurance Programme

*Achim Pross & Mark Johnson**

Tax administrations have at their disposal a number of tools to gain comfort that a group is paying the correct tax in a jurisdiction. These include advance pricing arrangements (APAs) and tax rulings to provide prospective legal certainty, risk assessment tools to identify groups or arrangements that pose greater potential tax risk (and to identify groups that pose less risk which can be de-selected from further enquiry), and tax audits to analyse specific arrangements and determine whether the position filed by a group in its tax returns is correct or if adjustment is needed. In cases where tax administrations differ in their positions with respect to a specific transaction, dispute resolution mechanisms can also be used, such as the Mutual Agreement Procedure (MAP) provided through Article 25 of the OECD Model Convention and, in some cases, binding arbitration.

The International Compliance Assurance Programme (ICAP), currently in a pilot stage, supports tax administrations in co-ordinating their risk assessment of a multinational enterprise (MNE) group's key international tax risks. The aim of the programme is to improve the effectiveness of these risk assessments and potentially provide MNE groups with multi-year comfort over all of their transfer pricing and permanent establishment issues, and possibly other international tax risks, in multiple jurisdictions where they have operations, including their head office jurisdiction.

Work to develop ICAP began in 2016 within the OECD Forum on Tax Administration (FTA) Large Business and International Programme (LBIP), under the co-sponsorship of the Canada Revenue Agency (CRA) and the Internal Revenue Service of the United States (IRS). Triggers that drove the need for such a programme at that time included the following:

---

* The opinions expressed and arguments employed herein do not necessarily reflect the official views of the member countries of the OECD.

- The G20 tax certainty agenda, which provides a political imperative for greater transparency and co-operation between tax administrations, and between tax administrations and MNE groups.
- The commitment by jurisdictions under BEPS Action 14 to improve the effectiveness and efficiency of dispute resolution through MAP.
- The availability of better and more standardised information for transfer pricing risk assessment as a result of BEPS Action 13, in particular the country-by-country (CbC) report, master file and local file.
- Tax administration experience in engaging with taxpayers through domestic co-operative compliance programmes, and with each other through FTA initiatives such as the LBIP and the Joint International Taskforce on Shared Intelligence and Collaboration.

§2.01 THE FIRST ICAP PILOT

Tax administrations from Australia, Italy, Japan, the Netherlands, Spain and the United Kingdom joined Canada and the United States and, together with the OECD Secretariat, worked throughout 2016 and 2017 to develop a handbook which became the basis for a first pilot of ICAP. This was launched at an event hosted by the CRA and IRS in Washington DC in January 2018, bringing together the eight participating tax administrations and MNE groups headquartered in their jurisdictions that had volunteered to be part of the pilot.

The first pilot was based on a standardised approach that was applied across all MNE groups:

- Each risk assessment was co-ordinated by the tax administration in the jurisdiction where an MNE group's ultimate parent entity was resident (the lead tax administration).
- A comprehensive documentation package was provided by an MNE group to the tax administrations participating in its risk assessment (the covered tax administrations) via a secure virtual data room maintained by the MNE group.
- Approximately six weeks after delivery of the documentation package, a two-day face-to-face kick-off meeting was held at the MNE group's headquarters, which provided an opportunity for senior management to present on aspects of their business, value chain and tax controls, and for tax administrations to ask initial questions (in practice the timing of these meetings was often co-ordinated so that meetings within a geographic region could be held back-to-back).
- Following the kick-off meeting, the lead tax administration organised regular calls between all covered tax administrations to discuss risk assessment findings, and to gather requests for additional information or clarification, which were communicated to the MNE group by the lead tax administration with a timeframe within which the information should be provided either to the lead tax administration or via the virtual data room.

- Once all covered tax administrations had concluded their risk assessments, each prepared an 'outcome letter' setting out their risk assessment findings, which were provided to the MNE group, typically by the lead tax administration.

Kick-off meetings were held between March 2018 and October 2018 and the last MNE group received its outcome letters in August 2019. Throughout the pilot, feedback was obtained from participating tax administrations and MNE groups, initially in writing and then at a face-to-face workshop in Paris, to identify aspects that worked well and those where improvements were needed.

§2.02 OUTCOMES FROM THE FIRST ICAP PILOT AND THE LAUNCH OF ICAP 2.0

In general, the core elements of the pilot received positive feedback from participants. In particular, MNE groups welcomed the central role played by the lead tax administration, which provided them with a single point of contact despite the fact that multiple tax administrations were involved in their risk assessment. MNE groups also appreciated the clear timeframes that were set for the provision of questions by covered tax administrations and within which responses should be provided which meant that, while risk assessments were ongoing, there was a sense of progress and an awareness of which issues remained outstanding. The use of a single documentation package by all covered tax administrations was also praised, which largely contained information that MNE groups already had available or could obtain reasonably easily, though concerns were raised that it did require some information to be provided on transactions that were not ultimately reviewed by a tax administration (e.g., because the MNE group already had an APA in place). The other main concerns raised were around a lack of flexibility in the ICAP process as described and the resources needed by both tax administrations and MNE groups participating in the programme, and these were taken on board in updating the handbook.

MNE groups in the pilot operated in a range of sectors and varied considerably in terms of their size, complexity, footprint and the materiality of their intercompany transactions but, in general, and in part as a result of multilateral discussions held as part of the pilot, covered tax administrations were aligned in their risk assessment conclusions. That said, a specific benefit was identified where tax administrations were able to recognise differences in views that could give rise to a potential dispute and deal with them within the programme. For example, cases arose where there were transactions between entities in jurisdictions of covered tax administrations and it was possible to agree with the MNE group off-setting transfer pricing adjustments in two jurisdictions, providing certainty to the MNE group and avoiding the time and expense of a tax audit and possibly a MAP case.

Other benefits that have been highlighted by some MNE groups, in addition to the comfort provided in the outcome letters, include an improved relationship with covered tax administrations, the opportunity to make improvements to tax controls reflecting input received from tax administrations, and the ability to share outcome letters, as evidence that the MNE group is viewed as low risk by covered tax administrations, with tax administrations outside ICAP.

In early 2019, it was agreed by the FTA that the first pilot had demonstrated benefits from ICAP, but further work was needed to revise the programme to take on board the feedback from participating tax administrations and MNE groups. At the FTA Plenary held in Santiago, Chile in March 2019 a second pilot (ICAP 2.0) was announced that incorporated a number of improvements:

- While elements that received strong support in the first pilot, such as the single documentation package and the central role of the lead tax administration have been retained, in general, greater flexibility has been provided for an MNE group and the covered tax administrations to agree the structure and timeframe for an ICAP risk assessment. For example, there may be cases where an up-front kick-off meeting is needed as was done in the first pilot, but there may also be cases where participants agree that a face-to-face meeting would be more beneficial if held later in the risk assessment process, or even that no meeting is needed. This allows a risk assessment to take into account the needs and circumstances of each MNE group and covered tax administration, improving the efficiency and effectiveness of the programme and potentially reducing the resource burden for all participants.
- A new scoping stage has been added, which takes place once it is confirmed that an MNE group will participate in the programme, to determine whether any covered transactions will be excluded from a covered tax administration's ICAP risk assessment, if appropriate (e.g., because a transaction is not material or certainty is already provided under an APA and so a further review is not needed). This ensures that an MNE group is only required to provide documentation relevant to transactions covered by its risk assessment.
- MNE groups participating in ICAP 2.0 will be asked to complete a CbC Reporting Tax Risk Assessment Questionnaire, which provides an opportunity to explain the presence of potential indicators of possible risk in their CbC report. Based on the risk indicators set out in the FTA's *Country-by-Country Reporting: Handbook on Effective Tax Risk Assessment*, this will aid covered tax administrations in interpreting the information they hold more effectively, in light of the context and explanations provided by the MNE group.
- A specific option for issue resolution is now included in the risk assessment stage, to allow covered tax administrations to work with an MNE group, within the ICAP process, to identify any changes that are needed to allow them to conclude that one or more of the covered risks are low risk.
- A greater number of tax administrations have indicated a willingness to participate in ICAP 2.0. Compared with the eight in the first pilot, seventeen tax administrations confirmed in March 2019 that they would participate in the second pilot, with France and the Russian Federation (Russia) joining the pilot in September 2019 and November 2019, respectively. While the number of covered tax administrations for a particular MNE group's ICAP risk assessment will remain limited, this increases the likelihood that an MNE group will be

able to obtain comfort over a greater proportion of its operations. The full list of nineteen tax administrations participating in ICAP 2.0 is set out below:

Australia	Austria	Belgium	Canada
Denmark	Finland	France	Germany
Ireland	Italy	Japan	Luxembourg
Netherlands	Norway	Poland	Russia
Spain	United Kingdom	United States	

MNE groups that wished to participate in ICAP 2.0 were asked to contact their possible lead tax administration by June 2019, and a tax administration workshop to discuss participation in – and the scope of – each risk assessment was held in Paris in September 2019. The first risk assessments in ICAP 2.0 commenced in January 2020.

§2.03 ICAP AS A TOOL TO IMPROVE TAX CERTAINTY

In considering ICAP as a tool to improve tax certainty it is necessary to understand the goals of the programme and how these differ from, and complement, the other tools available to tax administrations mentioned above.

ICAP is first and foremost a unique and innovative approach for tax administrations to work co-operatively and collaboratively with each other and with an MNE group at the risk assessment stage, allowing some tax audits to be avoided entirely or, where this is not possible (either because a group is not found to be low risk or because a tax administration is required to conduct an audit), for an audit to be more targeted and completed more quickly and efficiently. Tax administrations use their own risk assessment processes and tools to determine whether a particular MNE group poses a risk to their jurisdiction, and with respect to which transactions or arrangements, ensuring that each tax administration retains autonomy over its risk assessment outcomes. However, ICAP provides an opportunity for an MNE group to engage actively with the covered tax administrations at the risk assessment stage, to respond to questions and provide clarity around the content of its CbC report and other documentation. It also enables tax administrations to discuss their risk assessment findings with each other, gain confidence where these are aligned, and identify possible disputes early where views differ. As a result of working more closely together, tax administrations also gain a better understanding of how each other define and detect possible risk, and the specific tools used and information relied upon. Moving forward, a further potential benefit of the programme will be greater convergence in these practices and consistency in outcomes.

Where, as a result of an ICAP risk assessment, a tax administration concludes that an MNE group poses a low risk either generally or in particular areas, this will be included in the outcome letter it issues to the MNE group. The precise language used varies between tax administrations depending upon domestic legal or administrative requirements or restrictions over what can be said, but in general the level of comfort provided is that there is no expectation that further enquiries will be needed with respect to the tax years looked at in the risk assessment, plus the following two tax years on the condition there are no material changes. In terms of legal certainty, this is less than that provided by an APA, but this should not be viewed as a weakness of the programme – in many cases, an MNE group is able to request an APA if it feels that this is needed. On the contrary, there are a number of advantages to an MNE group from choosing to obtain comfort from participation in ICAP rather than absolute certainty under an APA:

- An ICAP outcome letter potentially covers all of an MNE group's transfer pricing risk in a jurisdiction rather than only specific transactions.
- Comfort may be provided with respect to the existence of a permanent establishment and, in future, potentially wider international tax risks, which may not currently be possible under a jurisdiction's APA programme.
- Comfort is provided simultaneously by all covered tax administrations, rather than just two tax administrations under a bilateral APA (multilateral APAs are possible but remain uncommon).
- The time taken to complete an ICAP risk assessment, and the corresponding resource commitment in terms of staff time, is significantly less than that is typical to agree a bilateral APA (potentially six-nine months, compared with up to three-four years or longer).
- The level of documentation required in ICAP is lower than that needed for an APA.
- As with the comfort provided by an ICAP outcome letter, the certainty provided by an APA will typically be conditional upon no material changes with respect to the transactions covered.

As such, ICAP has the potential to be a useful complement to traditional APAs, and may be viewed as such by MNE groups considering participation in the programme. For example, an MNE group may have specific transactions that are of a strategic nature or materiality, or that the group is aware may lead to dispute, where it feels the investment of time and resources for a bilateral or multilateral APA is merited in light of the legal certainty obtained. However, ICAP may be an appropriate tool to gain a valuable level of comfort over a broad range of other transactions at significantly lower cost.

§2.04 THE FUTURE OF ICAP

The second ICAP pilot is still at an early stage, and any plans for the future will need to take into account further learnings as the programme progresses. The future success of ICAP as a voluntary programme will also rely on MNE groups coming forward as participants, which it is hoped will increase as awareness of the programme grows and more tax administrations become involved. More complex MNE groups that, as a result of this complexity, may not have been considered low risk in the past should not be discouraged from applying to ICAP, so long as they have operations in participating jurisdictions and are willing to work openly with the tax administrations involved. As set out in the ICAP 2.0 handbook, factors that any MNE group should take into account in considering whether it is suitable for an ICAP risk assessment include the following:

- Whether the MNE group's ultimate parent entity is resident in the jurisdiction of a participating tax administration.
- The footprint of the MNE group and the volume and materiality of the group's covered transactions in jurisdictions of participating tax administrations.
- Whether the MNE group is subject to a CbC reporting filing requirement.
- Whether the MNE group has a group tax strategy which is clearly documented and owned by senior management at board level, and internal structures to set and manage its tax policies.
- Whether the MNE group has an effective tax control framework (or equivalent) over the covered risks at a global level.
- Whether the MNE group is willing to commit to engaging co-operatively and transparently throughout the ICAP process.

Learnings from ICAP also have the potential to benefit other programmes to improve tax certainty for groups, both domestically and multilaterally. For example, tools developed for the purposes of ICAP, including the standard documentation package and the CbC Reporting Tax Risk Assessment Questionnaire, may be incorporated into domestic compliance programmes, potentially improving the effectiveness of risk assessments conducted outside ICAP and reducing the burden on MNE groups that would be able to provide the same information to multiple tax administrations. In addition, Commissioners at the FTA Plenary in March 2019 agreed that, in addition to ICAP, a number of projects should be undertaken to further advance the tax certainty agenda, including to identify improvements to the APA process, to examine the potential for wider use of multilateral APAs and MAPs, and to explore the possible use and sharing of benchmarks for standard transfer pricing situations. While these new projects go beyond the scope of tax risk assessment, the ICAP experience of developing a standard process for greater multilateral working between tax administrations and with MNE groups could feed into this work as a model for how improvements could be made in other areas.

The first ICAP pilot has demonstrated benefits from tax administrations working together to provide multilateral comfort to MNE groups through co-ordinated risk assessment, avoiding the time and expense of either an APA or a tax audit. There will still be cases where an APA is appropriate or a tax audit is required, but there are advantages to both tax administrations and MNE groups from focussing those more intensive interactions on areas or transactions where they are needed. Work remains to be done to improve the scalability of ICAP to ensure the benefits are available to as broad a range of MNE groups as possible, and this is ongoing at the OECD. Once complete, and alongside other work being undertaken currently by the FTA, tax administrations will be in a stronger position than ever to provide MNE groups with greater certainty over their international tax risks, with a suite of tools that can be used for each case as appropriate.

CHAPTER 3

The ICAP Experience: From a Tax Authority Perspective

Hans Rijsbergen

§3.01 INTRODUCTION

In 2018, eight tax authorities started a pilot project called the International Compliance Assurance Programme (ICAP). This pilot project (ICAP 1.0) was unprecedented. Never before tax authorities had tested if and how they could jointly do a risk assessment and provide tax assurance to multinational enterprises (MNEs). It was also unique that MNEs volunteered to participate in this pilot, with a new untested process and an unpredictable outcome. The scope of the tax assurance regards transfer pricing risks and permanent establishment (PE) risks of the participating MNEs. The expected value of ICAP lies in the combination of tax assurance and international co-operation in two tiers. The first tier stands for the coordinated co-operation between an individual MNE and tax authorities of several countries leading to tax assurance on relatively short notice, as close to real time as possible and also forward looking. The second tier consists of the multilateral co-operation between tax authorities in a joint process, partly face-to-face, all using the same information and documentation. The meaning of this step taken by tax authorities and facilitated by the Organisation for Economic Co-operation and Development (OECD) should not be underestimated. This multidimensional and multilateral form of working together is unprecedented in the world of international taxation of MNEs. In their co-operation, the participating tax administrations and MNEs entered uncharted areas and had to resolve questions they had never faced in earlier work.

Because this work was new, many lessons were learned. The MNEs gave feedback, tax authorities decided to make changes to the programme and organize a second pilot, ICAP 2.0.

This chapter describes the background and goals of ICAP, how the tax administrations worked together in ICAP 1.0, what they achieved and learned, and it gives some insight on the possibilities of further development of the programme.

§3.02 BACKGROUND

In 2017, representatives of eight tax authorities[1] came together to explore how they could follow up on the "Tax Certainty" report that the OECD and the International Monetary Fund (IMF) published in 2017.[2] In the previous years the BEPS-action items[3] had been launched and good progress was made in fighting tax evasion and aggressive tax avoidance through more robust legislation and increased transparency, for instance as a result of country-by-country reporting and the exchange of advance rulings. The OECD and the IMF concluded that it was equally important to focus on tax certainty, because it supports trade, investment and economic growth. BEPS could lead to more tax disputes. These create uncertainty, because taxpayers are confronted with tax authorities taking different positions with regard to the same set of facts and circumstances. Many tax disputes concern transfer pricing arrangements and PEs of MNEs and will have to be resolved in Mutual Agreement Procedures (MAPs). Although MAPs are very important international instruments, tax authorities and MNEs have a shared interest in avoiding them. MAPs have several disadvantages. The first is that a MAP is a procedure between two tax authorities, without direct involvement of the taxpayer. The second is that uncertainty can exist for a long time as a MAP can take multiple years. Besides, not all MAP cases lead to a resolution that is satisfying for all parties or to a solution at all, which could lead to double taxation. The aim of ICAP is to prevent disputes and provide assurance to MNEs with a compliance record that can be classified as low or medium risk. The tax authorities in ICAP recognized that low-risk compliance behavior should be recognized and promoted. ICAP builds upon earlier work in the area of taxation of MNEs, specifically the work in BEPS items 13, Country-by-Country Reporting and 14, Dispute Resolution. The other important pillars of ICAP are Co-operative Compliance programmes in the participating countries and also the urgency, in the globalized world, that tax authorities work together to avoid duplicating work and unnecessary disputes. ICAP is a voluntary programme designed to facilitate a coordinated, multilateral risk assessment of MNEs' transfer pricing and PE risks. Its aim is to provide assurance on certain activities and transactions while

1. The participating tax authorities in the first ICAP pilot included Australia, Canada, Italy, Japan, the Netherlands, Spain, the United Kingdom and the United States.
2. IMF/OECD (2017). *OECD/IMF Report on Tax Certainty*, Paris, www.oecd.org/tax/tax-policy/tax-certainty-report-oecd-imf-report-g20-finance-ministers-march-2017.pdf. This report was updated in 2018 (www.oecd.org/ctp/tax-policy/tax-certainty-update-oecd-imf-report-g20-finance-ministers-july-2018.pdf) and 2019 (https://www.oecd.org/tax/tax-policy/imf-oecd-2019-progress-report-on-tax-certainty.pdf).
3. In 2015 the OECD launched the Base Erosion and Profit Shifting (BEPS) Action Plan, that consisted of 15 actions items, measures to tackle tax avoidance, improve the coherence of the international tax rules and ensure a more transparent tax environment. In 2020, 135 countries and jurisdictions are working together on the implementation of the action items.

isolating compliance risks which require further attention. The handbooks that the tax authorities used in ICAP 1.0 and 2.0 are published on the website of the OECD.[4]

§3.03 THE PILOT CHARACTER OF ICAP

It is important to emphasize the pilot character of ICAP 1.0 and ICAP 2.0. The pilots are important to test not only the efficiency and effectiveness of the newly designed process but also the expectations that MNEs and tax authorities may have from the programme and from each other. A few examples may illustrate this. During ICAP 1.0 it became clear that the designed process in practice worked out differently from what was expected. For instance, the ICAP 1.0 process had two levels. The idea was that for really low-risk MNEs the risk assessment work could be done in a short period of time, on a relatively high level (level 1). Only if on level 1 certain risks would arise, a level 2 risk assessment was foreseen. The level 2 risk assessment would be more in-depth. During ICAP 1.0 it proved difficult to make a distinction between level 1 and level 2, so the tax authorities decided to abandon the difference between the two levels. Another experience was that the process in ICAP 1.0 was not flexible enough, given the differences between the participating MNEs, in terms of industry, but also in size and complexity. A new process with various stages was introduced in ICAP 2.0 that should help to solve these issues (Figure 3.1). An important lesson of the first pilot was that it would be beneficial to include Issue Resolution as part of the Risk Assessment Stage. This decision was taken because in ICAP 1.0 some cases were identified that could be resolved within the ICAP or selected for fast-track resolution in Advance Pricing Agreements (APAs) or even a Mutual Agreement Procedure (MAP).

4. *See* https://www.oecd.org/tax/forum-on-tax-administration/publications-and-products/international-compliance-assurance-programme-pilot-handbook.pdf and https://www.oecd.org/tax/forum-on-tax-administration/publications-and-products/international-compliance-assurance-programme-pilot-handbook-2.0.pdf.

Figure 3.1 Target Timeframes for an ICAP Risk Assessment

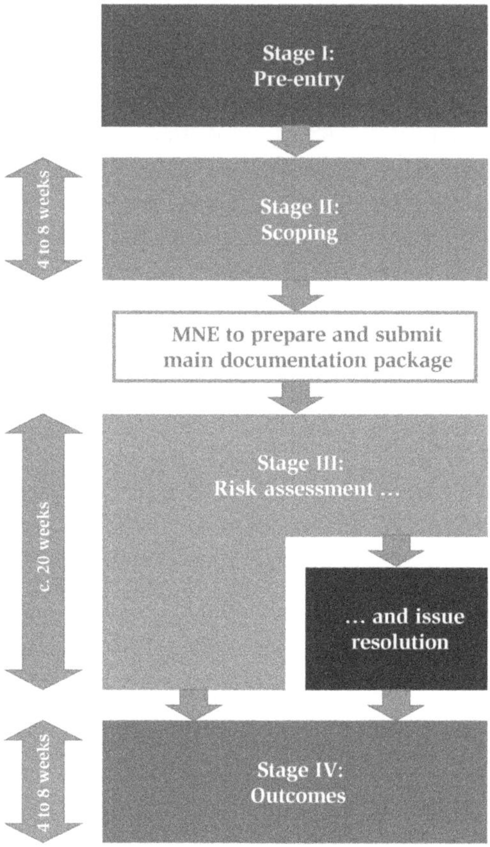

Very likely, more changes will follow after ICAP 2.0.

ICAP Pilot Handbook 2.0 OECD 2019, p. 46. Available at: https://www.oecd.org/tax/forum-on-tax-administration/publications-and-products/international-compliance-assurance-programme-pilot-handbook-20.htm.

§3.04 ICAP 1.0: PARTICIPATING MNEs AND JURISDICTIONS

Tax administrations of eight jurisdictions participated in ICAP 1.0. The scale of the pilot was kept small, the principle being that each jurisdiction would bring one MNE into the risk assessment process. The MNEs that volunteered to participate in ICAP operated in a range of industries and varied considerably in terms of assets, revenue, complexity of operations, footprint in the covered jurisdictions, materiality of intercompany transactions and PE risks. Not all tax administrations were involved in the risk assessments of all MNEs. The most simple reason for non-participation was the absence of any activities in a jurisdiction. Other reasons were that the activities in a jurisdiction were not material, that the tax authority had labelled the MNE as "high risk" or that the tax authority has decided, due to capacity constraints, to participate in ICAP 1.0 only in a limited number of risk assessments. In addition, both in ICAP 1.0 and in ICAP 2.0, MNEs could exclude jurisdictions from the scope of the risk assessment.

The following matrix makes it clear that in ICAP 1.0 risk assessments for individual MNEs were performed by three to six tax authorities, but also that only one country was involved in all risk assessments in the pilot:

	MNE 1	*MNE 2*	*MNE 3*	*MNE 4*	*MNE 5*	*MNE 6*	*MNE 7*	*MNE 8*
Country A	Lead	√	√	X	X	√	X	√
Country B	√	Lead	√	√	√	√	√	√
Country C	X	X	Lead	Lead	√	√	X	X
Country D	X	X	X	X	√	X	X	√
Country E	X	X	X	√	Lead	√	√	√
Country F	X	X	X	√	√	Lead	X	√
Country G	√	√	√	X	X	√	Lead	X
Country H	X	√	√	√	X	X	X	Lead

[A] Timelines ICAP 1.0

The first ICAP pilot was launched in Washington D.C. in January 2018 and concluded in August 2019. During this period, the eight tax authorities completed eight multilateral risk assessments. The start dates for the risk assessments were staggered from March 2018 to October 2018. The average time to complete the multilateral risk assessment process was approximately 12.5 months. Risk assessment timelines varied based on several factors, including the size and complexity of the MNEs' operations, the nature and materiality of the covered activities and transactions and the extent to which tax authorities identified potential risks (thus requiring additional documentation and/or further dialogue with the participating tax administrations and the MNE). In many cases the tax administrations completed their substantive risk assessment efforts prior to the timelines specified above, but additional time was needed to formally close the risk assessment process. Issuing the outcome letters in the pilot took several months. An explanation for this prolonged period is that tax authorities performed this process for the first time.

[B] Documentation and Information

During the pilot ICAP 1.0, many practical issues had to be resolved. An example is the way in which the extensive documentation packages could be made available to the participating tax authorities by the MNEs. The documents (in some cases hundreds) could not be easily shared using traditional channels for communication and exchange of information between a tax authority and taxpayers, but also between a tax authority and other tax authorities. Parties found a practical solution for this issue by using data rooms that were set up by the MNEs, where the tax authorities could download the information and documentation. This way of working proved to be a good practice that is also used in ICAP 2.0. Advantages are that the MNE is "in control" with regard to the information and can track if tax administrations downloaded the documentation.

After ICAP 1.0, the tax authorities concluded that the initial pre-entry documentation package can be reduced for ICAP 2.0. Another change is that the documentation package is not made available in one extensive package at the start of the process, but in stages and more targeted and tailored to the decisions made by tax authorities and taxpayers in the scoping stage that was introduced in ICAP 2.0. These amendments to the process should reduce the documentation burden for taxpayers and the time needed for processing of the documentation by tax authorities.

[C] Role of the Lead Country

The role of the lead country is crucial to make the ICAP process work. It includes engaging with the tax departments of the MNE, help them through the ICAP process but also manage expectations. Although this may seem obvious, it is important to note that all tax authorities in the ICAP work on the basis of their domestic legislative frameworks and their practical possibilities. Each tax authority operates in a different environment, and the compliance approaches depend on this environment. Although the compliance approaches are similar in some aspects, there are also many differences. The differences between national tax systems have an impact on the compliance behavior of both taxpayers and tax authorities. An example: the Netherlands have a strong tradition of consensus-based policy making, co-operation despite different interests, sometimes referred to as the "polder model".[5] This is a logical breeding ground for the Dutch "horizontal monitoring" variation of Co-operative Compliance.[6] In other jurisdictions the tax system works differently and as a result the working relationship between tax authorities and taxpayers will be different as well.

The lead country also has to engage with the other participating tax authorities. The ICAP-process involves organizing conference calls, in different time zones, organizing the documentation package, leading the risk assessment work and coordinating the process of issuing the outcome letters. The lead country in some cases took

5. The "polder model" or "polder culture" is characterized by consultation, consensus, co-operation and bottom-up innovation. The "polder culture" exists in many policy areas in the Netherlands.
6. Known in the Netherlands as Horizontal Monitoring.

an intermediary position between the MNE and a participating tax authority and helped the risk assessment work in other countries.

[D] ICAP 1.0: Achievements

The most important achievement in ICAP 1.0 was multidimensional transparency and understanding between all participating parties. The co-operation between tax authorities and MNEs in all cases worked out satisfactorily. A first dimension is that tax authorities invested in their working relationships. They multilaterally informed each other about their respective large business compliance approaches. It not only helped to understand the peculiarities of the different national tax systems but also improved the understanding of the positions of the other participants and the way they engage with large taxpayers.

Another obvious dimension is the transparency between MNEs and tax authorities. MNEs made documentation packages available. The practical solution to work with virtual data rooms was considered of great importance because it was efficient and contributed to trust and transparency between all parties. Tax authorities combined their questions and addressed them in one batch to the MNE. This process was led by the lead tax authority of the jurisdiction where the MNE had its head office. MNEs made their answers available to all tax authorities at once. As a result, tax authorities and the MNEs were able to oversee the activities and transactions in the ICAP process. In addition, the tax authorities and MNEs agreed on how to resolve certain material tax risks that were identified during the risk assessment process in ICAP. Despite the differences in MNE profiles, the tax authorities were generally aligned in many of their risk assessment conclusions.

§3.05 OUTCOMES

All eight risk assessments in ICAP 1.0 led to concrete outcomes in the form of (varying levels of) assurance for the participating MNEs. In certain situations, the tax authorities and MNEs collaboratively decided to resolve a material transfer pricing risk through the bilateral APA process. This process can be accelerated as a result of the information gathered and the preliminary discussions that occurred during the ICAP. In a limited number of situations, the risk assessment process in ICAP 1.0 has led to compliance interventions where the tax authorities and MNEs were unable to agree on measures to mitigate an identified transfer pricing risk. It is also important to mention that in some cases the tax authorities collaborated with the MNEs to improve their tax control frameworks (TCF), to ensure more accurate reporting of tax return data going forward, and to ensure that the outcomes as set forth in the MNEs' transfer pricing policies were achieved. Additional steps may need to be considered to ensure the effectiveness of TCF in practice.

Some high-level observations can be made with regard to the substantive findings of the risk assessments. Services transactions, in general, proved to be the least contentious transfer pricing issue in ICAP 1.0. In this pilot, transfer pricing issues associated with the purchase and sale of tangible goods were characterized by the tax authorities as low risk. More interestingly, the tax authorities generally reached a low-risk determination regarding the licensing of intangible property. It is important to note that in certain cases MNEs had obtained (or applied for) APAs with respect to material transactions. As a result, these transactions were treated as out-of-scope for ICAP purposes. The tax authorities in several cases were unable to reach low-risk conclusions with respect to certain financial transactions (e.g., intercompany loans, cash pooling arrangements, and guarantee fees). In general, the tax authorities concluded that the MNEs effectively mitigated the risk of creating an unintended PE in their respective jurisdictions and the risk of an incorrect attribution of profits to the PEs. Last but not least, the tax authorities found that most MNEs had set up their transfer pricing control framework in an adequate way, but in some cases concluded that the monitoring of the outcomes of the framework needed more attention.

Accordingly, adjustments (including corresponding adjustments in other jurisdictions) were made in ICAP, thus potentially avoiding resource-intensive future compliance interventions (e.g., tax examinations, preparation and filing of amended income tax returns) and subsequent resolution through a MAP.

§3.06 OUTCOME LETTERS

In all cases, the participating tax administrations, and the lead tax administration, issued outcome letters to the MNEs, formalizing their findings from their risk assessment efforts. The outcome letters provided feedback to the MNEs regarding the risk level posed by the covered activities and transactions (i.e., transfer pricing and PE issues) and expectations regarding the likelihood of compliance interventions during the period covered by the risk assessment, which was the year 2016. Anticipative tax authorities expressed that compliance resources were unlikely to be dedicated to a transaction deemed to be low risk for the 2017 and 2018 tax years. The approaches regarding outcome letters differed by jurisdiction. Some countries were legally obliged to send the outcome letters in their national languages. The length of the outcome letters was different, ranging from a more holistic approach to a specified list of assessed transactions. The language in the outcome letters followed the approach of the jurisdictions. All countries made explicit or implicit reservations that in a case of changed facts and circumstances it is in the spirit of ICAP that the MNE informs the tax authorities and discusses the consequences for the outcome letter.

The outcome letter of the Netherlands Tax and Customs Administration was an example of a holistic approach and was issued in English. In ICAP 1.0 tax assurance was provided as follows:[7]

7. This is just an example of the language used in the outcome letter. Depending on the individual case, additional language was used in the outcome letter to describe specific transactions that were excluded from this conclusion, because they were out of scope of were not assessed as low or medium risk. Furthermore, it is important to note that this language will develop in ICAP 2.0 and later programmes.

> Taking the above into consideration we conclude that the covered risks are adequately identified and controlled. Therefore it is not anticipated that extra compliance resources will be dedicated to a further review of the covered risks for the fiscal years 2016 up to and including 2018 regarding the covered risks.

It should be noted that, in line with the Netherlands' approach toward Co-operative Compliance, the NTCA does not assure that there will be no tax inspection activities. Based on the information from the risk assessment, and assuming that the compliance behavior of the taxpayer remains on a high level, the NTCA concludes that its resources can be deployed in a more efficient way, for instance with other taxpayers. However, if the compliance behavior of the MNE changes, or if relevant information which was not previously made available leads to other conclusions, the Dutch tax authorities are entitled to execute appropriate review activities.

§3.07 LESSONS LEARNED AND REMAINING ISSUES

The participating tax authorities have learned a lot from ICAP. They also found solutions for surfacing problems and dilemmas. Still, the exploration continues and issues have been identified that should be discussed and resolved before it is decided that ICAP will be a standard global programme. Some of these issues are described in the following.

- The concept of materiality

Experience in ICAP 1.0 proved that materiality is a complex factor, as it influences the level of assurance that both tax authorities and MNEs perceive. Materiality is also connected to the level of details in the risk assessment of the tax authorities. An MNE might not see a transaction as material where tax authorities take a different position. There are also differences between tax authorities. A particular transaction risk might not be material for the MNE or for the tax authority of one country, but it may be very material for another country. Explanations for these different positions are the sizes of the economies of the countries and the importance of the presence of an MNE in a country, the national legal frameworks, and also different concepts of materiality in national audit approaches. From a tax authority perspective it seems inconceivable to work with the materiality applied by the MNE for its annual accounts or by the tax administration of the country in which the MNE has its largest footprint. If tax authorities would do that, possibly all transactions involving smaller countries would be out of scope. Another aspect of materiality, at least in the Netherlands, is the difference between the materiality used to select risks and transactions for the assessment and the materiality that is used to determine if an error identified in the risk assessment should lead to adjustments. In the Netherlands, tax authorities have no discretionary powers to refrain from an adjustment in case of a known error, even if the error is not material in the context of risk assessment. As a result, it is possible to conclude that the overall transfer pricing position of an MNE is de facto low risk and still make one or more adjustments.

In each given case, it is therefore important to understand and do justice to the positions of all parties and the concepts of materiality they use.

• The high-level character of the ICAP risk assessment

ICAP was designed as a high-level risk assessment process. Participating tax authorities took time at the start of the programme to understand their mutual national risk assessment approaches. In practice, the tax authorities performed the ICAP risk assessment using their (diverging) national approaches. Some approaches were holistic and top-down, started with a general overview of the MNE, knowing the business and the relevant industry, the governance framework and control measures. The Dutch tax administration used this approach. Other tax authorities had more of a bottom-up approach as they connected to specific transactions. Both methods can lead to a high-level risk assessment; however, there is also the risk in both methods that the work has more characteristics of a tax audit than a high-level risk assessment. In ICAP 2.0, mechanisms were built in to avoid this risk. If within ICAP 2.0 more information is needed that exceeds the high-level character of the risk assessment, the tax authorities should decide to exclude transactions or risks from the scope of the assurance given, or in rare cases, stop the ICAP process, if it is unlikely that this process will lead to the expected tax assurance.

• ICAP in relation to other instruments

ICAP 1.0 was designed as a holistic programme with a broad coverage: all risk areas and all transfer pricing transactions were meant to be covered, unless one of the tax authorities involved or the MNE decided that certain activities or transactions would be out of scope. In this respect ICAP 1.0 differed from other instruments such as unilateral, bilateral or multilateral APAs that cover specific transactions. The focus on transactions also leads to less attention for the overall risk profile of the MNE and the measures it has taken to mitigate these risks, for instance, in their TCF.

In this respect one could ask what the added value of ICAP is for both MNEs and tax authorities. This is a relevant issue because we have had difficulties in ICAP 1.0 (and ICAP 2.0) to attract MNEs. MNEs seeking tax certainty have multiple options: APAs, Joint Audits, or unilateral certainty from a tax administration. The MNE can also simply decide to accept certain tax risks, and not apply for tax assurance or comfort. Each MNE chooses its own strategy. For instance, experiences from ICAP 1.0 have taught that some MNEs have a more proactive strategy than others. Some MNEs have concluded multiple APAs, where other MNEs have made no or only limited use of this instrument.

§3.08 EVALUATION AND SCALABILITY

During and after ICAP 1.0, the MNEs gave mildly positive feedback. They valued the initiative, the working together but also saw possibilities to improve the efficiency of the programme and to increase the level of assurance.

MNEs and tax authorities together agreed that ICAP 1.0 was resource intensive. The changes in the set-up of ICAP 2.0 are meant to make the process more efficient. A thorough evaluation of this second pilot programme will be necessary before tax authorities can decide to make ICAP a standard programme. In this evaluation both the efficiency, effectiveness and attractiveness will have to be weighted and analyzed.

More efficiency seems possible in the international co-operation if tax authorities can make better use of the work of their colleagues in other countries. A common understanding about risks and risk assessments is crucial. Here the work on CoRA (Comparative Risk Assessment Initiative)[8] is promising. There is a risk that in the ICAP tax administrations deploy resources to risks or taxpayers on which, given their low or medium risk profile, they would normally not spend capacity. In those cases extra work within ICAP does not make sense. Also, MNEs that have chosen a low- or medium-risk profile will ask themselves what the added value of the comfort level provided by ICAP is. More differentiation in the approach by tax authorities could help. As mentioned before: MNEs come in different sizes, are very complex or not complex at all, are active in many countries or only in a few jurisdictions. If tax authorities could agree on a "lighter touch" or "fast track" ICAP approach for MNEs that are considered low risk by all tax authorities, this would also help for the scalability of the process, and time would be saved, allowing more focus on the less straightforward and more complex cases. This could make the programme more attractive for all parties.

ICAP 1.0 certainly has been rewarding for the participating tax authorities. All tax authorities worked with dedicated ICAP teams that grew toward each other during the risk assessment work. The ways of working and compliance approaches of the countries that have joined ICAP 2.0 will have to be merged into the existing co-operation between the countries participating in ICAP 1.0. This will require time but also mutual trust, transparency and understanding. Additional dimensions are that the MNEs do not have extensive activities in the new ICAP countries and that the economies of those countries in some cases are relatively small with consequences for the co-operation and the perception of material activities and transactions.

§3.09 ICAP AND CO-OPERATIVE COMPLIANCE

ICAP has inspired the approach of the Netherlands Tax and Customs Administration toward large multinational taxpayers and the project of further development of Co-operative Compliance (Horizontal Monitoring) in the Netherlands. The largest MNEs will be asked to actively supply their master files to the NTCA for review. In the domestic programme, assessing and scoping the risk of activities and transactions will become more important and MNEs will be asked to show the results of their internal

8. *See* https://www.oecd.org/tax/forum-on-tax-administration/publications-and-products/forum-on-tax-administration-annual-report-2018-2019.pdf: "Through the development of a compendium of countries' approaches to risk assessment and a risk register, the CoRA initiative aims to enhance mutual understanding of key risks and approaches, understanding of business transactions and overtime to examine where international convergence around views and interpretation can be achieved."

monitoring activities. ICAP has made it clear that monitoring is a very important link in the risk assessment process.

§3.10 CLOSING WORDS

ICAP is an important innovative programme. It is unprecedented, because it brings together tax authorities in a joint process to assess tax risks and provide tax assurance to MNEs that voluntarily participate in the programme. The programme also stands for an important paradigm shift following the BEPS action items. Many lessons were learned in the first ICAP pilot. Promising aspects are the international co-operation, the solutions that were found for practical issues, the resolution of substantive tax issues in the process. ICAP adds to the mutual understanding between tax authorities and MNEs, and as a result can be expected to contribute to more awareness within tax authorities and a higher quality of risk assessment with regard to transfer pricing and PE. However, the improvements to the process that were made after the first pilot have to be tested in ICAP 2.0 and evaluated to allow a well-informed decision about the future of the programme. Although the ICAP process probably will undergo further adjustments, it is certain that the road to more international co-operation between tax authorities is now open. Obstacles on this road are inevitable but will more easily be removed as a result of the experience in ICAP. Hopefully, in five or ten years the conclusion will be that this co-operation works well for all parties. Certainly, for those involved in the launch of ICAP in 2018, the first pilot was a very interesting and rewarding experience.

CHAPTER 4

Co-operative Compliance Programmes in Australia: Working Towards Justified Trust

Celeste M. Black

This chapter provides an overview of the current programmes in Australia that foster co-operative compliance of taxpayers, with an emphasis on large companies and corporate groups. The focus is on voluntary schemes but the discussion also includes mandatory disclosure rules that apply to corporate taxpayers. In most cases these mechanisms have been developed by the Australian Taxation Office (ATO) as administrative arrangements under the general power to administer taxation laws that has been granted to the Commissioner of Taxation ('the Commissioner'). The source of the information in this report is therefore, for the most part, a publicly available guidance provided by the ATO, generally through its website. If a taxpayer achieves an overall high assurance rating with respect to relevant taxes, in other words if the taxpayer has obtained 'justified trust', the expectation is that future ATO engagement will be 'lighter touch'. The Justified Trust programmes all operate on a voluntary basis.

Australia was an early adopter of a co-operative compliance model and the ATO's compliance model was highlighted as an illustrative example in the Organisation for Economic Co-operation and Development's (OECD's) 2013 report on co-operative compliance.[1] According to the history compiled in Whait's academic research,[2] a compliance model that combined responsive regulation theory[3] and motivational

1. OECD (2019). *Co-operative Compliance: A Framework – From Enhanced Relationship to Co-operative Compliance*, pp. 24-26.
2. Robert Whait, *Developing Risk Management Strategies in Tax Administration: The Evolution of the Australian Taxation Office's Compliance Model*, 10:2 eJournal of Tax Research 436, 438 (2012). *See also* Robert Whait, *Let's Talk about Tax Compliance: Building Understanding and Relationships Through Discourse*, 13:1 eJournal of Tax Research 130 (2015).
3. Ian Ayres and John Braithwaite, *Responsive Regulation: Transcending the Deregulation Debate* (Oxford Univ. Press 1992).

posturing theory[4] was first developed and recommended by the ATO's Cash Economy Task Force in 1998,[5] to complement the Taxpayers' Charter, which was adopted in 1997. This co-operative compliance model was then adapted to suit large businesses[6] and this revised model was formally released in 2000.[7] A guidance booklet on the ATO's approach to tax risk management and compliance for the large business segment was issued in 2003. However, a review conducted in 2004-2005 gathered anecdotal feedback from the largest companies and revealed dissatisfaction with the ATO's perceived reluctance to engage co-operatively with taxpayers.[8] The ATO responded with a number of new initiatives in 2005, including the implementation of a Forward Compliance Arrangements (FCA) model, based on the principles of transparency and real-time collaboration.[9] Entry into this programme required a low-risk rating and a high standard of corporate governance and resulted in a written commitment between the ATO and the taxpayer regarding the future management of tax compliance matters.[10]

A further round of ATO initiatives in 2008 saw the introduction of Annual Compliance Arrangements (ACAs)[11] (its current form is detailed in sub-section §4.02[B][2][a]). The key features of the original ACA product were confirmation of compliance with corporate governance guidelines, a commitment to transparency that includes the ATO and the taxpayer working together to assess tax risks across the year in relation to major transactions and uncertain tax positions, and joint review of the tax returns and other information post-lodgement.[12] These features all continue to be key elements of the Justified Trust programme.

By 2011, as an alternative to an FCA or ACA, a less formal process of disclosure and workshopping of potential tax risks at or near the time of lodgement had been developed, which also fostered a co-operative relationship and greater certainty for both taxpayers and the ATO.[13] These became known as Pre-lodgement Compliance Reviews (PCRs) (detailed in sub-section §4.02[B][2][b]). FCAs were still available at

4. Valerie Braithwaite, Kristina Murphy and Monika Reinhart, *Taxation Threat, Motivational Postures, and Responsive Regulation*, 29 Law & Policy 137 (2007).
5. *See* Valerie Braithwaite, *A New Approach to Tax Compliance* in *Taxing Democracy: Understanding Tax Avoidance and Evasion* (Valerie Braithwaite ed., Ashgate, 2003) 1-11.
6. *See* John Braithwaite, *Large Business and the Compliance Model* in *Taxing Democracy: Understanding Tax Avoidance and Evasion* (Valerie Braithwaite ed., Ashgate, 2003) 177-202.
7. Commonwealth of Australia, *Cooperative Compliance: Working with Large Business in the New Tax System* (2000).
8. Kevin Burges, *Report on the Concerns of a Number of the Largest Companies in the Large Business Segment, with ATO Audit, Investigation, and Advice Procedures* (2005). This report was compiled at the request of the ATO and with the support of the Corporate Tax Association and was based on interviews with senior tax officers at a number of Australia's largest companies.
9. Australian Government, Inspector-General of Taxation, *Report into the Australian Taxation Office's Large Business Risk Review and Audit Policies, Procedures and Practices* (2011) at 21.
10. *Ibid.*
11. *Ibid.*, at 22.
12. *Ibid.*
13. *Ibid.*

this point in time but were no longer publicised by 2014. The principles behind the FCAs are still apparent, however, in the Justified Trust programme.[14]

The ATO participated in the first International Compliance Assurance Programme (ICAP) pilot in 2018 and is participating in the second pilot that commenced in 2019. Aside from stating that the ICAP complements ATO compliance programmes, there are no further details publicly available regarding the ATO's involvement.[15] The ATO sees a number of advantages from the ICAP initiative: targeted and consistent interpretation and use of country-by-country (CbC) reports; better use of both revenue authorities' and taxpayer resources; coordinated and transparent engagement; faster multilateral certainty; and fewer disputes entering into tax treaty mutual agreement procedures.[16] According to a public disclosure by the company, Computershare Limited, an Australian electronic share registry business with activities in twenty-one countries, participated in the first ICAP pilot.[17]

§4.01 OVERVIEW OF AUSTRALIA'S APPROACH TO CO-OPERATIVE COMPLIANCE

[A] Justified Trust

The ATO has adopted the OECD's concept of 'justified trust' as the level of assurance sought that the right amount of tax is reported and paid by a taxpayer. The 'tax assured' is, therefore, 'the proportion of the tax base where the ATO has justified trust that the right amount of tax has been paid'.[18] The ATO applies this approach to income tax, indirect taxes (Goods and Services Tax (GST) and excise) and petroleum resource rent tax (PRRT). The ATO's most recent annual report provides an estimate that 45.6% of total tax for the 2016-2017 tax year and 47.4% of the total tax for 2015-2016 was assured, with around 30% of the tax assured being so by virtue of direct engagement with larger taxpayers.[19]

In order to gain confidence that the correct amount of tax has been paid, there are four key focus areas of Justified Trust:[20]

(1) understanding and evaluating the taxpayer's tax governance framework;

---

14. The 2014 edition of the ATO's, *Large Business and Tax Compliance Publication* includes discussion of ACAs and PCRs but not FCAs.
15. ATO, *International Compliance Assurance Programme* (last modified 22 May 2019) https://www.ato.gov.au/Business/International-tax-for-business/In-detail/International-Compliance-Assurance-Programme-(ICAP)/.
16. Speech of Mark Konza, Deputy Commissioner International, ATO, '*Transfer Pricing*' (keynote address at TPMinds Australia, 29 May 2018) https://www.ato.gov.au/Media-centre/Speeches/Other/Transfer-Pricing/.
17. Computershare Limited, *Voluntary Tax Transparency Code Report* (for the year ended 30 Jun. 2018).
18. ATO, *CTA ATO Workshops: Justified Trust and Key Taxpayer Engagement Outcomes Document* (last modified 15 May 2018) https://www.ato.gov.au/business/bus/cta-ato-outcomes-document/.
19. ATO, *Annual Report 2018-19* (2019) at p. 31.
20. *Ibid.*

(2) identifying tax risks (in relation to arrangements that have already been highlighted to the market more broadly by the ATO through public advice and guidance materials);
(3) understanding the taxpayer's significant and any new transactions; and
(4) understanding why accounting and tax results vary (including an analysis of effective tax borne (ETB)).

The ATO prepares an annual tax assurance report (TAR) in relation to a taxpayer's affairs that shows the overall level of assurance achieved for that year, with a rating also given for each of the focus areas, and highlights any change in ratings over time. The Executive Summary of the TAR explains the ATO's conclusions regarding the level of assurance and outlines future plans for improving or maintaining that level.

[B] Relevant Taxpayer Segments

A version of the Justified Trust strategy applies to each of the following taxpayer segments: the Top 100; the Top 1,000; and the Top 320 private groups. The ATO was provided with specific funding to establish a Tax Avoidance Taskforce in 2016 in order to enhance and extend compliance activities.[21] Parts of these efforts are directed at taxpayer engagement leading to voluntary disclosures. As part of the budget measures for 2019-2020, the Australian Government announced an additional AUD 1 billion of funding for the Tax Avoidance Taskforce over the next four years, some of which will be used to bolster the Justified Trust initiative.[22]

The Top 100 consists of public and multinational businesses and superannuation (retirement savings) funds that have substantial economic activity in Australia.[23] They are initially identified based on the size of Australian operations but other factors may also be taken into account, such as the amount of tax paid and the influence of the business on their market segment. The ATO website suggests that members of the Top 100 would have total business income exceeding AUD 5 billion or would be a market leader.[24] The full Justified Trust programme applies to this segment.

The Top 1,000 consists of large public and multinational businesses and superannuation funds. The ATO website suggests that members of the Top 1,000 would generally have total business income exceeding AUD 250 million.[25] A streamlined assurance review (SAR) programme has existed in some form for this segment since 2016 but has been enhanced in the past twelve months (*see* section §4.04).

21. ATO, *Tax Avoidance Taskforce* (last modified 12 Dec. 2018) https://www.ato.gov.au/General/Tax-avoidance-taskforce/.
22. Australian Government, *Budget Measures 2019-20 – Part 1: Revenue Measures* (2019) at p. 24.
23. ATO, *Top 100 Risk Categorisation Approach* (last modified 18 Jun. 2019) https://www.ato.gov.au/Business/Large-business/Top-100-risk-categorisation-approach/.
24. ATO, *Action Differentiation Framework* (last modified 8 Jul. 2019) https://www.ato.gov.au/Business/Large-business/Action-Differentiation-Framework/.
25. *Ibid.*

The Top 320 private groups are identified using turnover and net asset criteria and include those groups that meet any of the following tests:[26]

- more than AUD 350 million turnover;
- more than AUD 500 million in net assets;
- more than AUD 100 million turnover and more than AUD 250 million in net assets;
- market leaders or groups of specific interest.

The tax performance programme for this segment is an engagement and assurance approach under the auspices of the Tax Avoidance Taskforce (*see* section §4.05).

[C] Relationship with Other Taxpayer Engagement Products and Mechanisms

The Justified Trust methodology works alongside pre-existing early (voluntary) engagement products and mandatory disclosure regimes. These mechanisms are described in more detail below in sub-section §4.02[B][2]. The main early engagement products are: ACAs; PCRs; and Advance Pricing Arrangements (APAs). Relevant mandatory disclosure regimes (i.e., disclosures required by law) include the Reportable Tax Positions (RTPs) schedule to the income tax return.[27] Significant global entities (SGEs) must meet country-by-country reporting (CbCR) obligations[28] and may also need to provide general purpose financial statements to the ATO.[29] *See* section §4.03 for more details.

[D] Corporate Tax Transparency

Since the 2013-2014 income year, the ATO has been required by legislation to publicly report information about certain corporate taxpayers on an annual basis.[30] This disclosure applies to Australian public and foreign-owned entities with total income exceeding AUD 100 million for the income year as well as Australian-owned private entities with total income exceeding AUD 200 million.[31] The most recent report available (for the 2016-2017 income year) includes information in relation to more than 2,000 entities. The Commissioner must report only the most basic data: the name and Australian Business Number of the entity; total income; taxable income; and income

26. ATO, *Top 320 Private Groups Tax Performance Program* (last modified 23 Oct. 2018) https://www.ato.gov.au/Business/Privately-owned-and-wealthy-groups/In-detail/Top-320-Program/.
27. The legal mechanism to require the lodgement of schedules to the returns in through the power given to the Commissioner to determine the approved form of the return: AU, *Income Tax Assessment Act 1936* (Cth) s. 161A.
28. AU, *Income Tax Assessment Act 1997* (Cth) subdiv. 815-E.
29. AU, *Taxation Administration Act 1953* (Cth) s. 3CA.
30. AU, *Taxation Administration Act 1953* (Cth) s. 3C.
31. AU, *Taxation Administration Act 1953* (Cth) s. 3C(1).

tax payable.[32] The full data set can be accessed electronically,[33] and the ATO also publishes a corporate tax transparency report that analyses various aspects of the data.[34]

Corporate taxpayers are also encouraged to take up a voluntary Tax Transparency Code, developed by the Board of Taxation and endorsed by the Australian Government.[35] The level of minimum disclosure is dependent on Australian turnover. Medium and large businesses should provide a reconciliation of accounting profit to tax expense and from tax expense to tax paid, identify material differences (temporary and non-temporary), and calculate the effective company tax rates for Australian and global operations.[36] At the time of writing, 260 entities had prepared and published a tax transparency report under the voluntary Code.[37]

§4.02 THE TOP 100 POPULATION

[A] Risk Categories

The ATO has adopted an approach called 'key taxpayer engagement' for the Top 100 that aims to establish a whole-of-tax virtual team of ATO officers so that engagement can occur in an integrated and coordinated way.[38] The ATO's risk differentiation framework identifies three categories for Top 100 taxpayers:[39]

(1) key taxpayer (lowest risk category);
(2) key taxpayer with significant concerns; and
(3) higher risk.

A 'key taxpayer' would have, comparatively, a lower risk level, though not necessarily no risk, and would engage early and often with the ATO to identify significant and potentially controversial tax positions in order to work towards a resolution. Ongoing co-operative engagement and a goal of a high level of assurance are expected. To facilitate this, these taxpayers are offered an ATO Senior Relationship

32. AU, *Taxation Administration Act 1953* (Cth) s. 3C(2).
33. The report of entity tax information is available through the Australian Government website https://data.gov.au/.
34. ATO, *Corporate Tax Transparency Report for the 2016-17 Income Year* (last modified 13 Dec. 2018) https://www.ato.gov.au/Business/Large-business/In-detail/Tax-transparency/Corporate-tax-transparency-report-for-the-2016-17-income-year/.
35. ATO, *Voluntary Tax Transparency Code* (last modified 20 Sep. 2016) https://www.ato.gov.au/Business/Large-business/In-detail/Tax-transparency/Voluntary-Tax-Transparency-Code/.
36. Australian Government, The Board of Taxation, *A Tax Transparency Code* (2016), at p. 18.
37. The report of entities preparing tax transparency code submissions and links to the reports are available through the Australian Government website https://data.gov.au/.
38. ATO, *Key Taxpayer Engagement* (last modified 2 Jul. 2018) https://www.ato.gov.au/Business/Large-business/Compliance-and-governance/Key-taxpayer-engagement/.
39. ATO, *Top 100 Risk Categorisation Approach* (last modified 18 Jun. 2019) https://www.ato.gov.au/Business/Large-business/Top-100-risk-categorisation-approach/.

Manager who will coordinate high-level engagement across the ATO.[40] There is also a Large Service Team that is more generally available and dedicated to assisting large market taxpayers. Key taxpayers with significant concerns also have a positive relationship with the ATO but their affairs raise multiple and more complex risks that involve larger amounts of tax.

Higher risk taxpayers have a very different relationship with the ATO. They generally do not engage in an open and transparent way and are less likely to seek to resolve differences co-operatively with the ATO. There is also a suggestion that they may be involved in tax avoidance arrangements. The description used in the ATO documentation is that 'a higher risk taxpayer may have a structure that appears unnecessarily complex or may enter into arrangements that objectively make little sense other than for the tax benefit'.[41] These taxpayers are likely to have a low level of assurance and the ATO is more likely to resort to comprehensive audits and formal information gathering powers.

The ATO has announced that this risk classification approach will soon be replaced by an Action Differentiation Framework that will work in conjunction with the Justified Trust approach. The information currently available regarding this new framework suggests that ATO engagement will be tailored to taxpayers based on the complexity of their affairs, size, transparency in dealings with the ATO, choices and behaviours in relation to tax affairs, and the level of risk shown.[42] This tailored approach will apply to both Top 100 and Top 1,000 taxpayer segments and may involve 'partnering' to maintain good compliance, 'encouraging' to urge taxpayers to address the concerns of the ATO, or 'influencing' for those taxpayers that are not transparent or who take high risk positions. These three levels of engagement are similar to the current three taxpayer risk categories.

[B] Justified Trust Process and Key Focus Areas

The application of the Justified Trust methodology across the four areas described below leads to a determination of tax assurance outcomes that are communicated to the taxpayer in the TAR. An overall assurance rating is given as well as ratings for each of the four focus areas. The TAR covers the twelve months that have been reviewed and is updated each year as an annual report. It is expected that there will be regular engagement throughout the review process so that the ultimate rating should not come as a surprise. TARs are not released to the public due to privacy and secrecy laws.[43]

The assurance ratings issued as part of a TAR inform ATO decisions regarding the application of compliance resources and allow for tailored engagement. The relevant ATO client engagement team will keep a taxpayer updated on the progress of the TAR

40. ATO, *Relationship Management* (last modified 2 Jun. 2015) https://www.ato.gov.au/Business/Public-business-and-international/Customised-service-for-Australia-s-largest-taxpayers/Relationship-management/.
41. *Ibid.*
42. ATO, *Action Differentiation Framework* (last modified 8 Jul. 2019) https://www.ato.gov.au/Business/Large-business/Action-Differentiation-Framework/.
43. ATO, *CTA ATO Workshops*, *supra* n. 18.

but the ATO is very clear in its statements that the TAR 'is not a jointly authored document'.[44] A draft of the Executive Summary 'may' be provided in advance and taxpayers may provide feedback on the report,[45] but there is no legal mechanism to challenge the rating determination. Access to the usual merits review system for tax-related decisions is not available as this must be specifically provided for in legislation and the Justified Trust programme is purely a set of administrative arrangements.[46] In addition, as the rating or risk assessment does not in itself have a substantive impact on the taxpayer, but rather informs other decisions regarding compliance and enforcement activities of the ATO, it could not be the subject of a judicial review application.

[1] Justified Trust Focus Area 1: Tax Risk Management and Governance (Tax Control Frameworks)

The distinguishing feature of the Justified Trust methodology in comparison to earlier co-operative compliance approaches of the ATO is the emphasis on tax risk management at the corporate level. This also reflects Australia's contribution to the OECD's work on developing expectations and testing mechanisms for tax control frameworks.[47]

The ATO has developed and released a detailed *Tax Risk Management and Governance Review Guide* (the 'Guide'), primarily directed at large and complex corporations, to assist taxpayers in developing a tax governance and internal control framework, testing that framework against the ATO's best practice guidelines and demonstrating the operational effectiveness of the controls.[48] A separate set of guidelines has been prepared for privately owned groups (described below in section §4.05).

The Guide has been updated so that it now applies to both direct and indirect taxes administered by the ATO. The Guide specifies that certain control objectives will be the ATO's initial areas of focus and each of those nominated controls is aligned with a Justified Trust focus area (JT FA). For each control, the Guide provides details of how better practice in this area can be demonstrated.

By way of overview, the controls are as follows, with the link to a JT FA identified where relevant:[49]

44. *Ibid.*
45. *Ibid.*
46. AU, *Taxation Administration Act 1953* (Cth) pt IVC.
47. *See*, e.g., OECD (2016). *Co-operative Tax Compliance: Building Better Tax Control Frameworks.* OECD Publishing.
48. ATO, *Tax Risk Management and Governance Review Guide* (last modified 18 Apr. 2018) https://www.ato.gov.au/Business/Large-business/In-detail/Key-products-and-resources/Tax-risk-management-and-governance-review-guide/.
49. This table has been constructed from the guidance provided by the ATO in the *Tax Risk Management and Governance Review Guide, supra* n. 48.

Level	*Control*	*Nature*	*Link to Justified Trust*
Board	1	Formalised (board endorsed) tax control framework	
	2	Directors' roles and responsibilities are clearly understood	
	3	Board is appropriately informed on tax risk matters and effectiveness of tax control framework	JT FA 2
	4	Periodic internal control testing (should be independent but may be internal)	JT FA 1
Management	1	Staff, management and board roles and responsibilities regarding tax compliance and risk management are clearly defined and documented	JT FA 1
	2	Senior management are confident in the capacity and capability of tax governance processes and personnel	
	3	Transactions and arrangements with a significant tax impact are systematically identified, categorised and reported on	JT FA 3
	4	Data integrity as a result of data transfer between various accounting and subsidiary systems is subject to internal control processes	
	5	Record keeping policies are in place and available and compliance is verified	
	6	Documented control frameworks to ensure complete and accurate flow of information from accounting records to tax returns	JT FA 1
	7	Procedures in place to explain significant differences between accounting disclosures, financial statements and tax returns	JT FA 4
	8	Complete and accurate tax disclosures	
	9	Tax corporate governance policies and procedures are regularly reviewed and updated for law and administrative changes	

The tax control framework must be tested and evaluated. This is to include two components: testing the design effectiveness of the controls and then testing the operational effectiveness of the controls. The Guide provides walk-though examples and nominates minimum sample sizes for controls testing.

The Guide also includes detailed 'self-assessment procedures for reviewers' which are stated to be used by large corporates when self-assessing against the ATO better practices in the Guide and professional firms engaged to perform a review, as well as ATO client engagement teams when they undertake tax governance reviews.

For each Board and Management control item, sub-items or steps are identified as well as an accepted procedure for performing the step and relevant evidence to be included in the report.

ATO client engagement teams have close regard to the Guide during Justified Trust engagement but it is recognised to represent 'best practice' and should not be used as a check-list.[50] The following rating system is applied:[51]

- red flag: not evidenced or significant concerns;
- stage 1: tax control framework exists;
- stage 2: tax control framework is designed effectively;
- stage 3: tax control framework is working in practice.

In ATO guidance dated November 2018, stage 2 was considered a good rating for governance for Top 100 taxpayers.[52] Moving from stage 2 to stage 3 requires evidence of a periodic tax control testing system and the outcomes of that testing. The ATO requires an independent review and testing of tax controls. This can be undertaken by either internal or external auditors,[53] though the ATO does recognise that external auditor testing may be more reliable.[54]

[2] Justified Trust Focus Areas 2: Identifying Tax Risks and 3: Understanding Significant and New Transactions

Although the Justified Trust methodology is relatively new, identifying tax risk and seeking to understand significant and new transactions have been part of the ATO's early engagement approach for some time through ACAs and PCRs. These products continue to be used as alternatives within the Justified Trust framework in determining the tax assured.

[a] Annual Compliance Arrangements

As an alternative to post-lodgement risk reviews and audit activities, the ATO has developed a number of products that encourage early disclosure and resolution of tax issues. ACAs were first made available in 2008 and continue to be a key component of the co-operative compliance approach.

The Australian National Audit Office (ANAO) assessed the effectiveness of the ATO's administration of the ACA system and found that, as of June 2014, there were

50. ATO, *CTA ATO Workshops, supra* n. 18.
51. ATO, *Reviewing Tax Governance for Large Public and Multinational Businesses* (last modified 19 Jun. 2018) https://www.ato.gov.au/Business/Large-business/Compliance-and-governance/Reviewing-tax-governance-for-large-public-and-multinational-businesses/.
52. ATO, *Large Business Stewardship Group Key Messages* (29 Mar. 2019) (last modified 15 Jul. 2019) https://www.ato.gov.au/General/Consultation/In-detail/Stewardship-groups-minutes/Large-Business-Stewardship-Group/Large-Business-Stewardship-Group-key-messages-29-March-2019/.
53. ATO, *Reviewing Tax Governance, supra* n. 51.
54. ATO, *Tax Risk Management and Governance Review Guide, supra* n. 48, at p. 31.

only 24 ACAs in place in relation to the 158 potentially suitable taxpayers and, of those, only 18 were with companies.[55] The main reason given to the ANAO by taxpayers for not entering into an ACA was the relatively high cost, especially at the entry phase.[56] More recent statistics on the number of ACAs in place have not been found.

ACAs are voluntary administrative arrangements offered to 'key taxpayers' that have tax corporate governance practices in line with the Guide developed by the ATO (considered above) and a history and commitment to transparency and collaboration in resolving tax issues and risks.[57] An ACA can relate to a single tax (income tax, GST, excise, PRRT or Fringe Benefits Tax) or can be a 'whole-of-tax ACA' (the ATO's preferred option) and typically have a three year duration.[58] The ACA includes a tax governance letter from the taxpayer and the terms of arrangement between the ATO and the taxpayer, setting out expectations and obligations of both parties. This would generally include, for example, points of contact and escalation, disclosure obligations, any penalty and interest concessions, how unresolved issues will be managed, and schedules for each of the taxes covered.[59]

A number of benefits can flow from the development of an ACA including the speedy and real-time resolution of technical issues, administrative solutions to 'compliance irritants', and concessional treatment for penalties and interest. The 'sign-off' letter provided by the ATO will confirm that the tax return for the particular year is closed from further review and no further compliance activities will be undertaken with regard to tax risks rated as low, subject to noting any conditions for tax risks rated as high where mitigation strategies will be developed between the ATO and the taxpayer.

There may, of course, be some instances where the ATO and the taxpayer will 'agree to disagree' with respect to a specific issue and the issue will need to be resolved through more formal channels outside of the co-operative compliance products. As one option, Australian law provides a private ruling system whereby the taxpayer may apply for determination that will then be binding on the Commissioner.[60] If the taxpayer disagrees, they may object against the ruling and seek independent merits review of the decision by an administrative tribunal and/or the courts.[61] Alternatively, the issue may be the focus of post-lodgement review and audit processes. Dispute resolution may be sought via in-house facilitation or other alternative dispute resolution options. Where the issue is still unresolved, the audit team would ordinarily issue a position paper. Large public and private groups (turnover of more than AUD 250 million) can seek an independent review of the position paper by an ATO officer from

55. Australian National Audit Office, *Annual Compliance Arrangements with Large Corporate Taxpayers*, ANAO Report No. 5 2014-15 (2014) at pp. 13 and 16.
56. *Ibid.*, at p. 16.
57. ATO, *Annual Compliance Arrangements: What You Need to Know* (last modified 8 Nov. 2018) https://www.ato.gov.au/Business/Large-business/In-detail/Compliance-and-governance/Annual-Compliance-Arrangements---what-you-need-to-know/.
58. *Ibid.*
59. *Ibid.*
60. AU, *Taxation Administration Act 1953* (Cth) Sch. 1, div. 359.
61. AU, *Taxation Administration Act 1953* (Cth) pt IVC.

the Review and Dispute Resolution area (which is separate from the audit function).[62] Ultimately, the issue can be raised for external consideration through an objection against the tax assessment or amended assessment and then further reviewed by a tribunal and/or the courts.[63]

From an ongoing compliance perspective, having an ACA protects the taxpayer from post-lodgement risk reviews and audits in relation to periods covered by the ACA, from needing to complete the RTP schedule for the ACA years, and not being subject to PCRs (*see* below).[64] However, the 'sign-off' is not legally binding but is instead based on good faith and may be subject to conditions, so the level of certainty obtained is qualified.[65] Greater certainty on issues can alternatively be obtained through the binding private rulings system.

However, a taxpayer with an ACA in place is required to maintain a high level of interaction with the ATO and the ANAO report suggested that, at least at that time, many taxpayers did not see the benefits of having an ACA (in comparison to engaging in other compliance approaches) as being worth the extra costs.[66] The taxpayer must still make ongoing disclosures of any major transactions or tax positions that have a level of uncertainty and work with the ATO to resolve any new tax risks as they arise.[67] Tax risk governance processes must be maintained and all lodgement obligations met. And an annual review must be completed each year before the sign-off letter (potentially subject to conditions) can be issued. Any party can exit an ACA at any point, though the ATO suggests written notice, with reasons, should be given.[68]

[b] Pre-lodgement Compliance Reviews

As an alternative to the 'premium' ACA, PCRs were introduced in 2011 for high consequence large corporate taxpayers. The goals of the PCR are similar: 'to assure the right tax outcomes, and identify and manage material tax risks through early, tailored and transparent engagement'.[69] A PCR may also be extended to lower consequence taxpayers if the view is taken that more timely compliance assurance is desired.[70]

A PCR generally spans a two-year period, so includes the relevant income tax year (during which real-time disclosures are expected to be made) as well as the following year, to allow for the lodgement of the annual return plus a period of up to five months to allow the ATO and the taxpayer to analyse, discuss and hopefully

62. ATO, *Resolving Disputes* (last modified 26 Sep. 2018) https://www.ato.gov.au/Business/Public-business-and-international/Tailored-engagement/Resolving-disputes/.
63. AU, *Income Tax Assessment Act* 1936 (Cth) s. 175A and *Taxation Administration Act 1953* (Cth) pt IVC.
64. *Ibid;* and ANAO Report, *supra* n. 55, at p. 32.
65. ANAO Report, *supra* n. 55, at p. 52-3.
66. *Ibid* at pp. 65-66.
67. ATO, *Annual Compliance Arrangements: What You Need to Know, supra* n. 57.
68. *Ibid.*
69. ATO, *Engaging Early with You* (last modified 29 Feb. 2016) https://www.ato.gov.au/Business/Public-business-and-international/Excellent-working-relationships/Engaging-early-with-you/.
70. *Ibid.*

resolve any outstanding issues.[71] Discussions during the year and during the pre-lodgement period when the return is being prepared allows for issues to be identified and for a resolution to be sought. Alternative dispute resolution mechanisms may be accessed in the pre-lodgement period. A GST PCR will involve real time reviews of monthly business activity statements for a twelve-month period, again with the emphasis on resolving issues pre-lodgement where possible.

At the completion of the PCR, the ATO provides a letter to the taxpayer that sets out the issues that have been identified and activities planned to address any outstanding issues outside of the PCR.[72] The ATO notes that a PCR does not provide the same level of certainty as an ACA (the PCR finalisation letter is not a sign-off letter) but the ANAO report suggested that, at least in 2014, the PCR process was considered satisfactory to many taxpayers.[73] Issues identified but not resolved by the PCR may be the subject of post-lodgement review and audit, which may ultimately require litigation to resolve more contentious issues.

[c] Advance Pricing Arrangements

The ATO sets out the details regarding the mechanism for obtaining an APA in an administrative practice statement.[74] An APA allows for specifying in advance the appropriate set of criteria to determine the transfer pricing of a controlled transaction. This is a separate administrative process to an ACA.

The practice statement recognises that APAs can be unilateral, bilateral or multilateral and have a usual term of between three and five years. APAs are seen as 'a pragmatic strategy that foster co-operative tax compliance and prevent escalation of transfer pricing issues into disputes'.[75] The taxpayer must lodge an annual compliance report over the term of the APA.

An APA will not prevent a risk review or audit but if an APA is in effect, the ATO will not engage in such actions in relation to the cross-border dealings unless there is a reason to believe that the taxpayer has omitted material information or provided incorrect material information.[76] Compliance with the APA is managed through an annual compliance review.

[3] Justified Trust Focus Area 4: Understanding Why the Accounts and Tax Results Vary

Little public guidance from the ATO is currently available in relation to this final focus area. An analysis of ETB has been identified as a key part of understanding the

71. *Ibid.*
72. *Ibid.*
73. ANAO Report, *supra* n. 55, at p. 65.
74. ATO, PS LA 2015/4 *Advance Pricing Arrangements* (originally issued 2015, update 2017).
75. PS LA 2015/4 at para. 4C.
76. PC LA 2015/4 at para. 25B.

variation between accounting and tax results.[77] The ATO will, when possible, use information already available to it in undertaking the ETB analysis.

The ATO will seek a 'holistic understanding of the taxpayer's business operation and financial performance' and then compare that to its tax performance, including an analysis of the global value chain and sales and acquisitions data.[78] According to a recent speech by Jeremy Hirschhorn, Second Commissioner, Client Engagement, ATO:[79]

> The [ETB] methodology identifies an economic group's worldwide profit from Australian-linked business activities and the Australian and offshore tax paid on that profit. As an adviser, ETB is another tool which will provide you with an early insight into how your client may be profiled and risk assessed by the ATO, in an effort to establish justified trust. As above, it is also a useful sense check on any transfer prices and whether they are giving plausible, common sense outcomes. Further, it may flush out any upstream hybridity or non-taxation relevant to the anti-hybrid rules or the MAAL [Multinational Anti-Avoidance Law] or DPT [Diverted Profits Tax]. Importantly, it will also flush out what I describe as 'transfer mis-pricing arbitrage' structures, where one methodology is chosen for the 'true' exporting company, another methodology is used by the 'true' importing company, but a low or un-taxed entity is inserted into the middle to book the residual channel profit.

Further from ATO guidance, 'the ETB determines the weighted average of the cash tax paid ratios (cash tax paid over Australian-linked profits) for each jurisdiction' and understanding a taxpayer's ETB assists in identifying risk.[80]

[C] Benefits of Obtaining Justified Trust

Where a high level of assurance (justified trust) is obtained, the ATO identifies the following benefits for the taxpayer:[81]

- reduced compliance costs in future years (provided business arrangements remain largely the same);
- Board of Director's confidence in the entity's tax compliance;
- greater certainty;
- 'lighter touch' (less intense) engagement going forward; and
- maintenance of ATO corporate knowledge through the retaining of the permanent file for the taxpayer.

---

77. ATO, *CTA ATO Workshops, supra* n. 18.
78. ATO, *Justified Trust* (last modified 2 Jul. 2018) https://www.ato.gov.au/Business/Large-business/Justified-trust/.
79. ATO, *Jeremy Hirschhorn, Second Commissioner, Client Engagement, Welcome Address and Opening Remarks at the Tax Institute National Transfer Pricing Conference, 'Transfer Pricing a Key Focus for ATO'* (Sydney, 14 Aug. 2019) https://www.ato.gov.au/Media-centre/Speeches/Other/Transfer-pricing-a-key-focus-for-ATO/.
80. ATO, *We Assist and Assure the Tax Compliance of Large Corporate Groups* (last modified 13 Dec. 2018) https://www.ato.gov.au/General/Tax-and-Corporate-Australia/In-detail/We-assist-and-assure-the-tax-compliance-of-large-corporate-groups/.
81. ATO, *CTA ATO Workshops, supra* n. 18.

The less intense engagement would usually mean less frequent and less in-depth interactions with the ATO where there are no material changes, reviewing only significant transactions and/or not reviewing the tax control framework again for two years.

The ATO has also been working on a Justified Trust credential that is proposed to be issued along with the TAR when there is a high rating achieved.[82] This document would allow the taxpayer to promote their high rating to the public. The ATO has reported an expectation that a majority of the Top 100 would achieve justified trust by 2020.[83]

§4.03 MANDATORY DISCLOSURE OBLIGATIONS

[A] Income Tax Return Schedules

There is a requirement under the income tax legislation for the Commissioner to provide an annual notice specifying those taxpayers required to lodge a return for the year[84] and this generally includes 'full self-assessment taxpayers' (defined to include all companies as well as trustees of trusts)[85] and partnerships that are either residents of Australia or derive income or gains taxable in Australia.[86] The legislation further grants the Commissioner a broad power to specify the 'approved form' of the return.[87] The Commissioner uses this power to require taxpayers meeting certain criteria to lodge, along with their main tax return, additional schedules. The two schedules highlighted here as most relevant for current purposes are the International Dealings Schedule (IDS) and the RTP Schedule.

Civil and administrative penalties may apply if a taxpayer fails to provide a document as required by the Commissioner[88] or lodges it late.[89] Penalties also apply if false or misleading statements are included in any disclosures.[90]

[1] International Dealings Schedule

Business taxpayers engaged in international transactions or dealings with related parties valued at more than AUD 2 million are required to complete and lodge the IDS. Other circumstances will also trigger the requirement to lodge the IDS, such as having

82. ATO, *Large Business Stewardship Group Key Messages*, *supra* n. 52.
83. *Ibid.*
84. AU, *Income Tax Assessment Act 1936* (Cth) s. 161.
85. AU, *Income Tax Assessment Act 1936* (Cth) s. 6.
86. Australian Government, Legislative Instrument F2019L00675, *Notice of Requirement to Lodge a Return for the Income Year Ended 30 June 2019*, registered 13 May 2019 (available on the ATO legal database as LODGE 2019/1).
87. AU, *Income Tax Assessment Act 1936* (Cth) s. 161A.
88. AU, *Taxation Administration Act 1953* (Cth) s. 8C.
89. AU, *Taxation Administration Act 1953* (Cth) Sch. 1, s. 286-75.
90. AU, *Taxation Administration Act 1953* (Cth) s. 8K and Sch. 1, s. 284-75.

overseas branch operations or where the thin capitalisation rules have an impact on the taxpayer.[91]

The IDS requires specified information be disclosed in relation to the following areas:[92]

- international related party dealings;
- financial arrangements;
- interests in foreign entities;
- thin capitalisation;
- financial services entities; and
- hybrid mismatches (new for 2019).

[2] RTP Schedule

The RTP schedule was first piloted in 2012.[93] Initially it only applied to those taxpayers from the largest business category who had been advised in writing of the requirement, but its application has been gradually extended to additional corporate taxpayer segments. The RTP schedule now applies to both the Top 100 and Top 1,000 companies, and the ATO has signalled its intention to extend the obligation to companies in the large private groups segment for the 2020-2021 financial year.[94] A taxpayer with an ACA covering the relevant year is not required to lodge the RTP schedule and a particular issue does not need to be disclosed on the RTP schedule if the taxpayer has already applied for a private ruling in relation to the issue.[95]

There are three categories of reportable positions:

(1) Category A: tax uncertainty in the income tax return.
(2) Category B: tax uncertainty in financial accounts.
(3) Category C: specifically identified RTPs.

A materiality threshold applies to Categories A and B, which is defined as the greater of AUD 3 million and 5% of current tax expense as calculated for accounting purposes.[96] There is no materiality threshold for Category C.

A Category A reportable position is a position taken in relation to the income tax return where 'it would be concluded in the circumstances, having regard to relevant

91. ATO, *International Dealings Schedule Instructions 2019* (last modified 30 May 2019) https://www.ato.gov.au/Forms/International-dealings-schedule-instructions-2019/.
92. *Ibid.*
93. ANAO Report, *supra* n. 55, at p. 65.
94. ATO, *Private Groups Stewardship Group Key Messages* (29 Mar. 2019) (last modified 29 Apr. 2019) https://www.ato.gov.au/General/Consultation/In-detail/Stewardship-groups-minutes/Private-Groups-Stewardship-Group/Private-Groups-Stewardship-Group-key-messages-29-March-2019/.
95. ATO, *Reportable Tax Position Instructions 2019* (last modified 20 May 2019) https://www.ato.gov.au/Forms/Reportable-tax-position-instructions-2019/.
96. *Ibid.*

authorities, that what is argued for is about as likely to be correct as incorrect, or is less likely to be correct than incorrect'.[97] If the position taken in the return is later found to be incorrect, the taxpayer may be subject to a penalty for failing to take a reasonably arguable position,[98] where this is defined as a position that is 'about as likely to be correct as incorrect, or is more likely to be correct that incorrect'[99] (though note the overlap between a reportable position and a reasonably arguable position when the case is evenly balanced). Category B covers situations where there is uncertainty about taxes payable or recoverable that is recognised or disclosed in the taxpayer's or a related party's financial statements.

Category C disclosures are much more directed. Each year the ATO produces a list of questions that identify certain types of transactions or arrangements and the taxpayer must disclose any involvement in such dealings. The list of questions is updated each year and includes arrangements identified through the ATO's Taxpayer Alerts and Practical Compliance Guidelines as involving higher tax risk. The 2019 RTP schedule identifies twenty-two higher risk arrangements that must be disclosed.[100] These include offshore marketing and procurement hub arrangements, research and development tax incentive arrangements, cross-border related party debt funding and derivative transactions, and inbound distribution arrangements. In relation to most of these arrangements, the ATO has issued Practical Compliance Guidelines that provide a framework for taxpayers to self-assess their risk category, which must then also be disclosed as part of the RTP schedule.[101]

[B] Country-by-Country Reporting

SGEs are required by Australian tax law to make disclosures through CbCR for income years commencing on or after 1 January 2016.[102] An entity covered by these rules is required to lodge all three CbCR statements with the ATO within twelve months of the end of the reporting period. The three statements correspond to the CbC report, master file and local file as outlined in the OECD guidance. For Australian purposes, the SGE threshold is AUD 1 billion.[103]

The approved forms of the CbC report and master file follow the requirements of the OECD guidance (Annexures III and I, respectively). The information requirements of the local file starts with the OECD guidance but some taxpayers are only required to

97. *Ibid.*
98. TAA, Sch. 1, s. 284-75(2).
99. TAA, Sch. 1, s. 284-15.
100. *Ibid.*
101. For example, *see* ATO, Practical Compliance Guideline PCG 2017/1 *ATO Compliance Approach to Transfer Pricing Issues Related to Centralised Operating Models Involving Procurement, Marketing, Sales and Distribution Functions* (2017, updated 2018).
102. AU, *Income Tax Assessment Act 1997* (Cth) s. 815-355. *See also* ATO, Law Companion Ruling LCR 2015/3 *Subdivision 815-E of the Income Tax Assessment Act 1997: Country-by-Country Reporting* (2015; last modified 29 Feb. 2018).
103. AU, *Income Tax Assessment Act 1997* (Cth) s. 960-555.

file a 'short form' version of the local file.[104] Irrespective of whether an ACA or APA is in effect, international related party dealings must still be included in the local file.[105]

The Commissioner can exempt an entity or class of entities from CbCR obligations.[106] For example, tax exempt entities are automatically relieved of these obligations and SGEs can apply for an exemption.[107]

§4.04 TOP 1,000 TAX PERFORMANCE PROGRAMME: SARs

The Top 1,000 tax performance programme was established in 2016 to seek tax assurance for this group of large public and multinational economic groups not otherwise included in the Top 100 programme. Designed as a variation of the Top 100 Justified Trust programme, the approach is referred to as SARs. Since February 2019, this programme now also specifically includes large regulated superannuation (retirement savings) funds within the Top 1,000.[108]

The ATO makes available the typical questions asked in a SAR so that taxpayers can begin to prepare before being officially contacted and these questions are updated from time to time.[109] The questions fall under the same four focus areas used for Top 100 Justified Trust method and the reviews cover a period of the last four income years. Taxpayers are now often given early notification up to four months before the commencement of a SAR so that they can begin to prepare responses to the questions. The ATO has produced a 'client experience roadmap' for the SAR that estimates that the process would generally be completed within four months, resulting in either a Letter of Assurance or a Finalisation Letter that identifies issues for further reviews of assurance.[110]

104. ATO, *Local File/Master File 2019* (last modified 26 Jun 2019) https://www.ato.gov.au/Business/International-tax-for-business/In-detail/Transfer-pricing/Country-by-Country-reporting/Local-file/master-file-2019/.
105. ATO, *Country-by-Country Reporting Guidance* (last modified 23 May 2019) https://www.ato.gov.au/Business/International-tax-for-business/In-detail/Transfer-pricing/Country-by-Country-reporting/Country-by-Country-Reporting-Guidance/.
106. AU, *Income Tax Assessment Act 1997* (Cth) s. 815-365.
107. ATO, *Country-by-Country Reporting Guidance*, *supra* n. 105.
108. ATO, *Streamlined Assurance Reviews for Large APRA-Regulated Super Funds* (last modified 22 Feb. 2019) https://www.ato.gov.au/Business/Business-bulletins-newsroom/Large-business/Streamlined-Assurance-Reviews-for-large-APRA-regulated-super-funds/?BusBulNewsroomLanding.
109. ATO, *Typical Questions in a Top 1000 Streamlined Assurance Review* (last modified 6 Jun. 2019) https://www.ato.gov.au/Business/Large-business/In-detail/Typical-questions-in-a-Top-1000-streamlined-assurance-review/.
110. ATO, *Top 1000 Multinationals and Public Companies Tax Performance Program: A Guide to Assist Taxpayers Engaging with the ATO Through the New Streamlined Assurance Reviews* (2016).

[A] SAR Focus Areas: The Links to the Justified Trust Programme[111]

Under the heading of tax governance and risk management, the starting point is for the taxpayer to describe the approach taken by it to the ATO's tax risk management Guide (i.e., whether there has been a gap analysis comparing current controls to the ATO's Guide). The most recent documents evidencing the tax control management framework are to be provided as well as details of any internal or external reviews and their findings. The SARs focus on the six controls set out in the Guide that are specifically linked to Justified Trust objectives (*see* sub-section §4.02[B][1] above).

Under tax risks flagged to the market, the taxpayer group is asked whether it has any RTPs, any errors or omissions in a tax return not yet disclosed, and the details of any research and development tax incentive claimed. The taxpayer is also asked to provide the details regarding any hybrid instruments held and any dealings with a related party hybrid entity or interests in any hybrid entity.

The significant and new transactions section requires a diagram of the worldwide group structure, including details such as an identification of all jurisdictions where economic activity is undertaken, any changes in the group structure during the review period and any permanent establishments or flow-through entities. Details are sought regarding new business lines, significant new transactions, restructures or reorganisations within the group and any acquisitions or disposals of interests in another entity, in all cases during the review period.

Finally, under the heading of alignment between accounting and tax results, the ATO seeks financial information including the statement of taxable income and working papers and trial balances as well as the reconciliation between accounting profit before income tax as shown in the financial statements to profit before tax shown in the tax return. The working papers supporting the tax return schedules and disclosures and explaining the income tax note in the financial statements should be provided, as well as the details of any elections or choices made under the Australian income tax law.

[B] SAR Experience to Date

In March 2019, the ATO published a findings report based on more than 280 SARs that had been completed to date.[112] In the SAR report given to taxpayers at the end of the review process, taxpayers are given a rating of high, medium or low reflecting the overall level of assurance that the taxpayer had paid the right amount of income tax. The ATO finding report shows that 31% received a high rating, 52% received a medium rating, and 17% received a low rating.[113] The SAR reports also identify steps that taxpayers should take to obtain a higher assurance rating.

Within the four sub-categories corresponding to the JT FAs, a different rating categorisation applies: stage 3 (green); stage 2 (yellow); stage 1 (amber); and red flag

111. The summary in this section is based on the ATO's, *Typical Questions*, *supra* n. 109.
112. ATO, *Findings Report: Top 1,000 Tax Performance Program* (income tax) (March 2019).
113. *Ibid.*, at p. 4.

(no evidence or significant concerns). In the area of tax governance, for this taxpayer group the most common rating was stage 1 (70%), suggesting that these taxpayers are in the early stages of developing robust tax control frameworks.[114] Tax risks flagged to market and significant and new transactions are grouped together in the report. The area found to be of greatest concern is transfer pricing, with nearly 40% of reviewed entities receiving a low rating or red flag.[115] The ratings for this taxpayer group were highest in relation to alignment of tax and accounting outcomes, where 88% of taxpayers received a high rating.[116] The ATO reported in March 2019 that another 300 SARs were then in progress.[117]

BDO Australia, an accountancy and advisory firm, undertook a survey of taxpayers' views and experiences with the ATO's Justified Trust initiatives, focussing on the Top 1,000 reviews process. The results were published in March 2019.[118] Although the sample size and description and response rates are not available, the survey provides at least anecdotal insights into taxpayers' understanding. Of interest, only approximately 25% of taxpayers with turnover levels that would put them in the Top 1,000 group rated their understanding of the concept of justified trust and how to achieve it as 'very well understood' and about 65% only thought that they 'somewhat understood' it. The survey indicates that 87% of those who had not yet been contacted by the ATO did not have a documented tax governance framework in place and, of those who had been contacted, nearly 70% believed that the cost of undergoing a Justified Trust review would exceed AUD 100,000.

§4.05 TOP 320 PRIVATE GROUPS TAX PERFORMANCE PROGRAMME

As was noted above, under the auspices of the Tax Avoidance Taskforce, the ATO has put in place an early engagement and assurance programme for the Top 320 private groups. The ATO's published materials describe this as part of the Justified Trust strategy,[119] but there is less detail available regarding this programme compared to the other taxpayer segments. This may be at least in part due to the diversity of taxpayers in this segment and therefore a diversity in the tailored approach to engagement.

Where the ATO has established justified trust with the taxpayer, and that the taxpayer has effective tax governance systems in place, then the ATO suggests that more streamlined engagements should follow that reduce the costs of compliance.[120]

114. *Ibid.*, at p. 5.
115. *Ibid.*, at p. 7. Rating for other areas are also given in the report: research and development; consolidation and MEC structuring; thin capitalisation; and related party financing.
116. *Ibid.*, at p. 9.
117. ATO, *Large Business Stewardship Group Key Messages*, *supra* n. 52.
118. BDO Australia, *Survey: BDO ATO Justified Trust Survey Results* (11 Mar. 2019) https://www.bdo.com.au/en-au/insights/tax/surveys/bdo-ato-justified-trust-survey-results.
119. ATO, *Tax Avoidance Taskforce* (last modified 12 Dec. 2018) https://www.ato.gov.au/general/Tax-avoidance-taskforce/.
120. ATO, *Tailored Engagement with Privately Owned and Wealthy Groups* (last modified 28 Sep. 2018) https://www.ato.gov.au/Business/Privately-owned-and-wealthy-groups/What-you-should-know/Tailored-engagement/Early-engagement-with-large-privately-owned-and-wealthy-groups/.

Areas of risk are identified, along with mitigation strategies, and early engagement is aimed at identifying and resolving potential tax risks prior to lodgement.[121]

The greatest amount of information is provided regarding tax governance in the private group context. The ATO has identified seven principles of effective tax governance to guide these taxpayers:[122]

(1) accountable management and oversight;
(2) appropriate controls and processes to recognise tax risks;
(3) seek advice through published ATO guidance, private advisers and, where needed, the ATO;
(4) integrity in financial and tax reporting;
(5) professional and productive working relationship with the ATO;
(6) timely lodgement and payments; and
(7) ethical and responsible behaviour.

Further detail is provided regarding 'key governance steps and processes'[123] some of which more explicitly than others match to the seven principles.

To assist taxpayers in the private group segment in improving their tax governance, the ATO developed and has now publicly released an Information System Risk Assessment (IRSA) tool (available for download through the ATO website since 1 July 2019).[124] This tool allows taxpayers to self-assess the integrity of their information technology (IT) systems, to evidence whether the appropriate controls to meet tax reporting obligations are in place, and to identify where there are areas of risk.[125] The tool asks questions across five key areas of the IT systems and produces a report along with a risk rating of low, medium or high.[126] The tool is aimed at testing the IT systems to see if the internal controls are sufficient to ensure that accurate and complete information is available for reporting and lodgement purposes.[127]

---

121. *Ibid.*
122. ATO, *Seven Principles of Effective Tax Governance* (last modified 31 May 2016) https://www.ato.gov.au/Business/Privately-owned-and-wealthy-groups/Tax-governance/Tax-governance-guide-for-privately-owned-groups/Corporate-governance-and-tax-governance/Seven-principles-of-effective-tax-governance/.
123. ATO, *Key Governance Steps and Processes* (last modified 18 Jun. 2019) https://www.ato.gov.au/Business/Privately-owned-and-wealthy-groups/Tax-governance/Tax-governance-guide-for-privately-owned-groups/Corporate-governance-and-tax-governance/Key-governance-steps-and-processes/.
124. ATO, *New Information System Risk Assessment Tool (ISRA)* (last modified 1 Jul. 2019) https://www.ato.gov.au/Business/Business-bulletins-newsroom/General/New-Information-System-Risk-Assessment-tool-(ISRA)/?BusBullNewsroomLanding.
125. ATO, *Information System Risk Assessment Tool* (last modified 18 Jun. 2019) https://www.ato.gov.au/Business/Privately-owned-and-wealthy-groups/Tax-governance/Information-System-Risk-Assessment-tool/.
126. ATO, *How the ISRA Tool Works* (last modified 18 Jun. 2019) https://www.ato.gov.au/Business/Privately-owned-and-wealthy-groups/Tax-governance/Information-system-risk-assessment-tool/How-the-ISRA-tool-works/.
127. *Ibid.*

Other early engagement products that are available to public groups are also available to private groups, including ACAs and APAs.[128] The ATO also offers this taxpayer group the option of seeking a pre-lodgement compliance agreement for a specific 'commercial deal', which is defined as a significant business transaction that affects the business structure.[129] Such an agreement does not offer the same level of protection as a binding private ruling but the ATO suggests that if an agreement is reached and the return is lodged in accordance with it, they will not conduct a review or audit of that commercial deal.[130]

§4.06 CONCLUSIONS

Australia's early adoption of a co-operative compliance approach to taxpayer engagement in 2000 has provided the ATO and taxpayers with the opportunity to develop and refine engagement models and products across various taxpayer segments. Although this chapter has focussed on the large business taxpayer segments, the ATO encourages early and co-operative engagement with all taxpayers, as reflected in the *Taxpayers' Charter* and the ATO's general compliance model, which combines behavioural insights principles with a responsive regulation pyramid.[131]

More recently, the ATO has grouped the co-operative compliance mechanisms under the umbrella of Justified Trust and adopted tax assured as a performance measure, with the first published estimates in the 2017-2018 ATO Annual Report. The most developed and sophisticated version of the Justified Trust model now operates with respect to the Top 100 segment, with the earlier developed ACA and PCR products now forming the foundation of focus areas 2 and 3. The Justified Trust model has been adapted for the Top 1,000 segment through the introduction of SARs and some evidence now exists in relation to its extension to the Top 320 private groups segment through the tax performance programme.

The ATO has been particularly active in relation to developing taxpayer guidance on tax control frameworks, culminating in the *Tax Risk Management and Governance Review Guide*, which now covers indirect taxes and well as income tax. Although the Guide is designed for large business entities, the six key controls that link to Justified Trust objectives are being assessed as part of the Top 1,000 SARs, with early results showing this to be an area requiring more work for nearly all taxpayers. Further assistance has also been recently released for the Top 320 private groups through the

128. ATO, *Mutual Arrangements for Certainty* (last modified 24 Jan. 2019) https://www.ato.gov.au/Business/Privately-owned-and-wealthy-groups/What-you-should-know/The-right-services/Mutual-arrangements-for-certainty/.
129. ATO, *Commercial Deals* (last modified 6 Sep. 2019) https://www.ato.gov.au/Business/Privately-owned-and-wealthy-groups/What-you-should-know/The-right-services/Commercial-deals/.
130. *Ibid.*
131. ATO, *Compliance Model* (last modified 11 Apr. 2019) https://www.ato.gov.au/About-ATO/Managing-the-tax-and-super-system/Strategic-direction/How-we-help-and-influence-taxpayers/Compliance-model/? = redirected_compliancemodel.

ATO's downloadable IRSA tool. The ATO's work in this area may be of particular interest to other jurisdictions seeking to assist taxpayers in developing and testing tax control frameworks and thereby bringing greater rigour to their co-operative compliance programmes.

CHAPTER 5

Co-operative Compliance: An Austrian Point of View

Simon Hofstätter

§5.01 INTRODUCTION

January 1, 2019 marks another milestone in the history of Austrian fiscal policy. On this day, a change in Austrian procedural law gave birth to the so-called Begleitende Kontrolle (bK), which translates best to "Guided Audit." What started as a project in 2011 was implemented into Austrian law, to create an alternative way of approaching Austrian taxpayers.

I want to give a quick summary of the new procedural law regulations, as well as some background information which led to said law and an overview of Co-operative Compliance in Austria in general. Furthermore, the Austrian Tax Administration chose to take part in the International Compliance Assurance Programme (ICAP) 2.0 pilot project, an undertaking by the Organisation for Economic Co-operation and Development (OECD) on multilateral risk assessment. I want to present you with the motives behind the decision for participating as well as trying to point out possible connections and chances to integrate the multilateral approach into our unilateral compliance programme.

§5.02 BEGLEITENDE KONTROLLE

[A] From Project to Law: Project Overview

The ambition in 2011 was to create some kind of proactive co-operation between the tax administration and large-scale enterprises. This co-operation should be on a regular basis with the aim to communicate at eye-level.[1] To give this ambition a wider acceptance, several key stakeholders, such as the Austrian Chamber of Commerce, the Austrian Chamber of Tax Auditors as well as the universities of Vienna and Graz, were involved from the beginning.

To represent the idea of communicating at eye-level the project was named "Horizontal Monitoring (HM)." It was clear from the start that such a relation between authority and taxpayer would need open-minded participants on both sides. The target group of the project were large-scale enterprises, willing to be compliant with Austrian tax regulations. The reward for these corporations should be legal certainty and timely processing of their tax returns. Although the Austrian Tax Administration was open-minded to such developments from early on, it has to be said that the origins for "HM" came from the OECD's Forum on Tax Administration (FTA) as well as several ideas taken from a similar approach by the Netherlands. The ideas gathered at an international level were combined with an Austrian Fair-Play-Program in 2010. This programme had three major goals:[2]

(1) Progressive increase of Tax Compliance by proactively involving taxpayers.
(2) Secure Austrian financial/fiscal interests.
(3) Secure fair conditions of competition for the economy.

HM was developed in 2011 as a follow-up. The three goals were amended with key objectives:[3]

- Promotion of Tax Compliance in reference to large-scale enterprises.
- Guarantee of timely and correct tax collection.
- Give the Austrian Tax Administration room to focus on risks rather than routine auditing.
- Reducing compliance costs for taxpayers involved.
- Staff development toward compliance, ethical behavior and trust for all parties involved.
- Create role-model behavior and improve the reputation of taxpayers involved.

The project was finally commissioned in June 2011 by the then Minister of Finance Dr. Maria Fekter. It was agreed that this project should be evaluated and the evaluation report should be made public, in order to guarantee transparency throughout the process. Afterward, a formal decision should be made, whether to incorporate regulations into procedural law, to put HM on a legally binding basis. At this point, it is important to mention that already at project stage HM had a partial legal basis, as § 144 Bundesabgabenordnung (Austrian Procedural Law) allowed the auditing of enterprises under the title of "Nachschau" which translates best to "Small Inspection." The

1. Müller & Reinweber in Müller & Woischitzschläger & Zöchling, *Co-operative Tax Compliance in Österreich*, 8 (2019).
2. Müller, *Fair Play—Steuerpolitik und Abgabenmoral, in Einkommensteuer Körperschaftssteuer Steuerpolitik—Gedenkschrift Peter Quantschnigg*, 279ff (2010).
3. Elmecker, *Evaluation Horizontal Monitoring* (2016).

slight disadvantage for corporations involved in the project was that a "Nachschau" does not provide full legal certainty in connection to tax returns filed and inspected. Therefore, a project agreement was signed with each of the participating corporations, to the effect that HM would ensure legal certainty once legislated.

Over the course of the project from 2011 to 2016, seventeen corporations or corporate groups (more than one entity) were involved. As two left in the course of the project and a few joined only in 2016 just twelve participants were finally evaluated.

[B] From Project to Law: Evaluation

The full result of the evaluation (evaluation report) was published on the homepage of the Austrian Ministry of Finance (www.bmf.gv.at).[4]

The evaluation mainly consisted of three methods:

(1) hard facts comparison.
(2) process workshops.
(3) interviews with stakeholders.

The aim was to decide possible incorporation into law on the basis of hard facts, but complemented with views and experiences from stakeholders. The evaluation should analyze whether the key objectives mentioned above were met within the project or not.

Hard Facts Decision: The report analyzed the twelve evaluated corporations on an inner comparison basis. This means that stats from the time these corporations were traditionally audited (*ex post* audit) were compared to stats from auditing through HM (*ex ante* audit). To summarize the result, the evaluation showed improvement in almost every fact evaluated. Not only was the number of appeals against tax assessments substantially reduced, the evaluation also showed that the time span between the filing of tax returns and the final assessment declined significantly. This led to the conclusion that legal costs must have been lower for the corporations, as appeals and court trials, usually represent a substantial amount of legal expenses.

On the other hand, evaluators found out that the twelve corporations participating account for around 5.5% of the total Austrian Corporate Income Tax Revenue and almost 6% of research premium paid out (state subsidy on research). Therefore, the Austrian Tax Administration was able to collect substantial amounts of Corporate Income Tax (CIT) correctly, as well as directly overseeing significant part subsidies paid. Furthermore, the analysis showed that HM gave tax auditors relief from routine functions (checking the correct basis for tax returns, procedural checks, etc.), and gave them opportunities to focus on risks and processes.

Process Workshops: Workshops were organized on a SWOT-Analysis base. These workshops covered all of the twelve participating corporations, as well as the auditing

4. *Horizontal Monitoring Evaluationsbericht Oktober 2016* (October 25, 2019), https://www.bmf.gv.at/services/publikationen/BMF_Evaluationsbericht_Horizontal_Monitoring.pdf?63xfqc.

office for large-scale enterprises and also involved local tax administrations (jurisdiction depending on the headquarter location of participating taxpayers). The strengths found were that permanent contact between taxpayer and authority is a big advantage for both sides and gives them the opportunity to focus resources on analyzing certain risks collectively and to discuss possible solutions right away. Weaknesses were found with personal resources on the authorities' side and increased requirements on documenting processes for taxpayers.

All stakeholders agreed that public approval of HM could only be gained if HM were put on a fixed legal basis, making it available on a large scale rather than focusing on selected companies (project participants). Another threat found was the change of key personnel, as trust is a big driver within the HM process. Also the danger of operational blindness was voiced, and legal requirements should be implemented to avoid this risk and to prevent the image of sweetheart dealing. But there was a collective agreement that HM is a big chance for both sides if circumstances generate an environment of trust and transparency.

Online Interviews: Interviews were held anonymously throughout the HM project. Employees of the Austrian Tax Administration were asked questions on three several occasions, whereas HM project participants and involved tax advisors were interviewed twice. One separate survey in 2015 covered corporations not involved in the project, to gather "outside opinions." Participants were asked to express their personal opinions and interpretations on several HM-dimensions:

- Information: Self-perception of knowledge about HM.
- Attitude: Personal opinion on image, co-operation, and efficiency connected to HM.
- Identification: Personal Identification with HM.
- Skills: Personal qualifications to take part in HM.
- Effects: Opinion on HM's effect on transparency, disclosure, fiscal reliability etc.

Within the survey, participants had to express their agreement in relation to positive and negative statements about HM on a scale from 1 to 9 with the possibility to support the grading with comments. Developments of HM should be made visible by repeated surveys throughout the process.

The result was multilayered in many ways. Within the Tax Administration, personnel involved in the project viewed HM more positively than non-involved personnel. Especially non-involved employees felt they were lacking knowledge about the process and were raising concerns of sweetheart dealing and possible corruption. Surprisingly, there was almost no evolution throughout the three different surveys. Whereas involved personnel viewed the process very positively from the beginning and stuck to their opinion, non-involved personnel commented more negatively on a continuous basis. It was therefore decided that a possible incorporation of HM into procedural law should be guided with information campaigns within the Tax Administration, to gain support from employees on a broader scale.

The result was much less diverse between involved and non-involved taxpayers. Both parties viewed HM and Co-operative Compliance very positively. The main difference was that involved taxpayers felt more knowledgeable and interested.

Conclusion: The evaluation led to the following general conclusions:

- *HM is an appropriate tool to encourage tax compliance:* All stakeholders involved stated the working environment created by HM superior to *ex post* auditing. Especially mutual understanding and respect were mentioned on both sides.
- *HM increases legal certainty and planning security for corporations involved:* The only amendment was that the inclusion in procedural law and a clear statement of the legal requirements would be sufficient.
- *HM can guarantee timely and correct collection of taxes for large numbers of Austria's fiscal revenue:* Ideally, HM should generate an environment where overdue taxes are reduced to a minimum.
- *HM gives tax authorities opportunities to focus on risk:* It was agreed though that participating taxpayers would need tax control frameworks (TCFs) to cover routine supervision both for themselves and on behalf of tax authorities.
- *HM needs to ensure constant personal development:* Evaluation showed that deficits in communication, information and qualification need to be fixed and constantly improved.
- *HM is beneficial for the corporations involved and strengthens Austria as a business location:* Involved corporations are taking action on their corporate social responsibility and are rewarded for their initiative.

To summarize, the evaluation report recommended the continuation of HM but based on its incorporation into procedural law.

[C] Legal Incorporation: Legislative Process

Upon implementation, HM was changed to "bK," which translates best to "Guided Audit." The incorporation into Austrian procedural law (Bundesabgabenordnung) was effected in 2018, becoming effective on January 1, 2019. Draft papers and general guidance can be taken from the Homepage of the Austrian Parliament (Legislative Authority).[5]

The Guidance reveals that bK should be an alternative to *ex post* audits, with the possibility to opt-in for taxpayers complying with various requirements. The most complex requirement is the implementation of a TCF (Steuerkontrollsystem), which needs certification from tax advisors. This TCF should free tax authorities from performing routine fiscal control functions. Certification from tax advisors should guarantee legal accuracy and conformity in terms of operational implementation.

5. *Erläuterungen zum Jahressteuergesetz 2018* (Oktober 26, 2019), https://www.parlament.gv.at/PAKT/VHG/XXVI/I/I_00190/fname_698480.pdf.

[D] Procedural Law: Requirements

This subsection deals with the new procedural legal regulations and BK is stated within Austrian procedural law called "Bundesabgabenordnung" in § 153a-§ 153g and transition regulations in § 323 subsection 55, all in wording effective after January 1, 2019.

General Requirements: The following general requirements have to be fulfilled to apply for bK:

- *Applicant:* The applicant must be an entrepreneur according to §§ 1-3 Austrian Corporate Law (UGB) or private trusts with shareholdings of over 50% in said entrepreneurs. This means that applicants can be individuals, legal entities of private law, legal entities under public law, registered partnerships or private trusts. Applicants must have their domicile in Austria.
- *Corporate Group Application:* Apart from single entities, so-called corporate groups can apply. The requirement is a shareholding of over 50% of the applicant on members of the corporate group. As an additional condition, if the Austrian group taxation benefit (fiscal unity regime) is applied every participant has to be included in bK. Apart from that, corporations fulfilling the shareholding requirement may choose to join the corporate group or not.
- *Revenue Threshold:* At least one of the applicants needs to have made EUR 40 million in revenue over the past two years prior to application. This threshold requirement does not apply to banks and insurance companies as they will be audited by the future Tax Administration for Large-Scale Enterprises (effective July 1, 2020) regardless of their revenue.
- *Accounting Standards:* All participants of bK need to comply with the accounting standards stated in Austrian Corporate Law (§ 189 UGB).

Special Requirements: Apart from the overall requirements two additional special requirements need to be met:

(1) *Fiscal Criminal Integrity:* No conviction within Austrian Tax Offence Law (Finanzstrafgesetz) over the past five years prior to application, for felonies committed within the past seven years. This rule applies equally to all participants.
(2) *TCF:* At the time of application, a certified TCF needs to be in place. Certification can be obtained for a single entity or for a corporate group at once.

Further Evaluation: The legislator decided that bK needs to be further evaluated. Therefore, another evaluation has to be processed no later than December 31, 2024. Based on that evaluation the effects of bK on taxpayers and the administration have to be analyzed and a decision has to be made on whether the revenue threshold has to be amended.

[E] Procedural Law: Procedure upon Participation

If a certified TCF is in place and all other requirements apply, a single entity or corporate group may choose to apply for bK. It is important to note that until January 1, 2021 the application has to be filed at the competent authority (Tax Administration), which will then formally order the office for auditing large-scale enterprises, to perform the audit upon entrance. Due to a restructuring within the Austrian Tax Administration effective January 1, 2021, a new Tax Administration will be created, the Tax Administration for Large-Scale Enterprises (Finanzamt für Großbetriebe), which will then be the only competent authority regarding bK applications and large-scale enterprises in general.

Application: Applications have to be filed via FinanzOnline, the online platform of the Federal Ministry of Finance. The parent company has to apply, for corporate groups. Application can be filed directly or via a tax advisor (who then needs power of attorney).

Inspection of Application: There is a check on whether all the necessary requirements are met.

Audit upon Entrance: Before switching to bK, one last *ex post* audit is performed, covering the past five years prior to application. If an audit already took place within the past five years, only the years not yet audited will be covered.

Appraisal of Fiscal Reliability: Additional to the requirement that the applicant maintains certified TCF, the Tax Administration will have to evaluate the applicant's fiscal reliability and decide whether to allow the applicant to enter bK or not. Allowance or refusal has to be communicated via formal notification (Official Decision). This decision can be challenged (Appeal against Official Decision).

Figure 5.1 Pathway to bK

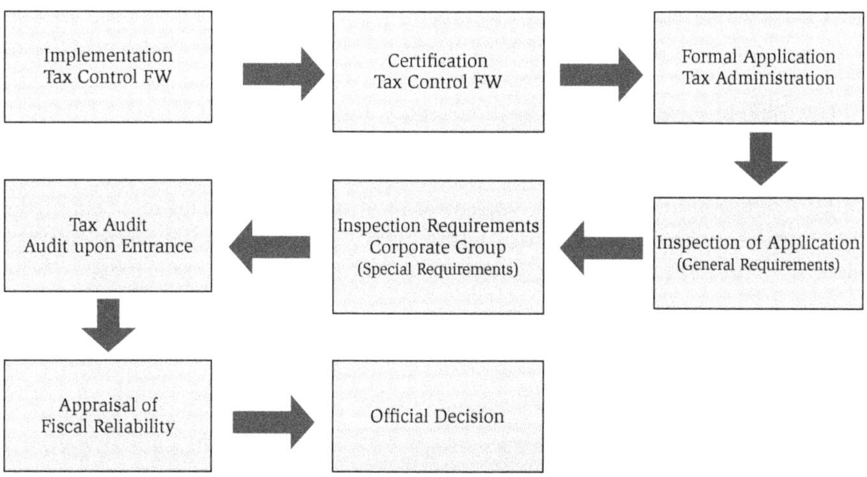

Author's representation from Austrian Procedural Law § 153c BAO.

[F] Procedural Law: TCF

As the tax control frame work represents an integral part of bK, I would like to explain the mechanics in some more detail at this stage. As explained already, the TCF should certify that applicants bear little risk in connection with timely and correct declaration of taxes and can thus be trusted to perform and oversee these matters themselves. As a logical consequence, the tax auditor within bK is freed of routine functions (checking the abovementioned risks) and can focus on processes rather than checking single records and receipts.

The TCF is defined in procedural law (§ 153b BAO, effective January 1, 2019). The wording, translated to English, sums up the most important parts:

> TCF is the sum of measures taken (Processes and Process Steps), that guarantee a correct determination of each tax base and therefore the correct and timely declaration of said taxes. It derives from the identified tax related risks covered and has to be amended frequently on account of changing conditions. TCF has to state a risk analysis and actions deriving from it, as well as the control mechanisms needed.

The TCF needs to be re-certified at least every three years, and procedural law gives the Austrian Minister of Finance the power to give further directives. This was done by a TCF-Regulation which became effective on the same day as the procedural law.[6] This regulation further explains, what a TCF should cover and how tax-related risks should be identified. It also covers the process of certification as performed by tax advisors. Deriving from this regulation, the chamber of tax advisors has released an expert opinion to give their members guidance for the certification process.[7]

From my experience, tax-related risks are mostly identified with a risk matrix, measuring risks by probability and financial implications. Deriving from that matrix, an applicant determines a process with checks and double checks as well as digitally supported actions, to prevent those risks from materializing. One important step in the context of possible certification is the creation of detailed documentation of every internal process related to taxes. This makes it easier to determine risks and gives tax advisors the opportunity to oversee and certify.

The TCF may not only be used to apply for bK but also it has a variety of advantages for taxpayers. First and foremost, it improves certainty by reducing tax-related risks and also, as a result, accounting risks as well as other related risks. It could also be a tool for taxpayers to optimize their organization and increase digitalization.[8] Some Austrian corporations, such as the BUWOG Group (real estate industry), publicly state their motives to implement a TCF by giving three major reasons:[9]

6. *SKS-Prüfungsverordnung*, effective January 1, 2019, *BGBl. II Nr. 340/2018*.
7. *Expert Opinion KFS/PE29*, effective June 5, 2019.
8. Rosar & Helnwein in Müller & Woischitzschläger & Zöchling, *Co-operative Tax Compliance in Österreich*, 225 (2019).
9. Seuß & Plott in Müller & Woischitzschläger & Zöchling, *Co-operative Tax Compliance in Österreich*, 262 (2019).

(1) BUWOG Group wanted to change its organizational structure to adapt to changed circumstances in real estate business.
(2) Due to this change tax-related risks evolved.
(3) Increased need to control tax-related risks and additionally manage financial and liability risks as BUWOG is also under stock market regulations.

This example shows, how the legal incorporation of TCFs has changed the approach of some taxpayers toward handling risks and also highlights different purposes TCFs may have. From my experience, more and more large-scale enterprises are currently working on the implementation and certification of a TCF. How many of them will take a further step and apply for bK remains to be seen.

[G] Procedural Law: Appraisal of Fiscal Reliability

Even if an applicant fulfills all formal requirements, there is still one last barrier that needs to be taken before the entrance into bK. Applicants must pass an inspection of their fiscal reliability. The procedural law indicates, how fiscal reliability could be measured (§ 153c BAO, effective January 1, 2019):

- Compliance from applicant in connection with tax audit upon entrance.
- Significant findings in tax audits five years prior to application.
- Fiscal compliance (disclosure, obligation to notify, etc.) five years prior to application.
- Delayed tax declarations five years prior to application.
- Fiscal criminal court cases/trials ongoing.
- Criminal cases regarding social security fraud.
- Measures undertaken by applicant after significant findings/fiscal penalties.

The Tax Administration has to explain their approval or objection with respect to the applicant's fiscal reliability in the official decision (formal notification) for admission into bK (appeal possible). The appraisal has to be made in the context of the overall view of the applicant. This means that failure on one of the indicators given does not automatically result in denial of participation.[10] As project participants already had this appraisal executed in the project phase and the legal incorporation happened effective as of 2019, tax authorities are currently working on guidance for appraising fiscal reliability. Experience will do its part, but it is important to note that the Austrian Tax Administration is very determined to treat taxpayers equally in order to fulfill the constitutional principle to that effect.

10. Dirnbacher & Vock in Brandl, *SWK-Spezial Begleitende Kontrolle*, 119 (2019).

[H] Procedural Law: bK Procedure

Within the process, following taxes and subsidies are covered by bK (§ 153e BAO, effective January 1, 2019):

- Income Tax, Corporate Income Tax.
- Value-Added Tax (VAT).
- Vehicle Tax, Electricity Tax, Natural Gas Tax, Coal Tax and Energy Tax Refund.
- Advertising Tax, Standardized Consumption Tax, Stability Fee.
- Research Premium/Refund.

You may notice that bK does not cover customs duties or payroll tax. This is due to the fact that bK only covers taxes and refunds within the jurisdiction of the future Tax Administration for Large-Scale Enterprises (effective July 1, 2020), to create a single point of contact (jurisdiction).

After switching to bK, the taxpayer is obliged to disclose all tax-related matters actively to the tax authority, i.e., without prior notification (§ 153f BAO, effective January 1, 2019). This will be done in meetings with the tax authority. At least four meetings are mandatory per tax year. One of these meetings has to concern the annual tax return which is discussed and processed. This also marks the formal end of the annual tax audit, so the final tax assessment can be completed, to provide legal certainty as soon as possible. It is still thinkable for the taxpayer to disagree with the assessment, and to formally appeal against tax bills. Meetings have to be documented by a signed protocol as evidence. While it is not the intention of bK to generate appeals, in case of ongoing disagreement it is possible to obtain a judgment from court.

[I] Procedural Law: Termination of bK

As bK represents an opt-in process, it also has an opt-out procedure (§ 153g BAO, effective January 1, 2019). BK can be terminated both by the participant and by the tax authority. Each member of a corporate group can terminate individually or the corporate group may terminate as a whole. Only if the group taxation benefit (fiscal unity regime) applies the possibility is restricted to either all-in or all-out. The Tax Administration has to declare the end of bK via formal notification (appeal possible). It is important to note that bK will end with the last tax year finished before termination. For the following years, the normal *ex post* audit procedure applies again. The tax authority needs to give its reason for terminating bK. Reasons stated within law are:

- Certain requirements are no longer met (e.g., a shareholding is reduced to less than 50%).
- The tax authority no longer accepts the taxpayer's fiscal reliability (e.g., as a result of a failure to disclose).
- The TCF has proven to be insufficiently effective.

[J] bK from an Auditor's Point of View

Performing tax audits under bK has influenced auditors' work in various ways. One change that comes to my mind immediately is that much of the auditing is focused on processes instead of events. A well-functioning TCF is a blessing for tax auditors as it gives them a chance to look behind the scenes and have a closer look at connections, communications and relations within large-scale multinational enterprises (MNEs). From my experience as a tax auditor, performing bK audits as well as *ex post* audits, I am familiar with both options and I want to explain the difference with an example. Imagine a corporation without either bK or a TCF. What would be an appropriate way of auditing VAT-related transactions within the European Union single market? I would have to audit based on documents (mass routine function), because the corporation has no certified way of giving me confidence to proceed with more complicated issues. Imaginable steps would be:

- Is the correct amount, with the correct VAT included on invoices?
- Has the corporation done checks on UID numbers?
- Has the corporation done a recapitulative statement?
- Has the corporation declared said VAT?

Whereas a process orientated audit would lead me to following considerations:[11]

- Who (which department, person) is providing the numbers, calculating taxes and generating invoices related to VAT?
- What skills do these persons need to have? (Education, degrees, in-house instruction)
- Who is ultimately responsible? Who does the double check?
- Who does the documentation?
- Are these processes digitally supported?

From reading these possible questions, the different approach is already visible. But does bK work? And how is possible sweetheart dealing prevented? From my experience, I can affirm that bK works and that it has shaped the relationship between taxpayer and authority in a tremendously positive way. As to possible sweetheart dealing, I can assure that proceedings within the Tax Administration prevent that from happening. Not only do meetings during bK happen under a "four-eyes" principle, additionally the bK audit teams are frequently rotated too.

From my perspective I can strongly recommend participation into bK, as it does not only create an audit environment built on trust, transparency and disclosure but more importantly, it gives the opportunity to solve tax-related problems in real time and not years later. This has several advantages. On the one hand, it is always more assuring to discuss possible problems together, rather than confronting taxpayers with issues years later, coming up with a completely different legal appraisal. Moreover, it

11. Macho in Müller & Woischitzschläger & Zöchling, *Co-operative Tax Compliance in Österreich*, 214 (2019).

gives the audit team opportunity to discuss matters with the person responsible for this decision. Because personnel may change, this is often not the case in *ex post* audits. And the feedback from involved companies underlines my opinion. Verbund AG, an Austrian energy provider listed on Vienna Stock Market (ATX), highlights legal certainty on tax issues, that would require public disclosure if not accepted by tax authorities, as a major improvement from bK.[12] With bK such issues, like goodwill depreciations or changed energy prices can be discussed with tax authorities timely and prevent adjustments and possible liabilities in connection to capital market law in later years. The assumption that bK saves time for companies proves to be wrong, however. Key personnel from Verbund AG, mentioned a shift in their workload toward active issue detection (as a result of the control processes that are part of the TCF) and furthermore to the disclosure of tax-related matters, compared to answering selected questions from auditors. In connection with the aspect of trust, they highlight the importance of integrity on the side of the tax auditors, as tax-related issues discussed during meetings can be relevant for public disclosure according to stock market law. I can only support this view, and highlight fiscal integrity and tax secrecy as key factors for generating trust from the authority's side. I think that Austria has made a big step in the right direction by implementing bK and I am hopeful that an increasing number of taxpayers will recognize the advantages and apply.

[K] bK Summary

Rounding up the first part of my report, I summarize the most important takeaways of bK:

- bK is a legal approach incorporated into Austrian Procedural Law as an alternative to *ex post* audits;
- bK is open to all taxpayers fulfilling the requirements (revenue threshold, certified TCF, etc.);
- bK is accessed voluntarily by formal application, hence it is not mandatory;
- bK is built on trust, transparency and disclosure;
- bK is intended to create legal certainty for taxpayers at the earliest stage possible;
- bK can be terminated by the taxpayer at any time and by the tax authority if the legal requirements are not fulfilled anymore.

§5.03 ADVANCE RULING IN AUSTRIA

A few years prior to bK, on January 1, 2011, Austria incorporated another Co-operative Compliance regulation into its procedural law. Originating from the Advance Ruling initiative, Austria created a notification called "Auskunftsbescheid" (§ 118 BAO,

12. Rohrer in Müller & Woischitzschläger & Zöchling, *Co-operative Tax Compliance in Österreich*, 187-192 (2019).

effective January 1, 2011). As this report should cover Austrian Co-operative Compliance programmes in comparison with initiatives from other OECD Member States, and the Advance Ruling is an integral part of said programme, I give a quick overview and highlight some updates from recent years.

[A] Application for an Advance Ruling

As with bK, an Advance Ruling also needs to be applied for. Entitled to apply for Advance Ruling in Austria are:

- Individuals or companies that are subject to tax.
- Tax-transparent Business Partnerships.
- Persons requesting a Ruling upon incorporation of an entity, which will then be subject to tax.

The application has to meet the following requirements:

- Comprehensive statement of circumstances not yet effectuated.
- Statement of the particular interest of the applicant.
- Clear statement of the legal problem.
- The specific legal question to be covered by the Advance Ruling.
- Statement of the legal interpretation advocated by the applicant.
- Statement of coverage of the administrative contribution.

[B] Coverage of Advance Ruling in Austria

Originally, the Advance Ruling was only possible for legal questions regarding:

- Restructuring.
- Group Taxation Benefit.
- Transfer Pricing (TP).

With effect from January 1, 2019 the eligible legal questions were amended and extended with the following topics:

- International Tax Law in general (including TP).
- Abuse of legal possibilities.
- VAT (effective January 1, 2020).

The reports of the parliamentary discussion show that these changes were made in order to widen Co-operative Compliance possibilities for taxpayers. Furthermore, an amendment was made to create a possibility for making minor modifications to applications, without having to pay additional administrative fees.[13] Further reflecting

13. *Erläuterungen zum Jahressteuergesetz 2018* (Oktober 26, 2019), https://www.parlament.gv.at/PAKT/VHG/XXVI/I/I_00190/fname_698480.pdf.

the aim of widening Co-operative Compliance, a side paragraph to § 118 BAO was incorporated into procedural law in 2013 (§ 118a BAO, effective January 1, 2013). This regulation also allows Advance Ruling for legal questions regarding research premiums.

[C] Advance Ruling: Notification

To provide full legal certainty, Advance Ruling requires a formal notification from the Austrian Tax Administration. This notification has to contain the legal appraisal of the facts and circumstances as stated in the application, tax laws leading to the appraisal, taxes and tax years covered by this notification and reporting obligations imposed on applicant. The law explicitly provides legal certainty with respect to the facts and circumstances disclosed, and provided these will materialize as stated in the application. Legal certainty is created for the applicant and any legal successor as well as relevant partners (if partnership was the applicant) and any entities incorporated after the Advance Ruling was issued.

Depending on the taxpayer's sales revenues in the prior tax year, administrative fees rank from EUR 1,500 to EUR 20,000 per application. The fee for an Advance Ruling on research premium is EUR 1,000. The fee is limited to EUR 500 (EUR 200 for research premium) if a request is rejected by the Tax Administration or withdrawn upon processing.

To give applicants legal certainty as soon as possible, the Austrian legislative has imposed an additional regulation within § 118 BAO, effective July 1, 2019, requiring Tax Administrations to give their legal appraisal within two months after application, if possible.

§5.04 BEGLEITENDE KONTROLLE VERSUS ADVANCE RULING

Comparing Austria's main Co-operative Compliance approaches with each other leads us to observe several differences.

Difference in Entry Point: Whereas bK covers tax-related matters that have already materialized and aims to create legal certainty shortly after declaring taxes, Advance Ruling aims to create legal certainty before the event.

Difference in Coverage/Scope: BK is a legal process for auditing a taxpayer's footprint within Austria, whereas an Advance Ruling addresses separate legal questions.

Difference in Procedure: Whereas bK is a permanent auditing procedure after entering the programme, an Advance Ruling is an instant appraisal of a single tax-related issue.

Difference in Temporal/Monetary Expenditure: BK reflects a change-of-culture for taxpayers, requiring them to implement TCFs, as well as constantly discussing and disclosing tax issues with the relevant authority and consequently entails a continuous relationship as well as having an ongoing financial impact. Advance Ruling, on the other hand, is very predictable from a financial point of view, but then again does not allow as much relational involvement.

Depending on their specific needs, taxpayers may decide which instrument of compliance to use. For questions of permanent establishments or restructuring processes, for example, it is certainly advisable to apply for an Advance Ruling before final execution and not discuss it during bK. But bK and Advance Ruling do not exclude each other. So it is thinkable to participate in bK, with business decisions deriving from an Advance Ruling in the past. If a taxpayer is willing to communicate with tax authorities on an advanced level and willing to shoulder the burden of applying for bK, I would encourage them to do so.

§5.05 CO-OPERATIVE COMPLIANCE FOR SMALL BUSINESSES: SAF-T AND HM

Deriving from the OECD Guidance for further digitalization of tax administrations, Austria is currently working on a SAF-T (Standard Audit File-Tax) for small companies.[14] Austria already allows taxpayers to do accounting based on the OECD Standard Audit File-Tax xml-format.[15] The new concept should create a digital HM process, based on an optimized SAF-T. The current plan is to have an HM-Light process, with the advantage that a form of legal certainty is provided, together with other benefits such as fast-track procedures for VAT refunds. Key elements of the current project are:[16]

- Digital Audit of transacted SAF-T data with optimized checks.
- Legally binding period for transacting and auditing SAF-T data.
- Power of attorney for tax advisors to transact data (which entails the aspect of certification).
- Other measures regarding tax compliance to generate legal certainty both for taxpayer and for authority.

Remember that this effort is still in a project phase, and therefore in a discussion draft status, with the aim of the Federal Ministry of Finance to start in 2022. Until then, there will be further discussions between key stakeholders (Tax Authority, Chamber of Tax Advisors, Chamber of Commerce). The plan for possible incorporation into procedural law has not yet been revealed.

14. OECD, *Guidance for the Standard Audit File-Tax*, May 2005.
15. BMF, *Erlass BMF-010102/0002-IV/2/2009* (March 20, 2009).
16. Engelbert & Schwartz in Müller & Woischitzschläger & Zöchling, *Co-operative Tax Compliance in Österreich*, 102-103 (2019).

§5.06 CONCLUSION WITH RESPECT TO THE UNILATERAL CO-OPERATIVE COMPLIANCE APPROACH

As can be seen from the presented initiatives and regulations, Austria is implementing Co-operative Compliance as an optional addition to conventional procedures, with the perspective for taxpayers to enjoy certain benefits if they are willing to comply with the requirements. Initiatives of compliance always need to have an element of optionality, as it is impossible to force compliance. The aim is to facilitate model behavior and to steer as many taxpayers as possible in the direction of Co-operative Compliance. The main facilitating factor is the legal certainty which Austria is willing to give in return for compliance. As a logical consequence, almost all compliance approaches lead to incorporation into procedural law at some stage.

Having said this, legal incorporation can only generate a basis for compliant behavior. Another key factor is a change in approach from the tax authorities. Auditing in bK has to be done at eye-level, which is in many ways completely opposed to the traditional authoritarian approach and demands continuous communication, much time spent and constant training. One key advantage of bK is a change in the operational model. As routine functions are procedurally covered and all tax-related issues are made transparent, discussions can be had without restriction and are in many ways more productive in outcome.

§5.07 AUSTRIA AND ICAP 2.0

When Austria was asked by the OECD's FTA to join the second phase of the ICAP, it became clearer that Austria's history of Co-operative Compliance would once more be supplemented. Despite specifically targeting taxpayers with revenues exceeding EUR 40 million per year, primarily multinationals, therefore, first and foremost, bK is a unilateral approach to achieve compliant behavior. ICAP is a multilateral way of co-operating with multinationals. The aim of the project, which is risk assessment at a multilateral stage, requires tax authorities from different tax administrations to discuss and disclose risks together with willing MNEs.

As the FTA aims to secure tax revenues for participating countries, the ICAP approach is to take action against tax avoidance and tax evasion by compliance from taxpayers and additionally enhance cooperation among tax authorities. Returning from the ICAP 2.0 conference in Paris in September 2019, I will try to explain Austria's perspectives and desires regarding its participation in ICAP 2.0.

[A] ICAP 2.0: Status and Possibilities

The ICAP, by its name, is a voluntary programme to assess risks and obtain assurance. The voluntary nature applies to both the tax authorities and the taxpayers. The participating tax administrations agreed to implement the experiences and feedback from the first ICAP project and develop ICAP further. ICAP is intended to reduce the need for resources and avoid lengthy mutual agreement procedures.[17] The avoidance of lengthy procedures is paid for by the absence of legal certainty, however. The result of the ICAP process is an outcome letter, according to the ICAP handbook, as opposed to a possible legal notification.[18] It has to be mentioned though that several MNEs participating in ICAP 1.0 held the advantage in acceleration higher than the disadvantage in lacking legal certainty.[19]

[B] ICAP 2.0: Legal Classification under Austrian Procedural Law

A legally binding process for an outcome letter is non-existent within Austrian procedural law by now. Nonetheless, a notification from tax authorities to taxpayers, like the ICAP outcome letter, is not necessarily non-binding for the Austrian Tax Administration. Such notifications and especially actions from taxpayers resulting from them may give rise to a legally relevant instance of "Good Faith" (Treu und Glauben). In connection with "Good Faith"-behavior the Federal Ministry of Finance has given its views in a regulation effective April 6, 2006.[20] The view expressed by the authority with respect to this regulation is:

> Good Faith means, that everybody participating in legal affairs, stands by his words and actions, and will not change his views unless having valid reasons, especially if others trusted upon them.

The translation is taken from a judgment coming from the Austrian Higher Administrative Court, to explain the basic concept.[21] It is important to note though that the same court also published a judgment saying that the constitutional principle of legality is ranked higher than the principle of "Good Faith."[22] The Federal Ministry of Finance concludes in its regulation that these two judgments do not oppose each other. Moreover "Good Faith" should be given an interpretational or tie-breaker function when considering the principle of justice. MNEs, however, could apply for a formal Advance Ruling notification (Auskunftsbescheid § 118 BAO) after receiving an outcome letter, to obtain legal certainty for the future. Remember though that an administrative fee needs to be paid.

The OECD is aware of the ICAP's lack of legal certainty, but still included the ICAP in their Tax Certainty Agenda.[23] The conclusion is that the ICAP and Co-operative Compliance could create something called a "de-facto" certainty. The aim is that the ICAP represents a tool for dispute avoidance between Member States and reduces the amount of arbitration procedures at a later stage.

17. Macho, *Transfer Pricing International (TPI)* (2019), 268.
18. OECD, *ICAP Pilot Handbook* (2019), 17.
19. Feedback discussed during ICAP conference in September 2019.
20. BMF, Erlass BMF-010103/0023-VI/2006, April 6, 2006.
21. VwGH, March 15, 2001, 2001/16/0063.
22. VwGH, January 21, 2004, 2003/16/0113.
23. Pross & Altenburg in Müller & Woischitzschläger & Zöchling, *Co-operative Tax Compliance in Österreich*, 91 (2019).

The outcome letter states the conclusion from the risk assessment reached by each tax administration and should contain a classification of the transactions covered as low, medium or high risk. Based on this the OECD concludes that further assurance should be given if transactions covered are seen as low risk. A possible outcome could be the indication that further auditing is unlikely.[24]

[C] ICAP 2.0: Advantages

As Austrian tax authorities are changing their audit style from a "single-document-orientated" approach to a process orientated one, ICAP 2.0 represents the chance to gain experience on how to risk assess TP and on different situations in the context of international tax law. With the implementation of a TCF the risk assessment for national tax matters such as VAT and CIT has already improved vastly, but in connection to TP issues we are still on a learning curve. Also, the outcomes from the OECD's Base Erosion and Profit Shifting (BEPS) initiative (such as the Country-by-Country-Report (CbCR)) provide lessons on risk assessment, from which Austria is trying to gain experience. Until now, internal regulations require continuous auditing of large-scale enterprises, meaning that the next *ex post* audit starts where the last one has ended (if the enterprise is not within the bK process). If a risk assessment based on CbCR could enhance Austria's path to risk-orientated-auditing, ICAP 2.0 would be a success already. A very helpful tool for Austria could be another OECD project called CoRA (Comparative Risk Assessment). The OECD, specifically the FTA, is trying to assist national tax administrations in analyzing CbCR's and assessing risks based thereon, but it is also aiming to gain information from Member States on their experiences with risk assessment procedures so far.[25] CoRA should gain fundamental expertise on risk assessment regarding international taxation and function as a basis for initiatives relying on risk assessment, such as ICAP and Joint Audits.

On a different level, globalization and the resulting complex TP strategies demand a better understanding and co-operation between national tax authorities. The ICAP 2.0 is another initiative, which supports global thinking of administrations and gives tax authorities the chance to learn from the OECD and each other, and to use this experience in respect of MNEs that are willing to comply. It is very important to address though that participating in the ICAP does not protect an MNE from being audited in Austria (in terms of *ex post* audits). Only participation in the unilateral bK programme can generate that level of security. This is due to the fact that the ICAP risk assessment process has not been incorporated into Austrian procedural law so far. It has to be highlighted though that even Austria's unilateral bK procedure started as a project. The ICAP can best be described as a regulatory sandbox right now, meaning that the Austrian Tax Administration is testing the suitability. A possible incorporation into procedural law may be decided at a later stage, depending on project results.[26] With

24. Macho, *Transfer Pricing International (TPI)* (2019), 268.
25. Pross & Altenburg in Müller & Woischitzschläger & Zöchling, *Co-operative Tax Compliance in Österreich*, 88 (2019).
26. Anderwald, *Steuer- und Wirtschaft International (SWI)* (2019), 549.

procedures like that, it is possible to test the waters upfront and develop regulations suitable for all stakeholders alike.

[D] ICAP 2.0: ICAP Versus bK

Several differences occur, when comparing the ICAP to bK. The understanding of these differences is important, when talking about possible integration or mutual benefits:

Difference in Coverage/Scope: Whereas the ICAP international tax risks, bK covers all taxes within the jurisdiction of the newly incorporated Tax Administration for large-scale enterprises (effective July 1, 2020). Also, the approach of bK covers a business as a whole, with all applicable taxes.

Difference with Respect to Legal Certainty: As explained, the ICAP is not designed to be legally binding according to Austrian procedural law, as opposed to bK, which is.

Difference in Outcome: The ICAP produces an outcome letter, which is in fact the result of the risk assessment. A final tax assessment is the ultimate goal for bK after each tax year.

Difference in Scale: The ICAP is a multilateral approach, with the aim of covering countries with an interest to co-operate with MNEs that are willing to comply, whereas bK is unilateral. Furthermore, the ICAP is designed for MNEs with global revenues exceeding 750 million (coinciding with the obligation to publish CbCR), whereas bK has a threshold of 40 million in local revenues.

Despite these differences, I think the ICAP could well be integrated into the bK process, as an environment of compliance has already been created and international tax matters with local effects are covered. The integration of the ICAP into bK should not be very complex and the chance to interest more MNEs to bK is desirable from a national standpoint. Therefore, MNEs participating in the ICAP are invited to apply for bK in reference to their Austrian-based entities.

§5.08 CONCLUSION

Regardless of whether it has a unilateral or multilateral approach, Co-operative Compliance is a relatively new trend regarding relationship between the taxpayer and the tax authority. After years of trying to detect and to fight tax evasion by showing muscles and performing extensive criminal investigations, tax authorities came to the conclusion that in a globalized world taxpayers with enough resources and funds will always find a way of evading taxes, as long as tax systems are not unified on a worldwide basis. As the name Co-operative Compliance already indicated, the new approaches rely on two main factors, co-operation and compliance. Tax administrations are eager to grant certain benefits if taxpayers are willing to comply. On the other hand, the business culture of multinationals is transforming from strictly shareholder driven, and therefore from nurturing "tax optimizing" strategies, to more sustainable ones. This generates an ideal breeding ground for compliance initiatives. This breeding ground is a chance for enhancing co-operation and compliance by taxpayers but also represents a societal mission to offer solutions. Tax authorities in various OECD Member States have read the signs of the times and offer these new legal ways.

Austria sees itself as a nation wanting to reshape their administration in a modern, solution-oriented style. One of the changes involves proactive approaches of large-scale taxpayers. The learnings from prior projects were taken into account and led to changes in procedural law, offering compliance options to those willing to participate. The compliance initiatives should assist taxpayers with covering tax-related risks themselves and grant legal certainty at an early stage. The aim is to reward taxpayers willing to work together with tax administrations and the biggest reward authorities can offer to larger taxpayers is legal certainty. Our unilateral programmes are showing steady progress and have proven to be valuable. Despite this success, the future will put forward new challenges and the need to amend these programmes. One challenge arising for Austrian Tax Administrations is to process risk assessments and implement the results in day-to-day work. The ICAP and CoRA offer opportunities for learning experiences and are therefore considered important.

The BEPS action plan has once more directed tax collection toward beneficial as opposed to legal ownership and has put a burden on multinationals to document and disclose internal information to tax administrations around the globe. One documentation requirement was the CbCR. But how useful is the CbCR if it is not overseen and processed by tax authorities? The ICAP presents a chance to perform this processing at a multilateral stage and to obtain experiences and views from tax administrations all over the world. Even if income tax regulations are strictly national at the moment, co-operation between tax authorities will be an integral part of worldwide tax collection in the future. MNEs know no boundaries any longer and use this fact to their advantage. To face them at eye-level, tax authorities, especially those within the OECD, need to act and work together. On the other hand, MNEs willing to co-operate should be given the chance to work together with various tax administrations at once and not one after another.

I am well aware that the ICAP is one of many initiatives for multilateral tax collection and will not solve all challenges lying ahead. But in a world where digitalization is rethinking the permanent establishment approach and demands refocusing and fundamental amendments, the ICAP can be an important tool to get all stakeholders together and generate sustainable solutions, which will be supported by everybody, without the need for further dispute.

CHAPTER 6

Canada's Experience with the ICAP

Allison Christians & Tarcísio Diniz Magalhães

§6.01 INTRODUCTION

As tax administrations around the world continue to reform international tax rules to promote transparency and address the challenges of aggressive tax avoidance, base erosion and profit shifting (BEPS), and the digitalization of the economy, multinational taxpayers are increasingly expressing concerns about a rise in compliance costs and risks of double taxation.[1] In particular, some taxpayers have characterized the Canadian international tax system as excessively complex and anti-competitive, leading to calls for greater simplicity and certainty.[2]

To tackle these issues, Canada has, in the past years, implemented a series of administrative policies and initiatives of voluntary co-operation, aimed at increasing

1. *See*, e.g., Alicja Majdanska & Pedro Guilherme Lindenberg Schoueri, *Tax Compliance in the Spotlight: The Challenges for Tax Administrations and Taxpayers*, 71 Bulletin for International Taxation 11 (2017); Chris Evans, Philip Lignier & Binh Tran-Nam, *The Tax Compliance Costs of Large Corporations: An Empirical Inquiry and Comparative Analysis*, 64 Canadian Tax Journal 4 (2016); Ricardo García Antón, *The Fragmentation of Taxpayer's Rights in International Dispute Resolution Settings: Healing Anxieties Through Judicial Dialogue*, 10 World Tax Journal 1 (2017).
2. *See*, e.g., Fred O'Riordan, *Why Canada Needs a Comprehensive Tax Review*, 66 Canadian Tax Journal 2 (2018) (explaining that for large multinational corporations "compliance with increasingly complex provisions of tax legislation is much more challenging. And for many of them, self-assessment and filing a return is just the beginning of a long and protracted process of dealing with the tax authorities."); Canadian Chamber of Commerce, *50 Years of Cutting and Pasting: Modernizing Canada's Tax System* (February 2019) at 8 ("Canadian businesses and tax practitioners report frustration and a need to commit significant time, often at considerable expense, to deal with taxation and filing issues with the [Canada Revenue Agency]. Many of the business members consulted find themselves spending exorbitant amounts of time dealing with the [Canada Revenue Agency]. … During consultations, our business members told us that, in many cases, they pay to hire tax professionals to navigate through the complexities of Canada's tax system—and even professionals are challenged by the current circumstances.").

disclosure by large corporations for better compliance, while reducing risks.[3] But even as the Canada Revenue Agency expresses a preference for more persuasive rather than coercive interactions with corporate taxpayers,[4] Co-operative Compliance programmes have not yet been formally adopted in Canada,[5] as they have been in other jurisdictions.[6]

Despite not fully complying with the recommendations of the Organisation for Economic Co-operation and Development (OECD) on this issue,[7] the Canada Revenue Agency has expressed strong enthusiasm for the OECD's new pilot project: the International Compliance Assurance Programme (ICAP).[8] In fact, together with Australia, Italy, Japan, the Netherlands, Spain, the United Kingdom (U.K.) and the United States (U.S.), Canada was one of the eight countries that participated in the first round of the ICAP, and it continues to participate as the project moves into its second phase.[9]

3. For an overview, *see* Dan Misutka & Lauchlin MacEachern, *The Canada Revenue Agency's Tax Transparency Initiatives: Implications for a Corporate Governance Response*, 61 Canadian Tax Journal 3 (2013).
4. On these two approaches, *see* Zakir Ahkand & Michael Hubbard, *Coercion, Persuasion, and Tax Compliance: The Case of Large Corporate Taxpayers*, 64 Canadian Tax Journal 1 (2016); *see also* María Teresa Soler Roch, *Tax Administration Versus Taxpayer: A New Deal?*, 4 World Tax Journal 3 (2012); Asmita Singh, *Enforcement or Cooperation: An Analysis of the Compliance Psychology of Taxpayers*, 21 Asia-Pacific Tax Bulletin 1 (2015); Gracia Mª Luchena Mozo, *A Collaborative Relationship in the Resolution of International Tax Disputes and Alternative Measures for Dispute Resolution in a Post-BEPS Era*, 58 European Taxation 1 (2018); Martin Lagarden, *Behavioural Transfer Pricing: Towards Enhanced Transparency and Compliance?*, 26 International Transfer Pricing Journal 3 (2019).
5. Allison Christians & Vokhid Urinov, *Canada, in Improving Compliance in a Globalized World* (Chris Evans et al. eds., IBFD 2015).
6. *See* OECD, *Study into the Role of Tax Intermediaries* (2008) (hereinafter "OECD Intermediaries Study"). For attempts in defining enhanced relationship and co-operative compliance, *see* IFA, *Initiative on the Enhanced Relationship: Key Issues Report* (Jan. 22, 2012); Eelco van der Enden & Katarzyna Bronzewska, *The Concept of Cooperative Compliance*, 68 Bulletin for International Taxation 10 (2014); *see also* Katarzyna Bronzewska & Eelco van der Enden, *Tax Control Framework: A Conceptual Approach: The Six Nuances of Good Tax Governance*, 68 Bulletin for International Taxation 11 (2014); Lisette van der Hel - van Dijk & Maarten Singlé, *Cooperative Compliance: Tax Risk Management and Monitoring*, 44 Intertax 8/9 (2016); Kataryna Bronzewska, *Cooperative Compliance: A New Approach to Managing Taxpayer Relations* (IBFD 2016); Katarzyna Bronzewska & Alicja Majdanska, *The New Wave of Cooperative Compliance Programmes and the Impact of New Technology*, 59 European Taxation 2/3 (2019); Justin Dabner & Mark Burton, *Lessons for Tax Administrations in Adopting the OECD's "Enhanced Relationship" Model: Australia's and New Zealand's Experiences*, 63 Bulletin for International Taxation 7 (2009); Karen Boll, *Securing Tax Compliance with Collaboration: The Case of Cooperative Compliance in Denmark, in The Routledge Companion to Tax Avoidance Research* (Nigar Hashimzade & Yuliya Epifantseva eds., Routledge 2018).
7. *See* OECD, *Co-operative Compliance: A Framework: From Enhanced Relationship to Co-operative Compliance* (2013) (hereinafter "2013 OECD Co-operative Compliance"); OECD, *Co-operative Tax Compliance: Building Better Tax Control Frameworks* (2016) (hereinafter "2016 OECD Co-operative Compliance"); OECD, *Joint Audit 2019: Enhancing Tax Co-operation and Improving Tax Certainty* (2019) (hereinafter "2019 OECD Joint Audit").
8. *See* OECD, *International Compliance Assurance Programme: Pilot Handbook* (2018) (hereinafter "ICAP 1.0"); OECD, *International Compliance Assurance Programme: Pilot Handbook 2.0* (2019) (hereinafter "ICAP 2.0").
9. *See* generally Jose M. Calderón, *The OECD International Compliance Assurance Programme: Just a New Multilateral and Cooperative Model of Tax Control for Multinational Enterprises?*, 72 Bulletin for International Taxation 12 (2018); Björn Heidecke & Leonie Slagter, *The*

As of this writing, no official legal or other regulations, reports, studies or investigations, or indeed any information about the implementation in Canada of either the first or second rounds of the ICAP has yet been made available to the public.[10] As such, this chapter was developed by consultation with competent authorities from Canada Revenue Agency's International and Large Business Directorate, each of whom was directly involved in the ICAP 1.0 and the ICAP 2.0.[11]

§6.02 CANADA'S PREVIOUS COMPLIANCE INITIATIVES

As mentioned, Canada has not formalized compliance initiatives in the shape of OECD recommendations; it has chosen instead to develop its own version of enhanced tax relationships. These include the Voluntary Disclosures Program,[12] whistleblower programmes under the Offshore Tax Information Program launched in January 2014,[13] mandatory advance disclosure rules attached to significant penalties,[14] audit quality assurance programmes like the Continuous Program Integrity Review for large taxpayers,[15] and plans to educate the population, including persons at very young ages, about

International Compliance Assurance Programme and Joint Audits: A New Epoch of Transfer Pricing Tax Audits?, 25 International Transfer Pricing Journal 3 (2018); Ronald Russo & Mário Henrique Martini, *The International Compliance Assurance Programme Reviewed: The Future of Cooperative Compliance?*, 73 Bulletin for International Taxation 9 (2019); Francesco Cannas & Kristof Wauters, *The Rise of Cooperative Compliance Programmes and the Rule of Law: A Comparison Between Belgium and Italy*, 59 European Taxation 12 (2019).

10. For example, ICAP coverage has reached U.S. newspapers but not yet Canadian ones. *See* Sony Kassam, *Bigger OECD-Tax Risk Assessment Program May Be "Challenging"*, Bloomberg Law News (Jun. 5, 2019); Sony Kassam, *P&G Says OECD Pilot Program Boots Corporate Reputation*, Bloomberg Law News (Jun. 5, 2019); *see also* François Vincent et al., *International Compliance Assurance Programme: Oasis or Mirage?*, Bloomberg Tax (Aug. 16, 2018).
11. Consultation via conference call (Jun. 10, 2019) and exchange of e-mails with Canadian ICAP senior-level personnel, notes on file with the authors.
12. *See* Income Tax Act s. 220(3.1-3.2); Government of Canada, *Voluntary Disclosures Program: Introduction*, at https://www.canada.ca/en/revenue-agency/programs/about-canada-revenue-agency-cra/voluntary-disclosures-program-overview.html.
13. *See* Government of Canada, *Report Offshore Tax Cheating: Overview*, at https://www.canada.ca/en/revenue-agency/programs/about-canada-revenue-agency-cra/compliance/offshore-tax-informant-program.html.
14. *OECD Intermediaries Study* at 19, 20, 29; *see also* Gilles Larin, *Some Thoughts on Disclosure Rules in Canada: A Peek into the Future*, 61 Canadian Tax Journal (supp.) (2013); Gilles N. Larin, Robert Duong & Marie Jacques, *Responses to Aggressive Tax Planning: A Study Framework*, 58 Canadian Tax Journal 1 (2008).
15. *2013 OECD Co-operative Compliance* at 33, 58, 69; *see also* CRA, *Summary of the Corporate Business Plan: 2014-2015 to 2016-2017* (December 2013) at 32 ("Our Continuous Program Integrity Review (CPIR) process is used to strengthen the integrity of our international and large business audits. The CPIR process reviews completed audits to assess general quality and adherence with legislation, policy, procedures and programme quality objectives. These reviews often identify opportunities for programme improvement and the individual results are communicated back to senior management in the programmes and regions for follow-up. On an annual basis, the findings and general trends identified by the CPIR process are summarized and discussed in a comprehensive report that recommends best practices and identifies opportunities for program improvement.").

the importance of paying taxes.[16] In addition, Canada has been involved in some joint audits (e.g., with the U.S.),[17] but the Canada Revenue Agency reports that, for geographic reasons, these initiatives work better at the level of the European Union.[18]

Beginning in 2011, the Canada Revenue Agency phased in a five-year risk assessment programme called Approach to Large Business Compliance, which is mentioned in the OECD's 2013 report on Co-operative Compliance.[19] Targeting only big corporate taxpayers,[20] the Canada Revenue Agency sent out letters with a questionnaire, asking whether the taxpayer had a risk management committee and a formal framework for controlling and responding to major tax risks, how material risks were

16. Government of Canada, *Understanding Taxes*, at https://www.canada.ca/en/revenue-agency/services/tax/individuals/educational-programs.html; Government of Canada, *Students and Income Tax* (2018); OECD (2019). *Tax Administration: Cooperative Information on OECD and Other Advanced and Emerging Economies* at 153-157.
17. *2019 OECD Joint Audit* at 28, 34.
18. Information collected from the CRA; *see also* Linda Lizotte-MacPherson, *Interview with the Canada Revenue Agency*, Global Tax Policy and Controversy Briefing (February 2011) ("European countries already have some experience with joint audits; our understanding is the approach has worked quite well for certain businesses. We have stated our interest and are now in discussion with other countries towards the identification of prospective corporations to pilot the joint audit approach. Before taking joint audit plans too far, we will of course need to ensure the corporation is prepared to participate.").
19. *2013 OECD Co-operative Compliance* at 22, 29, 31 ("In 2010, Canada launched a New Approach to Large Business Compliance that relies heavily on closer and more collaborative relationship with taxpayers and tax intermediaries and is the foundation upon which a co-operative compliance approach is being based. ... In Canada, building on the progress and experience gained as a result of their Audit Protocol initiative, the 'New Approach to Large Business Compliance' relies heavily on an enhanced relationship with taxpayers and intermediaries, and a more comprehensive risk assessment process. ... Canada is currently contemplating a co-operative compliance arrangement that would be applicable to the entire population of the largest business entities (over 25 000 corporate taxpayers, clustered into just under 1 200 Large Business Entities (LBEs) with annual revenues in excess of CAD 250 million). The co-operative compliance arrangement initiative will be first piloted with some of the largest and most complex entities.").
20. Even though the Income Tax Act s. 225.1(8) defines "large corporations" as those exceeding CAD 10 million (as the sum of capital employed in Canada and the taxable capital of related corporations), internally the CRA has relied on the amount of CAD 250 million to target companies. *See* Forum on Tax Administration, *Compliance Management of Large Business Task Group—Guidance Note: Experiences and Practices of Eight OECD Countries*, at 7 (July 2009). Recently, other proxies have been explored in order to narrow the focus to specific taxpayers, such as: involvement in aggressive tax planning; use of unusual, complex and international transactions, including restructurings and transfer pricing; major acquisitions and disposals. *See* Paul Lynch, *Coping with Tax Controversy in Canada*, International Tax Review (Dec. 6, 2012); *see also* Forum on Tax Administration, *General Administrative Principles: Corporate Governance and Tax Risk Management: Information Note* (July 2009), at 15 ("The Canada Revenue Agency (CRA) is revising its audit program to recognize the differences among large businesses with respect to the strength of their governance and their willingness to deal with CRA in an open and transparent manner. In brief, audits will be eliminated or targeted to specific issues where there is evidence of strong governance and a willingness to work with CRA on an open and transparent basis. Agency resources that are saved from this reduction in auditing will be re-focused to address taxpayers whose governance is weak, or purposely risk tolerant, as well as taxpayers who do not operate in an open and transparent manner. An important feature of this approach will be that CRA will advise the taxpayer of how the Agency perceives their governance, openness and transparency, along with other risk factors and accordingly, the compliance approach that will be utilized.").

reported, managed, and monitored, whether tax and business strategies were consistent, etc.[21] In particular, not having a formal tax governance strategy for identifying and assessing major tax risks could negatively influence the assessment outcome.[22]

On the basis of the factors listed below, taxpayers were then classified into low-, medium- and high-risk of non-compliance:[23]

- audit history;
- corporate governance and structure;
- openness and transparency;
- participation in aggressive tax planning;
- unusual, complex, and international transactions;
- major acquisitions and disposals; and
- industry sector issues.

This programme was met with mixed reactions from the business community, even though the majority of taxpayers seemed to be satisfied.[24] Since its conclusion, the other measure targeted at big multinationals has been the Large Business Audit Manual, a supplement to the Income Tax Audit Manual previously developed by the Canada Revenue Agency's Compliance Programs Branch,[25] and the Large Business Audit Programme for businesses (considering the whole corporate group) exceeding CAD 250 million of annual revenue.[26]

§6.03 CANADA'S INVOLVEMENT WITH THE INTERNATIONAL COMPLIANCE AND ASSURANCE INITIATIVE

The Canada Revenue Agency describes the ICAP as an important new international mechanism the aim of which is to bring tax compliance and tax certainty together for both taxpayers and tax administrations.[27] The idea for this type of collaborative compliance effort came about following conversations among competent authorities at the OECD. The goal was to design a programme on behalf of both public and private parties. According to the Canada Revenue Agency, the impetus for the programme arose from a desire of the OECD Forum on Tax Administration to improve relationships

21. Fred O'Riordan, *The Canada Revenue Agency Takes New Approach to Large Business Compliance*, Global Tax Policy and Controversy Briefing 12 (July 2013) at 63.
22. Misutka & Lauchlin, *supra* note 3, at 19.
23. Vivien Morgan, *Risk-Based Audits and Mandatory Arbitration*, 19 Canadian Tax Highlights 4 (April 2011) at 1; O'Riordan, *supra* note 21, at 63.
24. O'Riordan, *supra* note 21, at 64.
25. *See* Government of Canada, *Large Business Audit Manual*, at https://www.canada.ca/en/revenue-agency/corporate/about-canada-revenue-agency-cra/access-information-privacy-canada-revenue-agency/virtual-reading-room/large-business-audit-manual-international-large-business-investigations-branch-ilbib.html.
26. *See* Government of Canada, *Large Business Audit Program*, at https://www.canada.ca/en/revenue-agency/programs/about-canada-revenue-agency-cra/internal-audit-program-evaluation/internal-audit-program-evaluation-reports-2006/large-business-audit-program.html.
27. Information collected from the CRA.

with multinationals.[28] The Canada Revenue Agency articulated three motivations for participation in the ICAP: to achieve better compliance, to make tax compliance and administration less burdensome, and to produce more tax certainty beyond the annual filing exercise.[29]

One of the ways in which these goals are expected to be achieved is by increasing clarity regarding the likely administrative responses to inter-company or related party pricing of transactions. In comparison with (bilateral or multilateral) advance pricing arrangements (APAs), simultaneous/joint audits and mutual agreement procedures (MAPs) and arbitration, the ICAP provides comfort, but not certainty. It is still only through tax rulings and audited processes that taxpayers may guarantee the outcome of a given tax position with respect to the Canada Revenue Agency. With an APA, the taxpayer can obtain certainty prospectively, while audit, MAP and arbitration procedures provide certainty only retrospectively. The ICAP, in turn, occupies a middle ground, allowing parties to work co-operatively to diminish the number of expected disputes through *ex ante* prevention or mitigation instead of *ex post* reaction and negotiation.

§6.04 ICAP 1.0

In 2018, Canada and the other seven participating countries convened in Washington D.C. under the auspices of the OECD Forum on Tax Administration, where they agreed that a multilateral co-operative risk assessment and assurance process could be of interest to large multinational taxpayers.[30] The OECD Secretariat launched the initiative in connection with its efforts to implement the BEPS project while also improving tax certainty and tax co-operation among participating nations. After the meeting, officials from each participating government went back to their respective jurisdictions to work separately in search of potential private sector participants for the programme.

[A] Acceptance

In Canada, the programme was not open to all taxpayer segments, but only to some ultimate parent entities of selected multinationals.[31] The Canada Revenue Agency

28. *Id.*
29. *Id.*
30. *See* OECD, *OECD International Compliance Assurance Programme (ICAP)*, at https://www.oecd.org/tax/forum-on-tax-administration/international-compliance-assurance-programme.htm. In the same year, a subset of the ICAP countries, namely Australia, Canada, the Netherlands, the U.K., and the U.S., formed the Joint Chiefs of Global Tax Enforcement to combat "international and transactional tax crime and money laundering." *See* Government of Canada, *Tax Enforcement Authorities Unite to Combat International Tax Crime and Money Laundering* (Jul. 3, 2018), at https://www.canada.ca/en/revenue-agency/news/2018/07/tax-enforcement-authorities-unite-to-combat-international-tax-crime-and-money-laundering.html. Previous international initiatives that Canada participated in include the Leeds Castle Group (2006), the Joint International Tax Shelter Information Center (2004), and the Seven Country Tax Haven Forum (1998). *OECD Intermediaries Study* at 30.
31. Information collected from the CRA.

participated in eight risk assessments involving companies that were willing to move forward with the ICAP. To identify Canadian ultimate parent entities interested in participating, the Canada Revenue Agency actively reached out to some companies, offering them the opportunity to be part of an entirely voluntary process. All of the eight risk assessments in which the Canada Revenue Agency was involved were carried out in accordance with the ICAP parameters set out by the Forum on Tax Administration.[32]

[B] Process

For this first round of the programme, there were four phases: provision of documentation packages and scheduling of a kick-off meeting (six weeks), level 1 risk assessment (eight weeks, plus additional four or eight weeks, and another eight weeks for documentation and three weeks for risk assurance), level 2 risk assessment (approximately five months, plus additional three weeks for risk assurance), and outcome letters (three weeks).

The Canada Revenue Agency used algorithms in its computerized taxpayer records to generate risk categories for each of the eight participating taxpayers.[33] Working on the audit side of the risk assessment process, this algorithmic system was able to generate risk categories based on the transactions put forward by the companies. The risks assessed strictly followed the OECD Handbook, that is, only risks related to transfer pricing and identification and profit allocation involving permanent establishments, as to situations in which the taxpayer was not sure about their tax positions, were covered.[34]

[C] Outcome Letters

Upon conclusion of the process, the Canada Revenue Agency issued outcome letters to the ultimate parent entities of the multinationals that voluntarily came into the ICAP.[35] The outcomes depended on the covered transactions, which were explained in letters with various information, including the classification of taxpayers and transactions into low- and non-low-risk categories.

A low-risk assessment indicated that modest audit resources were expected to be required. Since no specific tax risk had been identified, low-risk companies received letters stating that the Canada Revenue Agency felt that it should not put time and effort into Co-operative Compliance.[36]

32. *See*, e.g., EY, *OECD Launches International Compliance Assurance Programme Pilot*, Global Tax Alert (Jan. 26, 2018).
33. Information collected from the CRA.
34. *ICAP 1.0* at 11 ("The international tax risks to be covered as part of the pilot (the covered risks) are: transfer pricing risk; permanent establishment risk.").
35. Information collected from the CRA.
36. *Id.*

For non-low-risk profiles, it could still be in the interest of the taxpayer to come forward and continue discussions in order to obtain clarity about the circumstances surrounding any Canada Revenue Agency concerns. The Canada Revenue Agency was interested in seeing whether companies could be reclassified to a lower risk category or what could be done to assure their tax status. In one case referenced by the Canada Revenue Agency without disclosing any specific details, high-risk transfer pricing issues were identified, and the company decided to proceed with a bilateral APA rather than continue with the ICAP process.[37]

High-risk taxpayers are usually those in some line of audit or compliance action. For companies classified as non-low risk, the programme became a key tool to anticipate and address problems before they arose during an auditing process. Some taxpayers decided to continue working with the Canada Revenue Agency in order to gain certainty about their transfer pricing and/or permanent establishment positions.[38] In any case, the Canada Revenue Agency sees the ICAP as an opportunity to learn about what works well and what the challenges are.[39]

[D] Informality

No special regulations were established before the ICAP 1.0 pilot project was tested in Canada. The work was carried out exclusively as a risk assessment process and on a more or less informal basis. Accordingly, no unusual procedures were required for the Canada Revenue Agency to proceed in carrying out the programme with willing multinationals. The Canada Revenue Agency referred for guidance to the OECD Handbook, used as a basis for the ICAP by all participating countries.[40] This was intentionally done to build flexibility into the programme.

The Canada Revenue Agency is of the understanding that tax authorities may directly contact taxpayers for the establishment of enhanced relationships, without the need for previous formalized instruments or special legal authorization.[41] Section 241 of the Income Tax Act imposes confidentiality requirements on Canada Revenue Agency employees and others with access to taxpayer information, with penalties for unauthorized disclosure, but sharing taxpayer information with other governments is possible through an authorizing tax treaty.[42] However, treaty-based information exchange remains subject to certain confidentiality conditions as the Canada Revenue Agency is subject to the Privacy Act and associated Treasury Board policies and directives for the management and protection of Canadians' personal information.[43] It

37. *Id.*
38. *Id.*
39. *Id.*
40. *Id.*
41. *Id.*
42. Income Tax Act s. 241; *see also* Stephen J. Toope & Alison L. Young, *The Confidentiality of Tax Returns under Canadian Law*, 27 McGill Law Journal 479 (1982); Jim E.R. Ellis, *Tax Return Confidentiality*, 1 Canadian Taxation 29 (1979).
43. CRA, *Audit Report of the Privacy Commissioner of Canada: Section 37 of the Privacy Act—Final Report* (2013). This is the most recent audit of the CRA by the Office of the Privacy Commission.

is also subject to the Convention on Mutual Administrative Assistance in Tax Matters.[44] No party to this Convention may receive information unless it can show that it meets "the highest standards of confidentiality and data safeguards."[45] The preamble to the Convention emphasizes that in coordinating efforts to exchange information, countries must ensure "adequate protection of the rights of taxpayers."[46]

Accordingly, in agreeing to participate in the ICAP, companies are required to sign a memorandum of understanding, which includes a consent to disclosure, in order to allow the Canada Revenue Agency to share information with other jurisdictions.[47] The existence of a treaty makes it possible for Canada Revenue Agency officials to approach other governments to discuss specific taxpayers, since under all Canadian tax treaties the delegation of responsibilities to competent authorities is broad and allows for this kind of interaction.[48]

[E] Canada Revenue Agency's Experience

From the perspective of the Canada Revenue Agency, the ICAP 1.0 offered important opportunities to engage with taxpayers as well as with other tax administrations.[49] With respect to its dealings with multinational companies, tax officials were able to establish open discussions and explain why the administration might have concerns about specified transactions. The programme also provided a mechanism to contact

The Office of the Privacy Commission has more recently reviewed the Security of Canada Information Sharing Act, which facilitates information sharing across agencies, including the CRA. *See* Office of the Privacy Commission of Canada, *Review of the Operationalization of the Security of Canada Information Sharing Act—Final Report* (December 2017), at https://www.priv.gc.ca/en/opc-actions-and-decisions/audits/ar-vr_scisa_2017/#toc1.

44. Convention on Mutual Administrative Assistance in Tax Matters, as amended by Protocol (2011). This Convention was developed jointly by the OECD and the Council of Europe in 1988 and amended by Protocol in 2010 to incorporate more expansive exchange of information. Canada signed the original convention on Apr. 28, 2004 and the Protocol on Mar. 11, 2011; the latter entered into force on Jan. 3, 2014.
45. OECD, *Standard for Automatic Exchange of Financial Information in Tax Matters: Implementation Handbook* (2015) (explaining that "[t]he confidentiality of taxpayer information is a fundamental cornerstone to tax information exchange and is relevant to all of the ... requirements" for international tax information exchange, and stating that an administration that receives tax information from its information exchange partners must have the legal frameworks in place necessary to keep tax information confidential, "including limitations on use of the information only for tax purposes.").
46. Convention on Mutual Administrative Assistance in Tax Matters, as amended by Protocol (2011), Preamble.
47. Information collected from the CRA.
48. Thus, for example, in the Canada-U.S. tax treaty, consistent with the OECD model, the competent authorities are authorized to "consult together for the elimination of double taxation in cases not provided for in the Convention." Convention Between Canada and the United States of America with Respect to Taxes on Income and on Capital, Art. XXVI; *see also* OECD, *Model Tax Convention on Income and on Capital* (Nov. 21, 2017), Art. 25(3) (stating that in addition to enumerated tasks, the competent authorities of treaty partner countries "may also consult together for the elimination of double taxation in cases not provided for in the Convention.").
49. Information collected from the CRA.

other countries, setting parameters on how to negotiate with them.[50] Countries often diverge on how they see each company, how they assess risks, and who should be entitled to tax certain transactions.[51] Allowing for insight into what other governments see as risk-intensive or not, the ICAP seems to serve as a learning tool for intergovernmental negotiation over tax issues, allowing each jurisdiction to anticipate their counterparties' positions. According to the Canada Revenue Agency, the overall experience so far has been positive.[52]

§6.05 ICAP 2.0

The ICAP 2.0 was launched in 2019 following the 12th plenary meeting of the OECD Forum on Tax Administration. The meeting focused on four priorities: (1) delivering on BEPS and tax certainty; (2) improving tax co-operation; (3) supporting the continued digitalization of tax administrations; and (4) building capacity for developing countries.[53] The participating jurisdictions of the ICAP pilot programme called for revenue administrations to continue working together with multinationals to come to solutions for cross-border tax problems. For this second round, ten new countries joined the initiative (Austria, Belgium, Denmark, Finland, France, Germany, Ireland, Luxembourg, Norway and Poland), thus there are now a total of eighteen participating countries. As the ICAP 2.0 develops, the Canada Revenue Agency continues to work with representatives from the tax community as well as other experts in order to get an idea of which other jurisdictions might be potentially interested in participating in the future.

[A] Changes

The second pilot project substantially reformulated the ICAP. It now consists of four stages: pre-entry, scoping (four to eight weeks), risk assessment and issue resolution (no more than twenty weeks), and outcomes (four to eight weeks). Furthermore, while the ICAP 1.0 was restricted to transfer pricing and permanent establishment risks, the ICAP 2.0 can deal with any issues that the multinational company decides to submit, including value added taxes, hybrids, etc. The lead tax administration is in charge of

50. For a discussion of why and how states come to negotiate over taxation issues, *see* Allison Christians, *How Nations Share*, 87 Indiana Law Journal 1407 (2012).
51. *See*, e.g., OECD/G20 Base Erosion and Profit Shifting Project, *Neutralising the Effects of Hybrid Mismatch Arrangements: Action 2: Final Report* (2015) (discussing issues surrounding hybrid instruments and entities); Tarcisio Diniz Magalhaes, *What Is Really Wrong with Global Tax Governance and How to Properly Fix It*, 10 World Tax Journal 4 (2018) (emphasizing the pluralist nature of the international tax order on the grounds that "[c]ountries disagree on what global solutions are actually needed and how they should be implemented, as in the obvious case of what should be the appropriate criteria for dividing the global tax base").
52. Information collected from the CRA.
53. *See* EY, *OECD's Forum on Tax Administration Agrees on Collective Actions on Tax Certainty, Cooperation and Digital Transformation*, Global Tax Alert (Mar. 29, 2019); EY, *OECD's Forum on Tax Administration Announces International Compliance Assurance Programme (ICAP) 2.0 and Publishes New Pilot Handbook*, Global Tax Alert (Apr. 4, 2019).

sharing with other covered tax administration the issues included by the taxpayers. The governments that agree would then go into the scoping phase. This means that each revenue body is free to decide the risk level and which issues to address.[54]

[B] Persistency of Informality

Despite these changes, the new handbook published by the OECD maintained the voluntary character of the process.[55] For Canada, this seems to suggest that the ICAP 2.0, like its previous version, will also be an informal programme.[56]

The Canada Revenue Agency states that there will be a specific procedure for the ICAP 2.0, which will tend to become more standardized in the future.[57] This time, the Canada Revenue Agency chose to have a two-pronged approach: it contacted taxpayers directly, but also welcomed those who wished to come forward. Similar to the ICAP 1.0, the Canada Revenue Agency will provide companies with the opportunity to apply for the programme if they wish to do so. The agency holds the view that it is up to the independent discretion of each tax administration to decide whether to offer an application process in the future.[58] It also states that, given the experience in the ICAP 1.0 and the infancy of the programme at this point, the OECD Handbook acts as the governing guidance for the programme.[59]

[C] Issue Resolution

For the third stage of the process, the OECD Handbook provides for issue resolution, which was included together with the risk assessment. The understanding of the Canada Revenue Agency is that, because the ICAP 2.0 is entirely voluntary, there is no right to appeal the decision.[60] In the event that taxpayers get contradictory positions from the tax administrations involved, they can resume discussions with the tax authorities of each country in which they have a filing position.[61]

---

54. Information collected from the CRA.
55. *ICAP 2.0* at 5 ("The International Compliance Assurance Programme (ICAP) is a voluntary programme for a multilateral co-operative risk assessment and assurance process.").
56. Information collected from the CRA.
57. *Id.*
58. *Id.*
59. *Id.*
60. This may be contrasted with other Co-operative Compliance-like frameworks in Canada. *See 2013 OECD Co-operative Compliance* at 51 ("In Canada, taxpayers remain entitled to their right to recourse under the various legislative authorities that the CRA currently administers. The CRA does not anticipate that there will be significant changes or adoption of alternate dispute resolutions as a result of a co-operative compliance arrangement.").
61. Information collected from the CRA.

§6.06 CONCLUSION

Tax certainty is gaining more attention these days, as changes in international tax laws become more frequent.[62] In this context, Co-operative Compliance has emerged as a useful mechanism to minimize disputes and controversies, stabilizing the global tax system. Canada has been an active participant in tax-related projects at the level of the OECD and, although it has not until now formalized Co-operative Compliance, it has been very supportive of the ICAP, in both its phases.

Canada's initial involvement in the ICAP 1.0 was motivated by a desire to determine the scope of potential experience to be gained and to gauge how active it could be in such an initiative, with a view to refine the programme into the ICAP 2.0. The Canada Revenue Agency believes governments stand to gain by getting involved in open dialogues with multinational groups about what each stakeholder sees as risky in an international tax environment. A secondary benefit is to bring tax officials together to collectively discuss issues as a group, creating rapport with treaty partners, learning how to effectively use country-by-country reporting, and so on.

From the taxpayers' perspectives, the ICAP may be seen as a game-changing initiative that would help them improve their risk profiles.[63] By giving multinationals an opportunity to better understand how tax administrations conduct risk assessments, it promises to reduce uncertainty. From the perspective of intergovernmental relationships and disputes, the ICAP will likely be useful to states in terms of gaining insight into the approaches, and anticipating the likely revenue positions, of their peers.

62. *See* IMF/OECD, *Tax Certainty: Report for the G20 Finance Ministers* (March 2017); IMF/OECD, *Update on Tax Certainty: Report for the G20 Finance Ministers* (July 2018); IMF/OECD, *2019 Progress Report on Tax Certainty: Report for the G20 Finance Ministers and Central Bank Governors* (June 2019); OECD, *Tax Certainty Day*, at https://www.oecd.org/ctp/administration/oecd-tax-certainty-day.htm.
63. *See* Satoru Araki, *The OECD-Led International Compliance Assurance Programme: A Game Changer?*, Tax Notes International (Jul. 2, 2019); Mindy Herzfeld, *ICAP as a Tool for Addressing the Digital Economy*, Tax Notes International (Jul. 15, 2019).

CHAPTER 7

Does Co-operative Compliance Fit into the German Compliance Environment?

Andreas Kowallik & Wouter de Ruiter

§7.01 INTRODUCTION/SUMMARY

The International Compliance Assurance Programme (ICAP) 1.0 pilot began in January 2018 with participation from the tax authorities of eight jurisdictions. Although Germany was initially on the list of participating countries, Germany did not participate in the ICAP 1.0 pilot, but only had an observer status.[1] In spite of some remaining legal uncertainties related to the Tax Assurance Letter that is issued by the leading tax authorities following an ICAP 2.0 procedure, the Federal Ministry of Finance decided to participate in ICAP 2.0 to allow German multinational enterprises (MNEs) to benefit from the new Organisation for Economic Co-operation and Development (OECD) programme and decided to do so without implementing any domestic tax law changes.[2]

In this chapter we will discuss the compliance environment and culture in Germany and how ICAP fits therein (§7.02). Following the general tax compliance culture on the side of the taxpayer, we continue with the relationship between the tax authorities and taxpayers in Germany (§7.03). As Germany did not participate in ICAP 1.0, we look at similar developments in Germany in the tax field and which initiatives were deployed in recent years that can be compared to ICAP (§7.04). We will end with some remarks on the participation of Germany in ICAP 2.0 (§7.05).

---

1. Prof. Dr. Prinz and Ludwig, Der Betrieb, 2018 Page 477.
2. *Egner*, Tax Compliance, TLE-023-2019; https://www.tax-legal-excellence.com/icap-2-0-unter-beteiligung-deutschlands/.

§7.02 THE TAX COMPLIANCE ENVIRONMENT IN GERMANY

Both a company as a legal entity and its legal representatives are responsible for the fulfillment of the company's tax obligations in the form of tax filings and tax payments. The level of compliance with these tax obligations starts with compliance culture and tax morale. The government can use several strategies to influence compliance directly or indirectly and thereby improving tax morale. In this section, we will discuss the situation in Germany regarding the level of compliance.

[A] Compliance Culture and Tax Morale in Germany

The compliance attitude regarding taxes is often referred to as tax morale. The tax morale explains the subjective attitude of a taxpayer to comply with tax law and regulation even in the (theoretical) absence of strict controls or punishment in cases of non-compliance.[3] Tax morale impacts the attitude of taxpayers in their payment behavior and in their relationship with governing bodies (e.g., the tax authorities).[4] We will consider the following influences on the tax morale of companies in Germany:

- Compliance culture, consisting of social norms and the general attitude toward compliance with tax laws and regulation in a country.
- Perception of tax justice.[5]

The tax morale as an attitude of taxpayers is a subjective concept differing between taxpayers. Tax morale varies in accordance with personal characteristics, but also as a result of socio-demographic aspects.[6] Germany is widely known for a common belief in reliability, structures, regulations and law enforcement. This culture is focused on obeying rules and complying with regulations and laws. This culture of compliance is also reflected in the attitude toward tax compliance. The Socio-Economic Research Institute of Cologne confirmed in a study in 2014 that the morale of taxpayers in Germany is excellent and that 82% of taxpayers mentioned tax avoidance and tax evasion as being immoral. A total of 80% claimed to have never made false statements on their tax returns.[7]

In addition to the above, German citizens also expect the existence or the creation of regulations in new or unknown situations to ensure a clear process pertaining to the matter. This is reflected in the preference of 87% of German companies to have a relationship of trust with the tax authorities in a formalized form.[8] This aligns with the

3. Robert Helbig, *Das Steuersystem*, in Steuerkomplexität (2018), Springer Gabler, pp. 85-176.
4. Stephan Mühlbacher, *Die Psychologie des Steuerzahlens* (2018), Springer Verlag GmbH, p. 8.
5. Stephan Mühlbacher, *Die Psychologie des Steuerzahlens* (2018), Springer Verlag GmbH, p. 8.
6. Ignacio Lago-Peñas and Santiago Lago-Peñas, *The determinants of tax morale in comparative perspective: Evidence from European countries* (2010), European Journal of Political Economy.
7. Heinz Wirz and Reiner Holznagel, Bund der Steuerzahler Nordrhein-Westfalen e.V., *Steuerkultur und Steuermoral in Deutschland 2014* (2014), pp. 1-5, https://deutsche-wirtschafts-nachrichten.de/wp-content/uploads/2014/07/Statement_2014_Folien1.pdf.
8. Allen & Overy, *Global Tax Practice: Negotiating the Minefield: Managing Tax Risks in Challenging Times* (2017), p. 16.

statement of Kowallik and Pumpler that the advantages of a Co-operative Compliance approach should be formalized to make this approach interesting for (German) companies.[9] This implies that German taxpayers are looking for certainty in an alternative co-operative relationship and do not expect that trust and openness will in themselves implicitly create advantages.

Only 16% of the German taxpayers consider the German tax authorities to be reasonable. With this percentage, Germany can be compared to Italy (20%), France (19%) and Spain (9%). There is a big gap, however, with countries such as the Netherlands (76%), Belgium (56%), the United Kingdom (U.K.) (49%) and Australia (46%). An explanation for this could be that in Germany the shift to more transparency and more co-operation has just started and that there is still very little trust between the tax authorities and taxpayers.[10] Another explanation may be that two-thirds of taxpayers in Germany describe the (administrative) costs of tax compliance in Germany as being very high.[11]

The perspective of tax justice can also be impacted by the experience which German taxpayers have with global transactions conducted in other countries. Germany is a country with a comparatively high statutory tax rate for corporate income tax. This statutory tax rate negatively affects the perspective of tax justice. At the same time, the effective tax rate is relatively low by global comparison.[12] The Socio-economic Research Institute of Cologne found that 85% of German taxpayers viewed taxes as being too high.[13] Tax audit adjustments play an important role in the interaction between tax authorities and taxpayers. Their magnitude implies intense discussions and controversies between many taxpayers and the tax authorities putting strain and pressure on their relationship.

[B] (Personal) Liability in Cases of Non-compliance

Building on tax morale, the government can choose a strategy to enforce tax compliance. In this sub-section, we will also discuss a strategy used to increase compliance, which is the risk of (personal) liability. Further discussions on the relationship between taxpayers and the tax authorities and the tools the German tax authorities typically use to enforce tax compliance can be found in section§7.03.

Generally, both a company in its own right and its legal representatives on its behalf are responsible for the fulfillment of tax obligations in the form of filings and

---

9. Andreas Kowallik and Reinhard Pumpler, *Begleitende Kontrolle als Alternative zur Außenprüfung in Österreich* (2018), Der Betrieb, Heft 41, Beilage 02, pp. 13-16.
10. Allen & Overy, *Global Tax Practice: Negotiating the Minefield: Managing Tax Risks in Challenging Times* (2017), p. 14.
11. Heinz Wirz and Reiner Holznagel, Bund der Steuerzahler Nordrhein-Westfalen e.V., *Steuerkultur und Steuermoral in Deutschland 2014* (2014), p. 1, https://deutsche-wirtschafts-nachrichten.de/wp-content/uploads/2014/07/Statement_2014_Folien1.pdf.
12. Frank Hettich and Carsten Schmidt, Deutschland ein Steuermärchen (2000), Wirtschaftswissenschaftliche Diskussionspapiere, No. 05/2000.
13. Heinz Wirz and Reiner Holznagel, Bund der Steuerzahler Nordrhein-Westfalen e.V., *Steuerkultur und Steuermoral in Deutschland 2014* (2014), p. 1, https://deutsche-wirtschafts-nachrichten.de/wp-content/uploads/2014/07/Statement_2014_Folien1.pdf.

payments. The costs of non-compliance for a company can consist of penalties, indemnification payments, legal expenses and reputational implications.[14] The fear of personal liability, high penalties and reputational exposure are ongoing challenges for many German companies.[15]

In Germany, most sanctions for tax non-compliance are triggered at the level of the company's legal representatives or acting individuals, but not against the company. Penalties and indemnification payments may also include employees or other individuals involved with tax topics. The personal liability of general managers in case of tax non-compliance may include imprisonment in some cases, as described below.[16] The following provisions in German (tax) law impose sanctions for tax non-compliance:[17]

- Liability of directors (§ 69 AO[18]): The directors of a company are liable for its tax liability, including potential penalties and interest, in the case of willful intent ("Vorsatz") or gross negligence ("grobe Fahrlässigkeit").
- Personal liability for tax evasion (§ 71 AO): Any person can be liable to the amount of the advantage to the company, being the reduced tax bill resulting from tax evasion, in case this person conducts the tax evasion or assists in it. The liability also includes potential penalties and interest.
- Tax evasion (§ 370 AO)[19] is defined as a decreased payment of tax based on the provision of incomplete or incorrect information to the tax authorities, the withholding of information from the tax authorities, or the absence of tax references as required by tax law on documents. Hence tax evasion could come in play in cases with small amounts and/or "mistakes" in tax returns and is not only considered as the (non-lawful) tax planning to intentionally evade amounts of taxes. The penalty for tax evasion may include imprisonment (six months up to ten years) or fines.
- Liability in cases of sales receipts (§ 379 AO): In case of willful intent ("Vorsatz") or gross negligence ("grobe Fahrlässigkeit") relating to the preparation, sale or posting of receipts resulting in a decreased tax amount paid or a tax advantage received.
- Administrative offenses (§ 30, § 130 OWiG[20] and § 377 AO): OWiG is not tax-specific, but can also cover cases of tax compliance arising from organizational deficiencies ("Organisationsverschulden"). Non-compliance resulting from organizational deficiencies can be punished with penalties of up to EUR 10 million. OWiG is the only law that may result in sanctions against both

14. Corinna Ewelt-Knauer and Anastasia Bauer, *Compliance Management Systeme: Definition, Bedeutung und Berichterstattung* (2017), from: Langfristige Perspektiven und Nachhaltigkeit in der Rechnungslegung, pp. 75-87, p. 79.
15. Allen & Overy, *Global Tax Practice: Negotiating the Minefield: Managing Tax Risks in Challenging Times* (2017), p. 12.
16. Johanna Hey, Steuerplanungssicherheit als Rechtsproblem (2002), Verlag Dr. Otto Schmidt.
17. Tilo Künstler and Frank Seidel, *Tax Compliance* (2009), pp. 245-252 from Compliance in der Unternehmerpraxis.
18. The General Tax Law ("Abgabenordnung," "AO") covers the formalities and procedures for the collection of taxes, spanning across all specific tax laws.
19. *See also* section §7.04[B].
20. Administrative Offence Act ("Ordnungswidrigkeitsgesetz," "OWiG").

a company as a legal entity and its legal representatives or other acting individuals.
- Embezzlement (§ 266 StGB[21]): Abuse of power which results in a disadvantage for the company. This can result in imprisonment for up to five years.
- Indemnification (§ 93 AktG,[22] § 43 GmbHG[23]): Company law indemnification claims based on insufficient efforts regarding the legal obligation to ensure an adequate organization. In cases of willful intent or gross negligence for tax obligations, a liability of legal representatives applies (§ 34, § 35 AO, e.g., for a managing director, cf. § 69 AO).[24]

Due to the comparatively high exposure of personal liability, a German company's employees, and in particular its management, can be expected to have a strong personal motivation to ensure that the company observes and complies with all applicable (domestic and global) tax laws and all tax obligations.

[C] A Road to Co-operative Compliance?

Based on the tax morale of taxpayers in a country or the tax morale of specific taxpayers, the (tax) authorities can design a strategy for enforcing tax compliance. Some generally used theories in this respect are:[25]

- *Economic model*: based on the cost of non-compliance a taxpayer makes a decision to be compliant or not. With a high detection risk and/or high costs of non-compliance, the tax authorities can influence the taxpayer's decision to be compliant.
- *Decisions of taxpayers (a moral dilemma)*: The compliance behavior of single taxpayers has a limited impact on the financing and provision of public services. In case some taxpayers avoid the payment of tax, they optimize their tax as public services are still available. If all taxpayers avoid tax, no services can be offered. For a single taxpayer there exists a dilemma between the individual and collective interests.
- *Responsive regulation*: an adjusted approach of the tax authorities, based on the compliance behavior of a taxpayer. This also means that the tax authorities support and advise co-operative taxpayers.
- *Slippery slope framework:* This framework combines economic and psychological factors as an explanation for tax morale. By positively influencing the trust of taxpayers the tax authorities can create increased compliance on the

21. Criminal Code ("Strafgesetzbuch," "StGB").
22. Stock Corporation Code ("Aktiengesetz," "AktG").
23. Limited Liability Companies Act ("Gesetz betreffend die Gesellschaften mit beschränkter Haftung," "GmbhG").
24. Following the scope of ICAP, which only includes multinational companies, the list above is focused on the liability risks for employees and directors of such companies.
25. Stephan Mühlbacher, *Die Psychologie des Steuerzahlens* (2018), Springer Verlag GmbH, p. 3 and Chapter 6.

side of taxpayers. In case of lower trust, the tax authorities can force compliance by using controls and penalties.

Relying on the strong tax morale in Germany (as described in section §7.02[A]) and a strict application of the economic model (e.g., in the form of (personal) liability risks for employees and legal representatives (*see* section §7.02[B])), the options for increasing tax compliance can be explored in different areas. The German tax authorities could consider the responsive regulation framework (e.g., a Co-operative Compliance approach). This could strengthen tax compliance even further and, at the same time, increase efficiency in the tax collecting process for both the tax authorities and taxpayers.

§7.03 RELATIONSHIP BETWEEN THE TAXPAYER AND THE TAX AUTHORITIES

[A] Structure of Tax Administration

The legal basis for taxation in Germany is the constitution ("Grundgesetz"), which lays out the principles for the administration of tax laws, for tax collection rights, and for tax revenue allocation. The federal government ("Bundesregierung"), the states ("Länder"), and the cities ("Städte") and municipalities ("Gemeinden") may all levy taxes. Most taxation rights belong collectively to the federal government and the states (so-called shared taxes), some only to the federal level (e.g., customs duty), some only to the states (e.g., excise taxes, gift and inheritance tax, real estate transfer tax), and some only to cities and municipalities (e.g., real estate tax, trade tax ("Gewerbesteuer")). Cities and municipalities may levy their taxes only in defined areas (e.g., on dogs, hunts, horses, entertainment events, second homes used for leisure, and touristic use of hotel rooms). In practice, the federal level represents approximately 95% of all tax revenue.

Germany's tax administration is divided into the federal tax authorities and the state tax authorities. The federal government ("Bundesregierung") is in charge of tax legislation and oversees the federal tax authorities ("Bundesministerium der Finanzen") who oversee the state tax authorities ("Oberfinanzdirektion or Landesamt für Steuern") that, in turn, oversee the local tax offices ("Finanzamt") in their state. The tax offices in the states assess, collect and manage the shared taxes for the federation government and the states and process most tax returns. In 2018, the number of tax offices in Germany was approximately 535. Following reforms in 2006 and 2009, the federal government also assesses, collects and manages some taxes. The competent authority is the Federal Tax Office ("Bundeszentralamt für Steuern") that is also the competent authority for processing all tax refunds to non-residents.[26] The cities and municipalities maintain their own tax administration and collection system with their own personnel.

26. https://www.bundesfinanzministerium.de/Content/DE/Downloads/Broschueren_Bestellservice/2018-03-16-die-steuerverwaltung-in-deutschland.pdf?__blob=publicationFile&v=8.

[B] Relationship Between Companies and the Tax Authorities

For all income taxes—including individual income tax ("Einkommensteuer"), corporate income tax ("Körperschaftsteuer") and trade tax ("Gewerbesteuer")—Germany still follows a traditional four-step tax administration model. Taxpayers file income tax returns for each calendar year or fiscal year. Business income is generally determined from financial statements for the relevant accounting period. The tax office in charge of the tax return issues a tax assessment notice ("Steuerbescheid") after a desk review of the tax return ("Veranlagung"). Individual income tax returns may be e-filed while all corporate income tax returns must be e-filed. To date, Germany still does not use a self-assessment approach for income taxes. All income taxes are pre-paid in quarterly instalments during the year based on the last available tax assessment with a final payment or refund after the issuance of the tax assessment notice following the review of the tax return by the tax office. The cities and municipalities run their own parallel system for assessing, collecting and managing their own taxes.

All monthly or quarterly tax returns for payroll taxes, dividends, interest, royalties and value-added tax (VAT) must be e-filed. Here, self-assessment of all payments is the rule, and all taxpayers must make payments without receiving a tax assessment notice.

Most German taxpayers have limited interaction with the German tax authorities. Traditionally, the tax climate in Germany is characterized by the tax authorities' self-perception as being part of the government's executive administration system ("Eingriffsverwaltung"). Historically, the German tax authorities generally did not see themselves as providing a public service, but rather perceived themselves as being the executor of public rights to collect tax revenue from taxpayers who they often perceive to be unwilling to pay their fair share of taxes. In light of the traditional administration model, most desk reviews of income tax returns during the tax assessment tend to be superficial since this is an intermediate step ultimately followed by a tax audit ("Außenprüfung") performed by a different department of the tax office ("Betriebsprüfung").

[C] Tax Audits[27]

Reflecting the tax authorities' self-perception as being part of the government's executive administration system ("Eingriffsverwaltung"), Germany heavily relies on tax audits ("Außenprüfung") as a means of ensuring taxpayer discipline. For many larger businesses, the strongest regular interaction with the tax authorities occurs with the tax audit department ("Betriebsprüfung") of the tax office. Micro- and small businesses are tax audited on a random basis and most of them are statistically never tax audited; in 2018, only 1.1% of the 5.6 million micro-businesses and 3.2% of the 1.2 million small businesses were tax audited. Medium-sized businesses are generally tax

27. Prof. Dr. Robert Risse, Aktuelle Entwicklungen bei der Betriebsprüfung aus Unternehmenssicht, DB vom 12.10.2018, Heft 41, Beilage 02, Seite 2—10, DB1273510.

audited on a random basis and with respect to a limited number of years; in 2018, 6.3 % of the 792,326 medium-sized business were tax audited. Tax audits of larger corporations and of the local subsidiaries of foreign groups tend to be regular and tend to cover all their fiscal years with consecutive tax audits; in 2018, 21.6% of the 186,339 large businesses were tax audited. With some variations—the most notable exception from the rule being near-time tax audits ("zeitnahe Betriebsprüfung")[28] —tax audits are usually conducted at four- to five-yearly intervals, though not always with the same intensity for the entire audit period since the tax auditors' last visit (i.e., the tax audit procedure allows for focus areas and does not require the tax audit of the same focus areas or topics in each tax audit cycle).[29]

Tax audits tend to be very intense, being on-site field tax audits that often last for several weeks, sometimes several months and in larger cases even years.[30] Large companies subject to continuous tax audits tend to have tax auditors on premise all the time. Findings during tax audits may trigger further investigations by public prosecutors to search for data and information.[31] If the company is a member of an international group, its most important tax audit areas are usually its transactional taxes (e.g., VAT, customs duty, wage tax), its dealings with related foreign parties and its transfer pricing documentation. Companies with an international focus can expect significant tax audit emphasis on all aspects of their dealings with foreign related parties. Most taxes are tax-audited by the tax audit department of their local tax office. During tax audits, the tax auditors tend to involve a growing number of specialists (e.g., information technology (IT) tax auditors with deep Enterprise Resource Planning (ERP) knowledge and technical understanding). The cities and municipalities may conduct their own tax audits (e.g., for trade tax) in parallel to regular tax audits, which is often the case for larger taxpayers. Also dawn raids have become more frequent, with 31 % of companies in Germany being subject to a dawn raid during 2015-2017. At the same time normal tax cases were increasingly being criminalized with more tax audits triggering tax audit findings (e.g., tax deduction of kick-back payments) that were passed on to the public prosecutors who then initiated criminal investigations against companies' top management.[32]

28. *See also* section §7.04[A].
29. https://www.bundesfinanzministerium.de/Monatsberichte/2018/11/Inhalte/Kapitel-3-Analysen/3-7-ergebnisse-betriebspruefung.html.
30. Even though German tax auditors reportedly do not have a target number for each tax audit and do not receive a success fee or a percentage share of any extra tax revenue they collect, success in tax audits tends to be measured by extra tax revenue collected; *see* Sheppard, The Limits of Friendlier Tax Administration, Part 2, 2019 WTD 72-1.
31. An example with international press coverage were dawn raids on nineteen German banks (including Deutsche Bank) and a number of private homes occurred on occurred May 15, 2019 to search for tax evasion information from using offshore companies, https://www.theguardian.com/business/2019/may/15/tax-authorities-mount-raids-on-19-german-banks-and-homes.
32. Allen & Overy, *Global Tax Practice: Negotiating the Minefield: Managing Tax Risks in Challenging Times* (2017), p. 9.

[D] Risk Management System During Tax Audits

The tax authorities have long denied that they were building up a risk management system and that they were testing risk-based approaches for screening and classifying taxpayers.[33] Historically, the tax administration also did not take part in related surveys of the OECD.[34] Following a law change in 2016, the tax authorities now openly admit that they use risk-based systems for screening and classifying taxpayers, which they also use for tax audit pre-screening and selection.[35]

The tax authorities do not disclose their tax risk ratings to the taxpayers. This is different from the approach taken by many other countries that view tax risk management as being part of their tax control framework or Co-operative Compliance system. Both approaches aim at motivating taxpayers to comply with all applicable laws by making tax non-compliance more costly, unattractive and risky than tax compliance. However, if taxpayers do not know their tax risk rating and do not know the applicable criteria, it is at least doubtful whether a risk management system will change taxpayer behavior. Reportedly, the tax authorities use at least some of the following criteria for risk classification and tax audit case selection: tax audit history; industry and sector issues; exceptional or complex transactions; corporate structure; major acquisitions and disposals; cross-border activities; corporate governance; participation in aggressive tax planning; history of under- or overpaying tax; compliance or non-compliance tax history (e.g., timely tax filings); and openness and transparency.

It is known, but not officially confirmed, that the tax authorities use four tax risk classes. Class 1 includes all complex taxpayers with more than one type of income (e.g., employment income, business income, investment income, rental income), taxpayers with high incomes and taxpayers with business income from certain industries or activities; this group can expect thorough desk reviews of all their tax returns by the tax office. Class 2 includes taxpayers with deviations from predefined ranges and standards flagged by tax risk management software; this group will be subject to at least a high-level desk review, which shall be limited to flagged areas. Class 3 includes all other taxpayers. Class 4 includes all taxpayers selected for tax audits; this group is in practice limited to high-income and high-net-worth individuals (i.e., taxable income of EUR 500,000 or more) and taxpayers with business income who are pre-screened on their income tax returns and their standardized book/tax differences to flag tax audit areas.

33. *See* Kowallik, IWB 2014, 406; Kowallik, DB 2015, 2774; Kowallik, DB 2017, 385.
34. https://www.oecd.org/tax/forum-on-tax-administration/publications-and-products/33818568.pdf.
35. Gesetz zur Modernisierung des Besteuerungsverfahrens (StModG) vom 16.7.2016, BGBl. I 2016, 1679; https://www.betriebsausgabe.de/magazin/finanzamt-fuehrt-risikomanagement-fuer-steuerpflichtige-ein-4084/.

[E] Role of the Tax Authorities

Historically, neither the Federal Ministry of Finance nor the local tax authorities have seen themselves as providing a public service and have no real tradition of maintaining an open and co-operative collaboration culture with taxpayers, with only 18% of German companies working on a full disclosure basis with the tax authorities.[36] The level of trust between companies, advisors and tax authorities is increasingly being tested.[37]

[F] Relationship Programmes

On May 23, 2016, the Federal Ministry of Finance introduced control focused compliance elements when issuing a final version of a decree on the procedure for amending a tax return under section 153 of the General Tax Code (AO).[38] The final decree provided instructions on the complex distinction between a non-sanctioned simple tax return amendment procedure (section 153 AO) and a potentially sanctioned voluntary self-disclosure procedure (section 371 AO). In note 2.6, the application decree states that the tax authorities may take into account the existence of an adequate and effective tax compliance management system when evaluating intent or negligence of the taxpayer (i.e., when evaluating whether a relevant case is a non-sanctioned simple tax return amendment or a potentially sanction-able self-disclosure procedure).

The option for taxpayers to implement a tax control framework in order to obtain tax benefits or to ensure a more favorable tax treatment from the tax authorities is a real novelty in German tax law and an indication that the Federal Ministry of Finance is willing to practice-test Co-operative Compliance elements. On May 31, 2017, the German CPA Institute ("IDW") enhanced its pre-existing final audit standard on compliance management systems ("IDW PS 980") for tax considerations and published a final version of IDW Practice Guideline 1/2016 (Design and Audit of a Tax Compliance Management System according to IDW PS 980).[39] In Germany, IDW Practice Guideline 1/2016 is the de facto standard for designing and implementing an adequate and effective tax control framework in accordance with the Federal Ministry of Finance's requirements since note 2.6 of the decree dated May 23, 2016 does not provide any kind of practical guidance on the content of and for implementing a tax control framework.[40]

Despite the fact that the OECD has published a number of reports on Co-operative Compliance, there is still no domestic legislation on Co-operative Compliance, but only

36. Allen & Overy, *Global Tax Practice: Negotiating the Minefield: Managing Tax Risks in Challenging Times* (2017), p. 13.
37. Allen & Overy, *Global Tax Practice: Negotiating the Minefield: Managing Tax Risks in Challenging Times* (2017), p. 4.
38. http://www.deloitte-tax-news.de/german-tax-legal-news/mof-decree-emphasizes-importance-of-tax-compliance-management-system.html.
39. https://www.idw.de/idw/idw-aktuell/endgueltiger-idw-praxishinweis-1-2016-zu-tax-compliance-management-systemen/101304.
40. *See also* section §7.04[B].

guidance from the Ministry of Finance dated May 23, 2016 on tax control frameworks. In addition, there are near-time tax audits ("zeitnahe Betriebsprüfungen") in some states that rely on Co-operative Compliance and special relationship programmes. Neither note 2.6 of the Federal Ministry of Finance decree nor IDW Practice Guideline 1/2016 are legally binding upon taxpayers and thus force no taxpayer to implement a tax compliance management system or other form of tax control framework.[41] To date, there are still no tangible tax benefits—such as a legal right to a near-time tax audit or a legal claim to advance certainty via an accelerated tax ruling process—to taxpayers with a tax control framework. However, once a taxpayer has qualified for a near-time tax audit, which is only possible in certain states and for certain taxpayers, there are more tangible benefits since the tax control framework documentation in practice helps to expedite the tax audit process.

The advantages of a co-operative approach, like ICAP, are described by the Responsive Regulation theory. With responsive regulation the tax authorities adjust their approach toward a taxpayer based on the attitude and behavior of this taxpayer. On the one hand, this means an appropriate intensity of controls (tax audit). On the other hand, the tax authorities can also support co-operative taxpayers (more). This could be explicitly described in law or regulation, but also implicitly, following the decisions of the tax authorities in their daily operations.[42] For such an approach a change in culture, as described in sections §7.03[B] and §7.03[C], on the side of the tax authorities would be necessary.

[G] Conclusion: Relationship Between Taxpayer and Tax Authorities

Most taxpayers have very limited interaction with the tax authorities. As mentioned, historically, the tax authorities did not perceive themselves as providing a public service, but rather saw themselves as being the executor of public rights to collect tax revenue from taxpayers. The tax authorities' internal organization still follows a very traditional and hierarchical model with a four-tier structure for income tax. In light of this traditional administration model, many desk reviews of income tax returns performed by the tax assessment departments are very superficial since they will ultimately be followed by a tax audit undertaken by the tax audit department of the same tax office.

The Federal Ministry of Finance knows that the tax authorities need to quickly change the way they operate taxes and organize the tax collection system since they will, in only a few years, no longer be able to recruit sufficient officials to uphold their current model. The tax authorities therefore pursue a clear roadmap to automate,

41. Legally speaking, note 2.6 of the Federal Ministry of Finance decree is only internal administrative guidance issued by the Federal Ministry of Finance to the state tax authorities and to the local tax authorities on how to apply tax law consistently and uniformly. Nonetheless, taxpayers may rely on such self-binding guidance for their own affairs and may also have its application controlled in tax court (e.g., if a taxpayer believes that a tax office ignored his tax control framework).
42. Stephan Mühlbacher, *Die Psychologie des Steuerzahlens* (2018), Springer Verlag GmbH, Chapter 6.

modernize and digitize the tax system. This originally also included a domestic tax control framework (e.g., a Tax Compliance Management System (CMS)), applying global or regional standards (e.g., Country-by-Country Reporting (CbCR), joint audits, or Council Directive (EU) 2018/822 on reportable cross-border arrangements (DAC 6)), and experiments with Co-operative Compliance (e.g., ICAP 2.0). To date, however, these initiatives have not yet fundamentally changed or revolutionized the tax system, the organization of the tax collection process or the practical co-operation between the tax authorities and taxpayers.

§7.04 COMPLIANCE: NEW WAYS OF WORKING

In Germany, there has—to date—not yet been a Co-operative Compliance initiative that is comparable to ICAP or horizontal monitoring. However, in recent years the tax authorities have initiated several changes in their way of working with companies that resulted in a change of how companies handle their tax obligations. In this section, we will discuss a few of the major developments.

[A] Work in Near-Time: "Zeitnahe Betriebsprüfung"

Zeitnahe Betriebsprüfung	
Is the approach established in legal or other regulation?	Included in a tax administration procedure
Is the approach open to all taxpayer segments?	Only taxpayers in specific states can apply; however, they have no right to participate. Where available, the programme is open to all taxpayers that meet the formal qualifications
Is entry into the programme upon application or invitation?	Informal application of the taxpayer is possible; however, the programme is only available by admission by the tax office in charge of the taxpayer
What are the conditions for acceptance into the programme?	- Close all open tax audits - Enter into a co-operation agreement with the tax authorities - Prepared and e-filed all tax-audit-relevant tax returns and standardized book/tax schedules
Is the disclosure mandatory or voluntary?	The taxpayer commits to pro-actively inform the tax authorities about tax relevant corporate and business changes

With a tax administration procedure amendment in 2011 (§ 4a Betriebsprüfungsordnung), Germany introduced federal legislation allowing all state tax authorities to use near-time tax audits ("zeitnahe Betriebsprüfung"). This new procedure formalized and standardized previous local state pilots run on an informal basis. The objective of the near-time tax audit is to perform a timely tax audit for a maximum of one to two tax periods immediately after the taxpayer has filed all tax returns. Currently, taxpayers do not have a right to a near-time tax audit but can only apply for it. Some states (e.g., Lower Saxony (Niedersachsen), Hamburg and North-Rhine Westphalia (Nordrhein-Westfalen)) push near-time tax audits and pro-actively offer them to all their large taxpayers who meet the following criteria: (1) the taxpayer is subject to continuous tax audit; (2) the taxpayer has a history of tax compliance orientation (i.e., a history of timely tax filings, no tax fraud cases, no major tax audit disputes, no criminal investigations related to tax); and (3) the tax local office can staff and run a near-time tax audit.[43]

To qualify for a near-time tax audit, the taxpayer must first close all his open tax audits to reach the next near-time tax audit period; in practice, this is often a challenge for taxpayers. The taxpayer must then enter into a co-operation agreement with the tax authorities in which they agree to inform the tax office, pro-actively and in a timely manner, of all corporate and business changes with potential tax relevance (e.g., changes in the shareholder structure, restructuring transactions, intercompany transactions). The taxpayer must furthermore ensure that they have prepared and e-filed all tax-audit-relevant tax returns and standardized book/tax schedules, must commit to a handover of all financial statements, must confirm that all adjustments from the last closed tax audit cycle are included in all filed tax returns and all standardized book/tax schedules and must agree to continuous presentation of all legal documents with potential tax relevance.

For years, the trade and industry associations have voiced their members' growing frustration with the structure of the tax audit system in general and the disappointing practical experiences with the near-time tax audit regime in particular.[44] The near-time tax audit regime is under the sole control of the states, of which many do not offer a near-time tax audit regime. Thus, only a few companies are in practice able to benefit from the regime, which had raised high hopes in industry to help expedite tax audits following the introduction of standardized book/tax schedules ("E-Bilanz"), which provided the tax offices with standardized data sets for all taxpayers that can be used for tax-audit pre-screening. Many companies with continuous tax audits want quicker tax certainty, but cannot get access to the near-time tax audit regime.[45]

In light of the high investments made by many of their members into their E-Bilanz introduction (since 2011 or 2012) and more recently again into their tax control framework (since 2016), the trade and industry associations demand that the Federal Ministry of Finance increases tax certainty by codifying the minimum requirements for tax control frameworks. Furthermore, they demand that either a modernized

43. *See* leaflet published by the Lower Saxony regional tax office in English in January 2012, http://www.betriebspruefung.info.
44. This frustration is documented by letter sent by the so-called Round of Eight (i.e., the eight largest German trade and industry associations) to the Federal Ministry of Finance on Apr. 11, 2019 with the subject line "'Horizontal Monitoring' as an alternative to the [traditional] tax audit" ("Begleitende Kontrolle" als Alternative zur steuerlichen Betriebsprüfung).
45. Kowallik, Der Betrieb 2018, Beilage 2, 26.

version of the near-time tax audit regime is made available to all continuously tax-audited taxpayers (as a right of the taxpayer) or that the near-time tax audit regime be replaced by a new horizontal monitoring regime in line with a new regime in Austria.[46] Effective from January 1, 2019, qualifying companies in Austria may apply for a new voluntarily regime ("Begleitende Kontrolle") that no longer includes a traditional tax audit; instead, they discuss all their tax risks with the tax authorities on an ongoing and on a regular basis.[47] The Federation of German Industries ("Bundesverband der Deutschen Industrie") as the leading organization of the manufacturing industry and manufacturing-related service providers, representing about 40 associations and more than 100,000 companies with around 8 million employees, is augmenting and increasing its pressure on the tax authorities by organizing a tax audit event in October 2019.[48]

[B] Focus on Controls: Tax Compliance Management System ("Tax CMS")

Tax CMS	
Is the approach established in legal or other regulation?	Tax CMS is mentioned in administrative guidance (i.e., tax regulations)[49]
Is the approach open to all taxpayer segments?	Yes, all companies, independent of size, can implement a Tax CMS. the size and form of a Tax CMS varies depending on the size and complexity of a company
Is entry into the programme upon application or invitation?	No application is necessary, the implementation of a Tax CMS is voluntary
What are the conditions for acceptance into the programme?	Tax CMS is not a programme and the quality of the implemented Tax CMS will be assessed only during a tax audit or in a non-compliance situation in tax court
Is the disclosure mandatory or voluntary?	Disclosure of the Tax CMS occurs upon request of the tax authorities or in tax court

The main obligation of companies toward taxes is the fulfillment of obligations resulting from tax law and regulation, mainly involving the filing of tax return and the payment of taxes. "Tax Compliance" can be explained differently. The first and simplest interpretation is the timely and complete filing of all applicable tax returns and

46. https://www.deloittetax.at/2018/10/24/draft-regulation-addresses-requirements-under-new-horizontal-monitoring-procedure/.
47. Kowallik/Pumpler, Der Betrieb 2018, Beilage 2, 13.
48. The working title for the event, which will be attended by representatives from the Federal Ministry of Finance and the Federal Tax Office, is "Tax Audits—Best-Practice Reform Options for Companies and the Tax Authorities" (Steuerliche Betriebsprüfungen—zeitgemäße Reformoptionen für Unternehmen und Finanzverwaltung).
49. Anwendungserlass zu § 153 AO (2016/0470583).

the payment of all owed taxes.[50] The definition commonly used in German literature can best be described using the wording from the Sarbanes-Oxley Act section 404: "establishing and maintaining an adequate internal control structure and procedures for taxes."[51] Hence "Tax Compliance" in this form can be understood as implying a "Tax Compliance Management System." The Federal Ministry of Finance only introduced the concept in 2016 by including a short reference to an Internal Control System for Taxes ("Tax ICS")[52] in administrative guidance.[53]

As discussed above, the threshold for tax avoidance is relatively low under German tax law and can come with severe consequences. The existence of an implemented tax control framework is an indication that, in the case of a correction in the tax return by a company leading to an increased tax payment, the company or employee did not reduce the tax amount with willful intent ("Vorsatz") or gross negligence ("grobe Fahrlässigkeit") when preparing the original tax return. Hence, the existence of a tax control framework or tax compliance management system can protect a company's legal representatives against allegations of tax evasion by the tax authority.[54]

Although the concept of a Tax ICS was introduced by the Federal Ministry of Finance, the application decree does not provide any guidance on the concept itself nor the form of a Tax ICS. Instead, the Federal Ministry of Finance asked the CPA Institute (IDW)[55] to draft such guidance. The IDW did so in IDW Practice Guideline 1/2016 on audit standard PS 980, which provides best-practice guidance to all German CPAs for auditing a tax compliance management system.[56] IDW Practice Guideline 1/2016, which also refers to the "general acknowledged and other relevant concepts," must be considered by all German CPAs as a best-practice standard when auditing and/or certifying a tax control framework. IDW Practice Guideline 1/2016 makes explicit reference to "Co-operative Tax Compliance: Building Better Tax Control Frameworks" of the OECD and to COSO guidelines (e.g., Risk Assessment in Practice).

IDW Practice Guideline 1/2016 includes the following building blocks:

- Tax Compliance-Objectives;
- Tax Compliance-Culture;
- Tax Compliance-Organization;
- Tax Compliance-Risks.
- Tax Compliance-Program.
- Tax Compliance-Communication.

50. Tilo Künstler and Frank Seidel, *Tax Compliance* (2009), pp. 243-261 from Compliance in der Unternehmerpraxis.
51. Tilo Künstler and Frank Seidel, *Tax Compliance* (2009), p. 243 from Compliance in der Unternehmerpraxis.
52. In German: Innerbetriebliches Kontrollsystem für Steuern ("Steuer IKS").
53. Kowallik, Vom innerbetrieblichen Kontrollsystem für Steuern zum Tax Compliance Management System, Der Betrieb Nummer 8, Feb. 24, 2017.
54. Anwendungserlass zu §153 AO (2016/0470583).
55. Institut der Wirtschaftsprüfer ("IDW").
56. IDW Praxishinweis 1/2016: Ausgestaltung und Prüfung eines Tax Compliance Management Systems gemäß IDW PS 980.

- Tax Compliance-Monitoring and Improvement.

If a taxpayer wants to comply with note 2.6 of the Federal Ministry of Finance decree by implementing a Tax Compliance Management System (Tax CMS) in line with IDW Practice Guideline 1/2016, the minimum is comprehensive Tax CMS documentation on the company's tax-relevant processes, its tax-relevant risks, and its tax-relevant controls including a definition of roles and responsibilities. If a taxpayer wants to document their tax control framework (e.g., for an external expert review and certification by a public auditor), a detailed tax risk control matrix with a systematic identification of tax risks and the respective tax controls and a description of their implementation within the tax control framework is required. The taxpayer will also need detailed written documentation of all tax-relevant as-is processes including process and interface visualizations if they aim for a tax control framework that can be audited and certified as being adequate and effective according to IDW Practice Guideline 1/2016.

Although the IDW Practice Guideline 1/2016 refers to the Federal Ministry of Finance decree, there is no such direct reference to IDW Practice Guideline 1/2016 in the Federal Ministry of Finance decree. Even though note 2.6 of the Federal Ministry of Finance decree and IDW Practice Guideline 1/2016 are not legally binding, there is now a de facto expectation in tax audits that taxpayers have paid attention to the tax control framework standardization. In current tax audits, the tax auditors present tax questionnaires to taxpayers asking them to explain whether they have implemented a tax control framework, whether their tax control framework complies with IDW Practice Guideline 1/2016, and whether the tax control framework is adequate and effective. In inbound cases that involve non-German headquartered groups, the tax auditors also ask taxpayers to explain where their tax control framework deviates from IDW Practice Guideline 1/2016 and to explain such deviations (e.g., another global standard forms the basis for the tax control framework such as Chinese SOX, ISO, OECD, US SOX, or COSO). Taxpayers with non-compliance findings or historical tax compliance issues (e.g., tax control deficiencies, weaknesses in tax-relevant processes, high VAT adjustments, or errors in tax codes in the ERP system) are now expected to have responded with a well-documented and expert-reviewed tax control framework to protect their German management.[57]

A recent court case attaches some immediate advantages to a Tax CMS. In the case, the tax authorities detected tax evasion. The company started implementing a Tax CMS only during its legal dispute after the non-compliance finding. In its decision, the Federal Court ("Bundesgerichtshof")—to the benefit of the company—took this Tax CMS into consideration when determining its penalty.[58]

57. Andreas Kirsch and Jens Schäperclaus, *Tax-Compliance-Management-Systeme in der Betriebsprüfung* (2018), Der Betrieb, Heft 41, Beilage 02, pp. 17-21.
58. Urteil StR 265/16 from 7 Mai 2017.

[C] Working Digitally: E-Bilanz

E-Bilanz	
Is the approach established in legal or other regulation?	The filing of the E-Bilanz is mentioned in the German Income Tax (EStG) law[59]
Is the approach open to all taxpayer segments?	The filing of an E-Bilanz is mandatory for companies, independent of size and legal form
Is entry into the programme upon application or invitation?	N/A
What are the conditions for acceptance into the programme?	N/A
Is disclosure mandatory or voluntary?	The E-Bilanz is only to be disclosed to the tax authorities, hence comparable to a tax return

As part of a programme to modernize (i.e., digitalize)—and to decrease bureaucracy in—the tax collection system, the German tax authorities introduced the so-called E-Bilanz.[60] For all fiscal years starting after December 31, 2011, all taxpayers who use double-entry accounting records as a basis for their income tax returns are required to submit, as an appendix to their income tax return, a standardized electronic tax basis balance sheet with an income statement ("E-Bilanz") or a standardized electronic book/tax schedule with an E-balance sheet and E-income statement ("E-Überleitungsrechnung"). The mandatory technical format (taxonomy) for all related data sets is Extensible Business Reporting Language (XBRL).[61] A taxonomy is a hierarchically structured data scheme comprised, *inter alia*, of detailed balance sheet and income statement positions. Each value in an XBRL document is attributed to an element from the XBRL taxonomy, so that the document becomes fully machine-readable. An E-Bilanz data set requires tax information that is commonly not available in standard charts of accounts used by most businesses for financial accounting. To avoid changes to individual charts of accounts used by companies for financial accounting (e.g., German GAAP, IFRS or US-GAAP; "GAAP" refers to "Generally Accepted Accounting Principles"), the taxonomies include so-called fallback positions for all non-attributable items to be included in E-Bilanz data sets.[62] The tax authorities provide a taxonomy for the XBRL file on an annual basis.[63,64,65]

59. Einkommenssteuergesetz §5b.
60. "Steuerbürokratieabbaugesetz vom 28. Dezember 2008, BGBl. I 2850."
61. BMF-Schreiben vom 19. January 2010 (IV C 6—S 2133-b/0, 2009/0865962, BStBl. I 47).
62. http://www.esteuer.de, http://www.abra-search.com.
63. BMF-Schreiben vom 28. September 2011 (IV C 6—S 2133-b/11/10009, 2011/0770620, BStBl. I, S. 855).
64. http://www.esteuer.de/.
65. https://www.bundesfinanzministerium.de/Content/DE/Monatsberichte/2011/11/Artikel/analysen-und-berichte/b03-E-Bilanz/E-Bilanz.html.

The E-Bilanz provides the tax authorities with machine-readable data insights into all book/tax differences and into all movements in temporary differences for all taxpayers with double-entry accounting records. This information was previously included in a single box as part of tax return forms and was computed and documented in non-standardized spreadsheets. For 2017, the tax offices received about 7.8 million standardized E-Bilanz data sets for all taxpayers with business income that are used for tax risk management and for tax audit screening.[66] The tax authorities now openly admit that they rely on the E-Bilanz for their tax risk management system. Given these machine-readable data sets, all taxpayers with E-Bilanz preparation and e-filing obligations try to submit only plausible and consistent data sets that are reconcilable to and have been reconciled with all tax returns and all other tax filings. Here, the Federal Ministry of Finance's strategy of gaining more tax insights by using data management and of slowly changing taxpayer behavior by disclosing, at least in a very high-level manner, which validations the tax offices do run on E-Bilanz data sets, was reasonably successful. Most taxpayers tried to avoid questions during tax office desktop reviews or subsequent tax audits. From a change management perspective, the E-Bilanz introduction and rollout were no real success story and triggered a lot of frustration on the ground, both with the taxpayers and the tax offices.[67]

[D] Electronic Tax Audits

Electronic Tax Audits	
Is the approach established in legal or other regulation?	Providing data access to the tax authorities is mandatory on request by the tax authorities during a tax audit[68]
Is the approach open to all taxpayer segments?	All companies can be requested to provide data access during a tax audit
Is entry into the programme upon application or invitation?	Entry is only upon a request from tax authorities
What are the conditions for acceptance into the programme?	N/A
Is disclosure mandatory or voluntary?	The data access is only to be provided to the tax authorities, as part of a tax audit

The German tax authorities were early adopters of electronic tax audits, which also was part of the abovementioned programme to modernize (i.e., digitalize)—and to decrease bureaucracy in—the tax collection system. Since January 1, 2002, the tax authorities have far-reaching data access rights during tax audits. In addition to direct

66. https://www.bundesfinanzministerium.de/Monatsberichte/2018/11/Inhalte/Kapitel-3-Analysen/3-7-ergebnisse-betriebspruefung.html.
67. http://web.xbrleurope.org/wp-content/uploads/2017/01/ForThe15th-18thXBRLEuropeDay-AHEIDEMAN-SBR-E-BilanOnline.pdf.
68. §146 and §147 AO.

access (Z1) and indirect access (Z2) to the taxpayer's ERP and computer systems, they can also demand that the taxpayer hand over all tax-relevant data (Z3) on a data carrier (e.g., CD, DVD, USB stick). During the entire legal data retention period of ten years, all tax-relevant digital data must be available at all times, must be able to be set to read-access at all times and must be automatically processable. If a taxpayer cannot meet all these criteria, or is unable to provide the data demanded during a tax audit within a reasonable time, or if electronic data are held on a foreign server without written permission from the tax office, the taxpayer may be assessed with a penalty of up to EUR 250,000 for each non-compliance.[69]

A big practical challenge is to identify the tax-relevant data, which is the responsibility of the taxpayer. This includes, for example, information and data in financial accounting, fixed asset accounting, payroll accounting, or the ERP system. Tax-relevant data may also be located in other areas of the taxpayer's IT systems (e.g., company e-mails). In addition, the automatic processability as set out in section 14(4) sentence 2 VAT Code (UStG) and other digitized documents not submitted in hard copy (i.e., original digitally generated data) must also be ensured. Furthermore, proper documentation of all tax-relevant IT systems and processes used must be retained in a format fully compliant with the tax authority guidance on the electronic archiving of accounting and tax information and electronic data access (GoBD).[70]

[E] Joint Audits

Joint Audits	
Is the approach established in legal or other regulation?	Legal basis exists; however, joint tax audits are mainly based on administrative regulations
Is the approach open to all taxpayer segments?	Only companies with foreign activities
Is entry into the programme upon application or invitation?	Invitation
What are the conditions for acceptance into the programme?	Not formalized
Is disclosure mandatory or voluntary?	Voluntary

Germany was part of the OECD's Forum on Tax Administration (FTA) expert group that prepared and released an update of a 2010 OECD report on joint audit on March 28, 2019 (Joint Audit 2019—Enhancing Tax Co-operation and Improving Tax

69. https://docs.microsoft.com/en-us/dynamics365/business-central/localfunctionality/germany/process-for-digital-audits.
70. https://www.deloitte-tax-news.de/german-tax-legal-news/new-guidance-issued-on-electronic-archiving-of-accounting-and-tax-information-and-electronic-data-access-by-the-tax-authorities.html.

Certainty).[71] The tax authorities promote joint audits as an effective means of clarifying the facts of cross-border cases and of avoiding double taxation.[72] There is no legal right for taxpayers to apply for a joint audit.[73] With the Federal Tax Office in its court district, the tax court of Cologne has exclusive jurisdiction over all claims against a coordinated tax audit, joint audit or any other means of cross-border mutual assistance between the German and foreign tax authorities. Tax cases indicate that not all taxpayers are supportive of coordinated tax audits.[74] The tax court's jurisprudence shows a clear trend of allowing coordinated tax audits.[75] To date, Germany has conducted joint audits with more than twenty countries, mostly, but not exclusively, with European Union countries.

Germany and the Netherlands undertook a coordinated pilot audit programme that resulted in outcomes that avoided possible international tax conflicts. The pilot included five MNEs in different business segments: four were publicly traded companies and one was privately held. The tax administrations formed two unilateral audit teams with an agreed working language. Both tax authorities participated in defining the scope of the audit, including the audit period, the tax items under audit, the information to be requested, and the employees to be interviewed. The audit procedures, including the issuance of two identical joint audit reports and an agreement with the respective taxpayer, were concluded within twelve months. Upon conclusion of the audits, both the MNEs and the tax audit teams provided feedback. The MNEs gave positive feedback regarding the avoidance of Mutual Agreement Procedures, quicker issue resolution, and cementing agreements for the future, because following the joint audit, the taxpayer could apply for an advance pricing agreement. However, the MNEs also expressed that more co-ordination was needed between the two tax audit teams, and that the tax audit itself needed to go beyond simultaneous examinations. The tax audit teams had the following suggestions regarding the pilot programme: (1) tax auditors should be included in the taxpayer selection process; (2) differences in tax audit approach between the two teams should be resolved beforehand; and (3) all tax auditors should have language proficiency and transfer pricing skills. In addition, if reasonable, the taxpayer should have the opportunity to apply for a joint audit if international tax conflicts are likely to arise in a given case. This could help to avoid situations in which a country rejects any adjustments because of timing issues.[76]

71. http://www.oecd.org/tax/joint-audit-2019-enhancing-tax-co-operation-and-improving-tax-certainty-17bfa30d-en.htm.
72. *See* English guidance dated Jan. 6, 2017, https://www.bundesfinanzministerium.de/Content/DE/Downloads/BMF_Schreiben/Internationales_Steuerrecht/Allgemeine_Informationen/2017-01-06-Merkblatt-ueber-koordinierte-steuerliche-Aussenpruefungen-mit-Steuerverwaltungen-anderer-Staaten-und-Gebiete-englische-Version.pdf?__blob=publicationFile&v=1.
73. https://www.bzst.de/EN/Businesses/Joint_Audit/joint_audit_node.html.
74. Tax court of Cologne dated May 23, 2017 (2 V 2498/16) and Oct. 20, 2017 (2 V 1055/17).
75. Tax court of Cologne dated Sep. 12, 2018 (2 K 814/18).
76. https://www.tpweek.com/articles/joint-audits-icap-and-the-role-of-risk-assessment/arsjgwvp.

[F] Country-by-Country Reporting

	CbCR
Is the approach established in legal or other regulation?	Legal regulations (§ 138a AO)
Is the approach open to all taxpayer segments?	Only taxpayers with more than EUR 750 million of consolidated sales
Is entry into the programme upon application or invitation?	N/A
What are the conditions for acceptance into the programme?	N/A

Germany enacted the OECD's Base Erosion and Profits Shifting Action Point 13 by amending its General Tax Code (§ 138a AO). Germany fully applies the XML schema published by the OECD for all CbCR data sets. For a transition period, Germany required all CbCR data sets to be digitally submitted to the Federal Tax Office via a secure e-mail standard (De-Mail). Since 2019, the CbCR data must be transmitted digitally via the Federal Tax Office's online portal using a mass data interface (ELMA).

On July 11, 2017, the Federal Ministry of Finance published administrative principles on the German implementation legislation.[77] The guidance also summarizes the German requirements for filling and preparing each of the OECD's three CbCR tables:

- Table 1: Overview of the distribution of income taxes and operations by tax jurisdiction (§ 138a (2) [1] AO).
- Table 2: List of all companies and permanent establishments of the group according to tax jurisdiction with their most important operations (§ 138a (2) [2] AO).
- Table 3: Additional information (§ 138a (2) [3] AO).

[G] Conclusion on New Ways of Working

In this section, we discussed several developments in the way of working between the German tax authorities and German companies. The tax authorities follow a clear road to modernize and digitalize the tax collections system. These separate initiatives are embedded in the current playing field, without changing the general principles of the game. The timeline for tax audits and (potential) discussions about positions moves closer to the present ("zeitnahe Betriebsprüfung"). The information requirements within tax audits are more focused on digital documents (E-Bilanz and data access). So far, these developments have altered the tax collection system; however, they did not

77. https://www.deloitte-tax-news.de/german-tax-legal-news/bmf-circular-from-july-11-2017-related-to-country-by-country-reporting-in-germany.html.

yet fundamentally change or revolutionize it. Tax audits remain a central component in the tax collection process, with a heavy focus on checking the correctness of the tax return. The focus on the Tax ICS, which was introduced a few years ago, could trigger real change going forward. For the time being, such a tax control system is only relevant when the tax authorities dispute positions taken in a tax return. With the participation in joint audits, Germany slowly moves to a more international approach to taxation, following the global operations of Germany's large and globally active corporations. In the next sections, we will discuss the differences between the German initiatives and ICAP and what needs to change in the German tax collection system to prepare for a successful participation in ICAP 2.0.

§7.05 COMPARISON OF ICAP WITH GERMAN INITIATIVES

In the previous section, we described developments in the tax arena in Germany. In this chapter, we will compare these developments in Germany with the characteristics of ICAP. The below table shows this comparison. The only really new topic for Germany, introduced by ICAP, is for the tax authorities and companies to work on a basis of trust. As part of the efforts of the German tax authorities to modernize and digitalize their tax collection system (as discussed in §7.04, the other characteristics have largely already been addressed by the tax authorities). In recent years, there was a strong focus on tax control frameworks (called Tax CMS in Germany). With the implementation of a Tax CMS, a company implements tax risk management and internal controls for taxes and creates transparency in its tax organization. Thereby, a company with a Tax CMS has a solid basis for participation in ICAP.[78] The E-Bilanz and data access requirements created more transparency in (financial) data and give the tax authorities more possibilities to apply analytics on these data. Besides these datasets, a difference from ICAP exists on the side of transparency in tax relevant information, as there is no comparable initiative to share insights so far. Also, the idea to work in the present has not yet really been realized in Germany in practice. A timely tax audit ("zeitnahe Betriebsprüfung"), i.e., a tax audit for very recent years, means a shift to recent time, however is still an audit of closed periods and therefore not working in the present approach. This is also reflected in the fact that about half of the taxpayers never seek advance rulings from the tax authorities.[79] On the international collaboration, Germany is quite far with the participation in many joint audits. CbCR—the entry ticket to ICAP—has been implemented in Germany in a timely manner and is centrally managed and monitored by the Federal Tax Office.

78. Esterer/Eisgruber, Zum steuerlichen internen Kontrollsystem und der damit verbundenen Chance für einen Cooperative-Compliance-Ansatz, Der Betrieb 2017, p. 986.
79. Allen & Overy, *Global Tax Practice: Negotiating the Minefield: Managing Tax Risks in Challenging Times* (2017), p. 15.

	ICAP	*"Zeitnahe BP"*	*Tax CMS*	*E-Bilanz*	*Data Access*	*Joint Audits*	*CbCR*
Working in the present/ recent history	X	X					
Emphasis on the internal controls of the company	X		X				
Trust and contact between company and tax authorities	X						
Transparency and symmetry of information	X			X	X		
International collaboration	X					X	X
Working digital				X	X		X

§7.06 GERMAN PARTICIPATION IN ICAP: LEGAL FRAMEWORK/REQUIREMENTS

The ICAP 1.0 pilot began in January 2018 with participation from the tax authorities of eight jurisdictions (i.e., Australia, Canada, Italy, Japan, the Netherlands, Spain, the U.K. and the U.S.) and selected MNEs with activities in those jurisdictions. The risk assessment for the selected MNEs began in the first half of 2018 and was expected to last approximately twelve months. The publicly available feedback from MNE taxpayers who participated in ICAP 1.0 was very favorable and supportive.[80]

Germany did not participate in the ICAP 1.0 pilot, but only had an observer status.[81]

Reportedly, the main reason was the federal structure of the German tax system resulting in tax cases not being federal tax cases, but state cases; co-operation between the federal republic and the states would have been necessary, including a waiver by

80. https://www.internationaltaxreview.com/Article/3879943/Tax-heads-encourage-more-companies-to-use-ICAP.html?ArticleId = 3879943.
81. *See* Prinz/Ludwig, Der Betrieb 2019, 477.

the states of their right to render an initial decision in their own tax cases.[82] The second issue related to legal concerns whether ICAP 1.0 would comply with the constitutional requirement of equal treatment since it is benefitting only a few large MNEs.[83,84,85]

With regard to the second point, the Federal Ministry of Finance took the view that the risk assessment in ICAP 1.0 occurred on the basis of a prognosis without the facts having been realized by the taxpayer for which there was a lack of a legal basis. In addition, the ICAP 1.0 programme provided for communication of the consensus on the risk assessment to the taxpayer in Tax Assurance Letter. The Federal Ministry of Finance voiced constitutional concerns (e.g., equal treatment of all taxpayers) since ICAP 1.0 would have restricted the tax authorities' verification options and also argued that Germany did have a legal basis for issuing a Tax Assurance Letter to qualify as an administrative act.[86]

The OECD FTA Plenary held in Santiago from March 26-28, 2019 announced a second ICAP Pilot (ICAP 2.0). The tax administrations that participated in ICAP 2.0 are from Australia, Austria, Belgium, Canada, Denmark, Finland, Germany, Ireland, Italy, Japan, Luxembourg, the Netherlands, Norway, Poland, Spain, the U.K., and the U.S. For ICAP 2.0, the application deadline for taxpayers to their local tax authorities ended on June 30, 2019.[87] In spite of a remaining legal uncertainty related to the Tax Assurance Letter following an ICAP 2.0 procedure, the Federal Ministry of Finance decided to participate in ICAP 2.0 to allow German MNEs to benefit from the new OECD standard without any related local tax law changes.[88] Reportedly, the Federal Ministry of Finance has been able to procedurally align with the states on co-operation and state waivers, which removed the main practical barrier. It appears that the constitutional concerns (i.e., equal treatment) and the procedural matters (i.e., no direct legal basis, no clear legal status of the Tax Assurance Letter and the legal implications thereof) were not viewed as really being a practical hurdle once the practical barriers had been removed. It is not yet known whether German taxpayers have applied for participation in the ICAP 2.0 programme.

82. https://www.internationaltaxreview.com/Article/3858327/Joint-audits-ICAP-and-the-role-of-risk-assessment.html?ArticleId = 3858327.
83. Bundestag Drucksache 19/3842, Aug. 16, 2018; http://dipbt.bundestag.de/dip21/btd/19/038/1903842.pdf.
84. June 27, 1991, 2 BvR 1439/89.
85. March 9, 2004, 2 BvL 7/02.
86. Bundestag Drucksache 19/3842, Aug. 16, 2018; http://dipbt.bundestag.de/dip21/btd/19/038/1903842.pdf.
87. https://www.oecd.org/tax/forum-on-tax-administration/international-compliance-assurance-programme.htm.
88. *Egner*, Tax Compliance, TLE-023-2019; https://www.tax-legal-excellence.com/icap-2-0-unter-beteiligung-deutschlands/.

CHAPTER 8

From Tax Rulings to Co-operative Compliance: A New Deal Between the Taxpayer and the Italian Tax Administration?

Francesco Cannas & Mario Grandinetti[*]

§8.01 INTRODUCTION

The Italian Co-operative Compliance Programme is the outcome of a long development process, at both statutory and cultural level.

What we are all witnessing is a general trend toward a shift in the relationship between the taxpayer and the Tax Administration. Ideally, that relationship is moving from an authoritative model based on the subjection of the former to the latter, to a model framed around the idea that the two parties have to co-operate to achieve a common goal on an "equal footing." In reality, this shift is not always consistent and the path toward it is fraught with difficulties.

Under the new scheme, the taxpayer is expected to be a more active party in the relationship and, in exchange, can rely on a more supportive attitude from the Tax Administration. This is seen as a way to broaden the principle of legal certainty, which ceases to be assured simply through the wording of statutes and starts to be guaranteed also through the positions taken by the Tax Administration in one or more dedicated administrative procedures.

The current chapter is divided into three main parts. The first one is dedicated to some of the legal instruments that in some respects are similar to the Co-operative

* Sections §8.01, §8.02, §8.03 and §8.06 are attributable to Francesco Cannas; Sections §8.04, §8.05 and §8.07 are attributable to Mario Grandinetti.

Compliance Programme, even if only in the sense that their main purpose is to reduce the level of uncertainty of the tax system.

Within the Italian tax system, a key role in safeguarding the principle of legal certainty has always been played by the instrument known as "*interpello.*" Even if the word "*interpello*" is quite frequently translated as "ruling" or "tax ruling," the authors opted to leave it in Italian as there is an intrinsic difference between the English and the Italian terms: while a "ruling" is seen in the Italian literature as an agreement or an answer which is binding for both parties, the *interpello* is an "answer" which is binding for only one of the two parties.[1]

Moreover, a brief description of: (i) the Advanced Rulings for International Businesses, and (ii) of the possibility for the taxpayer to "discuss" certain matters with the Tax Administration, such as, the unilateral acceptance of transfer pricing adjustments operated by other jurisdictions, are offered to the reader for the sake of completeness.

Then, the Italian Co-operative Compliance Programme and its latest developments will be analyzed in order to give the reader a comprehensive overview of how the Italian tax system tries to reduce the level of uncertainty and establish a more balanced relationship with the taxpayer. It is worth noting from the very outset that one of the main "pillars" of the Italian Co-operative Compliance Programme is the *interpello* itself, of which an "accelerated type" is made available to the taxpayer who joins the programme.

Finally, some thoughts are provided with regard to the possible future developments in this field. In particular, attention is paid to the consequences that may arise as a result of Italy's adhesion to the Organisation for Economic Co-operation and Development (OECD) International Compliance Assurance Programme (ICAP).

§8.02 THE INTERPELLO AS AN INSTRUMENT FOR ACHIEVING LEGAL CERTAINTY AND PROMOTING A DIALOG BETWEEN THE TAX ADMINISTRATION AND THE TAXPAYER

[A] The Constantly Evolving System of the *Interpello* and Its New Dimension

Starting from the 1990s, various types of *interpello* have been introduced into the Italian tax system.

Within the Italian tax system, the word "*interpello*" (or "*ruling*") refers to an administrative procedure aimed at:

> enabling the taxpayer to obtain the Tax Administration's point of view, in general preemptively, on either facts that are not easily classifiable for tax law purposes or tax rules that are not easily interpretable with regard to specific cases.[2]

1. G. Zizzo, *Diritto di interpello e ruling*, in *Rivista di diritto tributario.*, 1992, I, 136.
2. This definition is given by F. Pistolesi, *Gli interpelli tributari,* Milan, 2007, 1. The one offered herein is a translation by the authors of the following wording: "[...] *consentire al contribuente di*

The taxpayer's right to consult the Tax Administration is widely acknowledged as being one of the most relevant forms of preemptive communication between these two parties.[3] As to the substance of that right, the statutes define it in general terms as the taxpayer's right to be assisted by the Tax Administration in understanding, interpreting and applying the law within a legal system that is extremely complex, uncertain and affected by uncoordinated layering and overlapping, all of which often make it difficult for the taxpayer to identify the correct action to be taken.[4]

Scholars consider the right to a preemptive consultation with the Tax Administration, allowing the taxpayer to apply the law correctly and avoid sanctions, as part of the more general right to be informed. According to such a right, the Tax Administration is obliged to "*make the tax compliances deriving from a certain transaction known in advance, so that the taxpayer is able to evaluate the impact on his/her private or business life.*"[5]

The "right to *interpello*" also constitutes the transfer, in the field of taxation, of some of the principles underlying Law 241/1990,[6] namely the statute that three decades ago fully re-shaped the relationship between the Italian public administration and the taxpayers. Indeed, although that statute is not specifically applicable to the relationship between the taxpayer and the Tax Administration, it is commonly regarded as the starting point for the affirmation, also in the tax field and along with the right to be informed, of the principles of transparency, good faith and legitimate expectation.[7]

These principles have been established in the Italian tax system by the "Taxpayer's Rights Charter" (*Statuto dei diritti del contribuente*, hereinafter also referred to simply as "Charter"),[8] of which Article 11 regulates the "right to *interpello*." The fact that the right to *interpello* is regulated under a statute establishing such general and founding principles is indicative of the central role that it is considered to have in the relationship between the taxpayer and the Tax Administration.

---

ottenere, di regola in via preventiva, il parere dell'Autorità fiscale in ordine ad eventi non agevolmente qualificabili dal punto di vista impositivo o su norme di non facile interpretazione in relazione a determinati casi concreti."

3. *See*, among others, S. La Rosa, *Principi di diritto tributario,* Turin, 2016, 289.
4. Explanatory Report of the Legislative Decree September 24, 2015, no. 156, 1 et seq.
5. G. Marongiu, *Riflessioni sul diritto di interpello,* in *Corriere tributario*, 2002, 1408 et seq. The original Italian wording used is "[...] *rendere noti gli adempimenti fiscali che conseguono ad una determinata operazione, per consentire, all'interessato, di valutarne l'impatto sulla propria vita privata o d'affari.*"
6. Law no. 241 of August 7, 1990, on "*Administrative procedures and the right to access administrative documents*" ("Nuove norme in materia di procedimento amministrativo e di diritto di accesso ai documenti amministrativi"). For a general overview *see*, among others, E. Casetta, F. Fracchia, *Manuale di Diritto Amministrativo,* Milan, 2018, 417 et seq.
7. A. Fazio, *L'interpello tributario nella prospettiva della responsabilità sociale dell'impresa,* in *Diritto e pratica tributaria*, 2/2019, 542 et seq.; M. Pierro, *Il dovere di informazione dell'Amministrazione finanziaria e il diritto al contraddittorio preventivo,* in *Rivista di diritto finanziario e scienza delle finanze*, 2016, 193.
8. Law no. 212 of July 27, 2000, "*Taxpayer's Rights Charter*" (Disposizioni in materia di statuto dei diritti del contribuente).

Article 11 of the Charter sets out the so-called ordinary *interpello* (*interpello ordinario*). It consists of the taxpayer's right to submit a query to the Tax Administration in order to receive its point of view on the tax consequences of either a fact, an act or a transaction, to increase the level of legal certainty and to avoid the negative effects of a future unfavorable assessment. In addition to that, Article 11 sets out three other types of *interpello*, namely the probative (*interpello probatorio*), the anti-abuse (*interpello anti-abuso*), and the anti-avoidance (*interpello dispapplicativo*), which are also briefly described hereinafter. Moreover, Law 136/2018[9] introduced the *interpello* on new investments from January 1, 2019. All together they form a complex system of administrative procedures.

The whole system is undergoing constant development and has always been characterized by a high degree of fragmentation and complexity. A major reform took place in 2015,[10] for the purpose, among others, of strengthening the role of the *interpello* as an instrument of tax risk management and corporate social responsibility (CSR).[11]

This is in line with the general trend, at a worldwide level, to review existing instruments and establish new ones aimed at incentivizing tax strategies based on the spontaneous fulfillment of tax obligations.[12] What we are all witnessing is a profound re-shaping of the whole relationship between the taxpayer and the Tax Administration, in which the role of the latter is becoming less and less that of an authoritative inspector and increasingly that of an impartial and collaborative consultant.

The *interpello* fits particularly well into this general trend due to its dual essence: first, it is an instrument the taxpayer can rely upon to know the Tax Administration's point of view in advance. Second, it is also an instrument to allow the Tax Administration to ensure the correct fulfillment of tax obligations and, in particular, to exercise preemptive control over the acts, facts and transactions with regard to which queries are submitted.

---

9. Law no. 136 of December 17 2018, on "*Urgent tax measures*" (Conversione in legge, con modificazioni, del decreto-legge 23 ottobre 2018, no. 119, recante disposizioni urgenti in materia fiscale e finanziaria).
10. Law no. 23 of March 11, 2014, on the "*Mandate to the Government for the promotion of a fairer, more transparent and growth-oriented tax system*" (Delega al Governo recante disposizioni per un Sistema fiscal più equo, trasparente e orientato alla crescita). As to the *interpello*, Art. 6 of that law, on tax risk management and corporate governance, identified three main issues: (1) the need for a higher degree of consistency among the different types of *interpello*; (2) the need to reduce the time taken by the Tax Administration to answer taxpayers' queries; (3) the need to rationalize the whole system, also through the abolition of the "mandatory types of *interpello*." Following the above, the Government passed the Legislative Decree no. 156 of September 24, 2015. For some comments made at the time the reform took place, *see*, among others, F. Pistolesi, *Dalla delega fiscale più omogeneità ed efficienza per gli interpelli*, in *Corriere tributario*, 2014, 1836 et seq.; A. Tomassini, *Riordino degli interpelli: un'occasione da non perdere*, in *Corriere tributario*, 2014, 1380 et seq.
11. On this point *see*, among others, M. Greggi, *Il diritto di interpello e la gestione del rischio fiscale*, in C. Glendi, G. Corasaniti, C. Corrado Oliva, P. de' Capitani di Vimercate (eds.), *Per un nuovo ordinamento tributario*, Milan, 2019, 1007 et seq.; and G. Glendi, *Disciplina dell'interpello*, in C. Glendi, C. Consolo, A. Contrino (eds.), *Abuso del diritto e novità sul processo tributario*—Part. II, Milan, 2016, 89 et seq.
12. *See*, among others, R.S. Avi-Yonah, *Corporate Taxation and Corporate Social Responsibility*, 11 N.Y.U. J.L. & Bus. 1 (2014-2015), 1.

In the context of the major reform that took place in 2015, the will of the Legislator to enhance the importance of the *interpello* within the new model of relationship between the taxpayer and the Tax Administration may also be seen in the amendment of the heading of Article 11 of the Charter, which was changed from "*Interpello* of the taxpayer" to "Right to *interpello.*" This suggests the intention to elevate the *interpello* fully to the level of a taxpayer's right.[13]

On the same note, the new significance of the *interpello* as a full taxpayer's right is entirely consistent with the general rationale of the Charter, the ultimate purpose of which is to actually achieve the constitutional values underlying the tax system.[14]

[B] The "Ordinary *Interpello*" and How It Works (Including Some Procedural Rules also Applicable to Other Types of *Interpello*)

Article 11, paragraph 1), letter a), of the Charter sets out, among others, the procedure for the "ordinary *interpello.*" As already mentioned, this is an instrument on which the taxpayer can rely in order to know what for the Tax Administration is the correct application of tax law in the case of uncertainty with regard to the interpretation or classification of facts for tax purposes.[15]

The answer given by the Tax Administration is not binding for the taxpayer, who may decide not to comply with it, while it is binding for the Tax Administration in the event of a subsequent assessment on the same matter.

The ordinary procedure at issue is not applicable where other types of *interpello*, like the one on new investments,[16] or the procedure for obtaining a ruling for international businesses,[17] are applicable. Moreover, in 2016 the Tax Administration (*Agenzia delle Entrate*)[18] listed a number of further matters with regard to which the

13. On the duty of the Tax Administration to take an official position, *see also* A. Fantozzi, *Il diritto tributario,* Turin, 2003, 236.
14. The Charter aims explicitly at fulfilling the general principles established under Arts 3, 23, 53 and 97 of the Italian Constitution. On this point, *see also*, among others, A. Fantozzi, A. Fedele (eds.), *Lo Statuto dei diritti del contribuente,* Milan, 2005; A. Bodrito, A. Contrino, A. Marcheselli (eds.), *Consenso, equità e imparzialità nello Statuto del contribuente, Studi in onore del prof. Gianni Marongiu,* Turin, 2012; A. Fazio, *supra* n. 7, G. Falcone, *Statuto dei diritti del contribuente e Cassazione tributaria,* in *Il Fisco,* 2003, 2221 et seq.
15. On this point, *see also* the following Circulars (*circolari*) issued by the Tax Administration (*Agenzia delle Entrate*) before the 2015 reform: Circular no. 50 of May 31, 2001, on "The Right to *Interpello*" (*Diritto di interpello.* Articolo 11 della legge 27 luglio 2000, no. 212); and Circular no. 32 of June 14, 2010, containing "New Instructions on How to Process the Queries from the Taxpayer" (*Nuove istruzioni sulla trattazione delle istanze di interpello*).
16. Article 2, Legislative Decree no. 147 of September 14, 2015, on "*Measures for the Growth and the Internationalization of Businesses*" (Disposizioni recanti misure per la crescita e l'internazionalizzazione delle imprese).
17. Article 31-ter, Presidential Decree no. 600 of September 29, 1973, on "*the Regulation of Tax Assessments*" (Disposizioni comuni in materia di accertamento delle imposte sui redditi). For a detailed overview, *see* M. Grandinetti, *Gli accordi preventivi per le imprese con attività internazionale,* in *Rassegna tributaria,* 3/2017, 660 ss.
18. Circular no. 9/E of April 1, 2016, on "*the Reform of the System of Interpello operated by Legislative Decree 24 September 2015, no. 156*" (Commento alle novità del decreto legislativo 24 settembre 2015, no. 156 recante revisione della disciplina degli interpelli).

right to *interpello* is not applicable, namely: (i) the existence of a permanent establishment abroad for the purposes of Article 168-ter of the Tax Code[19] (exemption of profit and losses attributable to the permanent establishment of a resident company); (ii) the existence of a fixed establishment for value-added tax (VAT) purposes; (iii) cases with regard to which the factual component is so relevant that it is impossible to provide a conceptual answer; (iv) cases for which the action of other branches of the public administration would be necessary.

As to the personal scope, virtually any taxpayer is entitled to submit a query to the Tax Administration.

As to the objective scope, the query must refer to the facts of a real case and purely hypothetical questions are not allowed. It covers practically any primary and secondary source of law, while administrative acts such as Circulars (*circolari*), Decisions (*risoluzioni*) and Notes (*note*) are excluded.

Due to the fact that the Tax Administration, and in particular the Customs Agency (*Agenzia delle Dogane*), is also responsible for the collection of taxes that are "traditional own resources" of the European Union, the queries that can be submitted by the taxpayer in this field are subject to specific rules established at European level. Article 22 of the Union Customs Code[20] regulates the procedure to be used by the Tax Administrations of Member States to deliver decisions relating to the application of the Customs legislation.

With regard to the procedure, it is a general rule, and therefore not limited to the ordinary *interpello*, that the query shall be submitted by the taxpayer in writing, without any formal requirement, and without paying any stamp duty.

As to the content, the query must necessarily include the taxpayer's identification data, reference to the type of *interpello* that is being submitted, reference to the statute for which the interpretation, application or disapplication is requested, the taxpayer's contact address, suggested answer and either the taxpayer's signature or the signature of one of the taxpayer's representatives.

The query shall be submitted to either the Regional Office (*Direzione regionale*) or the Central Office (*Divisione contribuenti*) in the case of large businesses[21] and non-residents. Once submitted, the Tax Administration shall process the query on a step-by-step basis.

First, the Tax Administration shall ascertain the admissibility of the query. Second, where any of the minimum contents is missing the Tax Administration shall notify the taxpayer within 30 days from submission and request the necessary completion. If that is the case, the taxpayer shall fulfill the requests within thirty days from notification.

---

19. Article 168-ter, Presidential Decree no. 917 of December 22, 1986, "*The Tax Code*" (Approvazione del testo unico delle imposte sui redditi, also abbreviated to "TUIR").
20. Regulation (EU) No 952/2013 of the European Parliament and of the Council of October 9, 2013 laying down the Union Customs Code (recast).
21. Referring to businesses with a turnover or profits of not less than EUR 100 million.

For the ordinary *interpello*, the Tax Administration shall take a formal position within 90 days from either the submission or the completion. For probative, anti-abuse and anti-avoidance *interpello*, the deadline is extended to 120 days.

As already mentioned, the position taken by the Tax Administration is binding for all its offices and branches.[22] This is due to the general principle of legitimate expectations and implies that any subsequent assessment or sanction contrary to the answer given to an *interpello* on the same matter is invalid.

On the other hand, being the *interpello* an "act of address" (*atto di indirizzo*) by the Tax Administration, the taxpayer is not obliged to comply with the content of the answer given and, should an assessment be served at a later stage on the same matter, the taxpayer is entitled to stand for his/her own point of view in court.

As the taxpayer has the right to receive an answer, if the Tax Administration should fail to provide one, it has the effect of a tacit agreement with the answer suggested by the taxpayer, which, as a consequence, becomes binding for the Tax Administration.[23]

Where the Tax Administration decides to rectify its answer, it shall notify the taxpayer using the very same channel of communication as that used to answer the query. In any case, the conduct adopted by the taxpayer in compliance with the answer previously given is never punishable.[24]

Finally, it is noteworthy that, again due to its nature of "act of address," the answer given to an *interpello* is not appealable alone in court. The underlying rationale is that, unlike a tax assessment, the answer to an *interpello* alone cannot affect the taxpayer in any way.[25]

Concerning the relationship between the ordinary *interpello* and the other forms of dialog between the taxpayer and the Tax Administration, Article 11 of the Charter explicitly excludes the possibility of submitting a query regarding situations where the procedure to obtain an Advanced Ruling for International Businesses (*see* paragraph 3) can be activated.

This point differentiates the Advanced Ruling currently in place from the "International Ruling" in place before 2016 and underlines that all the reforms that have led to the development of the instruments of dialog in this field have to be analyzed "jointly."

Under the previous regime, worries were expressed by scholars[26] about the possible overlapping of different instruments for dialog, and, in particular, between the "now-repealed" International Ruling and the *interpello*. The last developments were coordinated and designed according to a coherent framework, with the result that, at

22. On this point, *see also* L. Del Federico, *Autorità e consenso nella disciplina degli interpelli fiscali*, in S. La Rosa (ed.), *Profili autoritativi e consensuali del diritto tributario*, Milan, 2008, 155 et seq.
23. On this point, *see also* S. La Rosa, *Principi di diritto tributario*, Turin, 2009, 291 et seq.
24. On this point, *see also* M. Miccinesi, *L'interpello*, in G. Marongiu (ed.), *Lo statuto dei diritti del contribuente*, Turin, 2004, 91 et seq.
25. Nevertheless, it is noteworthy that some scholars advocate for the possibility to appeal in court an illegitimate declaration by the Tax Administration of inadmissibility of the query. *See*, among others, L. Del Federico, *supra* n. 22, 171.
26. F. Pistolesi, *supra* n. 2, 113.

present, some of the most complex matters can only be the subject of a dialog aimed at reaching a "binding agreement."[27]

[C] The "Probative *Interpello*"

This is a wide category of *interpello*. It is regulated under Article 11, paragraph 1, letter b), of the Charter and gathers all the types of query aimed at ascertaining the fulfillment of the requirements or the suitability of probative elements for access to certain tax regimes.

It is noteworthy that here "access to a regime" is understood in its broadest sense, thus also including the non-applicability of certain rules as, for example, in the case of the Controlled Foreign Corporations (CFCs) legislation (with regard to which, from a technical standpoint, the query is aimed at the "non-applicability" of transparency for tax purposes).

The tax regimes for which this type of *interpello* may be used are listed exhaustively at statutory level: (i) the disapplication of CFC rules under Article 167 of the Italian Tax Code (ITC),[28] (ii) as to participations in low tax countries, this type of *interpello* may be used also for: (a) profits attributed by virtue of a participation (Article 47, paragraph 4, ITC); (b) capital gains from shares (Article 68, paragraph 4, ITC); (c) participation exemption regime (Article 87 ITC); (d) dividends (Article 89 ITC); (iii) the continuation of the consolidation regime under Article 124 ITC after a group reorganization; (iv) access to the global tax consolidation regime under Article 132 ITC; (v) the exclusion from the special regime for "dormant companies"; (vi) application of the special regime for participations obtained by virtue of a bank credit recovery procedure under Article 113 ITC.

[D] The "Anti-Abuse *Interpello*"

This type of *interpello* is regulated under Article 11, paragraph 1, letter c) of the Charter. It allows the taxpayer to ask the Tax Administration about the application of anti-abuse legislation to specific facts.

In particular, it allows the taxpayer to know in advance the Tax Administration's position on the application of the general anti-avoidance rule (GAAR) set out by Article 10-bis of the Charter.

Under the Italian GAAR, a transaction can be considered abusive if it lacks economic substance, with the result that its tax consequences can be disregarded by the Tax Administration and treated accordingly.

---

27. M. Grandinetti, *Gli accordi preventivi per le imprese con attività internazionale*, in *Rassegna tributaria*, 3/2017, 660 et seq.
28. Article 167, Presidential Decree no. 917 of December 22, 1986, "*The Tax Code*" (Approvazione del testo unico delle imposte sui redditi, also abbreviated to "TUIR").

[E] The "Anti-Avoidance *Interpello*"

This type of *interpello* is regulated under Article 11, paragraph 2, of the Charter. It has to be used by the taxpayer who finds himself/herself in a situation described by a statute and seeks the disapplication of anti-avoidance rules limiting, among others, the right to deduct and the use of tax credits or losses.

The taxpayer can use the instrument at issue to prove that certain facts do not lead to tax avoidance and, therefore, the taxpayer is entitled to use the tax benefits mentioned.

It differs from the other types of *interpello* because it is the only one that is "compulsory," in the sense that if the taxpayer intends to use the tax benefits mentioned he/she shall submit a query to the Tax Administration.

Although the anti-avoidance *interpello* is conceptually very close to the probative one, they differ because the latter is applicable only to an exhaustively listed number of circumstances, while the first is "generally applicable" to any anti-avoidance rule that is or will be established in the tax system. Moreover, they also differ with regard to what the taxpayer has to include in the tax report and in terms of applicable sanctions.[29]

[F] *Interpello* on New Investments

This type of *interpello* was established by Article 2 of the so-called Internationalization Decree of 2015,[30] with the aim of attracting new investments to Italy.

Even if it is not expressly conceived for international investors and can also formally be used by resident taxpayers, its structure seems to be particularly suitable for non-residents.

Businesses intending to invest on the Italian territory have the right to submit their business plan to the Tax Administration in order to receive a comprehensive opinion on the tax treatment applicable.

Through a single submission, prospective investors are entitled to formulate multiple queries, even if they are attributable to different types of *interpello*.

The "Internationalization decree" does not provide a precise definition of what an "investment" is but mandates that: (i) it must be made on Italian territory; (ii) it must not be lower than EUR 30 million; (iii) it must have significant and lasting repercussions in terms of employment.

A more precise definition is provided by the Ministerial Decree of Implementation of April 29, 2016, of which Article 1, letter c), clarifies that an investment can consist

29. Circular of April 1, 2016, no. 9/E, on "*the Reform of the System of Interpello operated by Legislative Decree no. 156 of 24 September 2015*" (Commento alle novità del decreto legislativo 24 settembre 2015, no. 156 recante revisione della disciplina degli interpelli), paras 7-8, 50-54.
30. Article 2, Legislative Decree no. 147 of September 14, 2015 on the "*internationalization of businesses*" (Disposizioni recanti misure per la crescita e l'internazionalizzazione delle imprese; also known as "decreto internazionalizzazione"). A. Vicini Ronchetti (ed.), *Fiscalità dell'internazionalizzazione delle imprese,* Turin, 2018.

of: (i) a lasting economic initiative; (ii) the reorganization of an already-existing business; (iii) participation in the capital of a business.[31]

§8.03 FURTHER FORMS OF DIALOG AIMED AT INCENTIVIZING THE INTERNATIONALIZATION OF BUSINESSES

As part of its constant effort to encourage the internationalization of businesses, Italy recently introduced two pieces of legislation that enable taxpayers who are active in international businesses to dialog with the Tax Administration. In particular, where an agreement is reached at the end of the dialog, the taxpayer is given the possibility to obtain advanced rulings and an accelerated acknowledgment of transfer pricing adjustments operated abroad.

"Advanced Rulings" for International Businesses are regulated under Article 31-ter[32] of Presidential Decree no. 600/73[33] ("DPR 600/73") and the Order of the Director of the Revenue Agency of March 21, 2016. They are widely based on the "international model" of the Advanced Pricing Agreements,[34] but with the significant difference that their scope of application goes beyond transfer pricing.[35]

In particular, international businesses are entitled to rely on those advanced rulings with regard to the following matters: (i) transfer pricing; (ii) permanent establishments under one of the conventions of which Italy is a contracting State; (iii) the concrete application of conventions and laws concerning passive incomes; and (iv) the values for exit taxation purposes.

Nevertheless, because the law describes those areas of application as the "main ones" ("*principali*"), it is commonly accepted that advanced rulings can be obtained by the taxpayer in almost any context in which an international aspect is present.

The explanatory memorandum attached to Article 31-ter[36] clarifies that advanced rulings are a "form of shared exercise of taxing powers aimed at reaching a common knowledge of facts and taxable items, and/or a common interpretation of the law,"

31. For a detailed analysis of this type of interpello, *see*, in particular, G. Vanz, *Investitori esteri e interpello sui nuovi investimenti*, in *Rassegna tributaria*, 4/2017, 947.
32. This article was introduced into the DPR 600/73 in 2015 by the abovementioned "decreto internazionalizzazione" (D.Lgs. 147/2015). *See supra* n. 30.
33. Presidential Decree no. 600 of September 29, 1973, which is the main piece of legislation regulating the collection of taxes.
34. On this instrument from an Italian perspective, *see*, among others, R. Succio, *Advanced pricing agreements e procedure negoziate di determinazione del valore normale: la Cassazione nega il potere di veto dell'amministrazione finanziaria*, in *Rivista di diritto tributario*, 2016, IV, 19 et seq.; C. Romano, *Il ruling internazionale*, in F. Tesauro (ed.), *L'imposta sul reddito delle società*, Bologna, 2007, 991 et seq.; G. Gaffuri, *Il ruling internazionale*, in *Rassegna tributaria*, 2004, 488 et seq.; P. Adonnino, *Considerazioni in tema di ruling internazionale*, in *Rivista di diritto tributario*, 2004, I, 57 et seq.; L. Tosi, A. Tomassini, R. Lupi, *Il ruling di standard internazionale*, in *Dialoghi di diritto tributario*, 4/2004, 489 et seq.
35. M. Grandinetti, *supra* n. 27.
36. Explanatory Memorandum ("*Relazione illustrativa*") to the "*decreto internazionalizzazione*" (D.Lgs. 147/2015).

thus excluding the possibility for the Tax Administration to reduce the tax liability in any way.[37]

From a procedural standpoint, the main characteristics of these rulings are that: (i) in order to be relied upon by the taxpayer they have to be obtained before the tax return is submitted; and that (ii) it is never mandatory for the taxpayer to apply for such a ruling.

The entire pre- and post-filing phase is characterized by the dialog between the taxpayer and the Tax Administration and an agreement shall be reached between them, where possible, within 180 days from when the taxpayer applies and starts the procedure. Such an agreement then lasts for 5 years including the taxable year in which the agreement was reached.

As to the legal effects of advanced rulings, the main one is that they are binding for both parties and, unless circumstances or facts change, the Tax Administration is entitled to inspect the taxpayer only on matters other than those for which the agreement was reached. Moreover, where the ruling is based on an agreement that is reached between the Italian Tax Administration and a foreign Tax Administration under a Mutual Agreement Procedure (MAP) contained in a Double Taxation Convention, it can be applicable retrospectively up until the year in which the taxpayer submitted the application to start the procedure.[38]

Article 31-quater of the DPR 600/73 regulates the possibility for the Italian Tax Administration to unilaterally accept a primary transfer pricing adjustment operated by a foreign jurisdiction with which there is an adequate exchange of information and an agreement can be reached under either (i) a MAP contained in a Double Taxation Convention, or (ii) the Convention 90/463/EEC of July 23, 1990.[39]

Such an acceptance of the reduction of profits taxable in Italy may come at the end of a specific administrative procedure started by a resident company which either controls or is controlled by a foreign company ("associate") or which conducts its business abroad through a permanent establishment.

Furthermore, in this case the procedure is non-mandatory and inspired by the principle of co-operation and dialog between the taxpayer and the Tax Administration. Where the unilateral adjustment is not granted, either the relevant MAP or the Arbitration Convention is activated.[40]

37. S. Morri & S. Guarino, *Il ruling italiano, la certezza del diritto e ... il terzo incomodo: la disciplina comunitaria degli aiuti di Stato*, in *Corriere tributario*, 2017, 1031.
38. G. Zizzo, *Accordi preventivi e prospettive evolutive della cooperazione tra fisco e imprese*, in *Corriere tributario*, 2019, 66 et seq.
39. M. Antonini & R.A. Papotti, *La nuova procedura di eliminazione delle doppie imposizioni da rettifiche di transfer pricing in uno stato estero*, in *Corriere tributario*, 2018, 2089 et seq.
40. G. Formica & D. Lillo, *Transfer pricing e doppia imposizione: nuovi strumenti di risoluzione*, in *Il Fisco*, 2018, 2507 et seq.; and D. Liburdi, M. Sironi, *Rettifiche in diminuzione derivanti dal transfer pricing*, in *Il Fisco*, 2018, 1414 et seq.

§8.04 THE ITALIAN CO-OPERATIVE COMPLIANCE PROGRAMME

With regard to the Italian programme of Co-operative Compliance it was passed with Delegated Law no. 23/2014 and introduced into the Italian tax system with the subsequent Legislative Decree no. 128 of 2015.[41] It is not completely new, due to the fact that already in 2013 a pilot project was introduced following the OECD approach.[42]

In view of the focus of this chapter, we consider it useful to concentrate our attention on two main points: the personal scope and the legal consequences of the adhesion to Co-operative Compliance. For this very reason, we will not make an in-depth investigation into the requirements, other than the personal ones, unless it is necessary for an understanding of the legal consequences. In this context, among the requirements set out by Article 4 of Legislative Decree no. 128 of 2015 for the taxpayers willing to adhere to the Co-operative Compliance programme, an effective system of detection, assessment and management of the tax risk must be implemented, which has to be part of the internal controlling function of the company. This is known as the Tax Control Framework (TCF), with respect to which under Article 4, paragraph 1, of Legislative Decree no. 128 of 2015, the Italian legislator granted a freedom of choice as to organizational issues. In the authors' opinion, it is noteworthy that Article 4, paragraph 1, of Legislative Decree no. 128 of 2015 set, as a pre-requisite for adhesion to Co-operative Compliance, the presence of an adequate TCF that must already be in place when application is submitted. Nevertheless, the implementation of an adequate internal TCF can theoretically also be the outcome of a process developed together with the Tax Administration and can constitute the last step of the adhesion to the programme. For this very reason, in the authors' opinion, the implementation of an adequate TCF capable of guaranteeing what the legislator requests may also be postponed to a later stage. This point also seems to be shared by the Italian Tax Administration.[43]

As far as the personal scope of the Italian Co-operative Compliance is concerned, the starting point of our analysis is Article 7, paragraph 4, letter a), of Legislative Decree no. 128 of 2015. In particular, on the basis of this provision the programme at issue is dedicated to the large taxpayers, namely those whose turnover or profits are not below EUR 10 billion. Moreover, the personal scope is also extended to those taxpayers with a turnover or profits of not less than EUR 1 billion who joined the pilot project of 2013.

---

41. Legislative Decree no. 128 of August 5, 2015, on the "*certainty within the relationship between the taxpayer and Tax Administration*" ("sulla certezza del diritto nei rapporti tra fisco e contribuente, in attuazione degli articoli 5, 6 e 8, comma 2, della legge 11 marzo 2014, no. 23").
42. According to the Ministry of Finance, eighty-four businesses linked to fifty-five multinational groups (53% of them Italian and 32% European) have adhered to the project. As to the programme currently in place, at the time of writing, a total of forty-one taxpayers adhered to it. A public list is available and constantly updated at the official website https://www.agenziaentrate.gov.it/portale/web/guest/schede/agevolazioni/regime-di-adempimento-collaborativo/elenco-societa-ammesse-al-regime.
43. Circular of the Italian Tax Administration of September 16, 2016, no. 38, p. 21.

Therefore, at first sight this may seem quite a narrow personal scope, departing from foreign models that allow the adhesion of a wider range of taxpayers. Nevertheless, such a conclusion deserves a deeper analysis, both from a general standpoint and with regard to the wording used by the legislator in Legislative Decree no. 128 of 2015.

As to the first point, the special prudence adopted by the Italian legislator is of note. If one considers Legislative Decree no. 128 of 2015, it is easy to realize that it appears in the Italian legal system twenty-five years after the first OECD Study[44] and that, according to the data released by the Italian Tax Administration, only eighty companies, both Italian and non, actually meet the requisites for joining the programme. It is, therefore, possible to acknowledge, from a general policy standpoint, that the legislator's expressed intention is to start a step-by-step change, which is also a cultural change, within the Tax Administration, with the aim of shifting from an assessment carried out *ex post* to one carried out *ex ante* through a dialog with the taxpayer. The choice was to start this change with large companies,[45] requiring the presence of a TCF already in place, integrated with the internal control function, to enable companies joining the programme not only to gain a higher level of legal certainty, but also in a wider perspective of CSR.[46] Adhesion to the programme of Co-operative Compliance, therefore, also proves to be a reputational asset in the eyes of company stakeholders.[47]

This conclusion is grounded both in the explanatory memorandum on Legislative Decree no. 128 of 2015 and in Article 7, paragraph 4, letter a), of Legislative Decree no. 128 of 2015.

The explanatory memorandum clarifies that within the Italian legal system one of the main issues is how to manage the transition, confirming in a certain way what has been stated herein regarding the change of perspective, both for the Tax Administration and for the taxpayer. For this very purpose, it is opportune to promote a step-by-step implementation of the Co-operative Compliance programme, gradually extending its application to all companies that are able to implement an internal system of tax risk management.

One can find the described approach under Article 7, paragraph 4, letter a), of Legislative Decree no. 128 of 2015. This article starts with the wording "during the first period of application," the programme is reserved for the largest taxpayers and then continues by stating, under letter b) of the same provision, that by means of a Decree

44. OECD (1990). *Taxpayers Rights and Obligation. A Survey of the Legal Situation in OECD Countries.* Paris. For a comprehensive description, A. Tropea, *I profili giuridici dell'adempimento collaborativo*, in *Rivista Trimestrale di Diritto Tributario*, 2018, p. 794.
45. It has to be taken into consideration that a personal scope which is restricted only to large businesses provides a greater safeguard also to the Tax Administration. Suffice it to think, for example, about the higher reliability that these taxpayers are able to offer in terms of the alignment between corporate and taxable profits.
46. This conclusion is widely supported by scholars who have dealt with the topic, noteworthy of which, among others, are R.S. Avi-Yonah, *Corporate Social Responsibility and Strategic Tax Behavior*, in W. Schon et al. (ed.), *Tax and Corporate Governance*, Springer, Verlag-Berlin-Heidelberg, 2008, p. 183.
47. B. Ferroni, *Cooperative compliance: un regime sempre più attraente per le grandi imprese*, in *Il Fisco*, 2017, p. 2407.

issued by the Ministry of Economy and Finance, in other words with a secondary source of law, the criteria to be used to progressively extend the programmes to further taxpayers shall be defined. In this circumstance, in the Italian legislator's future perspective the turnover or profit threshold should not be lower than EUR 100 million and, in addition, persons who are members of a group may fall within the personal scope of Co-operative Compliance.

The extension of the personal scope to include persons other than the largest companies has already taken place, at least partially, even if by means of different legal sources. Indeed, by passing subsequent Legislative Decree no. 147 of 2015, also known as the Internationalization Decree, a new procedure was established dedicated to investors intending to bring their capital to Italy and wishing to consult previously with the Tax Administration, the so-called advance rulings on new investment ("*interpello sui nuovi investimenti,*" *see* section §8.02[F]).

In this context, where an application for an advance ruling on new investment is submitted and an answer is given, either explicitly or implicitly,[48] by the Tax Administration, the programme of Co-operative Compliance will become available to the taxpayer regardless of the size requirements established in Legislative Decree no. 128 of 2015. As is evident, this extension of the scope is operated by a primary source of law, namely a Legislative Decree.

In addition to that, a further extension of the personal scope of Co-operative Compliance was operated by the Tax Administration Director with the release of the first executive order on this topic.[49] The possibility for the Tax Administration Director to regulate the practical application of the Co-operative Compliance programme is set out under Article 7, paragraph 5, of Legislative Decree no. 128 of 2015. For this purpose, the executive order granted admission to the programme to both residents and non-residents, on condition that they have a permanent establishment in Italy that addresses and operates some sort of tax risk control, but only if its inclusion is necessary for a comprehensive representation of the business processes. This is an option that allows adhesion to the programme of those companies which, regardless of the size requirements, play a leading role in the tax risk management; in other words, those companies that are entitled to effectively address the internal control function. In such a case, also called "dragging," it is sufficient for the size requirements to be met by one single company of the group in order for any company of the group to be eligible to join the programme, on condition that even if it does not meet the turnover or profit requirements set out by the relevant legislation, it plays a leading role with regard to the internal control function. The rationale behind the extension of the personal scope is to

48. The subsequent Ministerial Decree for the implementation of the advanced ruling on new investments specifies that "The taxpayer complying with the contents of the Italian Tax Administration's reply may, regardless of the amount of turnover or proceeds, have access to the legal institute of collaborative compliance referred to in Articles 3 to 7 of Legislative Decree No 128 of 5 August 2015, provided that the other requirements necessary for access to the said institute are fulfilled," Art. 8, para. 1, Ministerial Decree of the April 29, 2016.

49. Executive order of the Tax Administration Director of April 14, 2016, Regulation on the requirements for access to the Co-operative Compliance programme under Art. 3 and following of Legislative Decree no. 128 of August 5, 2015.

be found in the need for the Tax Administration to acquire the widest possible overview of the tax risk of the group.[50] For this very reason, the author is persuaded that the provisions of the primary source of law have not been infringed. Indeed, the extension is explicitly permitted by means of a Decree of the Ministry of Economics and Finance (under Article 7, comma 4, letter a), of Legislative Decree no. 128 of 2015), and the aspects concerning the practical application are coherently regulated by one or more executive orders of the Tax Administration Director. In this case, the possibility to include a company of the group has to be evaluated in the light of the Tax Administration's opportunity to obtain a system of tax control which is in line with the purposes of the programme itself. It is not, therefore, an extension operated by the Tax Administration in conflict with the primary source of law.[51]

Finally, as already mandated by the lawmaker under Article 7, paragraph 4, letter a), Article 20, Decree Law no. 119 of 2018[52] extends the personal scope of Co-operative Compliance to those companies that are members of a VAT group. In particular, if one of the members of the VAT group joins the programme of Co-operative Compliance, this automatically (and mandatorily) means that the other group members must join it, regardless of whether they meet the size requirements under Legislative Decree no. 128 of 2015 on an individual basis.

Moreover, Article 1-bis of Law Decree no. 50 of April 24, 2017 introduced a specific procedure of enhanced co-operation and collaboration (named *procedura di cooperazione e di collaborazione rafforzata*) with the main aim of intercepting the income derived by non-resident entities (part of larger multinational groups) from the sale of goods and/or the provision of services on Italian territory, either directly or with the support of an Italian entity belonging to the same multinational group, through a hidden permanent establishment in Italy. If, after this procedure, non-resident entities have a permanent establishment in Italy, they may enter the Italian Co-operative Compliance programme regardless of their turnover.

In conclusion, the personal scope of the Italian Co-operative Compliance programme is heavily restricted, even if it is destined to be extended further to include more taxpayers, although not every type.

§8.05 LEGAL (AND NON-LEGAL) CONSEQUENCES OF ADHESION TO ITALIAN CO-OPERATIVE COMPLIANCE PROGRAMME

Article 6, Legislative Decree no. 128 of 2015, entitled "Consequences," states that adhesion to Co-operative Compliance allows, but does not oblige, the taxpayer to reach a shared view with the Tax Administration on the facts and circumstances that may give rise to tax risks before the filing of the tax return, by means of different forms of

50. D. Conte, *Dal controllo fiscale sul dichiarato al confronto preventivo sull'imponibile*, Padua, 2017, p. 173.
51. Contrary to D. Conte, *Dal controllo fiscale sul dichiarato al confronto preventivo sull'imponibile*, Padua, 2017, p. 174.
52. Law Decree no. 119 of October 23, 2018, *Disposizioni urgenti in materia di fiscalità fiscale e finanziaria*, converted, with amendments, into Law no. 136 of December 17, 2018. Article 20 introduced para. 6-bis, to Art. 70-duodecis, of DPR no. 633/1972 (VAT Decree).

participation and prior dialog.[53] Furthermore, adhesion to the programme entitles participants to a "shortened" procedure of ruling ("*interpello abbreviato*") with regard to the application of tax rules that imply tax risks.[54] Finally, a further consequence of adhesion to the programme concerns the imposition of penalties. Indeed, for risks of which the Tax Administration is made fully and promptly aware, according to the law, penalties are reduced by half and cannot be higher than their statutory minimum, where the Tax Administration disagrees with the taxpayer's view.

However, Article 6, paragraph 1 refers to a shared evaluation of the situations that could potentially give rise to tax risks but it does not clarify what means shall be relied upon in order to achieve this result. Nor can it be inferred that such an agreement should be reached by means of the "shortened" ruling procedure, because it is evident that both the Legislative Decree and the Ministerial Decree[55] and, in particular, Article 1, provide this ruling procedure as an (additional) possibility offered to the taxpayer admitted to Co-operative Compliance. Therefore, by considering the statutory rules passed by the delegated legislator, it is possible to pinpoint either the lack of advanced forms of interaction or a specific position of the legislator on the topic of legitimate reliance that should originate from adhesion to the programme. Indeed, Co-operative Compliance models are expected to offer a win-win situation for taxpayers and the Tax Administration.[56] From the taxpayer's perspective, in addition to a number of benefits, such as the speed with which answers are obtained from the Tax Administration or a reduction of penalties, the most interesting aspect of adhesion to the programme is the possibility to rely on a shared view reached together with the Tax Administration within a balanced, and not authoritative, relationship. Co-operative Compliance, as highlighted, is adopted (and works better) in those legal systems where trust in the positions of the Tax Administration is high[57] and what is agreed is not questioned later, unless there are changes in either the facts or the law. From this standpoint, regardless of the fact that the Italian Co-operative Compliance programme was implemented by means of a source of primary law, the legislator did not regulate these aspects.

In particular, in the authors' opinion, the statutory regulation on Co-operative Compliance lacks what the delegated legislator enacted with Delegation no. 23 of 2014 that expressly sets out two further options. Reference here is to the advance rulings for companies with an international business and the advance ruling for new investments,

53. According to the Italian Co-operative Compliance Programme if the taxpayer and the Tax Administration do not reach a shared view, they may "agree to disagree." In this case, it is possible to start a tax litigation on a specific issue, while continuing in the programme.
54. Under Art. 6, para. 2, of Legislative Decree no. 128 of 2015, in the case of a ruling dedicated to Co-operative Compliance, the deadline for answering taxpayers is reduced to 45 days instead of the usual deadline under Art. 11 of the Taxpayer's Bill of Rights, namely 90 or 120 days.
55. Decree of the Minister of Economy and Finance of June 15, 2016, "Interpello" (or ruling) for the taxpayers joining the Co-operative Compliance programme, under Art. 6, para. 2, of Legislative Decree no. 128 of August 5, 2015.
56. R. Szudoczky & A. Majdanska, *Designing Co-operative Compliance Programmes: Lessons from the EU State Aid Rules for Tax Administration*, 2017(2) Brit. Tax Rev., (2017), p. 207.
57. F. Amatucci, *L'adeguamento dell'ordinamento tributario nazionale alle linee guida dell'OCSE e dell'UE in materia di lotta alla pianificazione fiscale aggressiva*, in *Rivista Trimestrale di Diritto Tributario*, 2015, p. 17.

introduced into our tax system by Article 1 (Advance rulings)[58] and Article 2 (Advance ruling for new investments) of Legislative Decree no. 147 of 2015. In both cases, although an analysis of the personal and objective scope of these two arrangements would go beyond the purposes of this contribution, what is protected is the legitimate reliance of the taxpayer on the interpretation provided by (and agreed with) the Tax Administration. Indeed, for the advance rulings regarding companies with an international business, the law "binds" the parties for five years, unless there are changes in either the facts or the law, and the advance ruling for new investments has the same effect where the content of the answer given by the Tax Administration is binding until both the facts and the law on which it is based change. Conversely, in the case of advance ruling for new investments, it is Article 2, paragraph 3, of the Internationalization Decree that regulates the invalidity of any act of the Tax Administration that is in conflict with the answer previously given by it (or with its tacit consent). These consequences match with the provisions of Article 11, paragraph 3, of the Taxpayer's Bill of Rights,[59] especially with regard to one aspect that may be of relevance in the context of the present analysis and has already been dealt with by scholars.[60] In the case of rulings regulated by the Taxpayer's Bill of Rights, if the taxpayer has already carried out all the actions recommended by the Tax Administration, the latter cannot change its mind because otherwise this would nullify the act. On the other hand, as to the actions not already put in place by the taxpayer, the Tax Administration can change its position, but without affecting what was decided in the past. That possibility provided for by the Taxpayer's Bill of Rights is present neither in the legislation on new investments nor in the field of advance rulings,[61] because in both cases, unless changes occur in the facts or the law, the Tax Administration cannot change its opinion.

As far as Co-operative Compliance is concerned, in light of the statutory legislation, it has already been explained that the taxpayer who is admitted to the programme is entitled, during the interaction with the Tax Administration, to submit a ruling request to it in order to obtain an answer on the application of tax law regarding specific circumstances giving rise to tax risks. It is, therefore, a ruling dedicated specifically to the programme of Co-operative Compliance. Nevertheless, on closer inspection, the peculiarity of the ruling consists of the short time provided for the answer (or tacit consent), even in relation to the consequences of the answer. Indeed, Article 9, paragraph 1, of the Ministerial Decree likens that answer to the one given to a ruling submitted under Article 11, paragraph 3, of the Taxpayer's Bill of Rights. In these cases, the answer given is also applicable to the taxpayer's subsequent actions, unless the Tax Administration changes the answer, which can only be done with regard to future actions. As is evident, the wording used overlaps that of the Taxpayer's Bill of Rights. However, in addition to what is mandated with regard to the ordinary ruling, what in the authors' opinion distinguishes the procedure at issue is the consequences

58. Article 1 of the Internationalization Decree introduced 31-ter in the DPR no. 600/1973.
59. Legge no. 212 del 2000, *Disposizioni in materia di statuto dei diritti del contribuente.*
60. G. Vanz, *see supra* n. 31.
61. Although in the case of advance rulings the Tax Administration (as well as the taxpayer) is bound for five years only.

that arise if the Tax Administration is either late and does not meet the deadline or gives an answer that is different from those given previously. In such cases, unlike the general discipline, non-compliance with the interpretative solution given does not exempt the taxpayer from the payment of taxes and interests, but it does not give rise to the application of penalties.[62]

A second aspect that is worth investigating is the protection given to the other types of ongoing and advanced interaction contained in the legislation on Co-operative Compliance. According to what was established by the executive order of the Tax Administration Director,[63] after having defined what is to be understood as ongoing and advanced interaction on elements of fact,[64] Article 5 identifies three different ways in which the Tax Administration makes a commitment toward the taxpayer, in respect to the decision made in the context of interaction, and before the filing of the tax report.

The first hypothesis concerns the case in which the taxpayer communicates to the Tax Administration situations of potential risk and those transactions that may be classified as aggressive tax planning, as well as any other situation that the taxpayer itself considers potentially uncertain. In those cases, the position of the administration is formalized with a reasoned opinion, capable of guaranteeing a prior certainty of the facts that are the object of evaluation. Furthermore, a second way of formalizing the Tax Administration's standpoint may be constituted by the report of inspection findings. This occurs when the Tax Administration carries out an inspection in order to assess what the taxpayer has given notice of and is willing to communicate its findings in advance. Lastly, a further way of formalization is dictated for those scenarios where the issue (or the complex series of issues) presented to the Tax Administration is considered as being strategic for the taxpayer. In those cases, the Tax Administration invites the taxpayer for a consultation aimed at reaching a shared evaluation and eventually formalizes it in a so-called agreement of Co-operative Compliance.[65] In

62. In the authors' opinion, this is an interpretation that is consistent with the provisions of Art. 9, para. 3, of the Ministerial Decree of implementation, where it is mandated that "if the Tax Administration in answering does not meet the deadline under Article 7, paragraph 1, or gives a different answer to the one previously given, any non-compliance with the late answer or that changes it gives rise to the collection of taxes and interests, but not to the imposition of penalties, but only if, at the time when the answer is given, the taxpayer has not yet put in place the specific action dealt with by the ruling."

63. Order of 26 May 2017 (Disposizioni per l'attuazione del regime di adempimento collaborativo disciplinato dagli articoli 3 e seguenti del decreto legislativo 5 agosto 2015, no. 128).

64. Article 1, letter o), Order of 26 May 2017, "*Per interlocuzione costante e preventiva su elementi di fatto si intende il contraddittorio di carattere continuativo che consenta di addivenire ad un comune intendimento in merito agli elementi di fatto costitutivi della fattispecie.*"

65. It is worthwhile clarifying that regardless of the use of the word "agreement," this advanced interaction with the Tax Administration, also in the case of reasoned opinions and reports of inspection findings, does not constitute a consensual way of calculating the amount of tax due, but constitutes a procedure aimed at qualifying, in a shared and not unilateral way, the factual elements at the base of the tax obligation, including by means of consultation with the taxpayer. M. Versiglioni concentrates on this aspect, *Cooperative compliance, Equivalent Dispute Resolution (EDR) and Administrative Tax Agreement (A.T.A.)—Contributo allo studio delle disposizioni giuridiche a "funzionalità dipendente,"* in *Innovazione e Diritto*, 2017, p. 110. M. Trivellin, *Un'altra pronuncia della Cassazione esclude il recupero del tributo in violazione del principio di tutela dell'affidamento: alcune note sulle ragioni della scelta adottata*, in *Rivista di Diritto Tributario*, 2007, II, p. 283. The author's analysis is interesting because it concerns the

those cases, the Director's executive order mandates that the content of the agreement is binding for the parties for the tax period to which the shared solution is referred and for the subsequent ones, unless there are changes in the facts or the law on which the shared view is based.

As can easily be observed, the consequence described is the same as that deriving from the answer (or the tacit consent) to the advance ruling for new investments or in cases where an advanced ruling is granted under Article 31-ter, DPR no. 600 of 1973.[66] The taxpayer's reliance is safeguarded even in the context of the two ongoing and advanced forms of interaction set out by the executive order of the Tax Administration Director.

§8.06 THE PARTICIPATION OF ITALY IN THE ICAP

During the 12th plenary meeting of the Forum on Tax Administration (FTA) held in Santiago de Chile from March 26 to 28, 2019, it was decided, among others, to launch a second "ICAP Pilot" (also known as "ICAP 2.0").[67]

More specifically, the main outcome of the meeting is a handbook containing information on the programme,[68] which builds on the first pilot[69] and is a voluntary programme aimed at facilitating a multilateral co-operative risk assessment and assurance process.

The second pilot has been joined by the Tax Administrations of nineteen countries, including Italy, which already participated in the first pilot that started in January 2018.[70]

The fact that the Italian Tax Administration also joined the second pilot suggests that participation in the first phase of the programme received positive evaluation and the potential for a fruitful future co-operation with both taxpayers and other Tax Administrations has been envisaged.

On the one hand, there is no doubt that the ICAP has the potential to increase the level of certainty concerning the treatment of complex cross-border situations falling within the scope of the programme. On the other hand, it also seems to be undeniable

---

annulment of a tax assessment notice, by virtue of the safeguarding of the taxpayer's legitimate expectation, in contrast with a previous agreement between the Tax Administration and the taxpayer on the material elements of the tax obligation. The Author underlines that in that specific case the Tax Administration did not intervene on the tax credit, but rather evaluated the "goodness and seriousness" of the arguments put forward by the taxpayer, whose technical support had been decisive.

66. The similarity of the consequences is also underlined by F. Pistolesi, *Le regole procedimentali nel provvedimento di attuazione dell'adempimento collaborativo*, in *Corriere Tributario*, 2017, p. 2414.
67. OECD ICAP, *see also* the official OECD website at "https://www.oecd.org/tax/forum-on-tax-administration/international-compliance-assurance programme.htm."
68. International Compliance Assurance Programme Pilot Handbook 2.0, "www.oecd.org."
69. For an analysis of both the first and the second pilots, *see* in particular R. Russo & M.H. Martini, *The International Compliance Assurance Programme Reviewed: The Future of Cooperative Tax Compliance?*, 73 Bull. Int'l Taxn. (2019), 9, 452.
70. *See also* the press note released by the Italian Tax Administration on January 24, 2018, "www.agenziaentrate.gov.it."

that, as the advantage granted to the taxpayer is an "outcome letter" from the lead Tax Administration containing "nothing more" than an assessment of the tax risk present in a specific situation, the assurance that may potentially be reached is significantly lower than the certainty potentially reachable using other instruments, such as Advance Pricing Arrangements.[71]

Ultimately, the main guarantee from a taxpayer's perspective is that all the Tax Administrations participating in the procedure and "agreeing" with the content of the outcome letter will not allocate further resources to the assessment of the same risk. The decision on whether to apply for a multilateral assessment by multiple Tax Administrations within the ICAP is likely to depend on the bureaucratic burden and costs that this choice will imply.

From a Tax Administration perspective, it is reasonable to expect that participation in the programme will incentivize the development of consistent and coherent techniques of tax risk assessment. Moreover, given that a large portion of the information concerning "assessable situations" falling within the scope of the ICAP corresponds to information that shall be included in the Country-by-Country Report, it is also reasonable to expect that in many cases this will help with the analysis of the data that are in the hands of the Tax Administration.

§8.07 CONCLUSIONS

Considering all the above, the Co-operative Compliance Programme recently established by the Italian legislator may be seen as the last step of a long journey. More specifically, interaction between the Tax Administration and the taxpayer is allowed by means of a number of different procedures. Starting from the various types of *interpello* currently available and considering Italy's participation in the most recent programmes promoted by the OECD, the level of the taxpayer's participation in the process of tax levying has gradually increased.

The abovementioned journey has been significantly accelerated by the recent adoption of two delegated acts, which are commonly known as "certainty decree"[72] and "internationalization decree."[73] As previously explained, they have widened the spectrum of options that the taxpayer has for dialoging with the Tax Administration quite considerably, especially with regard to situations characterized by cross-border elements.

Nevertheless, the investigations and reasoning recently proposed by scholars[74] highlight how difficult it is, in reality, to consider the Tax Administration and the taxpayer as being on an equal footing. In certain circumstances, the analysis of which is beyond the scope of the present chapter, a taxpayer who joins the Co-operative

71. On the same note, *see also* P. Bonarelli, *Trasparenza e scambio di informazioni tra imprese e amministrazioni: ICAP*, in *Fiscalità & Commercio Internazionale*, 6/2019, 5.
72. *See supra*, n. 41.
73. *See supra*, n. 30.
74. G. Ragucci, *Gli istituti della collaborazione fiscale*, Torino, 2018. On this point *see also* F. Cannas, K. Wauters, *The Rise of Cooperative Compliance Programmes and the Rule of Law: A Comparison Between Italy and Belgium*, 58 Eur. Taxn. (2019), 12, 561, 571.

Compliance Programme (or accepts a solution proposed by the Tax Administration) may be seen more as someone who "accepts a proposal" than as someone who "agrees with a shared view of the facts underlying the tax levy," and this may depend on the guarantees legally granted to him/her.

For this reason, in the authors' opinion, the journey described herein demands, in addition to further legislative interventions, a profound change and renewal of the cultural approach to the relationship between the parties involved in the levying of taxes.

CHAPTER 9

Japanese International Compliance Assurance in Practice

Yasuyuki Kawabata

§9.01 INTRODUCTION

Even though Japan was one of the observer countries in the Organisation for Economic Co-operation and Development (OECD) International Compliance Assurance Programme (ICAP) since its beginning in 2016, and up until mid-2017, the Japanese Government is not actively implementing the ICAP under domestic law for the time being, because there might be several obstacles and shortcomings under its domestic tax laws. Even the current status of Japanese tax administrations in the ICAP, as a formal participant, is not clear, as there is no guidance nor legal procedures for the implementation of such pilot. Since 1986, Japanese international transfer pricing rules have been operated with the advance consultation dialog between taxpayer and the administrations, called "Pre-confirmation System (PCS)." From an early stage of its history, PCS is joined with the United States (U.S.) Advance Pricing Agreement (APA) practice into a single bilateral APA for international practice under the Mutual Agreement Procedure of the Income Tax Treaty between these countries. Japan is now legislating most of the Base Erosion and Profit Shifting (BEPS) Action Plans, including Country-by-Country Reporting, for the purpose of achieving international standards of taxation, in addition to being one of the signatory countries of the Multilateral Convention to implement Tax Treaty related Measures to prevent BEPS Multilateral Instrument (MLI).[1]

1. The MLI has become effective for Japan on January 1, 2019.

The Japanese tax administration, notably the national administration,[2] is centralized into the single hierarchy of the National Tax Administration (NTA), to which all Regional Tax Bureaus and Local Tax Offices belong. Most national tax affairs are processed through Local Tax Offices or Regional Tax Bureaus where these offices/bureaus have relevant legal authority to manage the tax affairs of taxpayers. However, at the top of this hierarchy of tax administrations, the NTA would handle certain significant domestic and international tax matters of both resident and non-resident taxpayers (individuals as well as corporations). The NTA in Tokyo is also in charge of policy making for all the nation's national tax offices/bureaus. In this context, the implementation of the International Cooperation Assurance Program by Japanese tax administrations would be planned and managed by the NTA[3] in close co-operation with, mainly, Japanese multinational enterprises and industry-based associations.

This chapter analyzes the status quo regarding the OECD ICAP in relation to the Japanese international tax policy and business practices. The Japanese government has participated in the ICAP project from the outset of that programme as one of observers within the Forum on Tax Administration (FTA) community.

§9.02 JAPANESE TAX ADMINISTRATION

Before turning to the ICAP as viewed by Japanese tax administrations, I would hereby like to refer to the traditional practice of Japanese tax administrations, especially on international tax matters, such as international transfer pricing or other tax issues of multinational enterprises.

The Japanese Constitution requires national and local taxation to have a legal basis, mainly in the statutes legislated by the National or Local Parliament,[4] although tax practices by the national and local tax administrations cover a broad range of administrative procedures, such as authoritative interpretations of tax laws, their application to specific facts and circumstances of taxpayers, and control of tax officials' human resources. For such administrative procedures, there might sometimes be no formal legal basis, because the scope of the statutes is too narrow for this purpose. However, such tax practices are adaptable, so that there have to be no conflicts of interests between taxpayers and tax administrations. Historically, Japanese tax practices have put a certain emphasis on such informal but flexible tax practices, especially before the end of World War II in 1945.[5]

---

2. For local taxes, all local governing bodies such as Prefectures, Cities or Towns, have their own administrative mechanisms.
3. https://www.nta.go.jp/english/Report_pdf/2018e_04.pdf (as of September 10, 2019).
4. Article 84, Japanese Constitution (May 3, 1947).
5. Taxation and the tax administration before 1945 were not controlled by the strict Constitutional rule of the "Principle of Taxation with Legal Basis." Article 62 para. 1 of The Constitution of the Japanese Empire referred to taxation under legal rules. The Constitution then only required a formal basis of taxation, not a substantive one. There were relatively fewer provisions under the tax statutes to provide rough and ambiguous rules. On the other hand, the current Constitution requires such a strict Constitutional rule as a basis for taxation and administration.

Currently, the main tax practice of this type is advance (*ex ante*) consultation made by taxpayers to the tax administrations (Jizen-sohdan). This is not a legal procedure, but a de facto advance administrative consultation between the taxpayer and the competent tax administrations on tax issues to be reported in future tax returns. This could, for example, be the case for Individual Income Tax as well as Corporate Income Tax. The result of the consultation is a justified expectation of the taxpayer, if they pursue their economic transactions in line with the agreed analysis.[6] Such taxpayers would disclose the expected facts and circumstances to the tax administration prior to the relevant taxable year(s) and ask for the possible tax outcome, as far as this de facto *ex ante* disclosure does not affect the taxpayer's position on these tax matters.[7] The tax administrations could make de facto suggestions to the taxpayer, within and in light of the tax laws, based on the taxpayer's disclosure of facts and circumstances. Thus, there is no legally binding agreement or relationship between the taxpayer and the administration.[8] Taxpayers could hope for or expect the administration to deal with the relevant transactions in line with the outcome of the advance consultation upon filing the annual tax return. This kind of administrative operation is also applied in case of an organizational consultation, in the form of a written query-sheet, by any of the industry associations in the representation of industry-wide interests. In that case, the administrations would provide their views on the application of the law to specified facts and circumstances in written form and this reply would be published through the NTA's websites or commercial tax journals, although these publications have no formal legal authority. The replies given by the administrations could be understood as ad hoc responses that are compiled on a case-by-case basis.

For the authoritative interpretation of tax laws, the NTA publishes part[9] of their legal interpretations and views regarding the statutory rules under, e.g., the Income Tax Act (ITA), as a series of administrative circulars called "Tsutatsu." These are published in advance for specific cases or issues as a general position of the tax administrators. This "Tsutatsu" is not legislative in character, but rather a kind of de facto guidance or position issued by administrations. Taxpayers are not legally bound by these circulars, although any tax official who belongs to the organizational hierarchy of the NTA will be, because the circulars constitute a kind of governmental order under the legal relationship between employee (public officials) and employer (the Government). In addition to such general guidelines issued by the NTA, there are

6. Generally, such de facto consultation or advise by the administration is labeled with "Gyosei-Shido." This "Gyosei-Shido" is a consultation or advice made by the competent administrative body with backing by legal authorities to regulate civilians' conduct.
7. There could be a legal issue on such *ex ante* disclosure of expected facts and circumstances by the taxpayers to the administrations, because tax laws sometimes put the burden of proof of facts and circumstances on the administration's side.
8. Under Japanese tax laws, the legal obligation to pay a certain amount of tax, that would be ascertained for certain time-periods, can only become by the passage of this term (e.g., taxable year). Until that time (end of taxable year), there is no legally binding agreement between taxpayers and administrations on the amount of taxes to be paid.
9. It is well-known to Japanese taxpayers that tax administrations have still unpublished legal interpretations on tax laws, in accordance with applicable office-regulations.

written or—in most cases—unwritten responses from the administrations to ad hoc consultations made by the relevant taxpayers on fact-specific legal issues. These responses are also based on advance consultation by taxpayers.

§9.03 INTERNATIONAL TRANSFER PRICING AND PCS

Under the Japanese tax system, the most developed area of co-operation between tax administrations and taxpayers happens to be in the field of international taxation because of time-consuming proceedings to file tax returns, complex statutory rules, heavy compliance cost and the huge amount of taxes involved. From this field of international taxation, the Japanese international transfer pricing system[10] has spill-over effects to foreign taxpayers as well as foreign governments. Thus, the Japanese government has begun to coordinate their tax position with those of foreign governments, especially after the anti-tax haven legislation, around forty years ago. The most impressive action by the Japanese government, even from Japanese tax academia's viewpoints, could be observed in the area of international transfer pricing after its domestic legislation in 1986.[11]

Transfer pricing rules were introduced into Japanese law in 1986, immediately before the U.S. legislation of the so-called super-royalty rule in the second sentence of section 482, Internal Revenue Code of 1986. The basic framework of the Japanese transfer pricing regulations follows the arm's length principle developed under U.S. laws and OECD guidelines. The basic methodology for arm's length pricing are the traditional methods of Comparable Uncontrolled Pricing, Resale Pricing and Cost Plus, although other methodologies such as Profit Split and Transactional Net Margin are also allowed when relevant for the case. From the beginning of their history, Japanese transfer pricing rules have been coordinated by means of domestic advance consultations between taxpayers and tax administrations. This advance consultation procedure is known as the "Pre-Confirmation System, PCS (Jizen-Kakunin Seido)."[12] It is not a legal institution, but a kind of domestic administrative practice, specific to international transfer pricing both for taxpayers and for domestic tax administrations. NTA has published its de facto procedure under this PCS to reach confirmation, between

10. Under Japanese tax laws, only international pricing is operated under so-called transfer pricing rules. "Domestic" pricing is settled through the application of traditional legal rules under domestic laws other than transfer pricing rules. There is no application of treaty-based transfer pricing rules for such domestic transactions. Technically speaking, Japanese international transfer pricing rules under the Special Tax Measures Act (STMA) Art. 66-4 would be applicable to the transactions made between corporations (legal persons) and "foreign related-parties (Kokugai Kanrensha)." Transactions between non-resident foreign corporations and their foreign related parties are regulated by transfer pricing rules under the STMA, if these non-resident foreign corporations have any business interest in Japan leading to Japanese tax consequences.
11. Article 66-4, Special Tax Measures Act (as revised in 1986).
12. National Tax Administration, "On the Confirmation of Methodology of Ascertaining Arm's length Price," (Sacho5-1hoka-nika-kyodo) (April 24, 1987), as revised by Sacho8-1hoka (October 25, 1999).

administration and taxpayer, on a pricing methodology.[13] Several major multinational business corporations have followed this procedure from the beginning of PCS.

The United States, on the other hand, adopted their Advance Price Agreement Procedure immediately after the Japanese introduction of PCS. In the early stage of these two national advance consultation procedures in the field of transfer pricing, both Governments of the U.S. and Japan determined to put together these two systems into one single advance consultation procedure, and launched the so-called Bilateral APA procedure based on Article 25 (Competent Authority Clause)[14] of the then effective Double Tax Convention of 1971 between the U.S. and Japan.[15] Thus, under the U.S./Japan Tax Treaty, a bilateral APA consists of a Japanese PCS on the Japanese side, a U.S. APA procedure on the U.S. side and the mutual agreement procedure between the Competent Authorities of both countries. Such a bilateral APA could be said to be an international "quasi-legal" agreement.

We can point out some material differences in the legal character of the early Japanese PCS and U.S. APA. According to U.S. administrative rulings issued by the Internal Revenue Service, U.S. APAs have a legally binding force on both parties to such agreement, i.e., taxpayers and administrations, whereas the Japanese PCS is, even now, only a de facto consultation[16] between the administrations and the taxpayers. The Japanese NTA only "confirms" expected facts and circumstances, especially the method for calculating the price of future transactions between related parties (TP methodology). Thus, there is no legally binding force either on the tax administrations or on the taxpayers under these confirmations. Relevant taxpayers can expect the future position of the administration to be in line with the contents of the confirmation. Such taxpayers will not be legally protected by the confirmations, because they have no legally binding power on the relevant parties. Thus, any taxpayer who utilizes Japanese PCS, even though it is called a bilateral or multilateral APA under tax treaties, will be in an uncertain position compared with foreign taxpayers that are parties to a legally binding APA under foreign tax treaties.

The Japanese tax legislator has already accepted the BEPS Action Plans as a new dimension of international tax standards, including County-by-Country Reporting

13. The Japanese Pre-confirmation System does not focus on the final outcome of the price itself of specific transactions, but rather focuses on the "pricing methodology."
14. This Art. 25 of 1971 U.S./Japan Tax Treaty corresponds to the current Art. 25 (Mutual Agreement) of 2017 OECD, Model Tax Convention on Income and on Capital (2017).
15. Article 25, Convention between Japan and the United States of America for the Avoidance of Double Taxation and the Prevention of Fiscal Evasion with respect to Taxes on Income (signed, 1971). It is needless to say that the current 2003 U.S./Japan Income Tax Treaty follows this MAP procedure for the communications between tax administrations of both countries.
16. The NTA published its position on the effect of a "confirmation" to be that each head of a regional tax office shall treat the confirmed transaction as having been executed at an arm's length price, if the requesting corporation files its returns in line with the confirmation. This means that the tax office would understand the effect of the "confirmation" to confirm the treatment of the transaction. "18. Effect of Confirmation," National Tax Administration, "On the Confirmation of Methodology of Ascertaining Arm's length Price," (Sacho8-1hoka) (October 25, 1999).

(CbCR) in the context of transfer pricing and treaty revision through the MLI against international tax avoidance.[17]

§9.04 TAX COMPLIANCE BURDEN UNDER THE JAPANESE TAX SYSTEM

Before the end of World War II, Japanese Individual and Corporation Taxes were both based on the "levy system," under which the taxpayer would receive an administrative assessment of their tax base (taxable income) and tax due for each taxable year, based on an initial tax audit or assessment by the relevant tax administration.[18] Under this levy (or assessment) system, no taxpayer had any initial involvement in the assessment of his/her taxable income. The system of Tax Levy is a kind of "administrative action" performed by the tax administrations. The compliance cost for the taxpayers might be far less than those in modern tax procedures based on self-filing of tax returns (self-assessment system). Income calculation by the administrations were sometimes based on estimated amounts of receipts and expenses derived from the tax administration's information and tax statistics, which would be gathered prior to the administrative assessment, because it is sometimes hard for the administrations to find real amount of receipt/expenses of specific taxpayer, if such taxpayer did not keep his/her books/records of the transactions[19] for the relevant taxable year.

Nowadays, by contrast, the major Japanese national taxes, e.g., Individual Income Tax, Corporation Tax, Inheritance Tax, Consumption Tax, are all based on taxpayers' self-filing of tax returns with the relevant tax administrations. In all these cases, the assessment of the tax base, as well as the calculation of the tax amount, depends on the taxpayer's correct and detailed understanding of tax rules and fact-finding. Every taxpayer must ascertain his/her taxable transactions, calculate the amounts of revenue and expenses and determine the character of such amounts (taxable, deductible, etc.). This is one of the sources for the high tax compliance burden. At the same time, the relevant statutes give tax administrations legal authority for tax audits. Thus, as a matter of legal course, tax administrations can exercise their authority to audit specific taxpayers and to verify the tax payment due by the taxpayer. In view of these possible tax audits by the administrations, taxpayers may consult the administrations about the correctness of their interpretations of the tax rules or fact-findings, before any tax audit is started. This is another source of the compliance

17. Because Country-by-Country Reporting (CbCR) is a new system of information gathering both for taxpayers and domestic tax administrations, previous domestic reporting requirements are still under adjustment and experience with the new system are is limited.
18. Because Japanese administrative law succeeded German administrative law, certain "administrative actions" were required to make the taxpayer formally liable to tax payment to the National or Local Government.
19. This was mostly after World War II, when Japanese economies accepted Western-style modernized double entry bookkeeping. Before accepting this modern accounting system from Europe and the U.S., even major Japanese industries utilized an old-fashioned single-entry system for accounting and record-keeping purposes. The development of accounting theory and practices had a significant influence on the tax practice of taxpayers and administrations.

burden on the taxpayers and creates a thin line between compliance and non-compliance. The more the facts and circumstances of a specific case become complex and numerous, the higher is the taxpayer's burden of compliance. In this light, the shock-absorbing device of advance consultation between taxpayers and tax administrations is vital for both parties. International tax structures are relatively more complex than domestic structures, because they relate to the tax systems of other countries and their legal structures are also generally more complex and multilayered. As a result of such complexities, tax compliance in the context of international taxation has been a crucial point of attention for both taxpayers and tax administrations for decades.

In general, taxpayers take it for granted that administrative tax procedures are legally complex and burdensome and, as such, taxpayers understand that they should accept this burden. Some taxpayers may hire tax professionals, such as certified tax accountants (Zeirishi), certified public accountants or attorneys at law to prepare and file their tax returns. Because most Japanese citizens are unfamiliar with the details of tax laws, such private tax agents are the most common way to avoid complex and burdensome tax compliance obligations. Individuals, in general, do not have deep concerns over their tax compliance, because their tax returns are often simple. It would be mostly entrepreneurs and corporations that have concerns regarding their tax compliance or other tax obligations, because they have more complex economic activities. In that respect, ICAP might be a useful instrument only for relatively big companies.

As one of the basic documents and records for income and consumption taxation, the NTA has developed long-standing standards of bookkeeping. These are widely applicable to many types of business, from big listed corporations to small or medium-sized privately owned corporations and individual sole proprietorships. The reason for developing these standards is that the financial accounts could be used as a starting point for tax audits, where those are needed. The ITA has categorized individual taxpayers into two classes: one consisting of taxpayers with white-colored tax returns, the other taxpayers with blue-colored tax returns. These have different relationships with the authorities. The first category is the principal one under the ITA, but no advantages derive from this class. The second category, in turn, offers some tax advantages, such as a special tax credit, less chance to be audited by the administration, etc. However, such blue-return taxpayers are obliged to keep books and records in accordance with the double entry system of accounting. With a view to enjoy such tax advantages, many individual taxpayers, especially taxpayers with business or other income for which the ITA requires to maintain books, have elected this treatment of the second category (blue-return taxpayer) and accepted the compulsory bookkeeping standards. To facilitate the needs of taxpayers, the Ministry of Finance asked several business associations, such as the Japan Chamber of Commerce and Industry (JCCI), to help small and medium-sized business corporations and individuals setting up the required bookkeeping process. JCCI has a long history of promoting double-entry bookkeeping through its educational activities for managers, employees and business owners, starting after the end of World War II. This popularization of modern bookkeeping can be described as a fundamental means of lowering the tax compliance burden for taxpayers. Today, standardized bookkeeping is a legal obligation under ITA for all taxpayers who earn business or other relevant income. Financial accounting has become a common basic language of record keeping for tax administrations and taxpayers.

For corporate income taxation, any corporation subject to the Corporation Tax Act is also subject to bookkeeping obligations under relevant laws other than tax laws. A business corporation, e.g., in the form of Kabushiki-Kaisha (United Kingdom type of company limited by shares, or U.S. type of any State's Business Corporation) is obliged to keep books and records for the annual settlement of accounts for purposes of the Company Act, and some of these corporations, when publicly traded on the security market, are obliged to file their annual financial statements with the security market under the Act on Transactions of Financial Instruments. Because of such organizational regulations, Japanese corporations are expected to have financial books and records in accordance with Japanese or International Accounting Standards. This reduces the tax compliance burden of business corporations in the context of keeping books and records.

§9.05 THE ICAP IN JAPAN

Generally speaking, the ICAP announced by the FTA/OECD is not operational in Japan, because Japan has just been an observer country for the programme from the outset until mid-2017.[20] However, Japanese large multinational enterprises (MNEs) (with the assistance of the Japan Business Federation,[21] Keidanren) and the Ministry of Finance (the NTA) have disclosed limited information on ICAP Projects, even about Japan formal status of participating country from the outset of 2018. The most common comments among them would be:

> If a long-term solution is to be implemented based on Pillar 1, a profit calculation method should be clearly agreed upon. In addition, a mandatory binding arbitration must be introduced as a minimum standard and its implementation must be monitored to ensure tax certainty. If a global residual profit split method is to be introduced, a multilateral dispute prevention and resolution mechanism will be required, as disputes may involve more than two jurisdictions. In addition to the International Compliance Assurance Program (ICAP) etc., we may need to consider establishing a permanent auditing institution and dispute resolution body.[22]

This Keidanren's view on tax complexity and tax certainty as discussed by the OECD Consultation Document may well be shared by most Japanese businesses, large

20. At the early stage of the discussions on international tax compliance, OECD was in a context of administrative control on the compliance response of large MNEs, although recent pilot programmes rather seem to be about co-operative relationships between taxpayers and tax administrations. *See*, e.g., OECD, Co-operative Tax Compliance: Building Better Tax Control Frameworks (2016).
21. Japan Business Federation, Comments regarding the Public Consultation Document on Addressing the Tax Challenges of the Digitalization of the Economy, 2(4) (March 6, 2019). http://www.keidanren.or.jp/en/policy/2019/017.html (as of October 10, 2019).
22. *Id.*

or small, international or domestic, although this view does not focus on *ex ante* certainty, but on *ex post* dispute resolution. The view refers to the ICAP as a starting point of critical issue resolution in the area of international tax rules, specifically the interaction of national tax regulations of the relevant countries and the application of tax treaties. Even without a U.S.-type Compliance Assurance Programme (CAP) practice in Japan, Japanese taxpayers and practitioners have continuous access to the relevant tax administrations and can ask the administrations if specific facts and circumstances are correctly reported in their tax returns. Generally speaking, thus, Japanese taxpayers feel limited need for an international CAP as a tool for maintaining good compliance. As a result, the practical focus of the ICAP would be on the conduct of large MNEs, because Japanese large MNEs would experience CAP or ICAP in the foreign countries where they have business operations such as subsidiaries or branches. A practical advantage of accepting ICAP methodologies would be that Japanese taxpayers and the Japanese tax administrations could communicate better with each other, using the common international "language" of ICAP, and thereby achieve a higher level of compliance with both Japanese and foreign tax laws in the relevant jurisdictions.[23]

However, the attitude of the Japanese government on the ICAP is unclear. For the time being, neither the Ministry of Finance nor the NTA have made any public announcement about the Japanese participation in the ICAP, even as an observer. There is no information in Japan regarding any ICAP pilot programmes within the FTA community. They have not yet arranged new legislation nor prepared administrative guidance for the implementation of OECD-type compliance assurance measures, either under the domestic tax system or under tax treaties.[24] The OECD ICAP represents a new approach to tax compliance issues in international tax matters and would require a comprehensive legal basis.

On October 9, 2019, the OECD has published its latest public consultation document entitled "Secretariat Proposal for a 'Unified Approach' under Pillar One," following its past reports on BEPS and digital taxation.[25] This report proposes a new so-called unified approach to the taxation of highly profitable digital MNEs and purports to revise existing traditional rules for business income taxation of large foreign MNEs in countries where they sell their products. At first glance, this new proposal on business income taxation would require more compliance exertions by the taxpayer-MNEs than ever. On the other hand, by implementing such a new proposal, the Japanese tax administrations could enhance the country's involvement in the ICAP.

23. Research in Japan on OECD/ICAP is exemplified with the following meeting. E.g., Prof. Keiji Aoyama, "On the OECD/ICAP Program" held on October 30, 2017 at the research meeting of Japan Tax Institute, Tokyo, Japan. Prof. K. Aoyama is ex-officio of National Tax Administration. http://www.japantax.jp/iinkai/kokusai/index.htm (as of September 10, 2019).
24. The legal basis/authority for ICAP under Japanese law is still unclear because of this passive position of the Ministry of Finance and NTA.
25. At the same time, OECD has published a report on digital taxation to G20 Finance Ministers and Central Bank Governors entitled "OECD Secretary-General Tax Report to G20 Finance Ministers and Central Bank Governors," October 2019.

§9.06 SOME COMMENTS ON THE QUESTIONS PRESENTED BY THE OECD 2013 ICAP REPORT

The following presents some comments on the questions presented by the OECD 2013 ICAP Report.[26]

First, there are many de facto or legal relationships between taxpayers and tax administrations in Japan that are regulated by de facto or legal programmes, other than the OECD "co-operative compliance model." Most of these relationships are established through Administrative Circulars under which both taxpayers and administrations have access to certain process relating to compliance with the relevant laws. Even for mutual agreement procedures under the Tax Treaties, there is no domestic legal framework regulating the procedure. Because there is, in general, no time limit for such a treaty process, taxpayers can, at any time, ask the administration for its view on the issue and also ask NTA to initiate treaty Mutual Agreement Procedure (MAP) with the other contracting State.

So far as any de facto or legal procedure is concerned, Japanese tax laws do not discriminate specific classes of taxpayers against others. Any taxpayer who has a relevant interest could ask the administration for access to such a de facto or legal procedure. Thus, such procedures can be said to be open to any taxpayer segment.

Most of such de facto or legal procedures can be initiated by the taxpayer that wish to apply them.

In the case of a de facto procedure, there are substantially no conditions or requirements for acceptance, because of the informal character of this procedure.

Taxpayers can disclose the facts and circumstances of specific tax matters to the tax administrations, depending on the legal character of such matters, e.g., pricing methodologies under transfer pricing regulations, deductibility of payments to foreign affiliates, Permanent Establishment recognitions, applications in respect of tax treaties, and so on. Although it is not compulsory for the taxpayers to do so, there might be negative consequences if no disclosure is made and the administrations therefore cannot make the correct tax analysis.

The outcome of such a de facto consultation may not be made public, because this is personal information to be protected by the Disclosure of Information Act. Tax officials, in their capacity as National Public Servants, are legally bound to secrecy.

Currently, there is no practical work in progress with regard to a Multilateral ICAP. The NTA might be prepared to research the practicability of a Multilateral ICAP, because all countries have their own framework of tax administrations and practices, based on different legal systems, resulting in many complexities and uncertainties for MNEs.

The only exception to the general absence of a Multilateral ICAP procedure could be the so-called Bilateral/Multilateral APAs under the Tax Treaties. Specifically, as referred to above, the Bilateral APA between U.S. and Japan in the field of transfer pricing has more than thirty years of history, even though both countries have different

26. OECD, Co-operative Compliance: A Framework—From Enhanced Relationship to Co-operative Compliance, at 30 et seq. (2013).

legal frameworks of PCSs or APAs under their domestic laws. Although Mutual Agreement Procedures under the treaties and domestic PCS/APAs are designed for bilateral negotiations, multilateral MAPs or APAs are considered practical from the perspective of the Japanese administrations. The NTA sometimes asks foreign countries that have involvement in a specific tax case, to initiate and proceed bilateral procedures simultaneously among three countries, including Japan. Thus, some types of multilateral MAP/APAs can be said to exist in practice, similar to a multilateral CAP.

A recent revision of income tax treaties includes actions to give the so-called simultaneous tax audit a common institutional background for the treaty-partners. With such a coordinated tax audit, tax administrations of relevant countries, including Japan, could collect common information on the facts and circumstances with respect to relevant taxpayers.

These de facto procedures are fully voluntary for both taxpayers and administrations, in the sense that they are not legally binding. Each of the parties could withhold their response to the other party. Only with respect to the Mutual Agreement Procedure, Japanese administrations publish the practical procedure that applies to them and to the taxpayer, in the form of in-advance administrative interpretations of treaty rules for domestic application. However, the initiation of such treaty procedure depends on the view and position of the tax administrations. The tax administrations that are asked to start the procedure could review and audit the facts and circumstances of the case. On the Japanese side, the NTA would deliver a short written letter of confirmation on the methodology of pricing between given corporations and their foreign affiliates, as a confirmation of the facts and circumstances but without substantive arguments. Thus, the taxpayer involved in the procedure can only presume that their TP methodology(-ies) for specified types of transactions will be acceptable to the administration in the relevant tax year, provided the facts and circumstances are substantially the same as those presented during the PCS process. This confirmation would practically be respected and maintained by the administrations for, in principle, three taxable years in the future. On this basis, the taxpayer who has received such a confirmation can expect no action by the administration for the confirmed years on the transfer pricing matter at issue. However, tax administrations may audit or review even these confirmed years, if the taxpayer applies a different pricing methodology from the one confirmed through PCS, or if the economic conditions around the relevant transaction(s) have significantly changed from the projections under the confirmation. There is no penalty applicable in these circumstances.

Generally, there are no legal requirements for corporate taxpayers to disclose their risk management policy, risk appetite and tax strategy and principles. Taxpayers may have a tax control framework in place, although this is not a requirement to join the relationship programme of the abovementioned PCS or other programmes. The presence of a tax control framework does not influence how the tax administrations interact with taxpayers. In the past, blue-return taxpayers could enjoy a reduced chance of being tax audited as a factual expectation, although nowadays there is no advantageous treatment in this respect.

Whether they participate in a relationship programme or not, any taxpayer can easily access the relevant tax administrations given the open relationship between them. The communication process is not regulated and tax authorities might sometimes take longer time to respond to taxpayers' queries, because they seek to prepare as precise a response as possible.

In the context of an informal relationship between taxpayers and the administrations, the programme[27] would not allow taxpayers to go to the judicial courts. So far the main role of judicial courts has been the judicial resolution of legal disputes. Any legal issues under the programme could be brought to the judicial courts to resolve, even by non-residents/foreign taxpayers, once taxpayers receive decisions by the administrations that determine their tax position.

Because of the "observer" status of the Japanese government, there is no governmental or civil study or investigation that evaluates the result of (any part of) the Japanese ICAP. Rather, there is a lack of information from the tax administrations about OECD/ICAP in the Governmental publications.

On the other hand, the NTA has been publishing its annual reports on the PCS (International APA) under Tax Treaties for a long time.[28] Close observation of these reports shows that both the NTA and Japanese corporate taxpayers have become more sophisticated as their experiences, including dealings with foreign governments and taxpayers, have progressed. Insofar as the initial contact from the taxpayer to the administration is concerned, the administration is open to accept any query from taxpayers on international transfer pricing issues and will actively initiate the treaty MAP procedure with foreign treaty-partner countries, in the context of relief from international double taxation. As a result, the number of cases brought under MAP procedures gradually increased in the past in around fifteen years.[29]

§9.07 CONCLUSIVE REMARKS

Even today, Japanese International Co-operative tax compliance is not a legally systematic process under the tax legislation. There are several ways in which the administrations facilitate contact or query opportunities for taxpayers as an informal matter, but those opportunities are not institutionalized. The unstructured nature of these procedures may be a source of additional compliance burdens for both taxpayers

27. There are no procedures named "Programme" under the Japanese Tax Laws. However, for the convenience of the readers, I refer to the various relationships between taxpayers and tax administrations as Programmes.
28. In September 2003, the NTA first published its report on International Advance Pricing Agreements under Tax Treaties. After that, the NTA continuously published its annual reports on APA practices under the Treaty. Until 2010, those reports were called "APA Program Report," whereas the current reports are known as "Mutual Agreement Procedure Reports (MAP Reports)," because the Japanese commitment to a bi-lateral APA is based on the Treaty procedure of Mutual Agreement. An English version of each Report is available at the English website of the NTA. https://www.nta.go.jp/english/publication/map_report/index.htm.
29. There are several cases where final agreements with relevant foreign countries could not be reached, although the reasons for such failure to agree are not made public.

and administrations. Because the OECD ICAP purports to improve compliance standards on an international level, Japan should actively and positively take part in drafting a statutory framework for an International CAP with the aim to spread such "good practices" in the international tax community.

CHAPTER 10

Co-operative Compliance in Norway

Benedicte Brøgger & Kiran Aziz

§10.01 INTRODUCTION

This chapter gives an account of Co-operative Compliance practices in Norway based on the research conducted in the FairTax project.[1] The Co-operative Compliance practices in Norway are shaped by guidelines and recommendations from the Organisation of Economic Co-operation and Development (OECD). According to the OECD guidelines, tax compliance is defined as filing on time, in an orderly fashion and for the correct amount. The idea of Co-operative Compliance has roots in earlier policies to enhance relationships with large taxpayers. The enhancement policies aimed to change the quality of the relationships from controlling and reactive to more responsive and proactive in order to increase compliance and distribute the regulatory burden. The Co-operative Compliance policy included tax intermediaries in the enhanced relationships. The OECD policy comes with the caveat that each country needs to acknowledge social, cultural and political conditions when implementing the policy.

The Co-operative Compliance policy calls for co-operative relations with compliant taxpayers and more adversarial treatment of recalcitrant taxpayers. It institutionalizes a separation between compliant and non-compliant taxpayers and a practice of differential treatment.[2] The policy is contested on various grounds. One is that "cooperation may lead to the risk that 'compliance' will be confused with submission

1. https://www.umu.se/en/fairtax/.
2. Dabner, J.H., & Burton, M. (2015). Lessons for Tax Administrators for the Introduction of the OECD's "Enhanced Relationship Model: The Australasian Experience." Available at SSRN 2707918.

to the dominant will."[3] Other concerns are that it violates the principle of equality before the law, and that it blurs the distinction between lawmaking and execution.[4]

The findings from the FairTax research indicate that the local form of Co-operative Compliance practices in Norway minimized such risks.

The following pages present the Norwegian context and the local practices. The chapter concludes with the reflection that in Norway co-operation takes place because of the parties' need to sort out ambiguities in the large grey area between certain compliance and certain non-compliance due to difficulties in interpreting the law. Co-operation is an outcome of a mutual need to find out what compliance means by interpreting the law in the specific cases.

The empirical material in the research was based on interviews, document analyses and observations by researchers according to an ethnographic approach.

§10.02 THE NORWEGIAN CONTEXT

Norway is a unitary state with a strong central government. This affects the quality and form of the Co-operative Compliance practices. The Central Tax Office for Large Enterprises (LTO) is responsible for the tax administration of corporations. The office has worked with Co-operative Compliance since the office was established. This section presents how this came to be, and how gradually the OECD guidelines were adapted to the local context.

Norway has not adopted the procedure of a prior agreement and the project organization form of enhanced relationships/Co-operative Compliance programmes recommended by the OECD. The description of the infrastructure of co-operation therefore must outline the institutional structure framing everyday practices.

LTO's jurisdiction includes Norwegian-owned large corporations and foreign-owned corporations operating in Norway, with more than NOK 3 billion in annual turnover (about USD 345 million/EUR 300 million) required in order to be classified as a large corporation. A reorganization of LTO took place in 2014-2016. The scope of LTO tripled (from 75 to 220) as mid-sized corporations were included; the number of employees more than doubled (from 54 to 130) and value-added tax (VAT) was included among its responsibilities. The changes were implemented gradually as managers were hired, employees trained and new teams formed. One of the main purposes was to unite the different work cultures. However, there were no changes in the management. The core objective/mandate is still to serve large corporations.

A large company or group of companies is now defined as one with more than NOK 1 billion in annual turnover (about EUR 100 million). Each company is considered as an individual taxpayer and responsible for its own obligations. Many corporations have a tax policy in place, which regulates the tax control framework. The last five years have seen increased professionalization and specialization of companies' tax

3. Burton, M. (2007). Responsive Regulation and the Uncertainty of Tax Law: Time to Reconsider the Commissioner's Model of Cooperative Compliance? *eJournal of Tax Research*, *5*(1), 71-104.
4. OECD 2013. Co-operative Compliance: A Framework. From Enhanced Relationships to Co-operative Compliance. Preliminary Version. Assessed November 15, 2016. OECD Publishing.

functions. This is due to the global tax landscape, which is changing, leading to new requirements for responsible tax practices, especially for multinational companies. Against a backdrop of slow economic growth, low commodity prices and constrained development aid budgets, advanced and emerging economies alike are looking for ways to ensure that multinational companies are paying their fair share of taxes as they generate massive profits.

[A] The LTO Way

LTO was established in 1992 as part of a major tax reform. The tax reform was a move from tax on production to tax on consumption. Corporate tax rates were lowered in order to encourage capital build-up in companies and increase investment in productive capacity. In the early 1990s, the Norwegian economy experienced the after-shocks of a severe homespun financial crisis, the result of badly timed changes in fiscal policies in the 1980s. Inflation, bankruptcies and unemployment rates had soared for several years and the economy was at a standstill. The two largest commercial banks had gone bankrupt and their capital bases had to be rebuilt.

Another impetus for the tax reform was that in 1992, Norway became a member of European Union's (EU's) internal market through the membership in the European Economic Area and needed to adapt to its free market policies. In terms of fiscal policy, the Norwegian currency krone was tied to a basket of European currencies, later to become the euro. This limited the government's policy choices. The EU area was in an economic slump. The open competition of the EU's inner market would place Norwegian companies at a disadvantage if national corporate tax levels were higher than in other EU countries. If Norwegian companies relocated to other countries because of this, national tax revenue would diminish. So company taxes were lowered. This was an early example of the tax policies colloquially known as "tax for growth" and "the race to the bottom," which were to be common features of tax regulations in the 1990s and 2000s. Norway was an only early adapter to the new regulatory approach, propelled by the need to deal with a financial crisis and to prepare for the necessary deregulation required to enter EU's internal market.

LTO was set up in the midst of this turmoil. Its initial task was to work out the immediate legal and practical consequences of the tax reform. Part of the job was to encourage and guide the largest corporations with their adjustments to the new tax regime. Part of the mandate was also to uncover legal wrinkles that needed to be ironed out of the law.

LTO operationalized co-operation as an integral part of its tax administrative practices from the beginning. The managing director of the new office decreed that the LTO employees should actively engage with the taxpayers, meet and talk with them to find out their perceptions of the tax reform, practical problems and compliance issues. A work pattern was established that still is functioning more or less according to the same basic design.

LTO recruited highly qualified tax professionals who were organized in self-managed teams. Each team was responsible for a limited number of corporations. One team member served as the point of contact with a limited number of corporations. He or she coordinated all interaction between the tax agency and the corporation. Each had a counterpart in the corporation. To ensure impartiality, the composition of teams and contact persons changed every few years. The new teams met with corporation representatives to learn about company routines, to disseminate knowledge about the rules and regulations in general and to work out the practical effects of the tax reform in particular. Through series of face-to-face meetings, the parties gained knowledge of each other and a mode of trust was established.

LTO also employed a number of legal specialists and set up a few specialist teams. These teams provided the corporation team with specialists according to the need on a case-by-case basis. Team members shared specialist expertise and practical knowledge about actual corporate routines when they worked together. Specialist and generalist knowledge were blended and disseminated throughout LTO as team compositions regularly changed. There was no division of corporations into compliant or non-compliant, and no differential treatment according to these kinds of definitions as far as we could ascertain. Some tax officials said that it was important not to become biased against a corporation, even in case of strong disagreements. Some added that it was hard not to be angry or feel cheated, but that a conflict in one instance was not allowed to have a negative influence on all other instances.

This work practice has resulted in a strong company culture, which they call "the LTO way." An LTO tax administrator who previously worked with small and medium-sized enterprises in a county tax office said that she had heard of the LTO way at a seminar and applied for a position in LTO. She had worked for eight years in the local office. She preferred the work alongside the corporations, in spite of the occasional hard fight over interpretations, they were professional and aimed to comply. The new job required a two-hour commute every day compared to the twenty minutes required in the old job.

The company culture of LTO is also well known among its external stakeholders. An interest group representative fondly referred to LTO as a place for the "nerdy" tax people, those who go in deep and whose main interest is corporate taxation for its own sake and not for the money or a career. A prominent tax lawyer said he found the LTO people accessible and competent. He would contact them when a client asked about a new tax planning scheme of which he was in doubt. His experience was that the LTO people were willing to talk such issues through without committing to or expecting commitment to any one solution. The "LTO way" is an early example of a Co-operative Compliance practice. Tax directors in companies knew about LTO. It was the hub in the large corporation tax infrastructure of collaboration.

The problem for all stakeholders was that tax legislation, especially for corporations with international operations, is quite complex. In the words of a tax administrator: "You cannot safely walk the line, because no one knows where it is." The "LTO way" is an acknowledgment of this uncertainty and allows corporations to turn it into more measurable risk factors.

§10.03 THE PARALLEL ASSESSMENT AND CONTROL ROUTINE

"The LTO way" is based on a policy of continuous assessment and guidance of the taxpayers. There are several controls at transaction level, but rarely full-scale audits. The teams responsible for a corporation engage with it continuously and react to unusual occurrences and news whenever these appear, regardless of what moment it is in the annual cycle of tax work and the risk status of the corporation. Also, if there is a change in the tax laws, that may be a reason for extra attention. In the words of one tax official: "it is better to help them get it right the first time." Contact may take the form of a phone call or an email or a letter, depending on the seriousness of the issue and the perceived openness and accessibility of the corporation's tax managers. The general view was that the corporations aimed to comply.

LTO's operations follow an annual cycle. In addition to the routine tasks, the teams are actively monitoring their corporations. They gain information from many different sources and are on the lookout for factors that may indicate non-compliance. LTO gets information about deviations from the corporation's normal order of operations from many sources. Low quality of the corporation's internal tax control framework is another indicator of risk of non-compliance. A number of different controls also reveal inconsistencies. In all, the compliance status of the taxpayer is assessed continuously. LTO is concerned that numbers do not tell everything, the tax administrator needs to know the stories behind the numbers to make an assessment about possible non-compliance. The teams have responsibility to follow up such information.

Contacts start either at the request of the corporations or their advisors or because LTO staff find something in the papers that they do not understand. Contact is made preferably by phone or email to ask for more information. All such activities are documented in a separate registry.

If it appears to be something to dig further into, letters are sent. If the written exchanges do not provide enough information there will be meetings. Experience and intuition are crucial to identify which cases will turn out to be complicated. Only after the checks and internal deliberations a decision will be made to open a case. A formal notification will be issued. This may mean an extension of deadlines. Subsequent decisions are made in the hierarchy of the tax administration and not by the teams. This has allowed tax agency people to call on the corporations to check on a suspicious transaction or clarify an issue of which there is doubt. Likewise, corporations and tax advisors have had the possibility to confer with the tax administration when they had any questions.

LTO would not immediately assume foul play if a suggestion turned out to be too close to the large grey areas between compliance and non-compliance. The LTO way demonstrates a number of the same practices as the enhanced relationship guidelines recommend: close relations with the corporations and due care to avoid adversarial relations. This is helped by the routine that if a corporation contests a ruling made by LTO, the case will be sent to the Legal department and taken over by one of its lawyers.

§10.04 RISK ASSESSMENT METHODOLOGY

In 2009, LTO began to implement the OECD methodology for tax risk management in its routines. According to the OECD definition, compliance is about filing on time, in an orderly fashion, and for the correct amount (OECD 2009). Tax officers from Norway knew the methodology well from their experience in various OECD groups on tax compliance in the 2000s. A number of projects and working groups in the tax authorities had spent several years operationalizing the recommendations and adapting them to the Norwegian context. LTO have further operationalized the recommendations and have identified a number of indicators for assessing the level of risk of non-compliance of the corporations in their census.[5] Risk assessment was made a part of the annual cycle of work.

A national survey was carried out to gain knowledge about Norwegian corporations' will to comply. The methodology classifies taxpayers into three categories: the majority who do comply, a smaller group of taxpayers who want to comply, but do not have a high enough quality in their internal tax management system, and the minority who do not want to comply. A color symbol system was added as a visual aid to classification. The high-risk taxpayers are colored red, the medium-risk taxpayers yellow, and the taxpayers that represent little risk for non-compliance are colored green. A tax vernacular seems to have evolved too, for example in talk about "red" or "green" taxpayers. The taxonomy is rough but has the advantage of being an economical way to convey a mass of information. The taxpayers were not informed of their methodology or their status. All corporations were categorized. It was the nature of the case that determined treatment and not assessment of the willingness to pay taxes.

§10.05 THE PILOT PROJECT IN ENHANCED RELATIONSHIPS

Part of the work to refine the risk assessment methodology was a pilot project. In Norway it was called an "Enhanced Dialogue" (Fordypet dialog). The project had a remarkable trajectory. Its aim was to increase compliance by more targeted and closer participation between LTO and large corporate taxpayers. It started in 2011 and formally ended in 2013. Twelve corporations participated. The corporations as well as LTO channeled best practice lessons into their own internal management systems as each saw fit. LTO used it to refine its risk assessment methodology and educate the teams about how to evaluate the qualities of the corporations' internal tax quality systems. An evaluation report summed up findings at the end of the project. The straightforward nature of the project is remarkable given the critique of enhanced relationship projects in other countries.[6]

5. The documents describing the risk assessment methodology are classified. The account here is therefore of a general nature.
6. "The Stevens report" 2012. Tax supervision—Made to measure. Flexible when possible, strict where necessary. Committee Horizontal Monitoring Tax and Customs Administration, The

What made the difference? The OECD guidelines are part of the answer. The main reason, however, was the already established pattern of responsive relations, the LTO way. There may also have been features in the design and management of the project itself that account for the smooth flow. Three design features of the project are possible explanations of why the project ran only briefly and caused little conflict.

First, project activities were kept strictly separated from tax filing and assessment. Participation in the project did not mean preferential treatment and it did not provide a temporary tax haven. The project team adhered strictly to this principle. This is illustrated by the fact that one corporation received a note about an audit during the project. The company did complain about having to deal with different units in Tax Norway, but accepted the reasons why, and continued to participate in the project.

Second, participation in the project was voluntary. The aim of the project was to improve compliance, but participation was neither a reward for being compliant nor a punishment for being non-compliant. The project team spent more than a year in advance of the project start to recruit participants. This was slow and hard work. Several corporations declined. The most common reasons given were lack of time or that they could see no benefits from it. The twelve corporations that in the end chose to participate had a mix of reasons for participating, from wanting to improve their own routines, to understand tax risks, or simply to use the opportunity to get to know LTO better.

Third, it was designed as a knowledge development project. It took the form of open-ended, participatory inquiry. A small, internal project team worked with the participating corporations. The project team had separate meetings with each corporation and arranged joint meetings with all participants. The tax administrators inquired about the setup of the corporations' internal control systems. They also conveyed information about tax regulations and tax administration routines and requirements. The dialogs enabled meta-communication about ambiguous definitions and conflicting demands, but stopped well short of discussing concrete cases. Hence, the project made it possible to thematize "compliance" as a relatively neutral topic and not as a morally or legally loaded pointer to some suspicious behavior of the corporation.

This was a dialog project to enhance dialog, and so it "walked the talk." The project design made it possible to avoid the problem that cooperative relations were a reward for a corporation's nice behavior. However, the project design may also be one of the reasons why the project went smoothly. There were no material conflicts of interest and no questions asked about actual compliance. It was a pilot project and its purpose was learning and development. The issues of differential treatment and of being non-co-operative were not relevant.

Hague, the Netherlands. http://download.belastingdienst.nl/belastingdienst/docs/tax_supervision_made_to_measure_tz0151z1fdeng.pdf Assessed September 2, 2016.

§10.06 THE "NORMAL" PROCESS AFTER THE EXTENSION OF THE CENTRAL OFFICE

The risk assessment methodology was implemented along with the extension of LTO, and the existing work processes were revised. While previously LTO annual work plan (called annual wheel) dictated that tax assessment should be done between May and September, the new routine shortened this time period. New employees were hired from other tax offices with other traditions of collaboration. A recurrent and contested internal issue in Tax Norway has been how to ensure tax compliance, with two schools of thought. One held that taxpayers should be subject to reviews after their filings, and if there are suspicions of non-compliance, then tax audits must be performed. This is the same as the traditional "command and control posture." The Regional Offices worked according to this principle. The people who ascribed to this approach were the ones most skeptical of enhanced relationships/Co-operative Compliance initiatives as well. The other school of thought was that a more real-time and responsive posture would be more efficient, i.e., to monitor the taxpayers continuously, be available to answer questions of a general nature, and follow up immediately whenever questions arose. This was the practice of LTO and its normal routine of "parallel assessment and control." The pros and cons of each were the subject of internal debates, explored by various committees and in various documents.

With the extension, these two cultures were brought together in the company teams, as new employees were placed in teams in the established Central Office practice. The team members were supposed to learn from each other and to contribute to the refinement of the risk assessment methodology in the process. The companies noticed the differences, but were uncertain about what to make of it and what kind of relationship the Central Office now wants.

After the extension of the Central Office, the companies noticed that they received letters inquiring about compliance issues dating years back. The companies found the requirements more burdensome than earlier inquiries as they increased the workload, disregarded earlier understandings and seemed to be based on unspoken assumptions of poor quality of their previous tax filings. The earlier trust and unspoken social contract between tax authorities and companies was questioned by the taxpayers. After the changes, the taxpayers' reactions were more systems-critical and they found the responses from the Central Office to be more adversarial.

This indicates a need for trust-establishing initiatives if the previous quality of the co-operation is to continue. In order to enhance collaboration, the parties also need to collaboratively establish the rules of the collaboration. This was not part of the design of the changes that were rolled out in front of the companies and their advisors. They were the result of decisions about the administrative routines in Tax Norway and Tax Norway only. How those changes should in fact occur is something the tax management systems of the companies were not very clear on, nor the advisors, the companies or the researchers. For example, in 2013, some months before the extension, one of the researchers asked about the companies' responses to the inclusion of VAT with the Central Office. Units working with VAT in companies are usually separate from units that work with corporate tax. Management of the two tax forms requires different routines, knowledge and skills. Had possible changes in the routines within the Central Office been discussed with the companies? Would it require change of contact persons? Someone versed in both tax forms perhaps? The Central Office had not considered informing the companies.

What the stakeholders have in common, even if there are different cultural logics that shape their understanding of taxes and how to comply, is an interest in maintaining their standing and public legitimacy. The stakeholders also have a shared interest in a level playing field, and open and transparent processes in order to create predictability. They therefore have vested interests in collaborating, which reduce the chances of conflicts to escalate, and for practices that are cost-effective, legal and civil.

§10.07 MEASURING COMPLIANCE

The level of tax compliance is not measured as the "tax gap," that is the gap between assessed and actual tax revenue, but by the quality of the tax filing process, its orderliness and predictability, and the quick and complete answering of questions.

Instead it is by implementing the risk assessment methodology that LTO aims to recover taxes that have been avoided. However, LTO's top management said that in their experience the large corporations aimed to comply. Responsible corporations aim to comply. There is high risk for them in not complying, because the loss of trust and reputation as a responsible business partner can be large. Getting a visit from the tax agency is in itself regarded as a sign that not all is well and something corporations try to avoid. Corporations regard taxes as a cost, a price for operating in Norway. They expect the tax authorities to maintain a level playing field so that competition is not skewed in favor of non-serious companies that can lower their prices because they avoid paying their dues.

The extensive mutual knowledge that was the result of the LTO way is another argument for not measuring the tax gap. The stakeholders have a fair idea of each other's roles and responsibilities in the work to assess, collect and pay corporate taxes. These relationships provide a platform of trust for identifying and sorting out uncertainties and risk factors in the corporations' dispositions before actual decisions are made.

A tax audit is costly, and so the logic is that by targeting high- and medium-risk taxpayers a number of benefits will follow. Productivity and efficiency of the tax administration will increase as correct and timely returns are submitted once the medium-risk taxpayers learn how and what to file. A higher level of compliance will close the gap between what should be paid and what is actually paid.

For LTO, one challenge is that there are too few people in the tax agency to go through the dealings and books of every large corporation every year. In Norway, corporations are taxed at the level of the individual company that is consolidated into its books, so even though each company has to file separately, limiting the contact points to the corporation was a way to outsource responsibility for tax compliance to the organization itself. The corporation has much of the same problem. The large corporations have to be reliable in their business dealings, need to have their books in order to manage the complex business efficiently, and there is too much at stake for them to risk an unreliable reputation.

The corporations have highly qualified personnel and as one tax administrator put it: "if they want to cheat they will." The point the tax administrator made was that even if they can cheat, it should not be assumed that they will. Only a small percentage of the corporations are unwilling to pay taxes, more often it is the case that they do not know the rules and interpretations and need guidance. In many cases, there is a problem of knowing beforehand where the exact line between legitimate tax planning and outright tax avoidance goes, not only for the corporations, but for the tax advisors and tax inspectors as well. Business deals do not come fully formed, they are developed and a lot of input is needed before a decision is made. Initially, there is a large degree of uncertainty. Therefore, the corporations and their advisors have an interest in knowing what LTO thinks about the tax aspects before committing to an arrangement that may later prove to be illicit. On the other hand, they do not want to be too committed in the early stages of a case, so there is a need for some sort of non-committing discussions between the corporations and the tax agency. If the signal from the tax agency is that the planned activities are on the wrong side of the line, it is better to withdraw before too much has been invested in preparations for a deal.

§10.08 SUMMARY

Co-operative Compliance policies and programmes have been in place in many countries for fifteen years. Programmes in twenty-one countries were surveyed.[7]The programmes differed in their criteria for corporations' participation in terms of:

(1) whether participation requirements were written into laws and regulations;
(2) whether participation was by application or invitation;
(3) whether disclosure was mandatory or voluntary;
(4) whether pending issues had to be resolved;
(5) other conditions.

The criteria are of limited use in a discussion of practices in Norway. First, the routines were not formally codified. They were described in internal, classified documentation that the taxpayers did not have access to. Second, corporations were required to participate, since there was no special project of Co-operative Compliance. Third, disclosure was mandatory, again because paying taxes is a duty. Fourth, pending issues did not have to be resolved. They were the responsibility of other units at LTO, not the administration. Other conditions were the same as in other countries and depended on the mandate. The LTO mandate was determined by parliamentary decisions about company and tax law. It separated corporations according to tax

7. OECD 2013. Co-operative Compliance: A Framework—From Enhanced Relationships to Co-operative Compliance. Preliminary Version. Assessed November 15, 2016. OECD Publishing.

regime, size, ownership and industry. The OECD caveat that Co-operative Compliance needs to take the national context into consideration proved to be a good precaution.

The survey also compared in terms of other practical consequences like:

(1) Information to taxpayers
(2) Culture changes
(3) Level of contact
(4) Tax control
(5) Availability of metrics.

In the Norwegian case, the situation was as follows: First, little general information about administrative routines was shared with taxpayers. Second, there were cultural changes. Some went in the direction of more adversarial relations, as quality of treatment more depended on assumptions about the motivations of taxpayers. Others went in the direction of more certainty and predictability due to better-developed control mechanisms that did not disturb the ongoing flows of interactions. Third, tax administrators said that the level of contact was hard to maintain after the reorganization, as there were more corporations and employees included in the "LTO way." This may be a passing problem though, as the new organization settles. Companies also experience that people they did not know or trust started to demand new things of them. Fourth, tax control did improve, routines became more efficient in the tax administration, and especially the less professional corporations implemented more professional tax management systems. Fifth, there was the recurrent problem of measuring tax compliance. This was the theme in a separate project to assess the effects of the reorganization. The project design combined formative and summative evaluations. Formative evaluations happened when people can share their own theories about compliance, use them to discuss current practices and results, and decide on how to use the findings from their internal investigation for making changes to their own practice. Summative evaluation does, as the term says, sum up results, most often by means of statistics.

In summing up the account of Co-operative Compliance practices in Norway and reflecting on how the OECD policy is adapted to it, there is one further issue that may be of consequence for development of new programmes.

The 2001 OECD study that first recommended co-operation refers to two main obstacles to compliance—motivation and ambiguity.[8] The co-operation initiatives are divided along the same lines but aim for different groups. Those aimed at reducing ambiguity are for internal use in OECD and national tax administrations, like the the Forum on Tax Administration, bilateral and multilateral agreements the mutual agreement procedure, and Transfer Pricing policies. The initiatives aimed at increasing motivation are designed to change the behavior of the taxpayers. The account demonstrated how the practices in Norway differ from this design. These practices aim to reduce ambiguity for taxpayers, and by extending a helping hand expect the same

8. OECD 2001. Compliance Measurement—Compliance Notice. Tax Guidance Series. OECD Publishing.

consideration in return. The differences in interests when it comes to how much tax to pay are acknowledged, but the interactions do not have the form of negotiations. The co-operative practices are a means to work out pragmatic solutions in acknowledgment of the differences in interests. This practice does get support from conclusion in the latest OECD study of compliance practices. It indicates that adversarial treatment may not have the positive effect on behavior that was anticipated, "research also suggests that in general, inspection frequencies and the imposition of sanctions do not exhibit a market correlation with the degree of compliance."[9] The condition of mutual recognition between the parties in Norway had not come easily or of its own accord. It was the result of tax managers' and lawyers' need to sort out ambiguity. It was spurred by their need for support to face opposition within their own organizations with programmes and systems disregarded or unpopular among managers with profit and loss responsibilities. Most of all, however, it was the result of a long and systematic investment in competent personnel and administrative routines by LTO, in the DNA of its tax administrative practice.

The Norwegian case is an example of a maximum variation case because of the much longer history of collaborative relationships and the outcome of the work with tax risk. The combination of a collaborative way of working and systematic risk management and monitoring may either reflect a most likely scenario of future tax administration or perhaps the least likely.

9. OECD 2013. Co-operative Compliance: A Framework—From Enhanced Relationships to Co-operative Compliance. Preliminary Version. Assessed November 15, 2016.

CHAPTER 11

Co-operative Compliance and ICAP in the Netherlands

Ronald Russo

§11.01 INTRODUCTION

In the Netherlands, Co-operative Compliance started in 2004-2005 as a result of an investigation by the tax administration into the then existing relationships between multinational companies and themselves. They found these relationships were based on lack of trust, working mostly on the basis of audits in the past and therefore not very efficient. The tax administration also took some societal developments into consideration (a report from the WRR, a scientific advisory institution on the future of the state, giving horizontalization as a desirable development[1]), as well as the research on responsive regulation. This led to the development of a new way of interacting with multinationals, known as horizontal monitoring (HT), which was tried as a pilot in 2005. From there, the concept of HT was further developed and widened to also encompass small and medium-sized enterprises (SMEs). Besides the programmes for multinationals and SMEs, the tax administration also engaged in covenants with specific sectors.[2] We will not go into details of these specific sectors' covenants, as their character is more of a general regulatory nature and as a rule they are not relevant for Co-operative Compliance. Where they are relevant, we will mention them.

In this chapter, we will first look at HT for multinationals in section §11.02, followed by the programme for SMEs in section §11.03. In section §11.04 we will discuss International Compliance Assurance Programme (ICAP) and we will finish with some concluding remarks in section §11.05.

1. https://www.wrr.nl/publicaties/rapporten/2002/10/29/de-toekomst-van-de-nationale-rechts staat.
2. *See* https://belastingdienst.nl/wps/wcm/connect/bldcontentnl/belastingdienst/intermediairs/toezicht/convenanten/convenanten_horizontaal_toezicht/.

§11.02 CO-OPERATIVE COMPLIANCE FOR MULTINATIONALS

As stated in the introduction, in 2004-2005, a new way of interacting between the tax administration and multinationals was shaped. The basis was that the new interaction should be more "horizontal" (i.e., equal), more based on trust as opposed to distrust and work more in the present than in the past.[3] This new relationship is formalized in a covenant which both parties sign. The traditional concept was in contrast referred to as vertical supervision. The new way of working (referred to as HT) was developed entirely within the discretionary mandate of the tax administration: there was and is no legislation on HT, so the following is based on guidelines published by the tax administration,[4] further to be referred to as HT Guidance. Another goal of the new way of working was efficiency: compliant taxpayers would consume less time which the tax administration could then use for less compliant taxpayers.

The HT Guidance defined the main elements of HT and presented instruments to deal with them. These elements are: trust, mutual understanding and transparency, which we will discuss separately. After that, we will discuss the HT process in more detail, as well as the possible challenges that exist within HT. We will conclude with some future developments. As a general comment HT is the preferred model of the tax administration, but the concept cannot function without vertical supervision. If HT does not work for some reason, the tax administration always has vertical supervision to fall back on.

[A] Trust

The element of trust was primarily introduced to mark the difference with the previous situation, which was one of distrust between multinationals[5] and the tax administration. The tax administration formalized this new approach by contacting the boards of multinationals and offering them initial trust in the way they managed their tax affairs. If a board was willing to participate, they were asked to return the trust by signing a covenant. The covenant is standardized (the same for all participants) and contains no other information than that the parties concerned promise to work in trust, understanding and transparency. The function of the covenant is mainly that the board of the company has signed an agreement with the tax administration, while in the old days taxes were more or less exclusively dealt with by the tax department. In the new approach, taxes appeared on the board's agenda. In the covenant, both parties stress that all existing legal instruments and obligations remain intact. In other words, the covenant does not change the legal framework in any way.

---

3. For more information *see* R. Veldhuizen in "Tax Assurance," Kluwer, Deventer 2015, ed R. Russo, Chapter 6.
4. *See* https://download.belastingdienst.nl/belastingdienst/docs/leidraad_toezicht_grote_ondernemingen_dv4231z1fd.pdf.
5. We use the term multinationals loosely here. We refer to section G for more precise current and future criteria. In practice the pilot for HT was aimed at the twenty-five biggest companies in the Netherlands, all multinationals.

Obviously the trust expressed by the tax authorities must be founded: this is accomplished by the participating company having (or intending to build) an adequate internal control framework regarding its tax position. This is commonly referred to as a tax control framework (TCF) and is one of the pillars of HT.

[B] Understanding

The understanding element of HT mainly deals with the notion that the parties involved take each other's position into consideration. This means that the tax administration will try to answer questions from the multinational within a reasonable timeframe (as speed is fundamental) and vice versa. Basically, a trust-based relationship will also be one of understanding, but this element is nonetheless always mentioned separately. For multinationals, things like reputation and publicity are very important and the tax administration should take this into consideration in maintaining the relationship. A danger might be that there is too much "understanding", as a result of which a multinational may receive preferential treatment (sweetheart deals). This should not be possible and safeguards should be implemented to prevent it without losing the benefits of understanding one another's position.

[C] Transparency

Transparency is another important pillar of HT. The multinational commits to sharing actively all relevant information with the tax administration. This obligation extends beyond existing legal obligations, which only state that a taxpayer must provide all information asked for by the tax administration. This is one of the ways parties want to achieve a situation of working in the present rather than in the past. Ideally, the multinational shares all relevant information and the tax administration responds by quickly giving its opinion. In this situation, the (formal) tax return will contain no surprises as all vital matters have already been discussed and, where possible, agreed.

The tax administration in its turn shares its plan of action with the multinational. Both parties therefore share information that, in the old days, they always kept to themselves, thus creating an atmosphere of mutual trust to generally "work this out." In practice this does not always work. One practical point is: what to share and what not? If a multinational were to share all details of their operations, the tax administration would be swamped by too much information. Ideally, parties would work on a trial and error basis to achieve a level of sharing that is workable for both. Another difficulty that can arise is that parties share information, but do not agree on the tax consequences. In such a case it must be possible to "agree to disagree" and bring the matter to a third party (for instance a court of law) to get a decision without effecting the relationship. In effect this is only possible if parties differ on the application of the law in a certain case, the facts should be clear.

Because multinationals are, as a rule, not keen on having a (substantial) provision for uncertain taxes, they might have a tendency to concede points of discussion to avoid disagreements. Alternatively, in discussing a disputed tax position, both the tax authorities and the taxpayer might make concessions in order to reach agreement. In this case, they have achieved a practical solution which is transparent for them, but not for the rest of the world. If there would have been a court case, the rest of the world could use the resulting case law to assess their positions. So this form of bartering under HT could mean less transparency for the tax world in general.

[D] The HT Process in Steps

[1] Initial HT Meeting

This meeting is intended to explore the possibilities for a company to enter the HT programme. The meeting must be attended by the board of the company. Strategic goals and values of HT are discussed and, if necessary, explained. An important item is the "tone at the top": the attitude and behavior of the board is important and should be in line with the values of the organization, as well as with the aims of HT. An organization that regularly seeks the boundaries of what is permissible in taxation is not suited for HT; we will come back to this in section §11.02[E][4].[6] The meeting may also be attended by external advisors, but that is for the company to decide.

[2] Compliance Reconnaissance

In this step the company and tax administration explore together in more detail whether or not HT is possible in this specific case. To this end key personnel is interviewed by the tax administration and a decision on the possibility of HT is formulated on the basis of the information thus provided. The organization must be dedicated to HT and must also be able to conform to the expectations of the tax administration. These expectations, along with the expectations of the organization, are discussed in some detail. It is possible that the admission into HT is conditional, for instance to an upgrade of the TCF within a certain time.

Other actions might include quick scans of certain areas or systems. If the company has a tax department, this department will be intensively involved in the compliance reconnaissance. Some issues to be discussed are:

- Mission and vision of the organization.
- Operational goals and key performance indicators.
- The level of compliance (in general).
- The risk appetite in relation to tax planning.
- The tax governance and principles.
- The policy on remunerations.

6. *See* Chapter 3 Guide HT.

Given their importance, the internal control processes relating to tax are discussed separately and in more detail. Specifically, one of the key elements to be discussed is how these internal controls are monitored, both internally and externally.[7]

[3] Dealing with Problems from Past Years

If a company and the tax administration enter into HT, they are mainly oriented toward the present and the future. The pre-HT era should be closed as much as possible. If at all possible, disputes should be resolved by either reaching a compromise or agreeing to disagree on a specific point *before* the HT covenant is entered into. As both parties should now have a new, forward-looking mindset under HT, it should be easier to resolve the differences that may have existed for many years. This outlook is beneficial for both parties: clearing up conflicts enables a fresh start. The added advantage for the company is the external visibility, as the provision for uncertain tax positions in the public accounts can be reduced or at least calculated more precisely.[8]

[4] Covenant and Evaluation

If the previous steps lead both parties to (still) want HT, parties enter into a covenant in which they agree to work according to the basic elements of HT: trust, understanding and transparency. The covenant is signed by the board of the company and by a representative of the management of the tax administration. The tax administration refers to the covenant as a gentlemen's agreement, but we feel that it is a civil law contract as a result of the fact that both parties now have more obligations than before the covenant. We will come back to this issue in section §11.02[E][5].[9]

[E] Challenges and Possible Friction Points

[1] Guidance with Respect to Internal Controls

The primary view of the tax administration is that the TCF is the responsibility of the company. Corporate governance rules demand internal control in key areas of the company and taxes are generally considered a key area, meaning that a TCF should in many cases be in place irrespective of HT.[10] Furthermore, in their opinion a TCF is always entity specific: there is no room for a uniform model. These circumstances have lead the tax administration to the conclusion that it is not their responsibility to provide guidance on how to set up a TCF.

7. *See* Chapter 4 Guide HT.
8. *See* Chapter 5 Guide HT.
9. *See* Chapter 6 Guide HT.
10. For more information *see* R. Russo, "Risk management, Internal Control and Cooperative Compliance in Taxation" in *The future of Risk Management*, Volume I, Palgrave Macmillan 2019, Cham Switzerland, editors P. De Vincentiis, F. Culasso, S. Cerrato, pp. 330/336.

Despite that conclusion, the HT Guidance does contain a separate chapter on tax controls (Chapter 7), in which the view of the tax administration on what constitutes an adequate TCF is expressed. Reference is made to the COSO[11] model, though only as an example. The Guide HT provides generic observations on the internal controls in general and the tax controls in specific. These have to be aligned with the strategic goals of the company, promote efficient operational management, enhance the quality of internal and external reporting and foster compliance. The guidance continues by expressing the key points identified for tax control purposes, presented as a table. These key points are not surprising, but we would like to highlight two.

Tax planning

Under this heading, the tax administration explains that tax planning is a necessary and normal action for a company to control its tax cost. It is important to distinguish between this type of rational tax planning and aggressive tax planning, the latter being branded as undesirable. Particularly in the popular press, but also in politics, the difference between the two terms is often lost. We refer to section §11.02[E][4] for further comments on aggressive tax planning.

Monitoring

Monitoring is mentioned in the table of key tax controls, but clarification in the Guide HT is very brief. In practice, however, it is one of the most important aspects of HT. Straightforwardly put, monitoring is assessing whether the internal controls of a company are actually effective. Even more importantly, if monitoring shows that something does not (completely) work, action should mandatorily be taken to amend the relevant processes. Monitoring reports are therefore extremely suited to form an opinion on the workings of a TCF and how adequate the company's improvement procedures are functioning. The techniques used for monitoring are often similar to generally accepted audit standards. For this reason, some guidance on monitoring can be found in the audit guidelines of the tax administration (CAB).[12] The CAB contains a table on the reduction of audit work. Theoretically, a reduction of 100% is possible if third party audits (or from the company itself) are available and can be relied upon.[13] The theoretical basis for this reduction can be found in the layer model (CAB, Chapter 2). Although the CAB is primarily applicable to tax audits, the tax administration links it to monitoring in HT.

[2] Different Covenants Apply

As described in section §11.02[D][4], HT is formalized in a covenant between the company and the tax administration. It is, however, possible that a company employs a tax service provider (TSP) (a professional party providing tax compliance services).

11. *See* https://www.coso.org.
12. *See* https://download.belastingdienst.nl/belastingdienst/docs/cab_dv4221z3fd.pdf.
13. *See* CAB, p. 24/25.

The TSP may also have a covenant with the tax administration. If so, their clients may be included in the provider's HT scheme (*see*, in more detail, Chapter 3). The covenants with TSPs are intended mainly as a means for SMEs (who cannot enter into an individual covenant) to join HT, but multinational companies can also use TSPs for specific services. The question arises which covenant should then be leading: the individual covenant of the company or the covenant of the TSP. There is a separate chapter in the Guide HT on this subject that deals with some practical issues (such as which part of the tax administration is competent in specific cases), but the main message is that this should be arranged on a case-by-case base.[14]

[3] Fines and HT

If a company has entered HT, both the company and the tax administration have the expectation that the TCF is adequate so that the resulting tax returns are free of material mistakes. In practice, however, mistakes can always occur and the question then is how to deal with them. As the standard covenant states, all tax rules and regulations are in no way restricted in their use, so mistakes that are discovered must be corrected according to standard procedure. The question is whether this correction may (or must) be accompanied by a fine. According to the general rules, this is the case, but the tax administration may always weigh the specifics of a case to limit the fine. Whether or not a company has entered in to HT might be such a specific factor, potentially leading to reductions.

There is also a distinction to be made regarding the sort of fine, relating to the nature of the error discovered. On the one hand, there are fines for a return that is too late or a payment that is too late. These are relatively minor affairs and the connected fines are imposed automatically. On the other hand, there are fines for willingly filing a wrong return. The behavior leading to such a fine does not really fit within the basic values of HT. It does not automatically mean that HT is terminated. The wrong return could be due to an action of an employee that was not known or condoned by the board, in which case the tax administration could still have trust in the board of the company.

And obviously, there is a difference if the company reports the mistake itself as opposed to the mistake being discovered in an audit by the tax administration. In the latter case trust will by definition be an issue, in the former much less so.

So, fines within HT are possible, but much depends on the circumstances, as described above.[15]

[4] Aggressive Tax Planning

As mentioned in section §11.02[E][1], tax planning is a normal, or even a necessary business activity. There is, however, a turning point where tax planning becomes so

14. *See* Chapter 11 Guide HT.
15. This issue is dealt with in Chapter 12 of the Guide HT.

aggressive that HT may no longer be possible. There are no formal requirements to the company's tax principles or risk appetite (e.g., in order to determine whether or not a company is low risk, as happens in other jurisdictions). In theory a company can enter HT with an aggressive tax policy, as long as it is transparent. In the Guide HT the tax administration draws some lines. Their first remark is that a tax inspector cannot demand that a company must pay its fair share. However, if a company applies so-called tax aggressive methods, the tax inspector must reflect on that behavior with the company. The covenant will as a rule not be ended by the tax administration because of aggressive structures. However, it clearly remains a difficult issue for the tax administration, as they remark that aggressive structuring may influence the way they deploy their monitoring and audit (meaning that these may increase in intensity). Although the difference between normal and aggressive behavior is very relevant, the Guide HT does not clarify it. In a footnote they give an example: deducting the same amount multiple times or claiming a deduction without a corresponding inclusion of taxable income. In fact, this approach quite resonates with the OECD's BEPS project.[16]

[5] Conflict Within HT or Regarding the Status of the Covenant

As mentioned in section §11.02[C], it is possible to have a difference of opinion within an HT relationship. In such cases, a third party (usually the competent tax court) will have to decide. Within HT this should be possible without damaging the relationship and existing trust between parties. Doubts have been raised at this point: although the relationship is called "horizontal," the tax administration still has all its legal instruments (such as tax audits) at its disposal. Would this not make the company inclined to agree quicker than perhaps desirable to propositions of the tax administrations, to avoid damage to the relationship? Another point is, as mentioned before, that fewer cases would be brought to court, thus resulting in less case law. Although this is in itself a good thing, it is not beneficial for other companies in similar conditions because they do not know what deals have been struck.

Another potential issue is a conflict concerning the HT process itself, i.e., not directly connected to the tax position of the company. For instance, a company may want to enter HT, but the tax administration denies it, or the tax administration may want to end HT and the company does not agree. In these cases, there is no possibility to go to a tax court, so the only way left for the taxpayer would be to go to a general civil law court on the ground that a contract (the covenant) has been breached.[17] In practice this has not happened yet, also because the tax administration seems to be handling matters cautiously. Covenants are not easily ended, but they are sometimes suspended pending certain specific circumstances (such as improvements to the TCF). Another example of the caution with which the tax administration operates is the possibility to

16. *See* Guide HT, section 2.5.
17. Civil law rules also apply in the pre contract phase.

co-operate with a taxpayer *as if* there was a covenant ("convenant-conform werken"[18]).

[F] Empirical Research on HT

[1] Stevens Committee

The Stevens Committee, which investigated the proper functioning of HT, published its report in 2012.[19] The committee's goal was to evaluate HT, identify challenges and suggest improvements. The committee found that HT rests on three hypotheses, which cannot all be proven effective. The committee states that the first hypothesis (more trust and responsibility for the company) has been proven correct. The same is true for the second hypothesis (HT can lead to more effective supervision by relying on control and audit activities of third parties: the layer model). The third hypothesis is that supervision is more cost effective for company as well as tax administration, through the first and second hypothesis. The committee found that this hypothesis cannot be (entirely) proven and differs for multinationals and SME's. It encourages more research on this issue. The committee offers some points for improvement: firstly, to give more guidance to the TCF, and secondly, for the authorities to make more use of the work of the external auditor.

[2] Review of the Large Companies Supervision Process

In June 2017, the tax administration published a report following its investigation of the dedicated supervision process applied to large companies.[20] The aim of the investigation was to reach insights on HT and on the tax compliance of these companies. For this investigation, the desired influence of transparency, tax control and tax strategy on compliance was defined in terms of correct, complete and timely returns and payments of tax. A sample of 350 large companies was taken. For each of these, both a representative of the tax administration and a representative of the company were asked to fill out a questionnaire. Subsequently, the company was audited and the findings were compared to the information from the questionnaires. The results are presented in the report and the main conclusion is that the relationship between the mutual representatives is the most important factor to predict compliance: the better the relationship, the higher the level of compliance of the organization. Although there has been some criticism of the report,[21] it is a useful example of empirical research into the influence of (elements of) HT on compliance. As another important fact, the

18. *See* Guide HT, section 6.2.
19. www.rijksoverheid.nl/documenten/rapporten/2012/06/20/rapport-van-de-commisie-stevens-over-horizontaal-toezicht-bij-de-belastingdienst.
20. www.rijksoverheid.nl/documenten/rapporten/2017/06/27/rapport-onderzoek-grote-ondernemingen.
21. F.C. de Groot, "Het rapport onderzoek grote ondernemingen: worden de beleidsverwachtingen omtrent het HT ook daadwerkelijk gerealiseerd?," WFR 2017/204, and I.T. van den Berg/M.F. de Ridder, "Het rapport onderzoek grote ondernemingen vertaald," WFR 2017/217.

Stevens Committee found that the tax administration did not measure compliance prior to introducing HT, so that their claim that HT is more efficient than the "vertical" model could not be measured. This report can be seen a (first) measurement of compliance levels and should therefore be repeated to establish whether or not the level of compliance has actually changed in the intermediary period.

[G] Future Developments

The tax administration is currently in the process of further developing HT. This process has not led to new guidance or amendments to the existing guidance yet. What is clear, is that the tax administration wants to reduce the number of companies that are eligible for an individual covenant.[22] At the same time, the 100 biggest companies will not have a covenant anymore. For them HT will be a programme to enter, which comes down to the same setup as for instance ICAP (*see* section §11.04). It is unclear what the differences compared to the existing programme will be as there is no new guidance yet. This is expected however as on November 11, 2019 the tax administration presented its yearbook 2020 to Parliament in which the new criteria are mentioned.[23] Another issue is that the tax administration wants to install a better mechanism for conflicts about HT. This would take the form of an internal administrative appeal, meaning that external appeal options are still lacking, but the new procedure would be transparent and therefore a lot clearer than the current situation.

§11.03 CO-OPERATIVE COMPLIANCE FOR SMALL- AND MEDIUM-SIZED COMPANIES (SMEs)

HT as applied to multinationals is not possible for SMEs for a number of reasons.[24] The most important one is that the sheer number of SMEs makes it impossible for the tax administration to deal with them on an individual basis, as they do with multinationals. Also, the internal control systems of smaller companies are generally not at the same level as those of multinationals, so they cannot be relied upon in the same way. SMEs usually have an inherent weakness in their internal controls: management is often also a main shareholder, so the natural checks and balances that exist between the management and shareholders of a listed company are not as a rule present in an SME. There is, however, a system of HT in place for SMEs, although the character

22. The current criteria for an individual covenant are not published, but refer to Art. 396, book 2 Civil Law Code: companies that must have a mandatory external audit report for their financial accounts (crudely put: turnover more than EUR 35 million, between 50 and 250 employees). The tax administration is planning to go to the criteria of Art. 397, which means turnover of more than EUR 40 million and more than 250 employees.
23. https://www.rijksoverheid.nl/documenten/publicaties/2019/11/20/jaarplan-2020-belastingd ienst.
24. For more information *see* B. Herrijgers in "Tax Assurance," Kluwer, Deventer 2015, ed R. Russo, Chapter 7.

differs from the individual approach applicable to multinationals.[25] The solution the tax administration came up with is to work through TSP. The quality control system of the TSP should make up for the shortfall in the internal controls of the SME. We will look at the process in more detail, discuss some possible challenges and look at future developments. As with HT for multinationals, special guidelines for SMEs were published,[26] hereinafter referred to as Guide HT TSP.

[A] The SME HT Process in Steps

[1] Compliance Agreement Discussions

This step is similar to the step described in section §11.02[D][1] in cases of individual covenants. The difference is that in this case the check is whether the TSP is able and willing to prepare acceptable returns (free of material errors). The focus is on the quality control system of the TSP (as opposed to the taxpayer's TCF in the case of an individual covenant). Many TSPs are a member of a so-called umbrella organization[27]. If this is the case, the tax administration will rely on the quality assurances offered by the umbrella organization. If not, the TSP must go through a more extensive process with respect to its own quality control system.

The quality referred to is not just the quality of the tax returns, but also of the financial data that they are based on. To date, all TSPs are accounting or auditing firms (which is easy to check, as all covenants with TSPs are published on the site of the tax administration[28]). Apparently accounting firms can deliver the quality desired according to the tax administration. This creates a difficult position for so-called niche tax advisor offices, which prepare tax returns but are not related to an accounting firm. In principle, they cannot be a TSP and cannot have a covenant.[29]

[2] Application and Cancellation for Companies

If the TSP has signed the covenant, the question arises which of their clients they will consider to participate in HT via the TSP's covenant. There is some risk involved for the TSP, because by letting a client participate they take at least some responsibility that they will be able to prepare acceptable returns for this client. The client has to sign an agreement with the TSP (a participating agreement) in which they basically promise to provide all information needed for compiling an acceptable tax return. There is some

25. There are currently also some large family owned businesses that have an individual covenant, but in the future this will further decrease with the new criteria, we refer to section §11.02[G].
26. https://download.belastingdienst.nl/belastingdienst/docs/guide-horizon-monitoring-service-providers-dv4071z3pl.pdf.
27. These organizations are usually formed by practitioners such as accountants or tax advisors and promote their interest.
28. *See* https://belastingdienst.nl/wps/wcm/connect/bldcontentnl/belastingdienst/intermediairs/toezicht/convenanten/convenanten_horizontaal_toezicht/fiscaal_dienstverleners/.
29. *See* Chapter 3 Guide HT TSP and annex II.

guidance on the processes used for the assessment of both the TSP as well as the participating client.[30]

[3] Preliminary Consultations

This is one of the advantages of HT for SME's: if the application of the tax law is not (completely) clear, the TSP can consult directly with the tax administration in order to obtain more assurance on the tax position. The TSP must seek advice from their own experts first before they can contact the tax administration (and they will by definition have access to such experts, because it is a mandatory part of the quality system). As in the case of an individual covenant, there is the possibility to "agree to disagree."[31]

[4] Filing and Processing the Tax Return/Randomly Selected Audit/Evaluation

If the tax returns submitted by the TSP do not have any technical shortcomings or inconsistencies, they are in principle accepted by the tax administration (no touch). Any returns on which no consensus has been reached with the client will have to be made recognizable by the TSP, so as to exclude these from the no touch approach. This does not mean that the no touch tax returns are never challenged. There is monitoring and evaluation of the TSP and its clients and a randomly selected audit is possible also. So there is an advantage for participating companies: in principle the returns are followed by the tax administration, but there is no guarantee as a result of the possible random audit.[32]

[B] Challenges/Possible Friction Points

One of the most heard complaints of TSPs is that they have to invest heavily in their quality control systems, leading to more work which leads to higher bills for their clients. They claim the advantage for the client is not clear enough as a tax audit always remains a possibility. A more fundamental challenge is that in this application of HT the TSP is placed between the tax administration, so the client might feel that the TSP is not just responding to their needs, but also to those of the tax administration. This is not easily solvable. It is a fact that the role of the TSP in HT is different from that of a traditional advisor and this has both positive and negative effects. The TSP has the benefit of direct access to the tax administration, but the tax administration wields more influence on the TSP than in non-HT situations. For some TSPs this is a reason not to enter in a HT covenant.

The participating agreement through which a client of a TSP can enter HT is a complex document. It is a contract between client and TSP, but also contains

30. *See* Chapter 4 Guide HT TSP.
31. *See* Chapter 5 Guide HT TSP.
32. *See* Chapters 6 and 7 Guide HT TSP.

obligations to the tax administration. If anything goes wrong, for example bankruptcy of the TSP, fraud by the client that is not (or cannot be) known by the TSP etc., the consequences are not clear. To our knowledge this has not yet happened, so there is no practical experience to build on.

Problems in the sense of conflicts concerning the covenant itself are similar to the situation with individual covenants, we refer to section §11.02[E][5].

[C] Future Developments

As observed earlier, the tax administration is currently in the process of further developing HT. From the ongoing discussions some points can be distilled. One is that the tax administration is thinking about officially aligning their supervision more closely with work already done by a TSP. If the TSP has done a full audit, supervision by the tax administration can be reduced, for instance by decreasing the chance that such a client will be subject to an audit. Another point of discussion is that the tax administration, as with HT in the context of individual covenants, wants to install a better mechanism for solving conflicts about HT.

§11.04 INTERNATIONAL COMPLIANCE ASSURANCE PROGRAMME

ICAP can in some respects be seen as a form of international Co-operative Compliance. If we compare HT to ICAP, some differences and some similarities are evident.

[A] Differences

Under ICAP, participating multinationals have to deliver a huge information package, which is not true for HT. ICAP has a clear time schedule and a conflict managing procedure, HT has not. ICAP leads to assurance, in HT there is constant dialogue that can lead to certainty or to an agreement to disagree. In ICAP, tax strategy plays a major role (with respect to the taxpayer's eligibility and in the assessment process), much less so in HT. A big difference is that ICAP operates cross-border and HT is limited to the Dutch situation. HT covers all tax issues, ICAP just some specific situations. Lastly, ICAP does not work on the basis of a covenant, a multinational can just enter the programme (or not).

[B] Similarities

Both ICAP and HT place great importance on risk management and internal controls of a participating company. Furthermore, in both approaches the financial accounts are important. For ICAP it is important whether or not a multinational is already participating in a local Co-operative Compliance programme. This suggests, at least, that ICAP is some form of international extension of a national programme.

§11.05 CONCLUDING REMARKS

In our opinion, HT in the Netherlands can be viewed as a form of Co-operative Compliance. The elements that constitute Co-operative Compliance according to the OECD report of 2013 are mostly present in HT, as described in this chapter. An important point with respect to the current state of HT is the fact that the presence of a low-risk tax strategy is not decisive to a company's eligibility (it is in principle possible to have HT with an aggressive strategy), but most probably this requirement will be added to bring HT more in line with for instance ICAP. Risk management and internal control are of vital importance in HT, and must culminate in an adequate TCF. The tax administration has the opinion that the TCF is entity-specific and will exist as a consequence of corporate governance regulations, so in principle they do not feel responsible to provide guidance in this respect. In matter of fact there is quite some guidance in various publications of the tax administration. Perhaps in the upcoming further development of HT, more guidance will be provided, or at least the currently available guidance from different publications will be bundled and given more formal status.

HT for SMEs is in effect a different form of supervision, as it is not the TCF of the individual company that plays the main part, but the quality control system of the TSP. The same elements that characterize HT for multinationals play a role for SMEs, but the details differ greatly. However, we believe that HT for SMEs system can also be categorized as a form of Co-operative Compliance.[33]

33. *See* for the same opinion J.L.M. Gribnau and E.A.M. Huiskers-Stoop, Co-operative Compliance and the Dutch Horizontal Monitoring model', JOTA 2019 5:1, 66-110, http://ssrn.com/abstract =3333347.

CHAPTER 12

Co-operation Programme: A Novelty in the Polish Tax System

Małgorzata Sęk

§12.01 INTRODUCTION

Poland does not yet have any operating Co-operative Compliance regime; however, this novelty will be introduced as of 1 July 2020.

Works on Co-operative Compliance have been originally undertaken by the General Tax Law Codification Commission (*Komisja Kodyfikacyjna Ogólnego Prawa Podatkowego*), appointed in 2014 and tasked with drafting a new tax ordinance (TO) (general tax law act)[1] to replace the currently applicable Act of 29 August 1997 TO.[2] The general assumptions for the new TO, submitted by the Commission to the Minister of Finance in 2015,[3] foresaw the introduction of Co-operative Compliance. A draft TO submitted in 2017[4] included five articles on Co-operative Compliance, providing the very basics of this regime. The draft compiled by the Commission has subsequently been modified by the Minister of Finance, which involved substantial extension of the

1. PL, Regulation of the Council of Ministers of 21 October 2014 on the establishment, organization and operation of the General Tax Law Codification Commission (*Rozporządzenie Rady Ministrów w sprawie utworzenia, organizacji i trybu działania Komisji Kodyfikacyjnej Ogólnego Prawa Podatkowego*), Journal of Laws of 2014, item 1471.
2. PL, Act of 29 August 1997 Tax Ordinance (*Ustawa z dnia 29 sierpnia 1997 r. Ordynacja podatkowa*), consolidated text Journal of Laws of 2019, item 900.
3. The General Tax Law Codification Commission, *Draft of 24 September 2015 of the general assumptions for the new tax ordinance* (*Projekt z dnia 24 września 2015 r. kierunkowych założeń nowej ordynacji* podatkowej) (21 October 2019) https://legislacja.rcl.gov.pl/docs//1/12274851/12300367/12300368/dokument185182.pdf.
4. The General Tax Law Codification Commission, *Draft of 6 October 2017 of the Act – Tax Ordinance* (*Projekt z dnia 6 października 2017 r. ustawy – Ordynacja podatkowa*) (21 October 2019) https://mf-arch2.mf.gov.pl/c/document_library/get_file?uuid=73b04e75-c59a-4ac3-81d8-4ab8eb351cd3&groupId=764034.

provisions on Co-operative Compliance (to over twenty-five articles), and the governmental bill on TO was introduced to the Parliament in June 2019.[5]

However, the new TO is generally regarded as a too extensive[6] and innovative piece of legislation to be adopted soon. Thus, Co-operative Compliance has been extracted from the draft TO and paired with other urgently needed instruments to form a less extensive legislative proposal introduced to the Parliament on 23 August 2019: *The government bill on the settlement of disputes regarding double taxation and the conclusion of advance pricing agreements* (*Rządowy projekt ustawy o rozstrzyganiu sporów dotyczących podwójnego opodatkowania oraz zawieraniu uprzednich porozumień cenowych*) (hereinafter: 'Co-operative Compliance Bill' or 'CC Bill').[7] The CC Bill was adopted by the *Sejm* on 16 October 2019 and submitted to the *Senat.*[8] The Senate discussed the CC Bill in record time and adopted it without any amendments on 18 October 2019. The Act (hereinafter: 'Co-operative Compliance Act' or 'CC Act') was signed by the President on 5 November 2019 and officially published on 14 November 2019.[9] However, the provisions on Co-operative Compliance will only enter into force on 1 July 2020,[10] as a new part of the currently applicable TO. The competent authority will be the Head of the National Fiscal Administration (*Szef Krajowej Administracji Skarbowej*) (hereinafter: 'Head of the NFA').[11]

Consequently, it must be clearly stated that this chapter describes the Polish Co-operative Compliance model, which has not yet been implemented in practice.

§12.02 PROSPECT OF REDUCED TAX UNCERTAINTY AS THE MAIN DRIVER TOWARDS CO-OPERATIVE COMPLIANCE

The tax compliance burden in Poland is high,[12] but this does not seem to be a factor capable of promoting Co-operative Compliance on its own. The burden connected with

5. PL, The government bill of 4 June 2019 – Tax Ordinance (*Rządowy projekt z dnia 4 czerwca 2019 r. ustawy – Ordynacja podatkowa*) *Sejm* (VIII term) print no. 3517 (*Sejm RP VIII kadencji, druk nr 3517*) (21 October 2019) https://www.sejm.gov.pl/Sejm8.nsf/druk.xsp?nr = 3517.
6. The government bill of 4 June 2019 – Tax Ordinance with explanatory statement and other required documents is 1,554 pages long.
7. PL, The government bill of 23 August 2019 on the settlement of disputes regarding double taxation and the conclusion of advance pricing agreements (*Rządowy projekt z dnia 23 sierpnia 2019 r. ustawy o rozstrzyganiu sporów dotyczących podwójnego opodatkowania oraz zawieraniu uprzednich porozumień cenowych*), *Sejm* (VIII term) print no. 3788 (*Sejm RP VIII kadencji, druk nr 3788*) (21 October 2019) http://www.sejm.gov.pl/sejm8.nsf/druk.xsp?nr = 3788.
8. For a description of the legislative process in Poland *see*: PL, The *Sejm* of the Republic of Poland, *Discover Sejm: Legislative process* (21 October 2019) http://opis.sejm.gov.pl/en/procesustawodawczy.php.
9. PL, Act of 16 October 2019 on the settlement of disputes regarding double taxation and the conclusion of advance pricing agreements (*Ustawa z dnia 19 października 2019 r. o rozstrzyganiu sporów dotyczących podwójnego opodatkowania oraz zawieraniu uprzednich porozumień cenowych*), Journal of Laws of 2019, item 2200.
10. Article 130(3) CC Act.
11. Article 13(2)(9) TO.
12. In Poland the time to prepare and pay taxes is estimated at 334 hours as per the year 2018, *see* The World Bank, *Time to prepare and pay taxes (2018)* (21 October 2019) https://data.worldbank.org/indicator/IC.TAX.DURS.

the adopted Co-operative Compliance regime seems rather high itself, with the necessity to design, implement and maintain an adequate and effective internal tax control framework, to undergo a thorough preliminary audit and then to co-operate with tax authorities on a continuous basis and fully transparently. Thus, for Polish taxpayers it is rather the prospect of reduced tax uncertainty, reduced risk of tax disputes and reduced hostility that are likely to be the main drivers towards Co-operative Compliance. Also, according to the Polish Ministry of Finance, the greatest benefit for the taxpayer participating in Co-operative Compliance is increased tax certainty and foreseeability of tax expenditure, which also reduces the need to keep reserves for financing additional tax liabilities resulting from future tax assessments.

As expressly stated in the newly adopted provisions, the new compliance programme 'serves to ensure that the taxpayer complies with the provisions of tax law in conditions of transparency of undertaken actions and mutual trust and understanding between the tax authority and the taxpayer, taking into account the nature of the business carried out by the taxpayer'.[13]

Theoretically, the basic principles behind Co-operative Compliance programmes should be very appealing to taxpayers: working in the present and not in the past, emphasis on internal controls of the taxpayer instead of external controls by tax authorities, trust and openness in contacts between the taxpayer and the tax authority.[14] The main problems that may hinder the actual development and implementation of the programme in Poland, resulting in insufficient taxpayer interest, are the low level of trust in public authorities, the long history of hostility and distrust between taxpayers (or their tax advisors) and tax authorities, as well as attachment to formalism and an intrinsic preference for the written form instead of direct exchange of views.[15]

According to the Ministry of Finance, the Co-operative Compliance programme is an alternative, a concurrent option, to aggressive tax planning. Benefits provided to taxpayers participating in the programme are meant to incentivize them to enter the programme and to undertake the obligation to become extraordinarily compliant, open and transparent. Taxpayers joining the programme will commit to a degree of transparency that goes far beyond statutory obligations, incurring significant financial outlays for the implementation and maintenance of the internal tax control framework in the form accepted by tax authorities, which is meant to ensure that the taxpayer effectively manages the tax function and is able to properly fulfil tax obligations. In order to balance the additional obligations and financial outlays, legal benefits and facilitations are foreseen so that from the economic point of view participation in the programme is attractive and profitable for the taxpayer. The Ministry believes that the benefits of participation will be a counterweight to aggressive tax planning.

13. Article 20s(2) TO.
14. *See* OECD, *Co-operative Compliance: A Framework, from Enhanced Relationship to Co-operative Compliance* (2013), pp. 29 et seq. (21 October 2019) https://read.oecd-ilibrary.org/taxation/co-operative-compliance-a-framework_9789264200852-en#page31.
15. For a wider discussion of cultural, sociological and historical aspects of the possible introduction of Co-operative Compliance in Poland *see* Katarzyna Bronzewska, *Cooperative Compliance: A New Approach to Managing Taxpayer Relations*, pp. 445-497 (IBFD 2016).

§12.03 THE POLISH CO-OPERATION PROGRAMME (WSPÓŁDZIAŁANIE) AND THE OECD 'CO-OPERATIVE COMPLIANCE MODEL'

[A] Legal Regulation

In Poland, the Co-operative Compliance regime (formally, the 'co-operation programme') will be established in legal provisions included in the TO, namely newly adopted section IIB of the TO entitled 'Co-operation' ('*Współdziałanie*') and including over twenty-five articles numbered 20s to 20zr.

In order to avoid an overly meticulous formalization of the co-operation programme, the TO will only provide a framework regulation of individual elements of the programme, i.e., the co-operation agreement (*umowa o współdziałanie*), the tax agreement (*porozumienie podatkowe*) and the tax audit (*audyt podatkowy*), while the specific shape of the co-operation will depend on the practice developed by the tax authorities upon entering into co-operation with individual taxpayers.

The legal regulation of the contents of the co-operation agreement to be signed between the Head of the NFA and the taxpayer provides the parties with considerable freedom to shape the details of their co-operation in the spirit of trust, informality and flexibility, adapting the conditions of co-operation to specific needs of the taxpayer and the tax authority.

[B] Eligible Taxpayers

As provided in the explanatory statement accompanying the CC Bill and reflected in the adopted provisions, the co-operation programme will be addressed only to the largest taxpayers in terms of economic importance, which is a solution also adopted abroad.[16] First of all, in the opinion of the Ministry of Finance, such taxpayers are able to ensure the proper functioning of the internal tax control framework, because they either already have a good internal tax control framework, or if not, they have the appropriate personnel, technical and financial resources necessary for the implementation and maintenance thereof. Another reason why the programme is intended solely for the largest taxpayers is that, in the view of the Ministry, aggressive tax planning is most often carried out by these very entities, as the economic 'profitability' of tax planning increases with the amount of income to which it relates. The programme is meant to reduce or even eliminate the profitability of aggressive tax planning by providing real-time tax certainty, which in the long term may be more beneficial to the taxpayer than risky participation in tax planning. Moreover, due to the amount of tax liabilities involved, the consequences of a tax error, both for taxpayers themselves and for the state budget, are the most severe in the case of the largest taxpayers. Therefore, the goal of the programme is to provide support to the largest taxpayers. As a result of timely and correct payment of taxes by the largest entities without the need for lengthy

---

16. About the use of the criteria of a 'large taxpayer' in other countries *see* Katarzyna Bronzewska, Alicja Majdańska, *Program Współdziałania z Dużymi Podatnikami – polski odpowiednik co-operative compliance. Czy warto?*, p. 49, 2 Przegląd Podatkowy (2019).

and costly disputes, tax revenue flows to the state budget will become more stable and reliable.

Eligible taxpayers will be indicated by reference to their annual gross income, as reported in the tax return for corporate income tax purposes, filed for the tax year preceding the tax year in which an application for joining the programme is submitted. Only taxpayers with gross income exceeding the equivalent of EUR 50 million in national currency (PLN) will be eligible.[17] It is estimated that circa two and a half thousand taxpayers meet this threshold.[18] However, in the period of three years from the introduction of the co-operation programme (i.e., from 1 July 2020 to 1 July 2023), the Head of the NFA will be authorized to limit the number of entities accepted into the programme to twenty[19] to ensure the efficient and timely performance of the tasks of the NFA.[20] When selecting the entities, the Head of the NFA will take into account the economic and social significance of these entities and the diversity of these entities in terms of their business activities, and may also take into account the order in which applications are submitted.[21] Thus, in what can be considered a pilot stage, the actual eligibility will depend on a combination of clear criteria (i.e., gross income, submission date) and vague criteria that are subject to interpretation (i.e., economic and social significance, diversity of business activities).

As emphasized in the explanatory statement, in the opinion of the Ministry of Finance, the adoption of 'gross income' criteria instead of 'taxes paid' criteria is better in selecting entities with significant impact on the economy and the state budget. High employment, production levels or an extensive supplier and customer base, associated with high economic turnover, tend to generate more significant social, economic and budgetary impact. As the Ministry of Finance points out, eligible taxpayers generate 50% of total corporate income tax revenue.

It is worth noting that only corporate income tax taxpayers will be eligible, thus a partnership or a self-employed entrepreneur with annual gross income exceeding EUR 50 million will not be able to enter the co-operation programme. The co-operation programme will only cover taxes remaining within the competence of the NFA (e.g., corporate income tax, personal income tax, tax on goods and services, excise tax), which excludes local taxes administered by local government bodies (e.g., immovable property tax, agricultural tax, forestry tax).[22]

Interestingly, the eligibility threshold corresponds with the amount of gross income which triggers the publication by the Minister of Finance (at the Ministry's website) of basic individual tax data of the largest corporate income tax taxpayers: name and taxpayer identification number, tax year, the amount of gross income, costs incurred, income earned or loss suffered, tax base and amount of tax due, as well as the

17. Article 20s(3) TO.
18. Explanatory statement to the CC Bill.
19. The Ministry of Finance foresees that due to negative results of preliminary audits or taxpayer's failure to implement recommendations resulting from the preliminary audit, the actual number of taxpayers accepted into the programme may drop to ten.
20. Article 122(1) CC Bill.
21. Article 122(2) CC Bill.
22. In Art. 20s(1).

effective tax rate (the amount of tax due relative to the gross profit of the taxpayer, shown in the financial statements).[23] As pointed out in the explanatory statement to the CC Bill, entities whose annual gross income exceeds EUR 50 million, as the most economically significant entities, are required to be publically transparent regarding certain data contained in their annual tax return. Both the co-operation programme and the publication of data are meant to encourage the largest taxpayers to refrain from aggressive tax planning.

For the sake of transparency, the refusal to accept a taxpayer into the programme will be issued in writing with grounds provided,[24] to inform the taxpayer about objective reasons which prevented the Head of NFA from entering into a co-operation relationship. The taxpayer will not be entitled to appeal against such refusal. As provided in the explanatory statement, the Head of the NFA when deciding whether to co-operate or not, should be guided by a consistent policy safeguarding equal treatment of eligible taxpayers, and should also provide taxpayers with feedback indicating rational decision-making premises applicable to all candidates for the co-operation programme.

[C] Entry upon Application

A co-operation agreement (*umowa o współdziałenie*), which is the basis for entering the co-operation programme, will be concluded by the Head of the NFA upon request of an eligible taxpayer,[25] following a positive result of a preliminary audit.[26]

An invitation from the tax authorities (i.e., the Head of the NFA) will not be necessary and in fact is not provided for in the provisions as such. However, the explanatory statement claims that the initiative to conclude a co-operation agreement can come from both the taxpayer and the tax authority. In the latter case, a consent from the taxpayer will be needed to start the preliminary audit, which will be treated as a request to sign the agreement. There is no legal basis for the tax authority's invitation, so it would be purely informal and absolutely not binding upon the taxpayer. Moreover, an invitation will not guarantee signing of a co-operation agreement, because this will always be dependent upon obtaining a positive outcome of the preliminary audit.

Entry into a co-operation programme will be entirely voluntary. As a consequence, each party (both the taxpayer and the Head of the NFA) will decide on joining or possibly withdrawing from the programme. The tax authority will not be able to require the taxpayer to enter into this relationship and assume specific obligations related to it. No negative consequences for the taxpayer will ensue from the fact that they are not interested in concluding a co-operation agreement. Symmetrically,

23. *See* Art. 27b(2)(2) of the Act of 15 February 1992 on Corporate Income Tax (*Ustawa z dnia 15 lutego 1992 o podatku dochodowym od osób prawnych*) (hereinafter 'CITA'), consolidated text Journal of Laws of 2019, item 865.
24. Article 20s(5) TO.
25. Article 20s(1) TO.
26. Article 20s(4) TO.

taxpayers will not be able to demand the conclusion of an agreement. Whether or not a tax authority enters into a co-operative relationship with the taxpayer will remain within the authority's discretion. However, as pointed out by the Ministry of Finance, in accordance with the general principles of tax proceedings - so as to preserve the principle of impartiality and equal treatment and not to violate the taxpayers' confidence in public authority - the authority should be guided by a coherent policy regarding the treatment of taxpayers when deciding whether and with whom a co-operation agreement is concluded.[27]

[D] Programme Entry Conditions

Apart from meeting the income threshold, in order to be accepted into the programme the taxpayer will have to pass a preliminary audit.[28] As pointed out in the explanatory statement, this condition is intended to ensure that the Head of the NFA signs an agreement with reliable entities expressing not only the desire to comply with tax law, but also actually having the ability to properly fulfil their tax obligations. A positive outcome of the preliminary audit is proof of such ability, especially taking into account the fact that clear rules on the tax audit (including the preliminary audit) will be provided for.

As described in the explanatory statement, the signing of a co-operation agreement, constituting the basis for taxpayer's participation in the co-operation programme, will be preceded by a verification of the maturity of the internal tax control framework implemented by the taxpayer and the fulfilment of tax obligations to date.

The preliminary tax audit will be carried out by the Head of the NFA, whose assessment will be based, among other things, on an independent audit of the tax function performed by tax advisers or statutory auditors (or tax advisory companies and audit companies acting through employed tax advisors and statutory auditors, respectively). For further details on the preliminary tax audit, *see* section *Pre-entry Evaluation of the Tax Control Framework* below.

Generally, entry into the co-operation programme will also be conditional upon the taxpayer's readiness to undertake the obligations ensuing from the co-operation agreement, namely the obligation to:

- voluntarily and properly fulfil obligations arising from tax law;
- have an effective and adequate internal tax control framework (i.e., a set of identified and described processes and procedures for managing the fulfilment of obligations arising from tax law and ensuring correct fulfilment thereof);
- report to the Head of the NFA, without request, any relevant tax issues that, judging reasonably, can become a source of dispute between the taxpayer and the tax authority - in accordance with the relevance thresholds set in the co-operation agreement;

27. As mentioned before the refusal to conclude a co-operation agreement will be issued in writing together with justification (new Art. 20s (5) TO).
28. Drat Art. 20s(4) TO.

- immediately forward to the Head of the NFA, without request, any relevant information on tax benefits obtained or to be obtained by the taxpayer – in accordance with the relevance thresholds set in the co-operation agreement.

[E] Mandatory Disclosure

Under the co-operation programme, disclosure is mandatory.

The taxpayer will be obliged to provide at the request of the Head of the NFA documentation and information necessary to conduct a tax audit.[29] Above all, by signing the co-operation agreement, the taxpayer will commit to informing the Head of the NFA of any relevant tax issues that, reasonably judging, can become a source of dispute, as well as any relevant information on tax benefits obtained or to be obtained by the taxpayer. These obligations will go well beyond what is required under the generally applicable rules, including mandatory disclosure rules regarding tax schemes.

In practice, the taxpayer will be required to disclose to the Head of the NFA without delay all information relevant for taxation, including any difficult tax issues that he is not able to resolve on his own, as well as identified tax risks, and to provide honest and reliable answers to questions asked by the Head of the NFA. On the other hand, transparency on the part of the NFA is reflected in openness in providing information about the circumstances related to questions addressed to the taxpayer and in the scope of implementing supervisory activities towards the taxpayer.

It is worth noting that, in order to protect the trade secrets of the taxpayer, documents and information recognized by the Head of the NFA as containing the trade secrets will be destroyed within two months: (1) from the date of termination of the co-operation agreement, and, in the case of failure to conclude a co-operation agreement, either (2) from the day of completing the preliminary audit or (3) from the end of verification if the taxpayer complied with the recommendations issued as a result of the preliminary audit.[30]

Moreover, in order to protect information obtained in the course of co-operation (including preliminary and monitoring audits), employees who perform a (co-operation) tax audit may not perform any (ordinary) tax inspection, customs and fiscal inspection and tax proceedings against the taxpayer for a period of three years from the date of its completion.[31]

[F] Multilateral Co-operative Compliance

Multilateral Co-operative Compliance is not regulated *expressis verbis* in the newly adopted legislation.

29. Article 20zh TO.
30. Article 20zh(2) TO.
31. Article 20zn(3) TO.

§12.04 OTHER FEATURES OF THE POLISH CO-OPERATION PROGRAMME

[A] Voluntary Character

As mentioned above, the co-operation programme will be entirely voluntary. Formally, no negative consequences will ensue from the fact that a taxpayer is not interested in joining the programme. Moreover, the taxpayer will be allowed to terminate the co-operation agreement and hence quit the programme at any time.[32] Termination of the co-operation agreement by the taxpayer will not be subject to any conditions.

[B] Co-operation Agreement

Signing a co-operation agreement will be necessary to establish the special co-operation relationship between a taxpayer and the Head of the NFA.

The co-operation agreement will be concluded in writing.[33] Elements of the co-operation agreement are described in the newly adopted provisions, but in very general terms. A co-operation agreement will include 'the parties' arrangements necessary for the proper fulfilment of contractual obligations, including a detailed specification of the rights and obligations of the parties resulting from the concluded agreement and the method of informing each other about authorized contact persons'.[34]

The general scope of rights and obligations arising from the agreement will be the same for all taxpayers who conclude a co-operation agreement.[35] They are listed in the new provisions (*See* section *Programme Entry Conditions*, above). However, as pointed out in the explanatory statement, the course of the implementation of the agreement will be individualized in accordance with the specific arrangements and the details of taxpayer's tax control framework.

Interestingly, taxpayers who signed a co-operation agreement will be listed in a publicly available (online) register,[36] which may bring publicity benefits to the taxpayer. Upon termination of the agreement, the taxpayer will be removed from this register.

[C] Legal Nature and Enforceability of the Co-operation Agreement

The legal nature of the co-operation agreement establishing this special co-operation relationship between a taxpayer and the Head of the NFA remains unclear. Theoretically the agreement is binding on both parties, but its enforceability has not been regulated and there are no legal instruments provided for forcing the other party to act

32. Article 20x(1) TO.
33. Article 20t(1) TO.
34. Article 20t(2) TO.
35. Article 20u TO.
36. Article 20za TO.

in accordance with the agreement. There are no specific penalties or sanctions which would differ from the generally applicable ones. The eventuality of termination seems to be the main enforcing factor.

[D] Validity and Termination of the Co-operation Agreement

The co-operation agreement will be concluded for an indefinite period,[37] which will add to the certainty and predictability enjoyed by the taxpayer. However, the taxpayer's legal successor will not enter his rights and obligations under the co-operation agreement.[38]

The taxpayer will be entitled to terminate the co-operation agreement at any time, not subject to any conditions.[39] In contrast, the Head of the NFA will terminate the co-operation agreement only in the case of: (1) breach of the agreement by the taxpayer, or (2) serious or repeated breach of tax law by the taxpayer.[40] The Head of the NFA will have to indicate the reasons for termination, providing justification. As indicated in the explanatory statement, when considering terminating the contract, the tax authority should be guided by objective reasons, which can be justified and understood, so that a coherent policy is followed.

If the agreement is terminated by the Head of the NFA, the taxpayer for the next two years will not be allowed to apply for re-entering the programme.[41] The purpose of this rule is to encourage actual compliance under the co-operation programme, to discourage taxpayers within the programme from gross or repeated violation of tax law or from failing to comply with the terms of the agreement.

Termination of the co-operation agreement will be effective on the day of submitting a written statement to the other party, unless a later term is indicated in this statement.[42]

[E] Risk Management, Risk Appetite and Tax Strategy Requirements

Taxpayers willing to enter and remain in the co-operation programme will have to commit to voluntarily and properly fulfil obligations arising from tax law. Such a commitment is a mandatory element of the co-operation agreement,[43] but it has not been further elaborated in the legislation itself. However, the explanatory statement clarifies that this obligation cannot be seen as a mere duplication of obligations already existing under the applicable law. As emphasized by the Ministry of Finance, the overriding goal of the co-operation programme is to ensure that the tax is paid in the correct amount and on time, without the need for coercive measures to be undertaken

37. Article 20t(1) TO.
38. Article 20w TO.
39. Article 20x(1) TO.
40. Article 20x(2) TO.
41. Article 20y TO.
42. Article 20x(3) TO.
43. Article 20u TO.

by the tax authorities. According to the Ministry, the voluntary nature of fulfilment of tax obligations also means that the taxpayer will not apply tax avoidance practices, including aggressive tax planning. To this end, already at the strategic level, i.e., in the tax strategy, the taxpayer should adopt appropriate assumptions aimed at preventing tax avoidance, and ensure supervisory mechanisms that guarantee minimization of tax risks, so as to voluntarily and properly fulfil tax obligations.

[F] Tax Control Framework as an Entry Condition

One of the conditions for entering into a co-operation agreement and remaining within the co-operation programme is to have an effective and adequate internal tax control framework agreed with the tax authority, which should ensure that the taxpayer exercises real control over his tax issues and is able to properly fulfil his tax obligations.

As emphasized by the Ministry of Finance, mutual trust cannot be naïve but must be legitimate, based on objective facts. The legitimate trust of the Head of the NFA towards the taxpayer will result from the fact that the taxpayer has implemented a tax control framework.

[G] Tax Control Framework Requirements

The normatively stated requirements for the tax control framework are its adequacy and effectiveness. Detailed information on the requirements regarding the internal tax control framework will be published in the form of guidelines at the website of the Ministry of Finance. No such guidelines have been published so far, but opinions from the public have been already collected under public consultation procedure. Moreover, within the co-operation programme it will be possible to determine details of the tax control framework in an instrument called tax agreement (*porozumienie podatowe*), expressing position agreed between the taxpayer and the Head of the NFA and having protective effects on the taxpayer.

As provided in the explanatory statement, the internal tax control framework is adequate when it is adapted to the size and structure and type of taxpayer's activity, including the economic sector and the scale of domestic and foreign transactions. An adequate internal tax control framework is to ensure high quality of records maintained, as well as the correct implementation of new systems and processes and any other changes in the existing system that affect the tax function, so that proper planning, risk assessment, implementation and post-implementation assessment is safeguarded.

According to the explanatory statement, an effective internal tax control framework is characterized by: comprehensiveness, documentation, monitoring and improvement, guarantee of certainty, adopted scopes of responsibility. The internal tax control framework should be regarded comprehensive if it covers the whole organization and takes into account various roles and responsibilities, which means that the framework must apply to the entire tax function, not only to the activities of the department responsible for tax issues. The guarantee of certainty within the internal tax control framework means the certainty that the taxpayer controls tax risk and effects ensuing from tax obligations, as well as a guarantee of exercising control over the entity's tax processes, ensuring timely identification of risks and timely submission of tax returns containing correct data.

[H] Pre-entry Evaluation of the Tax Control Framework

As mentioned above, a co-operation agreement will only be concluded with eligible taxpayers,[44] who passed a preliminary audit, i.e., received a positive opinion resulting from the preliminary audit.[45]

The newly adopted provisions contain extensive rules on tax audits (*audyt podatkowy*), including the abovementioned preliminary audit (*audyt wstępny*), carried out before the signing of the co-operation agreement, and a monitoring audit (*audyt monitorujący*), carried out after the signing of the agreement, as long as the co-operation relationship exists.[46]

The tax audit will be carried out by the Head of the NFA in order to check: (1) the correctness of fulfilment of tax obligations, and (2) the effectiveness and adequacy of the internal tax control framework.[47] The taxpayer will be obliged to provide documentation and information necessary to conduct a tax audit.[48] The Ministry of Finance has declared to publish guidelines on tax audit, but so far no such document has been made available.

The preliminary audit is meant to verify, in accordance with identified risks, the taxpayer's fulfilment of tax obligations to date and to determine whether the taxpayer has not only the desire but also the ability to exercise effective supervision over the tax function (i.e., whether he has an effective and adequate tax control framework).

The decision to carry out the preliminary audit and its scope will belong to the Head of the NFA, who will take into account the level of taxpayer risk,[49] as identified following a preliminary risk analysis (expected to last about two months) based on taxpayer data already available to the tax authorities or gathered from available sources. Therefore, the mere fact that a taxpayer declares a willingness to sign a co-operation agreement will not be tantamount to the obligation to carry out a preliminary tax audit. The taxpayer will be informed about the scope of the preliminary audit,[50] which will depend on the results of the risk analysis and will be targeted at specific problems.[51] The preliminary audit will cover the current tax year and two previous years, which in the view of the Ministry of Finance, will enable the Head of the NFA to learn the specifics of the taxpayer's activity and properly identify risks. The

44. Article 20s(1) TO.
45. Article 20s(4) TO.
46. Article 20zg(1) TO.
47. Article 20zg(1) TO.
48. Article 20zh(1) TO.
49. Article 20zj(1) TO.
50. Article 20zj(2) TO.
51. Article 20zj(1) TO.

schedule of activities will be determined by the Head of the NFA in consultation with the taxpayer.[52] It is expected that the preliminary audit will last about six months.

A tax audit in relation to the internal tax control framework will assess the ability to correctly fulfil tax obligations, by verifying implemented procedures and processes related to: the risk (including tax risk) management system, internal control (including control over tax issues), internal audit (including tax issues), supervision over the compliance with laws, internal regulations and voluntarily adopted standards (including the area of tax law), as well as mechanisms for external tax supervision (including an independent audit of the tax function, which plays the role of a tax audit carried out by tax advisers and auditors).[53]

The monitoring audit will be carried out on a continuous basis to supervise the proper implementation of the co-operation agreement on the side of the taxpayer, i.e., to check the correctness of the exercise of taxpayer's obligations under the co-operation agreement.

The tax audit (both preliminary and monitoring) will conclude with an opinion (positive or negative) or recommendations, indicating what measures should be taken by the taxpayer to remedy discovered irregularities,[54] e.g., to improve the internal tax control framework. The opinion or recommendations will require justification, but the taxpayer will not be entitled to lodge an appeal. The opinion and the recommendations will be immediately delivered to the taxpayer. The deadline and schedule for the implementation of audit recommendations will be agreed by the taxpayer and the Head of the NFA,[55] to adjust the implementation schedule to the capabilities of the taxpayer.

Participation in the co-operation programme and even an application to participate will potentially lead to reductions of default interest, tax sanctions and criminal fiscal liability.

If irregularities in the fulfilment of tax obligations, found during a preliminary audit, are remedied by the taxpayer within a specified period of time since delivery of audit recommendations, the rate of interest on tax arrears will be reduced by 50%.[56] Moreover, no interest on tax arrears will accrue and no criminal fiscal liability will apply, if a taxpayer being a party to a co-operation agreement timely remedies irregularities which appeared in a period covered by a monitoring audit. According to the Ministry of Finance, the granting of the said prerogatives results from the fact that after signing the co-operation agreement, the taxpayers will be subject to constant monitoring and will consult with the Head of the NFA on an ongoing basis any tax doubts and benefits, therefore their tax returns should generally be correct. The premise of the co-operation programme is to clarify disputable issues *ex ante* (for the future), even before submitting the tax return. Thus if the return needs to be corrected, it means that either the disputed issue was so complex or disputable that it was impossible for the parties to resolve it before filling the return, or both parties did not

52. Article 20zj(3) TO.
53. Article 20zl TO.
54. Article 20zi(1) TO.
55. Article 20zi(4) TO.
56. Article 20zm TO.

discover the error in the return before its filling. In addition, due to the deformalized nature of co-operation, it will be difficult to determine when the correction would be made on the taxpayer's own initiative, and when as a result of the activities of the NFA. Moreover, acting in accordance with the co-operation agreement will be considered as indicating taxpayer's good faith which may exclude the application of so-called additional tax liability (of 10%, 40% or even more of underreported tax liability or over reported loss).[57]

[I] Independent Audit of the Tax Function

An independent audit of the tax function will be a mandatory element of the taxpayer's internal tax control framework. It will be carried out at the request of the taxpayer by an independent tax auditor, i.e., a tax advisor, a statutory auditor, a tax consultancy company acting through employed tax advisors or an audit company acting through employed statutory auditors.[58] These persons are considered to have the necessary knowledge and skills to safeguard a high quality of the audit.

To ensure the actual independence of the auditor, the following entities have been excluded: a person who performs financial audits, provides tax or legal advice for the taxpayer (or a person who performs services for such a person), as well as a natural or legal person affiliated with the taxpayer or affiliated with a person who performs financial audit, tax or legal advice for the taxpayer.[59]

The purpose of the independent audit of the tax function will be the verification by an entity independent of the taxpayer and the NFA of the correctness of the fulfilment of tax obligations, and the effectiveness and adequacy of the internal tax control framework implemented by the taxpayer.[60] The Ministry of Finance has declared to publish guidelines on the independent audit of tax function, but so far no such document has been made available.

The independent audit of the tax function will end with a report containing its result.[61] The report, together with audit documentation containing tests and procedures carried out, will be immediately delivered to the taxpayer.

[J] Adaptation of Tax Authorities' Audit Intensity to the Characteristics of the Internal Tax Control Framework

Reduction in the number and intensity of audits is an intrinsic element of the Polish co-operation programme.

The Head of the NFA will be legally obliged to apply the principle of proportionality by adapting the form and frequency of actions verifying the correctness of the

57. Article 58a TO.
58. Article 20zo TO.
59. Article 20zo(2) TO.
60. Article 20zp(1) TO.
61. Article 20zp TO.

fulfilment of tax obligations[62] to the current level of effectiveness and adequacy of the tax control framework and to the quality of co-operation of the taxpayer with the tax authorities to date.[63] As provided in the explanatory statement, the level of supervision will also depend on the ethical standards implemented by the taxpayer, which are an important element of the organizational culture conditioning the proper application in practice of established procedures and processes of internal tax control.

In order to ensure the proper adjustment of the level of supervision exercised by tax authorities, only the Head of the NFA will be competent to initiate and carry out so-called customs and fiscal inspections (*kontrola celno-skarbowa*) of a taxpayer who has signed a co-operation agreement in the scope of taxes covered by the agreement.[64] Generally, no other tax authority will be able to carry out any kind of auditing activities.[65]

[K] Communication Within the Co-operation Programme

One of the obligatory elements of a co-operation agreement is the indication of the method of informing the other party about authorized contact persons.[66] The agreement should generally contain all arrangements agreed between the parties and necessary for the proper implementation of the terms of the agreement. Individual co-operation agreements will probably contain more specific rules on the interactions between the contact persons representing the parties, possibly including some deadlines. As underlined by the Ministry of Finance, the contents of the agreements will be individualized.

The Ministry declares that due to continuous transparency on the side of the taxpayer and the familiarity of the tax authority with the specifics of taxpayer's business, taxpayers will be able to learn the tax authority's response to disputable

62. In Poland verification of the fulfilment of tax obligations is carried within three distinct procedures: verification activities (*czynności sprawdzające*), tax inspection (*kontrola podatkowa*) and customs and fiscal inspection (*kontrola celno-skarbowa*). Assessments are issued in tax proceedings (*postępowanie podatkowe*). Verification activities, which generally may be considered documental checks, are less formalized and initiated ex officio with no formal notification. If no irregularities are found and there is no need to request further information from the taxpayer, the taxpayer may even remain unaware of verification activities. If irregularities are found, which cannot be corrected during the verification activities, tax proceedings may be instigated to correct or substitute the assessment of tax made by the taxpayer. If doubts cannot be cleared during the verification activities, a tax inspection or a customs and fiscal inspection can be instigated to carry further, more in-depth fact finding activities. Tax inspection or customs and fiscal inspection are initiated ex officio in forms differing depending on circumstances. Customs and fiscal inspection is aimed at more severe tax law infringements, also in terms of amounts involved and due to the size of eligible taxpayers is the preferred form of verification.
63. Article 20v TO.
64. Article 20v TO.
65. Article 28 (1)(7) of the Act of 16 November 2016 on the National Fiscal Administration (*Ustawa z dnia 16 października 2016 r. o Krajowej Adminstracji Skrabowej*), consolidated text Journal of Laws of 2019, item 768.
66. Article 20t(2) TO.

issues in a timely manner. However, no specific response deadlines are included in the legislation.

Generally, the Head of the NFA, acting through the authorized contact person, will on a regular basis consult on the disputable issues and expected tax benefits reported by the taxpayer. It will also be possible to consolidate or formalize agreed positions.

To this end, more specific rules are provided regarding the tax agreement (*porozumienie podatkowe*), which may be concluded within the co-operation programme between the participating taxpayer and the Head of the NFA to express their agreed position on disputable issues. This instrument is one of the key benefits available to participating taxpayers, aimed at providing actual certainty in a short time.

Tax arrangements will cover issues otherwise dealt with in the form of individual tax rulings, protective opinions against the application of the General Anti Avoidance Rule (GAAR), as well as Advanced Pricing Agreements (APAs). It will be possible to conclude a tax agreement forecasting the amount of corporate income tax liability for the tax year for the purpose of calculating lump-sum advance payments to be made monthly through the tax year and adjusted after the end of the tax year. Tax arrangements will also cover other issues necessary to ensure proper implementation of the co-operation agreement, including agreements on the internal tax control framework. As emphasized in the explanatory statement, the wide range of covered issues is meant to meet the needs of taxpayers who expect a comprehensive service under the co-operation programme.

The procedure for the conclusion of the tax agreement will be simpler and cheaper (50% in the case of protective opinions and APAs) in comparison with the generally applicable instruments. Moreover, the Ministry of Finance declares that answers will be provided faster than normally, but no exact deadlines are mentioned. As declared, the Head of the NFA will try to express their position on an ongoing basis, in the form of an agreement concluded with the consent of both parties, on significant (material) tax issues, which in turn will allow limiting disputes regarding the correctness of tax settlement. Only if the parties fail to reach an agreement, the disputed issue will eventually be resolved under ordinary procedures.

According to the explanatory statement, tax arrangements will be binding on the parties, but there are no specifics on the means of their enforcement against the taxpayer. The taxpayer will be entitled to terminate the tax agreement at any time. On the other hand, the Head of the NFA will only terminate the tax agreement if (1) the co-operation agreement is terminated, or (2) the position adopted in the agreement is found to be incorrect taking into account case law of the Constitutional Court, the Court of Justice of the European Union, resolution of the Supreme Administrative Court or general rulings, or (3) new facts or new evidence existing on the date of conclusion of the agreement are discovered, which were unknown to the Head of the NFA. The termination of the agreement by the Head of the NFA will be in writing, with reasons stated. The binding effect on tax authorities will actually be expressed in the protection enjoyed by the taxpayer who fulfilled their tax liabilities in accordance with the position included in the tax arrangement, which later turned out to be incorrect or was terminated due to the termination of the co-operation agreement. No interest on tax arrears will accrue, no criminal fiscal liability will be imposed and - in case of *ex ante* agreements - the taxpayer will be exempted from the obligation to pay tax exceeding tax calculated in accordance with the agreement. A taxpayer who has hidden relevant facts will not enjoy any protection.

[L] External Assistance in Improving the Quality of Actual Relationship

If the relationship built in the framework of the co-operation programme is regarded as unsatisfactory by any of the parties, either the taxpayer or the Head of the NFA, there will be no specific body or higher authority to complain to (e.g., a panel of independent mediators or a court). Termination of the co-operation agreement will be the ultimate expression of dissatisfaction.

Moreover, if an agreement cannot be reached, the taxpayer cannot appeal, as the tax authority cannot be forced to agree with the taxpayer on a disputable issue.

[M] Access to Means of Appeal

Participation in the co-operation programme does not deprive the taxpayer of access to any means of appeal, including access to the courts.

If the taxpayer and the Head of the NFA cannot reach an agreement, the taxpayer is free to apply for the generally available tax law instruments, including private tax rulings, protective opinions against the application of the GAAR, as well as APAs. The taxpayer may then use all means of appeal available to other taxpayers applying for these instruments.

If the disputable issue, not resolved by an agreement, becomes the object of a tax and customs inspection and tax proceedings and the assessment ensuing therefrom is unfavourable to the taxpayer, the taxpayer may use all generally applicable means of appeal: firstly an administrative appeal and if the administrative appeal is not successful - a complaint to an administrative court (judicial appeal).

§12.05 CHALLENGES TO THE DEVELOPMENT OF THE CO-OPERATION PROGRAMME IN POLAND

The Polish co-operation programme is not yet operating. At this point it is difficult to foresee the number of taxpayers interested in joining the programme and accepted into the programme and to assess if the expectations of both parties, i.e., the taxpayers and the tax authorities, will be met. As already mentioned, there are several issues that may hinder the actual implementation of the programme (i.e., the low level of trust in public authorities, the longstanding distrust between taxpayers and tax authorities, attachment to formalism). Additionally, tax authorities may encounter problems trying to hire additional, business experienced staff to operate the programme. Finally, there is no wide public or in-depth expert debate on the programme, with merely basic information being reported online, and also the Ministry of Finance is not promoting the programme extensively. But the largest taxpayers and their advisers are probably well aware of the forthcoming opportunities.

CHAPTER 13

Hard Law and Soft Law Measures Implemented by Spain Regarding Co-operative Compliance

J. Carlos Pedrosa López

§13.01 INTRODUCTION

This work analyzes the Co-operative Compliance phenomenon from a Spanish perspective. The Spanish Agencia Estatal de Administración Tributaria (hereinafter "Directorate of the Tax Agency" or "Spanish AEAT"), during the last decade has notably increased its efforts to propose new mechanisms for reaching consensus with companies regarding their tax obligations.

The measures proposed have been elaborated in accordance with the pillars of fiscal transparency and tax certainty. Companies have to explain that their tax strategies are not abusive or aggressive and, in return, the tax administration has to ensure greater certainty regarding the legal and tax treatment of those taxpayers.

The author has divided this work into two main parts. The first part exposes the reasons that have led to the rise of tax compliance programs. It also explains the historical background of these programs in Spain, making reference to reports, policy papers, and other projects by the Spanish tax administration. In that context, it is important to highlight the connection with documents published by the Organisation for Economic Co-operation and Development (OECD).

The second part analyzes specific questions in connection with the two most relevant national soft law documents, on the one hand, the Spanish Code of Best Tax Practices (hereinafter "the Spanish CBTP") and on the other hand, the so-called rule UNE 19602 (hereinafter "the Spanish Rule").

§13.02 GENERAL ASPECTS OF THE CO-OPERATIVE COMPLIANCE PHENOMENON

[A] Co-operative Compliance Phenomenon in Spain

Tax compliance issues have been receiving increased international attention. Especially since 2008, as a result of the financial global crisis,[1] tax administrations have adopted austere policies to reduce the level of public expenditure and have implemented fiscal reforms focused on the struggle against aggressive tax avoidance to enhance tax collection.[2]

Spain, like other States, has intensified its actions against aggressive tax planning with which companies, multinational (hereinafter "MNEs") or not, have managed to erode tax basis and shift profits. The State legislator and tax administrations have implemented new mechanisms for tackling fraudulent strategies,[3] with the intention to eliminate transnational tax planning structures based on a lack of coordination between the tax legislations of different countries.[4]

These developments have found their cornerstone in Co-operative Compliance. During the last decade, the OECD promoted models of tax compliance based on a collaborative approach between the parties involved (tax administrations, taxpayers and intermediaries, amongst others).[5]

Initially, in 2008, the OECD entered this new stage under the term enhanced relationship,[6] described as an improvement and strengthening of the relationship between taxpayers and the tax administration. Later, from 2013, it reconsidered the original term and changed it to "Co-operative Compliance,"[7] because the envisaged relationship not only supposes voluntary tax compliance by the taxpayers,[8] but also requires tax administrations to collaborate with and assist those taxpayers.

Therefore, Co-operative Compliance is different from other, more normative measures. Although the aim is similar, i.e., to eliminate abusive and aggressive strategies, Co-operative Compliance programs represent a voluntary opportunity for

1. José Manuel Carrero Carrero & Alberto Quintas Seara, *Cumplimiento Tributario Cooperativo y Buena Gobernanza Fiscal en la era BEPS*, 123-124 (Thomson Reuters y E&Y Abogados CIVITAS 2015).
2. Cristina García-Herrero Blanco, *Buen Gobierno Fiscal y Cumplimiento Cooperativo con las Grandes Compañías*, 2 Revista Quincena Fiscal 1 (2017).
3. José Carlos Pedrosa López, *El Arbitraje Fiscal Internacional. Un Nuevo Debate*, 12-13 Tribuna Fiscal 272 (2014).
4. José Carlos Pedrosa López, *Análisis sobre la Licitud de las Operaciones de Arbitraje Fiscal Internacional*, Revista de Contabilidad y Tributación 377-3278 (2014).
5. José Manuel Calderón Carrero, *The Concept of "Aggressive Tax Planning" Launched by the OECD and the EU Commission in the BEPS Era: Redefining the Border Between Legitimate and Illegitimate Tax Planning*, 206 Intertax 44 (2016).
6. OECD, *Study into the Role of Tax Intermediaries* (2008).
7. OECD, *Co-operative Compliance: A Framework. From Enhanced Relationship to Co-operative Compliance* (2013); OECD, *Co-operative Tax Compliance. Building Better Tax Control Frameworks* (2016).
8. José Manuel Calderón Carrero, *The Concept of "Aggressive Tax Planning" Launched by the OECD and the EU Commission in the BEPS Era: Redefining the Border Between Legitimate and Illegitimate Tax Planning*, 206 Intertax 44 (2016).

taxpayers and tax administrations to improve their relationship through transparency, mutual confidence and administrative assistance.[9]

The equality, legitimacy and fairness of international tax systems have attracted the full attention of society, resulting in zero tolerance in relation to fiscal fraud and tax evasion.[10] The level of tax compliance of large companies also possesses an important reputational dimension, since best practices and good governance in tax matters are substantive parts of good corporate governance.

The implementation of co-operative tax programs by the Spanish fiscal authorities was influenced by the continuing initiatives of the OECD. These reports, recommendations and other similar works are in line with the co-operative relationship as an essential element to eliminate aggressive tax planning strategies, while at the same time minimizing administrative cost and reducing risk and fiscal uncertainty.[11]

The efforts of the OECD have not been in vain, but in fact have induced Spanish parties with an interest in this matter to adopt such policies. The success of Co-operative Compliance programs at the domestic level also explains why the OECD has extrapolated this practice to the international level by the publication of the first pilot of the International Compliance Assurance Programme (ICAP) in 2018. The aim is to propose a quick and coordinated approach to provide more fiscal certainty to MNEs that are actively and totally transparent about their activities and transactions.[12]

Spain is one of the most actively engaged countries in that practice. The State legislator has introduced mechanisms to achieve a higher level of transparency, confidence, loyalty and responsibility based on good governance and leading to fiscal certainty. The Spanish tax administration has been active over the years improving this practice through hard law and soft law measures. The State legislator has introduced rules to ensure good governance of companies, not only in the (civil) legal field but also in the tax field. Spain has always been aware of the importance of this issue, both from an internal and an international perspective. That is demonstrated by the fact that Spain was one of the eight jurisdictions involved in the ICAP from its beginning.[13]

[B] Historical Analysis of the Co-operative Compliance Programs Implemented by Spain and Their Connection with the OECD's Reports

In Spain, Co-operative Compliance was born on July 10, 2009, when the State Agency of Spanish tax administration constituted the Forum of Large Companies (hereinafter

9. Valerie Braithwaite, *Taxing Democracy: Understanding Tax Avoidance and Evasion* 79 (Ashgate 2003); Roman Seer, *Voluntary Compliance*, 584 Bulletin for International Taxation 67, 11 (2013).
10. Jaume Menendez Fernandez, *El Tax Compliance: Un Escalón más Hacia la Transparencia Fiscal*, 8 Diario La Ley (2019).
11. OECD, *Study into the Role of Tax Intermediaries*, 39 (2008).
12. OECD, *International Compliance Assurance Programme*, 9 (2018).
13. The tax administrations from 8 Jurisdictions plough: Australia, Closes, Italy, Japan, the Netherlands, Spain, the United Kingdom and the United States.

"Spanish FLC").[14] The creation of this group followed the trail of the OECD Forum on Tax Administrations (hereinafter "OECD's FTAs"),[15] constituted by the Committee of Fiscal Affairs (hereinafter "OECD'S CFA") in 2002, with the aim that fiscal authorities could identify, debate and influence in relevant global tendencies in the sector and develop new ideas to improve the tax administration.

On July 20, 2010, in a plenary session the Spanish FLC approved the Spanish CBTP, which implicitly exposed a new concept in favor of the modernization of the tax administration. Both taxpayers and the tax authorities were aware of the importance to establish a close reciprocal relationship based on good faith, transparency, certainty and mutual trust.[16]

This document is also in line with guidelines established by the OECD in its meetings in 2005 in Dublin,[17] in 2006 in Seoul[18] and in 2008 in Cape Town,[19] all of which focused on the paper regarding fiscal intermediaries.[20]

In 2013, the Spanish FLC published a report with conclusions about the development of Spanish CBTP. The result exposed by this report was absolutely favorable, describing as useful and fruitful the initiatives of the Spanish AEAT and the companies that have adopted it.

The report positively commented on the two-way nature of the relationship. On the one hand, it involves a guarantee for the tax administration in relation to tax obligations that the company has to fulfill. This guarantee assumes management of risks, including measures to mitigate fiscal risks and avoiding the use of opaque structures which intend to minimize taxation.[21] On the other hand, the tax administration tries to collaborate with the taxpayer, reducing conflicts from the interpretation of applicable rules.

Therefore, the CBTP, with its successive modifications and updates, and the other documents elaborated by the Spanish fiscal authorities, emphasizes the need to pay attention to fiscal governance and fiscal awareness as important elements of the tax control framework. The establishment of a global strategy of risk management

14. More information on the Spanish Forum of Large Companies (2009) https://www.agenciatributaria.es/aeat.internet/inicio/_segmentos_/empresas_y_profesionales/foro_grandes_empresas/foro_grandes_empresas.shtml.
15. OECD, *Forum on Tax Administration* (2002) https://www.oecd.org/tax/forum-on-tax-administration/about/.
16. Spanish General Directorate of the Tax Agency, *Code of Best Tax Practices*, 3-4 (2010) https://www.agenciatributaria.es/static_files/aeat/contenidos_comunes/la_agencia_tributaria/segmentos_usuarios/empresas_y_profesionales/foro_grandes_empresas/cbpt_publicacion_web_es_es.pdf.
17. OECD, *Forum Tax Administration*, Dublin Meeting (June 1-2, 2005) http://www.oecd.org/site/fta/34872840.pdf.
18. OECD, *Forum Tax Administration*, Seoul Meeting (September 14-15, 2006) https://www.oecd.org/tax/forum-on-tax-administration/news/oecdtaxadministratorstojoinforcesinfightingtaxnon-compliance.htm.
19. OECD, *Forum Tax Administration*, Cape Town Meeting (January 10-11, 2008) https://www.oecd.org/southafrica/fourthoecdforumontaxadministrationcapetowncommunique.htm.
20. OECD, *Study into the Role of Tax Intermediaries* (2008).
21. José Carlos Pedrosa López, *Análisis sobre la Licitud de las Operaciones de Arbitraje Fiscal Internacional*, Revista de Contabilidad y Tributación 377-3278 (2014).

includes the correct fulfillment of tax obligations[22] and the promotion of business behavior management because, as indicated by the "OECD Guidelines for Multinational Enterprises" reviewed in 2011,[23] companies have to fulfill with the spirit of the law in countries where they operate, and should also cooperate with fiscal authorities by providing relevant information, even when not legally required.

Spanish CBTP also took into account the attributes, as identified in the 2008 OECD Report "Study into the role of tax intermediaries," regarding the definition of the term enhanced relationship. This term relates to the aim to boost collaboration between fiscal authorities and taxpayers through tax compliance programs based on confidence and fiscal certainty.

In this respect, the 2013 OECD Report "Co-operative Compliance: A Framework. From Enhanced Relationship to Co-Operative Compliance"[24] introduced the concept of Co-operative Compliance, in complement to the concept of enhanced relationship. It considered that the latter concept still implies retrospective control and should progress from mainly repressive to collaborative relationships between tax administrations and taxpayers, with an explicit view to cover discussions on tax treatment in real time, or even prospectively.[25] It proposed a tax compliance optimum ensuring efficient taxation, based on the input of transparency and resulting in the output of certainty.[26]

This approach implied the development of (elementary parts of) a tax control framework in order to ensure an efficient tax co-operation system between companies and tax administrations. With this aim, the OECD established new guidance to ensure that tax risks of companies are controlled in its report "Co-operative Tax Compliance: Building better tax control frameworks,"[27] published in 2016. One of the ways this is achieved is by documenting explanations of relevant transactions. Such documentation has to be regularly reviewed so as to guarantee its completeness and correctness to all interested parties.[28]

The updates and reviews of the CBTP took into account the OECD guidelines. Proof of this came in November 2015, when the Tax Spanish FLC agreed in a plenary session to reinforce the co-operative relationship under CBTP by making it optionally accessible to all companies willing to adopt CBTP, irrespective of their size and economic activity.[29]

---

22. Cristina García-Herrero Blanco, *Buen Gobierno Fiscal y Cumplimiento Cooperativo con las Grandes Compañías*, 4-5 Revista Quincena Fiscal 1 (2017).
23. OECD, *Guidelines for Multinational Enterprises* (2011).
24. OECD, *Co-operative Compliance: A Framework. From Enhanced Relationship to Co-operative Compliance* (2013).
25. Alicja Majdanska & Pedro Guilherme Lindeberg Schoueri, *Tax Compliance in the Spotlight: The Challenges for Tax Administrations and Taxpayers*, 637 Bulletin for International Taxation 71, 12 (2017).
26. OECD, *Co-operative Compliance: A Framework. From Enhanced Relationship to Co-operative Compliance*, 57 (2013).
27. OECD, *Co-operative Tax Compliance. Building Better Tax Control Frameworks* (2016).
28. OECD, *Co-operative Tax Compliance. Building Better Tax Control Frameworks* (2016).
29. AEAT, *Annex to the Code of Best Tax Practices* (2015) https://www.agenciatributaria.es/static_files/aeat/contenidos_comunes/la_agencia_tributaria/sala_de_prensa/03_11_2015_anexo_codigo_buenas_practicas.pdf.

Spanish CBTP was promoted to stimulate corporate social responsibility management of fiscal risk, in accordance with OECD guidelines and with the essential attributes identified for efficient tax co-operation.

These Spanish initiatives represented a degree of progress without precedent. This group of soft law reports, drafted by the Spanish FLC, promoting a new paradigm of co-operation, is in accordance with the OECD's proposals regarding tax compliance co-operation. In addition to these soft law guidelines, the Spanish CBTP also infers the connection between the Spanish AEAT with the OECD's recommendations in its so-called Action Plan on Base Erosion and Profit Shifting (hereinafter "the BEPS Plan"), composed from 2013 to 2015.[30]

In accordance with the principles and aims of the BEPS Plan, and especially Actions 12, 13 and 14, the Spanish CBTP established some indicators of best tax practices that, indirectly, force companies to identify their fiscal structure, as well as information on the most relevant transactions approved by the board of directors. In return, it commits the Spanish tax authorities to communicate administrative and legal criteria used in applying the tax laws, in order to minimize conflicts over the interpretation of applicable rules.

Tax transparency and fiscal certainty are the pillars of the co-operative relationship between taxpayer and the tax authorities. Companies communicate their attitude towards tax and explain how they are taxed and how they add assurance to their fiscal compliance management in the countries in which they operate. This supposes the provision of information beyond legal obligations.

In this sense, the position of the State Agency of the Spanish tax administration and its reports are in line with the main aim of the Mandatory disclosure rules report.[31] The rules force MNEs to provide the most relevant information on allocation of income, economic activity and taxes paid in each country.

Further proof of the importance of this practice in Spain is the recently published rule UNE 19602 "Systems of management of tax compliance. Requirements with guidance for their use." This rule followed in the trail of the Spanish CBTP. It was published on February 28, 2019 by the Spanish Association of Normalization and Certification (AENOR)[32] with the aim to design and to evaluate systems of management of tax compliance that allow to generate or improve a suitable Organizational culture, sensitive to the prevention, detection, management and reduction of fiscal risk.

---

30. OECD, *Action Plan on Base Erosion and Profit Shifting* (2013) https://www.oecd.org/ctp/bepsactionplan.pdf.
31. OECD, *Action 12 Final Report: Mandatory Disclosure Rules* (2015) https://read.oecd-ilibrary.org/taxation/mandatory-disclosure-rules-action-12-2015-final-report_9789264241442-en#page1.
32. The AENOR, from 1986 until 2017 the Spanish Association that devote so much to the tasks of creation of technical standards (normalization), as to tasks of evaluation of the compliance (certification). Nevertheless, in 2017 AENOR separated in two independent parts: on the one hand, it creates the current Spanish Association of Normalisation (UNE), that is the entity so-called by Spain to realize the activities of normalization in the country (rule UNE) and also participates in the normalization to international level (rules IN and ISO). On the other hand, the activities of evaluation of the compliance (certification) and other auxiliary activities, remain in hands of the new AENOR International, S.To.Or.

This rule, applicable to any entity, whether multinational, medium-sized or small, was a novelty in the context of tax compliance programs because, in addition to offering some guidelines to ensuring compliance with fiscal obligations, proper implementation of the rule is also a proof of good governance before the Spanish AEAT or even before the courts. Likewise, in case of an infraction, implementation can serve to demonstrate that there was no intention to commit a fraudulent act, which can reduce the sanction or even avoid litigation.[33]

This rule UNE 19602 represented a step forward in the field of tax compliance, because it tried to establish an autoregulation system which—through the establishment of internal control mechanisms to prevent fiscal risks—aims to avoid ex-post inspection by the tax administration, as well as corrective and coercive measures. It established a relationship of trust, leading to minimization of confrontations between taxpayers and the Spanish tax administration. It also resulted in more legal certainty, and swifter resolution of conflicts, the paramount aim being to protect the presumption of innocence and absence of fraudulent intention before any inspection and, by extension, before the courts.[34]

To sum up, all recommendations made by the Spanish tax administration and the rules implemented by the State legislator promote the development of best tax practices. These recommendations and rules are directly related to the principles, values and guidelines that define good tax behavior of economic agents, and promote an environment of transparency, co-operation, good faith and justified confidence in the legal relationship between companies and tax administration.[35]

The adoption of tax compliance programs in many OECD Member States has led this Organization to take a further step. Thus, on January 23, 2018 the OECD launched the first pilot of the project called "International Compliance Assurance Programme"[36] with the participation of tax administrations and MNEs from eight Member States,[37] Spain included. This program is designed to improve the level of legal certainty in fiscal matters through a multilateral coordination mechanism by which tax administrations analyze international fiscal risks of companies that develop business activities in those States.

In 2019, the OECD published another document[38] in which it analyzes in greater detail the instruments and measures on which it bases the application of this program,

33. Juan Calvo Vérgez, *La Evolución de los Programas de Cumpimiento Tributario: de la Norma UNE 19601 a la Norma UNE 19602*, 1 Revista Quincena Fiscal 7 (2019).
34. David Alvarez Barrios, Compliance Financiero o la Lógica Evolución del Compliance Penal: La Norma UNE 19602, Legal Today (December 7, 2018) http://www.legaltoday.com/practica-juridica/penal/penal/compliance-financiero-o-la-logica-evolucion-del-compliance-penal-la-norma-une19602.
35. Lorena Pérez Martínez, *UNE 19602. Sistemas de Gestión de Tax compliance. Entre el Cumplimiento Normativo y las Buenas Prácticas*, 9 Actualidad Jurídica Aranzadi 947 (2019).
36. OECD, *Forum Tax Administration: International Compliance Assurance Programme*, Pilot Handbook (2018) https://www.oecd.org/tax/forum-on-tax-administration/publications-and-products/international-compliance-assurance-programme-pilot-handbook.pdf.
37. Australia, Canada, Italy, Japan, Holland, Spain, United Kingdom and United States.
38. OECD, *Forum Tax Administration: International Compliance Assurance Programme*, Pilot Handbook 2.0 (2019) https://www.oecd.org/tax/forum-on-tax-administration/publications-and-products/international-compliance-assurance-programme-pilot-handbook-2.0.pdf.

and the phases outlined to reach the planned outcome. The OECD opted for a coordinated approach, because this Project was based, among other elements, on the transfer pricing documentation that MNEs have to produce as a consequence of the implementation of Action 13 of the BEPS Plan in domestic laws. It also took into account the recommendations of Action 14 of the BEPS Plan, which promotes the utilization of mutual procedure agreements to resolve tax disputes.[39] Thus, the ICAP Project tries to reduce the time spent on resolution of conflicts through an environment of mutual confidence, good faith and loyalty among all parties.

§13.03 CONTROVERSIAL ISSUES OF CO-OPERATIVE COMPLIANCE PROGRAMS

The Spanish tax administration has been active over the decades improving the co-operative relationship with taxpayers to ensure compliance with their tax obligations. As described in the previous section, the Spanish tax administration has implemented multiple mechanisms to reach consensus with taxpayers in a constructive way, so as to ensure that private companies do not commit administrative offenses or tax crimes.

Corporate transparency has been key to the change in favor of increased certainty in the tax field. The evolution of Spanish proposals in this matter can mainly be divided into two blocks:

(1) Tax compliance programs based on the Spanish CBTP, elaborated by the Spanish AEAT.
(2) The tax compliance model based on the rule UNE 19602, under which all companies with a qualifying tax management system meet the conditions to demonstrate the reliability of their tax information and their commitment to tax compliance.

[A] Approaches That Co-operative Compliance Models Can Be Based On

In Spain, the regulation of good corporate governance was always tackled from the legal perspective of companies, assuming that, if a resident company in Spain exceeds the minimum legal transparency threshold, it could also be considered sufficiently transparent from all other perspectives.

In the last decade, greater importance has been attributed to the fiscal appearances of companies and to their relationship with the Spanish tax administration, leading to the promotion of co-operative relationships, based on the principles of transparency and mutual trust, sharing information with the aim to reduce conflicts

39. OECD, *Action 14 Final Report: Making Dispute Resolution Mechanisms More Effective* (2015) https://read.oecd-ilibrary.org/taxation/making-dispute-resolution-mechanisms-more-effective-action-14-2015-final-report_9789264241633-en#page1.

and litigations. The object is to provide fiscal certainty to companies about the criteria applied by the tax administration regarding the tax consequences of business strategies, in return for greater transparency regarding the tax policy and fiscal planning strategies of those companies.[40]

The intersection of the commercial and tax law fields[41] is the result of continuous soft law initiatives of the Spanish tax administration, although it is also true that in this context the OECD has been fundamental. The ongoing proposals and recommendations of this organization, intended to improve the relationship between tax administrations and companies, have marked a turning point by facilitating the preparation of non-compulsory documents on good tax governance and best tax practices in Spain.

This convergence of civil and tax law makes sense, because both have the same focus, that is a high standard of behavior and appropriate practices of commercial enterprises. For this reason, it is not surprising that the State legislator successfully attempted to introduce compulsory tax compliance provisions for companies into commercial law. This mix of contexts has materialized in the reform of the Law of Entities of Capital that came into force on January 1, 2015 through the Law 31/2014.

The reform includes measures focused on guaranteeing good governance of companies. It demands of the Board of Directors to determine a fiscal strategy and to set out a policy regarding the control and management of fiscal risks, as well as to communicate any creation of or participation in entities resident in tax havens. In sum, companies are required to promote an appropriate policy of corporate social responsibility, based on transparency in respect of all information that is relevant to this aim, including the company's performance and financial results.[42]

Also, in 2015, the Spanish General Tax Law implemented in its Article 92 the principle of Co-operative Compliance in tax matters, making reference to the possibility that companies in any economic sector and any line of business may reach an agreement regarding their tax obligations with the tax administration.

However, with a few exceptions, the question of Co-operative Compliance at the fiscal level had always been tackled through recommendations and proposals formulated in soft law documents. As described in the previous section, the CBTP created by the Spanish FLC is the most representative document in this context. The Spanish CBTP, with its successive modifications and updates, has tried to follow the various initiatives by the OECD.

In the tax field, there have basically been no binding documents to regulate this practice between companies and the Spanish tax administration. The soft law regulation in the context of good fiscal governance has in fact become self-regulating with the issuance of the so-called rule UNE 19602. This soft law rule tries to facilitate the design and evaluation of tax compliance management systems that allow the prevalence of an

40. Jaume Menendez Fernandez, *El Tax compliance: Un Escalón más Hacia la Transparencia Fiscal*, 17 Diario La Ley (2019).
41. Some of other countries that have implemented a similar mixed approach: United States of America, United Kingdom, the Netherlands, Australia.
42. Cristina García-Herrero Blanco, *Buen Gobierno Fiscal y Cumplimiento Cooperativo con las Grandes Compañías*, 10 Revista Quincena Fiscal 1 (2017).

organizational culture that is sensitive to the prevention, detection, management and minimization of fiscal risks.

All this shows that, in the fiscal field, Co-operative Compliance mainly remains regulated by soft law. This is unlike other fields, like civil or penal law. This is illustrated by the origins of the previously commented rule UNE 19602. This rule—that in spite of its denomination is not compulsory—proceeds from the rule UNE 19601, which pertains to the penal field.

The rule UNE 19601 derived from the reform of the Spanish Criminal Code, realized in 2010 through the Fundamental Law 5/2010, of June 22. This introduced the possibility that legal persons, or their legal representatives and administrators, could be sanctioned for having perpetrated criminal acts resulting from a lack of adequate control. However, Article 31 Criminal Code also introduced the possibility that a legal person could be exempted from criminal responsibility when meeting the minimum standards set by the compliance programs.

In this context the rule UNE 19601 was created, which establishes normative requirements aimed at maintaining and improving compliance models for companies. The intention is to warn the commission of possible crimes at the earliest stage and to reduce the penal risk through a culture of ethics and compliance. Thus, in the tax field the rule UNE 19602 was created with a similar purpose, but with the difference that this regulation was, for that moment at least, restricted to soft law status. Nevertheless, it is no less true that this kind of soft law has a regulating character as well as a positive effect on consistency, meaning that—depending on the attitude of the tax administration and the courts—it could be applied as if it had force of law.

[B] Nature of the Disclosure Rules and Application by Taxpayers

In accordance with the explanations in the previous sections, the Spanish CBTP was designed mainly with a view to co-operation between large companies and the tax administration. Still, other companies were allowed access too. After all, the aim of this Code of Best Practices was to construct the co-operative relationship model on a voluntary basis and to stimulate an open style of communication between tax administration and all companies that have adopted the Spanish CBTP, irrespective of their size, economic sector or business activity.[43]

In the fiscal field, the rule UNE 19602 followed in the trail of the Spanish CBTP because, in addition to being voluntary, it integrates some measures at both the domestic and the international level that promote the fulfillment of tax obligations, the identification of fiscal risks and the effective compliance with all relevant tax legislation.[44]

---

43. AEAT, *Annex to the Spanish Code of Best Tax Practices* (2015) https://www.agenciatributaria.es/static_files/aeat/contenidos_comunes/la_agencia_tributaria/sala_de_prensa/03_11_2015_anexo_codigo_buenas_practicas.pdf.
44. Laura Campanón Galiana, *Análisis y Aplicación Práctica de la Norma UNE 19602 de Sistemas de Gestión de Tax compliance 1*, Carta Tributaria. Revista de Opinión 49 (2019).

This rule too is applicable to any company, whether multinational, medium-sized or small, allowing for individual circumstances and industry peculiarities, offering guidelines for a system that ensures compliance with all fiscal obligations.

[C] Conditions for Acceptance and Application of the Programs

This kind of mechanism, the purpose of which is to establish a co-operative relationship between the Spanish tax administration and resident companies, implies that these instruments are at the disposal of all companies, irrespective of size, economic sector and business activity. But by the same token, companies that decide to join the tax compliance programs accept the obligation to execute and support the agreements reached.

This does not go against the fact that the company interested in applying the CBTP or the rule UNE 19602 has to execute those programs in accordance with a definite procedure and fulfilling a series of set conditions. In that sense, the Spanish CBTP affirms that once the Board of Directors has agreed its adherence to the Spanish CBTP, the company has to remit the agreement to the Service of Planning and International Relations of the Spanish FLC Technical Office, which in its turn will communicate the agreement to the Central Delegation of Large Taxpayers. Finally, the Spanish AEAT will publish a list of companies that have adopted the program.

From this moment, companies that have adopted the program must ensure good corporate governance by complying with the tax practices agreed and must report about this annually. If they do not produce the annual report, the understanding will be that the company has decided to opt out.

The very fact that companies apply the Spanish CBTP implies the assumption of particular tax behavioral commitments to reflect their effective compliance with the conditions. In this sense, the fiscal strategy of the company as ratified by the Board of Directors has to be documented, also explaining any transactions and investments involving specific risks and detailing the measures adopted to mitigate the fiscal risks identified, including internal rules adopted to ensure good corporate governance.

The company has to show that it has not used opaque structures for tax purposes and has even collaborated in the identification of such structures, as well as proposing solutions concerning possible fraudulent fiscal practices it has detected in the markets in which it operates. With a view to possible future inspections, the company will try to reduce potential conflicts concerning the interpretation of the law, as well as setting up effective information systems and internal controls with respect to fiscal risks. The company has to be able to prove that it has effectively assumed and fulfilled the commitments from its acceptance of the Spanish CBTP.

In this context, companies can implement a system to comply with the fiscal obligations stipulated by rule UNE 19602. Companies can adopt, unilaterally and voluntarily, a system of compliance under the standards established by this rule that, in some respects, was inspired by the Spanish CBTP.

The acceptance of the rule involves the voluntary implementation of a tax compliance management system aimed to prevent fiscal risks, emphasize tax control, operate in accordance with good governance practices and avoid abusive tax behavior and aggressive fiscal strategies.

Logically, the level of exposure to fiscal risks will vary according to the circumstances that apply to the company. The rule UNE 19602 established a series of requirements that will have to be fulfilled by companies in accordance with their specific characteristics, including proposed mechanisms to warn about fiscal risk, fiscal control management, the identification of abusive practices and good tax governance. The rule proposes requirements which have to be adapted to the specific situation of individual companies and that have to be fulfilled in order to minimize fiscal risks and improve the management and tax control of companies.

[D] Communication Procedures Between the Tax Authorities and the Taxpayer Within the Co-operative Compliance Programmes

In the first meeting of the Spanish FLC, a proposal was made regarding the implementation of a mechanism of regular consultations on the acceptability of certain transactions with a tax impact. For this reason, the CBTP later established that "The Spanish AEAT will establish suitable procedures to allow taxpayers that have doubts on the tax treatment of specific transactions can know, as soon as possible, the criteria that the tax administration would apply."

The companies that have adopted the Spanish CBTP meet and communicate with the Spanish tax administration on the Commission. This group consists of members of the Spanish AEAT and participating companies and meets annually. Both parties debate about matters of the Spanish CBTP, consider the incorporation of new recommendations and identify the interpretative criteria for the benefit of common understanding, without prejudice to any other initiative that can contribute to and help implement the Spanish CBTP. The procedure to clarify the tax treatment of specific transactions is initiated by one of the parties. The company has to describe the transactions and the Spanish AEAT resolves the question in a written report, which has to contain the administrative criteria concerning the application of the tax legislation[45] and the treatment that would apply to those subjects that are involved in the described situation.

Furthermore, the Spanish AEAT can call occasional meetings with companies that have adopted the CBTP, either to obtain more information about a case or to clarify a particular action by the company. In that sense, the Spanish CBTP applies different and alternative means to ensure exchange of information and to ensure the fulfillment of tax obligations.

45. Royal decree 1065/2007 of July 27.
Article 63 "Performances of information," Art. 64 "Procedure of the application of information" https://www.boe.es/buscar/act.php?id=boe-a-2007-15984.

[E] The Agreements Reached by the Parties: Are They Binding?

The Spanish CBTP in its heading 2.2 commits the tax administration to the publication of its interpretations of fiscal rules and of criteria regarding transactions that might generate controversies. It also requires the tax administration to inform taxpayers about the most relevant practices regarding certain transactions.[46]

This duty is unilateral but, by implication, aims to promote legal certainty and a co-operative model regarding the fulfillment of fiscal obligations by companies through systematic, homogeneous and clearly defined performance guidelines. The publication of the administrative criteria is mainly carried out through a web portal of the AEAT, which contains a section on "criteria of a general character in the application of taxes." In this way, the tax administration makes the effort to issue interpretations with the intention to reward taxable subjects that act in accordance with the guidelines published.

In this context, the CBTP establishes in its heading 2.1 that the tax administration has to take into account relevant precedents and to determine a coherent interpretation of the fiscal rules. The Spanish AEAT has the obligation to address those questions that might give rise to significant controversies with taxpayers and has to communicate whether or not the Spanish General Directorate of Tax Agency has established generally applicable criteria.

Still, this initiative is not more than a non-exhaustive general orientation and source of information. It certainly does not represent a detailed and homogeneous database of the tax administration's applied views.

These mechanisms are unilateral. They are not the result of negotiations between parties, but of an interpretative exercise concerning the criteria that the tax administration applies to certain situations. They are soft law in the form of expert opinions.

The Spanish CBTP also covers in its heading 2.3 the implementation of a request procedure. The intention is that, upon request of the taxpayer, the tax administration interprets the facts of specific transactions and sets out its views of the tax consequences, in order to provide more legal certainty to taxpayers.

This request mechanism is in line with Article 87 Spanish Ley General Tributaria (hereinafter "Spanish General Tax Law" or "Spanish LGT") that instructs fiscal authorities to provide information on the taxation of certain sectors, activities or sources of income. It is also in accordance with Articles 63 and 64 Spanish LGT, which relate to overall effectiveness, controls and review procedures.[47]

These ad hoc reports from the tax administration have to be valued as soft law in the form of expert opinions regarding the acceptance or rejection of a transnational transaction. In accordance with heading 2.4 of Spanish CBTP, this process affirms that the taxpayer will not be liable to sanctions, provided the criteria and further guidance

---

46. General Tax Law 58/2003, of December 17. Article 87 "Communications and performances of information" https://www.boe.es/buscar/act.php?id=boe-a-2003-23186.
47. Royal decree 1065/2007 of July 27, which approves the General Regulation of the tax inspection procedures https://www.boe.es/buscar/act.php?id=boe-a-2007-15984.

of the tax administration are followed. This would even apply if certain tax obligations are not met.

This does not mean that these legal requests on specific cases constitute binding rules. The consultations are reciprocal mechanisms aimed at reaching consensus regarding the correct interpretation of the relevant tax obligation but can never be binding, not even for the taxpayer in question, because the tax administration cannot be aware of all the elements relevant to the taxation of the transaction.

[F] Tax Control Framework and Risk Management

The tax administration expects that, through a co-operative relationship and mechanisms for voluntary tax compliance, companies manage their tax positions with a low-risk level and maintain a corporate governance model in accordance with legal requirements, as well as an effective internal risk control framework.[48]

In Spain, the rules regarding risk management are in the CBTP and in other soft law documents, but they do not focus only on fiscal risk. This is due to the fact that there is not a separate prescribed control framework for each relevant business area, but uniform frameworks that apply to a different field. As a result, the tax control framework refers to internal controls of companies in such a way as to cover all processes and transactions with possible fiscal consequences.

On this basis, Article 116 Spanish LGT stipulates that the tax administration will annually set up a plan of tax control focused on identifying areas and business strategies with high-risk level. This has the purpose to create a structure to improve the co-operative relationship between tax administration and companies, in addition to restricting transaction risks by improving the knowledge of responsible management with respect to the way the tax administration interprets certain situations. This procedure is also in line with Article 93 Spanish LGT that allows tax administrations to demand reports and legally relevant documents regarding tax compliance from taxpayers.

The control of fiscal risk through different legally binding mechanisms as well as soft law measures and the increased emphasis on co-operative relationships serve to reduce the number of litigations and conflicts. In line with this development, the CBTP in its heading 3.1 supports the use of normative and binding mechanisms established in tax legislation.

Furthermore, heading 3.2 of this soft law document promotes settlements in the different phases of a procedure. For this purpose, it stresses the importance of delimiting the object of inspections, mutually providing all the necessary information and exchanging opinions.

The aim, as indicated in heading 3.3 of the Spanish CBTP, is that taxpayers face fewer fiscal issues and that the tax administration efficiently obtains the information it needs. The Spanish AEAT has to narrowly define the object of requests as well as the

48. OECD, *Co-operative Compliance: A Framework. From Enhanced Relationship to Co-operative Compliance*, 37-40 (2013).

scope of inspections in order to realize an effective level of control. For parties to reach agreements of this type, it remains fundamental that the taxpayer maintains a fully-fledged system of tax issue detection.

A co-operative relationship, characterized by mutual transparency, indirectly remains dependent on the existence of a minimum level of tax control. In this light, the tax compliance of companies and the requirements of tax administration have evolved to the extent that the authorities do not exert their powers too rigorously, while the taxpayers are seriously committed to maximum tax compliance.

With this aim the OECD proposed many measures of control,[49] among which a group of behavioral rules and values for the tax administration's personnel stand out, including work standards and operating systems to ensure consistent decision making. It also considers as fundamental that different functionaries of various hierarchical levels act in procedures, in order to avoid one-sided decisions.

BIBLIOGRAPHY

Articles, Chapters & Books

Alicja Majdanska & Pedro Guilherme Lindeberg Schoueri, *Tax Compliance in the Spotlight: The Challenges for Tax Administrations and Taxpayers*, Bulletin for International Taxation 71, 11 (2017).

Cristina García-Herrero Blanco, *Buen Gobierno Fiscal y Cumplimiento Cooperativo con las Grandes Compañías*, Revista Quincena Fiscal 1 (2017).

David Alvarez Barrios, Compliance Financiero o la Lógica Evolución del Compliance Penal: La Norma UNE 19602, Legal Today 7-12 (2018).

Eelco van der Enden & Katarzyna Bronzewska, *The Concept of Cooperative Compliance*, Bulletin for International Taxation 68 (2014).

Jaume Menendez Fernandez, *El Tax compliance: Un Escalón más Hacia la Transparencia Fiscal*, Diario La Ley (2019).

Joe Stanley-Smith, *Case Study: Repsol's Participation in ICAP*, International Tax Review (2019).

José Carlos Pedrosa López, *El Arbitraje Fiscal Internacional. Un Nuevo Debate*, Tribuna Fiscal 272 (2014).

José Carlos Pedrosa López, *Análisis sobre la Licitud de las Operaciones de Arbitraje Fiscal Internacional*, Revista de Contabilidad y Tributación 377-3278 (2014).

José Manuel Calderón Carrero, *The Concept of "Aggressive Tax Planning" Launched by the OECD and the EU Commission in the BEPS Era: Redefining the Border Between Legitimate and Illegitimate Tax Planning*, Intertax 44 (2016).

José Manuel Calderón Carrero, *El nuevo modelo de Control del Cumplimiento Tributario de los Grandes Contribuyentes: las Últimas Medidas Propuestas por la HMRC y su Potencial Impacto en España*, Revista Quincena Fiscal 19 (2015).

49. OECD, *Co-operative Compliance: A Framework. From Enhanced Relationship to Co-operative Compliance*, 70 (2013).

José Manuel Calderón Carrero & Alberto Quintas Seara, *Cumplimiento Tributario Cooperativo y Buena Gobernanza Fiscal en la era BEPS* (Thomson Reuters y E&Y Abogados CIVITAS 2015).
Juan Calvo Vérgez, *La Evolución de los Programas de Cumpimiento Tributario: de la Norma UNE 19601 a la Norma UNE 19602*, Revista Quincena Fiscal 7 (2019).
Laura Campanón Galiana, *Análisis y Aplicación Práctica de la Norma UNE 19602 de Sistemas de Gestión de Tax compliance*, Carta Tributaria. Revista de Opinión 49 (2019).
Lorena Pérez Martínez, *UNE 19602. Sistemas de Gestión de Tax compliance. Entre el Cumplimiento Normativo y las Buenas Prácticas*, Actualidad Jurídica Aranzadi 9 (2019).
Roman Seer, *Voluntary Compliance*, Bulletin for International Taxation 67, 11 (2013).
Valerie Braithwaite, *Taxing Democracy: Understanding Tax Avoidance and Evasion* (Ashgate 2003).

Reports (Spanish & OECD)

Spanish Forum of Large Companies (2009).
Spanish State Agency of Tax Administration, *Code of Best Tax Practices* (2010).
Spanish State Agency of Tax Administration, Annex to the Code of Best Tax Practices (2015).
Spanish Forum of Large Companies, *Proposal for the reinforcement of the best practices of company fiscal transparency by companies falling under the Code of Best Tax Practices* (2016).
OECD, *Action Plan on Base Erosion and Profit Shifting* (2013).
OECD, *Action 12 Final Report: Mandatory Disclosure Rules* (2015).
OECD, *Action 14 Final Report: Making Dispute Resolution Mechanisms More Effective* (2015).
OECD, *Forum on Tax Administration* (2002).
OECD, *Forum Tax Administration,* Dublin Meeting (2005).
OECD, *Forum Tax Administration*, Seoul Meeting (2006).
OECD, *Forum Tax Administration*, Cape Town Meeting (2008).
OECD, *Study into the Role of Tax Intermediaries* (2008).
OECD, *Guidelines for Multinational Enterprises* (2011).
OECD, *Co-operative Compliance: A Framework. From Enhanced Relationship to Co-operative Compliance* (2013).
OECD, *Co-operative Tax Compliance. Building Better Tax Control Frameworks* (2016).
OECD, *Forum Tax Administration: International Compliance Assurance Programme*, Pilot Handbook (2018).
OECD, *Forum Tax Administration: International Compliance Assurance Programme*, Pilot Handbook 2.0 (2019).

Legislation

Spanish Royal Decree 1065/2007, of July 27, which approves the General Regulation of the tax inspection procedures (2007).

Spanish General Tax Law 58/2003, of December 17 (2003).

CHAPTER 14

Co-operative Compliance: The U.K. Evolutionary Model

Dennis de Widt & Lynne Oats

§14.01 INTRODUCTION

[A] Background

The United Kingdom (U.K.) model of Co-operative Compliance can be described as evolutionary because it is not a clearly defined programme but is rather an amalgam of individual initiatives, as will be seen below. For the purposes of this chapter, we examine those initiatives from 2005 onwards, since that year marked a significant turning point in U.K. tax authority history. The U.K.'s tax authority, Her Majesty's Revenue and Customs (HMRC), was established by the Commissioners for Revenue and Customs Act 2005 as a merger between the two former tax departments, Inland Revenue (broadly dealing with direct taxes) and Her Majesty's Customs and Excise (broadly dealing with indirect taxes). The merged department deals with all nationally imposed taxes and the merger process provided an opportunity to reconsider operational procedures, including those relevant to dealing with large businesses. A number of modernizing and innovative processes were developed and crystallized in 2006.[1]

HMRC's current stated objectives are to:[2]

- collect revenues due and bear down on avoidance and evasion;
- transform tax and payments for our customers; and
- design and deliver a professional, efficient and engaged organization.

---

1. *See* below and also Tuck 2013, "The Changing Role of Tax Governance: Remaking the Large Corporate Taxpayer into a Visible Customer Partner," British Journal of Management 24, 116-131.
2. HMRC https://www.gov.uk/government/publications/hmrc-strategy.

HMRC has for a long time had a "customer centric" strategy[3] and regularly seeks the views of customers through surveys and commissions low-level market research.[4] Public consultations take place regularly and comments are invited in respect of new initiatives, including aspects of the Co-operative compliance regime. As a non-ministerial body, HMRC holds significant powers and is held to account by a number of formal oversight mechanisms including Parliamentary committees, the National Audit Office, the Parliamentary Ombudsman and the Adjudicator's Office. HMRC is relatively open in its operations; for example, internal manuals outlining processes and procedures are publicly available on the internet and annual reports produced detailing the department's performance.

[B] Administrative Compliance Burdens

There is no systematic process in the U.K. for measuring administrative compliance burdens and this is an area that has received little scholarly attention. Two features of the U.K. system do, however, seek to shed light on the compliance burdens of specific tax legislation, Tax Information and Impact Notices (TIINs) and the Office for Tax Simplification (OTS).

New legislation is accompanied by TIINs produced by HMRC that provide standardized information about the new measures including their rationale and historical background together with a summary of impacts.[5] The expected tax revenue impact of any new measure is quantified for the year of the change and the subsequent five years. In addition, narrative explanations are provided for the following categories:

- economic impact;
- impact on individuals, households and families;
- equalities impacts;
- impact on business including civil society organizations;
- operational impact (HMRC or other); and
- other impacts.

The OTS[6] was initially created as an independent office of Her Majesty's Treasury (HMT) in 2010 and put on a statutory footing in 2016. It was established to provide

3. *See* Tuck, Lamb & Hoskin 2011, "Customers? The Reconstruction of the Taxpayer in Inland Revenue Discourse and Practice," Accounting and Business Research 41:4, 357-374.
4. HMRC website research programme, *see* https://www.gov.uk/government/organisations/hm-revenue-customs/about/research. A recent report entitled "HMRC Stakeholder Engagement Research 2018" (HMRC Report No 518) provides insights into the views of influential stakeholder groups. The Department was found to be performing well against key performance indicators and on balance all stakeholder groups view the organization favorably.
5. https://www.gov.uk/government/collections/tax-information-and-impact-notes-tiins#finance-bill-2019-20-11-july-2019.
6. Zu & Oats 2019, "The Role of the Office of Tax Simplification in the United Kingdom and Lessons for Other Countries," in Evans, Franzsen & Stack eds. *Tax Simplification: An African Perspective*, Pretoria University Law Press.

advice on simplification of the tax system, including measures that will ease administrative burdens. It is funded jointly by HMRC and HMT and relies heavily on secondments from the tax profession.

[C] Ongoing Advice and Consultation

HMRC has a good record for ongoing consultation with businesses of all sizes in relation to how well, or not, the tax system is functioning.

For small businesses, HMRC has recently launched an online forum to allow small business owners to seek and receive direct tax advice.[7] The website includes a message board, discussions and a webchat.

For small and medium businesses, an Administrative Burdens Advisory Board[8] was established in 2006 and is a group of small and medium business operators and advisors who regularly meet with HMRC and report to the Financial Secretary to the Treasury. The body acts as a critical friend to HMRC with the aim of making tax compliance simpler and easier for small businesses. HMRC is developing a Master Customer Journeys approach which considers how taxpayers experience dealing with HMRC and other relevant government departments in respect of particular events.

[D] Large Business Tax Forum

HMRC sponsors a forum to bring together representatives of large businesses and HMRC and HMT officials to improve mutual understanding and foster a stronger relationship in relation to administration of the tax system. The group meets on a quarterly basis and the minutes of the meetings are available on the HMRC website.[9]

Also, for large businesses, HMRC has for many years run surveys seeking the views of tax directors of a sample of large businesses on aspects of HMRC operations and policy. As with much of HMRC's evidence gathering, the survey is carried out by an independent social research organization with little reference to academic work.

§14.02 TAX UNCERTAINTY

Tax uncertainty is perceived to be one of the most important drivers for Co-operative Compliance in the U.K. A 2007 document published by HMRC[10] that followed up on the 2006 Review of Links with Large Business,[11] was entitled "Making a difference: clarity and certainty."

7. HMRC https://www.gov.uk/government/groups/business-tax-forum#meeting-minutes.
8. HMRC https://www.gov.uk/government/groups/administrative-burden-advisory-board.
9. https://www.gov.uk/government/groups/business-tax-forum.
10. HMRC 2007, *Making a Difference: Clarity and Certainty*, London: The Stationery Office.
11. HMRC 2006, *Review of Links with Large Business*, London: The Stationery Office, U.K.

Writing in 2008, then Director General of HMRC Dave Hartnett[12] observed a commonality of interest between business and HMRC. Both were seeking a relationship based on mutual trust and it was recognized that delivery of improved certainty and effective dialogue required a commitment to change. Hartnett advocated bringing tax within the realm of corporate social responsibility principles.

HMRC's Large Business Strategy, published online in 2014, states, *inter alia*, that HMRC will seek to work in real time which brings earlier certainty, and further, will provide assistance to resolve uncertainty in relation to complex or significant transactions.

The 2016 Large Business Survey conducted by HMRC[13] in which tax directors of large businesses were canvassed on a range of issues, includes a "key driver analysis" to determine which elements of HMRC's service are most likely to contribute to a good rating of overall experience. 65% of respondents agreed that "HMRC provides certainty" which is seen as an important element for business.

A 2016 report by Ernst and Young[14] notes that throughout Tax Director Panel discussions it was clear that the number one priority for business is to secure certainty in relation to technical issues. HMRC was observed to be responsive in relation to large transactions, but less so in relation to more mundane transactions, which can impact on commercial decision-making.

Interviewees in the authors' recent research project[15] confirmed the importance of securing certainty as part of the Co-operative compliance relationship.

§14.03 U.K. CO-OPERATIVE COMPLIANCE IN OVERVIEW

The U.K. does not have a defined programme of Co-operative Compliance. Rather, the programme consists of a collection of laws, regulations and practices that in aggregate can be viewed as Co-operative Compliance, although in recent years several measures have been introduced that could be construed as running counter to the ethos of Co-operative Compliance.

Co-operative Compliance, in the sense of a programme defining the co-operative relationship between HMRC and taxpayers, applies only to the large business segment. For small and mid-sized businesses, different arrangements apply.

The U.K. model applies to all those businesses falling within the purview of the Large Business Directorate and so an application process is not required.

---

12. Hartnett 2008, "The Link Between Taxation and Corporate Governance," in Schön ed. *Tax and Corporate Governance*, Berlin: Springer 3.
13. *See* https://assets.publishing.service.gov.uk/government/uploads/system/uploads/attachment_data/file/536555/Large_Business_Survey_2015.pdf.
14. Ernst & Young 2015, "Building the Balance: Cooperative Compliance in Practice" https://www.eycomstg.ey.com/Publication/vwLUAssets/EY-Building-the-balance-Cooperative-compliance-in-practice/$FILE/EY-Building-the-balance-Cooperative-compliance-in-practice.pdf.
15. De Widt & Oats 2019, "Co-operative Compliance: The U.K. Case—Playing the Long Game," FairTax Working Paper Series No 22 http://www.diva-portal.org/smash/record.jsf?pid=diva2%3A1279990&dswid=-5400.

The application of Co-operative Compliance to all businesses falling under the Large Business Directorate means that no conditions of acceptance are required. The model applies to all businesses identified as "large" for this purpose. It should be noted, however, that this is not a fixed population and businesses may be included in or removed from the Large Business Directorate as their circumstances alter over time. Large businesses are managed through a process of risk assessment which allocates a risk status that determines the level and frequency of engagement with HMRC. Companies designated as low risk are deemed more trustworthy and subjected to lower levels of supervision and monitoring. High-risk companies are monitored more closely.

The U.K. has a formalized disclosure programme for tax avoidance arrangements; however, this is not confined to large businesses and applies to the whole taxpayer population. The Disclosure of Tax Avoidance Schemes (DOTAS) regime was introduced in 2004.[16] HMRC sought the views of advisors to help shape the legislation. In evidence to the 2006 Lords Economic Affairs Committee, Hartnett said:

> "we built a trusted group as well whom we tried out our ideas on quite frequently, continually going back to them." ... "We listened and we actually spent a huge amount of time with them, with solicitors and barristers, accountants and others, and one of the so-called big four firms of accountants actually invited us into their tax planning center to see how they do business, and that helped us enormously to frame the rules differently than we actually started out. That has helped us keep out the huge number of disclosures we were promised that would be of no value."

The House of Commons Committee on Public Accounts (PAC) considered the 2007 National Audit Office (NAO) report[17] in January 2008 and in the process took evidence from Hartnett, by this time Acting Chairman of HMRC. When asked by the Chairman whether the Department was "simply, not to mince words, being taken for a ride by some big companies?" Hartnett responded as follows:

> I do not think so, Chairman. I really do not believe that is a serious proposition. With the introduction of tax disclosure rules in 2004 and with Government having closed a great number of tax avoidance schemes, what we are learning from both business and their advisers is that marketed schemes are substantially in the past, although clearly not entirely. We are seeing fewer disclosed and we test to make sure disclosure is made. I think we have been very effective in countering avoidance. Am I complacent, of course not I think there is scope for us to do more.

The DoTAs regime is designed to provide intelligence to HMRC about tax avoidance schemes and requires promoters of schemes to disclose arrangements that fall within one of a number of descriptions or "hallmarks."[18] Since its introduction in 2004, the DoTAs rules have been changed on several occasions to expand their scope.

16. Part 7, Finance Act 2004.
17. NAO 2007 HM Revenue & Customs: Management of large business Corporation Tax, report by the Comptroller and Auditor General HC 614 Session 2006-2007, July 25, 2007.
18. The hallmarks are contained in regulation 6 to the Tax Avoidance Schemes (Prescribed Descriptions of Arrangements Regulations 2006 (SI 2006/1543)). The latest version of HMRC guidance on DoTAS can be found here https://assets.publishing.service.gov.uk/government/uploads/system/uploads/attachment_data/file/701190/DOTAS-March.pdf.

In 2013 two consultation documents[19] were published by HMRC, following which additional measures were introduced in 2014 to ensure that disputed tax in relation to avoidance schemes is paid in advance.

Additionally, the U.K. has a long history of co-operation both with taxpayers and with other tax authorities. The U.K. was one of the founder members of the Joint International Tax Shelter Information Centre.[20] In evidence to the PAC in 2008, for example, Hartnett explained:

> We did that because the four international countries could see that major firms of tax advisers which were global in their nature were saying: "We have got something that works in Australia; we know the U.K. rules are different; but why do you not have a look at it and see how you can make it work?" In the past it might have taken years of exchanging information under a double taxation treaty to give us insight into that; now we have seen arrangements where that exchange happens quite literally within days of something becoming clear in one country.

§14.04 U.K. CO-OPERATIVE COMPLIANCE DESIGN FEATURES

In the U.K., HMRC has only relatively recently started referring to the programme as Co-operative Compliance. HMRC led the Organisation for Economic Co-operation and Development's (OECD's) Intermediaries study[21] in which the term "enhanced relationship" was first mooted, however, and Co-operative Compliance is mandatory for all large businesses falling within the Large Business unit. The model was, until recently, collaborative and based on trust, openness and transparency. In recent years some diminution of trust and openness has been perceived by large businesses.[22]

The U.K. model does not include the conclusion of individual agreements with individual taxpayers, such as the covenants adopted in the Netherlands. The model was described by HMRC in the International Federation of Accountants 2012 study[23] as an informal way of working, generally in real time and in a transparent manner.

Two programmes specifically target large businesses and are designed to tackle high-risk businesses with known compliance deficiencies.

---

19. HMRC 2013 "Raising the Stakes on Tax Avoidance" https://assets.publishing.service.gov.uk/government/uploads/system/uploads/attachment_data/file/275071/Raising_the_stakes_on_tax_avoidance.pdf and "Tackling Marketed Tax Avoidance" https://assets.publishing.service.gov.uk/government/uploads/system/uploads/attachment_data/file/785551/tackling_tax_avoidance_evasion_and_other_forms_of_non-compliance_web.pdf.
20. Subsequently expanded in terms of membership and rebranded as Joint International Taskforce on Shared Intelligence and Collaboration, *see* https://www.oecd.org/tax/forum-on-tax-administration/jitsic/.
21. OECD 2008, *Study into the Role of Tax Intermediaries*, Paris: Organisation for Economic Co-operation and Development.
22. De Widt & Oats 2019, "Co-operative Compliance: The U.K. Case—Playing the Long Game," FairTax Working Paper Series No 22 http://www.diva-portal.org/smash/record.jsf?pid=diva2%3A1279990&dswid=-5400.
23. IFA 2012, *Initiative on the Enhanced Relationship: Key Issues Report*, International Fiscal Association, Amsterdam.

The first is the High Risk Corporates Program which was launched in 2006 and as of 2007 overseen by a Program Board chaired by the Director of the then Large Business Service who were required to approve settlements where the total tax under consideration exceeds GBP 100 million. A set of criteria is used to identify the highest risk cases and inclusion of corporates in the programme is discussed at corporate board level.

A further special measures regime, introduced in 2016, is described by Freedman and Vella[24] as "tortuous." It was first described in HMRC's December 2015 policy paper and is designed to target a very small number of large businesses that persistently engage in aggressive behavior and are uncooperative. Such businesses are given twelve months to improve their behavior after which time a review will take place and if no improvement has been made, the business will enter special measures for twenty-four months after which time an exit review will take place. Sanctions include removing defense of having taken reasonable care to be accurate in order to mitigate penalties otherwise applicable and ultimately naming and shaming.

The U.K. model of Co-operative Compliance has two key features. First is the single point of contact, currently referred to as a Customer Compliance Manager (CCM), allocated to each large business within the Large Business Directorate (*see* section §14.06 below). Secondly, it is a risk-based model. The "resource to risk" approach that was formalized in April 2006 emphasizes the allocation of staff and other resources to those cases which represent the most significant risk to tax collection in terms of the amount of tax under consideration. In the early years these businesses were described as high risk. HMRC's strategy was to encourage voluntary behavior change so as to reduce the risk rating.[25] The risk rating is shared and discussed with the business, and low-risk businesses given lighter touch treatment. At that time there were 1,300 very large businesses managed by the Large Business Service. In May 2007 new guidelines were issued to define lower risks and refine the risk scoring process. The guidelines distinguish between seven risk factors in total, and, except for one, they are divided between inherent and behavioral risk factors. Inherent risk factors are risks that are inherently linked to a company, which in itself creates risks. The behavioral risk dimension is assessed against three factors: the corporate's governance; its previous fiscal compliance track record (referred to as "delivery"); and its tax strategy. In addition, companies were assessed on their tax contribution and whether their tax declarations reflect what is known about the business and the sector it operates in.[26]

24. Freedman & Vella 2016, "Finance Act 2016 Notes: Section 161 and Schedule 19: Large Businesses: Tax Strategies and Sanctions for Persistently Uncooperative Behavior: Further Commentary," British Tax Review, 5, 653-663.
25. NAO 2007 HM Revenue & Customs, *Management of Large Business Corporation Tax*, report by the Comptroller and Auditor General HC 614 Session 2006-2007, July 25, 2007.
26. De Widt and Oats 2017, "2017 Risk Assessment in a Co-operative Compliance Context: A Dutch-U.K. Comparison," British Tax Review, 2, 230-248.

Figure 14.1 HMRC Business Risk Review Audit Trail

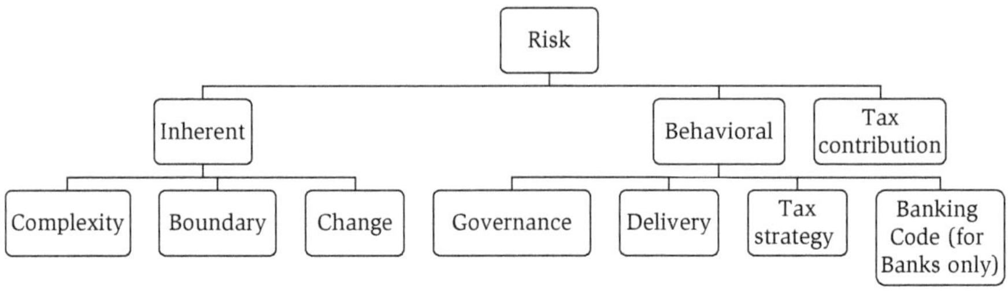

Source: www.hmrc.gov.uk (gds › tcrm › attachments › tcrm6000_brrat_temp).

The two-tier model of high risk and not high risk that has evolved has been criticized for lack of nuance and in 2017, HMRC embarked on a review of the business risk rating process, which resulted in the Business Risk Review (hereinafter: BRR) (Figure 14.1).

HMRC is open about the way in which risk is evaluated and the factors that are taken into consideration. The risk assessment rests in the first instance with the Customer Compliance Manager (CCM). It is the CCM's responsibility to try to understand the "customer's" business and the overall level of risk.

HMRC emphasizes that where possible BRR should be a collaborative process with the customer forming their own view of how they match up to the risk criteria, comparing their findings with the CCM and discussing any differences. In any event the CCM should invite the customer to discuss the BRR and try to come to an agreed view of the correct risk rating.[27]

During the consultation period in relation to the new BRR, HMRC embarked on an intensive publicity campaign holding roadshows, public webinars and attending external events hosted by practitioners and large business forums. Overall most respondents felt the existing risk review process worked well, however, several areas for improvement were identified including the binary low-risk/non-low-risk classification, which was perceived as too narrow to reflect the differences across the large business population, and the need for the risk review process to be more interactive and iterative. In addition, respondents highlighted the need for risk monitoring to take stronger account of the tax risk management work already required of large businesses, such as the Senior Accounting Officer (SAO) provisions, while respondents also highlighted the importance of clear advantages and disadvantages being connected to the different risk categories.[28]

In 2017, HMRC's Large Business Directorate also began sending letters to businesses setting out the principles of its "Framework for Co-operative Compliance" and expectations for organizations to demonstrate lower risk behaviors including

27. https://www.gov.uk/hmrc-internal-manuals/tax-compliance-risk-management/tcrm3200.
28. HMRC 2018, *Large Business Compliance: Enhancing Our Risk Assessment Approach. Summary of Responses*. London: The Stationery Office.

adherence to the risk review framework and other rules outlined below in section §14.05. HMRC was also asking large business to undertake "governance reviews."

In 2018, a pilot of the new BRR process, developed following the consultation outlined above, began with fifty-eight participating large corporates taken from a range of sectors.

Following the pilot, on which generally positive feedback was received, HMRC largely included the pilot methodology in its updated compliance risk management manual. The manual explains the new process for new large business customers which has been in force since October 1, 2019 as follows:[29]

For a new large business customer the Tax Compliance Risk Management process will involve the CCM:

- developing an understanding of the customer;
- carrying out an initial BRR to determine the customer's overall risk status; and
- classifying the customer as Low Risk, Moderate Risk, Moderate—High Risk or High Risk.

If the customer is classified as Low Risk, the CCM will not carry out another BRR for three years but will maintain an understanding of the customer over this period. If subsequent BRRs result in the customer being classified in one of the three not-low-risk categories, they will enter the cycle for not-low-Risk customers set out below:

> If the customer is classified as not Low Risk, either Moderate Risk, Moderate—High Risk or High Risk, the CCM will carry out Risk Assessment activity which may lead to Risk Working. They will carry out a BRR every year. If subsequent BRRs result in the customer being classified as Low Risk, the company enters the cycle for Low Risk customers set out above.

The revised tax compliance risk management process for both types of businesses is set out diagrammatically in Figure 14.2. This is a simplified diagram as HMRC will also occasionally undertake activity on low-risk customers in between BRRs.

29. *See* https://www.gov.uk/hmrc-internal-manuals/tax-compliance-risk-management/tcrm2300.

Figure 14.2 Overview of the Tax Compliance Risk Management Process

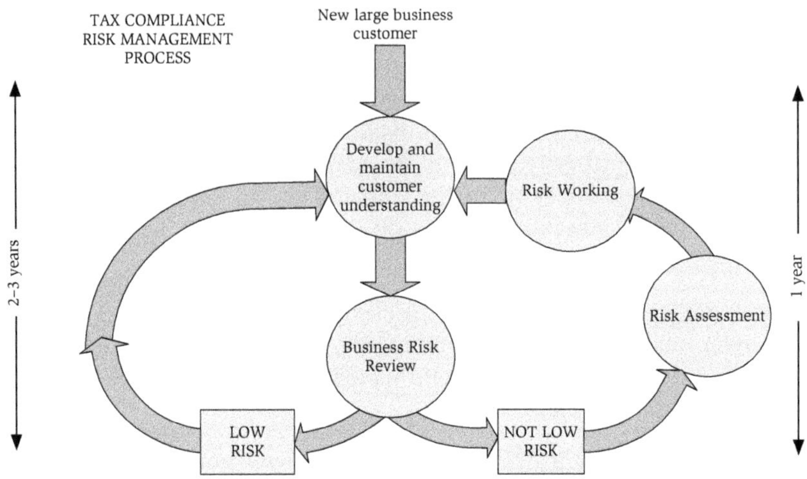

Source: www.gov.uk/hmrc-internal-manuals/tax-compliance-risk-management/tcrm2300.

As part of the risk rating process, the CCM is expected to work closely with the individual tax specialists and audit specialists in HMRC, who do conduct a risk rating of the company in regard to their own specialist area.[30] HMRC emphasizes that the overall risk rating is not a straight combination of the individual regime ratings but instead is a representation of the CCM's knowledge of the group as a whole with the individual regime scores and commentary from HMRC specialists feeding into the company's overall risk rating. HMRC will subsequently present the overall risk rating, and individual regime ratings, to the business using a standardized risk review template.[31]

Large businesses that are designated low risk are given greater autonomy with infrequent HMRC's intervention and are trusted to manage their tax risks appropriately. For this category of taxpayer, BRRs will only be conducted every three years, or longer. There is, of course, an expectation that areas of uncertainty will be disclosed to HMRC promptly. Large Businesses which are not considered to be low risk are recognized as having a wide range of tax compliance behavior and are generally reviewed more regularly; annually in the case of those representing the greatest risk. Those businesses that are deemed to represent ongoing and significant risk will be dealt with by a team of HMRC specialists who will engage at board level to encourage behavior change.

30. Specialists of the following tax areas provide their own risk rating: corporation tax, employment duties, indirect tax, excise tax, and a rest category for specialist roles/niche taxes (e.g., environmental taxes).
31. The templates are available on HMRC's website https://www.gov.uk/hmrc-internal-manuals/tax-compliance-risk-management/tcrm6000.

While the BRR methodology is intended to introduce more flexibility by increasing the number of risk categories, and thereby the level of resource HMRC devotes to large businesses with different risk levels, it remains to be seen how the new methodology will work in practice. HMRC is planning to continue to carry out annual risk reviews for companies in the moderate, moderate-high and high-risk categories, which makes that the benefits are not obvious for companies to try to move between these not-low-risk categories.

One aspect of HMRC's updated guidance concerning the new BRR that has been welcomed by corporates and tax advisers is a clear statement by HMRC that complex businesses can still be low risk if they mitigate their higher level of inherent risk by meeting the behavioral risk indicators. While this has always been HMRC's view centrally, many CCMs have expressed the view that complex businesses cannot be low risk because of inherent factors.[32]

§14.05 TAX CONTROL FRAMEWORK

There are two ways in which concern with internal controls is evident in the U.K. system. Both are statutory requirements; the first to provide assurance directly to HMRC through the SAO regime and the second to provide public assurance through publication of a tax strategy.

[A] Senior Accounting Officer

The SAO regime was introduced in 2009.[33] The provisions apply to qualifying companies which are U.K. incorporated companies with a minimum turnover of GBP 200 million, or a balance sheet of more than GBP 2 billion. The main duty of the SAO is to ensure that the company has in place appropriate tax accounting arrangements and to provide a certificate to HMRC attesting to this. The SAO does not need to be a tax specialist and will generally be a senior finance person who must attest that the data and other systems in place enable tax returns to be accurate. The SAO provisions are designed to fit within the overall BRR process by which CCMs determine where a group is situated on a compliance risk spectrum, part of which is to consider compliance with the requirements.

There is some evidence that prior to the introduction of the SAO rules, there may have been an abrogation of duties by Financial Directors, confirming that its implementation had signaling power as part of the general push to raise the profile of tax decision-making within large businesses.[34]

---

32. KPMG 2019, *HMRC: Revised Business Risk Review* https://home.kpmg/U.K./ en/home/insights /2019/09/tmd-hmrc-revised-business-risk-review.html.
33. By Schedule 46 of the Finance Act 2009. For a discussion of its introduction, *see* Freedman (2009).
34. De Widt & Oats 2019, "Co-operative Compliance: The U.K. Case—Playing the Long Game," FairTax Working Paper Series No 22 http://www.diva-portal.org/smash/record.jsf?pid=diva2 %3A1279990&dswid=-5400.

According to HMRC's SAO Manual,[35] a CCM should discuss with the company any areas of uncertainty about the operation of the SAO provisions but must not give any assurance that the tax accounting arrangements are adequate.

[B] Publication of Tax Strategy

Following a consultation process, Finance Act 2016 introduced a strategy publication requirement for the same group of businesses subjected to the SAO regime. The act specifies the content required to be published and failure to comply results in a penalty.[36]

Freedman and Vella[37] observe that "[t]he new tax strategy provisions go beyond Co-operative Compliance in the relationship between the revenue authority and the taxpayer ... It is based on the optimistic view that not only will businesses write meaningful strategies which the public will be able to successfully decode but also that this will trigger a reputational mechanism through which a change in corporate behavior will be achieved."

While tax control frameworks (TCFs) have not specifically been discussed as such in the context of Co-operative Compliance outside of the specific legislation mentioned above, the revised BRR now explicitly aligns itself with the TCF model. The consultation document issued by HMRC in 2017[38] in which the revised risk assessment process, BRR, was mooted, addresses the alignment of BRR with a TCF, which is described as able to "provide a verifiable assurance that the information and returns submitted by a taxpayer are both accurate and complete." The document observes that one of the key features of Co-operative Compliance is an emphasis on disclosure and transparency, including sharing information about internal control systems.

An article produced by accountancy firm BDO in 2017[39] takes stock of expectations for clients at this time as follows:

> Looking at the key measures, we are seeing leading practice behaviors as:
>
> - **SAO**: demonstrate to HMRC that your SAO compliance processes are integral to your overarching tax operating framework. Based on HMRC's recent SAO guidance, you should demonstrate that you have "*monitored key U.K. tax risks throughout the year*" and have "*implemented, maintained and monitored a risk-based testing programme ... and evidenced what has been done.*"
> - **Tax Strategy:** share your tax strategy with HMRC before you publish it. Avoid "motherhood and apple pie" statements[40] (HMRC has specifically railed against

35. *See* https://www.gov.uk/hmrc-internal-manuals/senior-accounting-officers-guidance/saog16200.
36. *See* Freedman & Vella 2016, "Finance Act 2016 Notes: Section 161 and Schedule 19: Large Businesses: Tax Strategies and Sanctions for Persistently Uncooperative Behaviour: further commentary," British Tax Review, 5, 653-663.
37. *Ibid.*
38. HMRC 2017, *Large Business Compliance: Enhancing Our Risk Assessment Approach.*
39. https://www.bdo.co.uk/en-gb/insights/business-edge/business-edge-2017/new-framework-for-co-operative-compliance.
40. Such statements are regarded as unquestionably good and so beyond criticism.

this) and demonstrate how your tax strategy aligns to your risk profile and wider group CSR statements and, most importantly, that policies in your tax strategy can be evidenced by actual tax working practices.

- **Governance:** HMRC wants to see how tax risk is understood in the business, who makes tax decisions, and how you define your tax risk appetite in terms of demonstrating—where possible—that these decisions are *"aligned with commercial and economic activity."*
- **Cooperative Compliance:** being able to demonstrate the above and then sharing your strategy and governance framework with HMRC will go a long way in meeting your responsibilities as set out in the Framework.

§14.06 COMMUNICATION PROCEDURES

The U.K. model includes the appointment of a relationship manager who is designated as the first point of contact for large businesses. In 2007, HMRC noted that:[41] "[w]e have recognized that we need to manage our relationship with our large business customers more effectively, and that their needs and service requirements can vary widely. All of our largest businesses, dealt with by our Large Business Service, have a dedicated Client Relationship Manager, and the majority of feedback has been that this service has improved their working relationship with us."

Early criticism of client relationship managers included a lack of industry knowledge and understanding of the practical issues faced by businesses, particularly those with international operations (NAO 2007).

Client Relationship Managers were subsequently rebranded as Customer Relationship Managers, and then in 2017, as part of the BRR reassessment, as Customer Compliance Managers (CCMs). HMRC's internal manual states that:[42]

> For all our customers we will aim for a relationship in which HMRC:
>
> - Is knowledgeable about their business and appreciates their commercial and business drivers
> - Is joined up as an organisation in its interactions with them
> - Focuses on significantly identified risks
> - Responds proportionately to those risks
> - Provides clarity to them about the process and timeframe in which areas of dispute will be resolved
> - Makes clear and targeted requests for information
> - Communicates professionally and uses appropriate channels.

Securing certainty is a frequently mentioned advantage of Co-operative Compliance arrangements. In the U.K., an Advance Agreements Unit was launched in 2007 following a public consultation "Giving certainty to business through clearances and advance agreements." A clearances pilot ran from January 2008 to help identify common areas where guidance is unclear.

41. HMRC 2007, *Making a Difference: Clarity and Certainty*, London: The Stationery Office.
42. *See* https://www.gov.uk/hmrc-internal-manuals/tax-compliance-risk-management/tcrm2200.

There has been some suggestion that HMRC should enter into service level agreements to formalize the relationship and concomitant expectations.[43] If such a process were to be introduced, it would bring the U.K. closer to the Netherlands' model of covenants, but to date this suggestion has not been taken up by HMRC.

§14.07 DISPUTE RESOLUTION

There are no special arrangements for dispute resolution through the courts for large businesses within the U.K. system. The dispute resolution processes apply to all categories of taxpayers. HMRC has a published Litigation and Settlement Strategy (LSS) which sets out the approach to resolution of inquiries likely to be settled other than by prosecution, i.e., by civil law processes.

Following media disclosures about alleged inappropriate dispute settlements with specified large businesses, the PAC in 2011 probed the processes in place at the time and expressed concern the large companies were being treated more favorably than other categories of taxpayer. A Tax Assurance Commissioner role was established in 2012. Edward Troup, the first Commissioner, commented in his 2015 report that the Commissioner is responsible for seeing that tax disputes are resolved appropriately with greater transparency about our processes and a strengthened decision-making model for our largest and most sensitive disputes".[44]

In 2018, the House of Commons Treasury Committee commenced an inquiry into HMRC's dispute resolution procedures. The ensuing report[45] notes that advisers to large businesses observed that there is now a perception that HMRC takes a harder line with large business, in contrast with previous perceptions of "cozy deals." In evidence to the Committee, for example, Slaughter and May expressed a view that increased external scrutiny had led to a "more aggressive and inflexible approach" and that inflexibility in the LSS leads to litigation in cases where a mutually acceptable settlement is otherwise possible. Other witnesses to the inquiry observed that HMRC is now also taking a harder stance in relation to penalties for large businesses, with penalties being applied more frequently.

A report by the Confederation of British Industry (CBI) suggests that a range of factors have had a deleterious impact on the culture of HMRC including new and complex legislation, additional reporting burdens, and reduced resources within HMRC. The report further identifies a regression toward a more dogmatic approach by HMRC to issues, which is reflected by HMRC's approach to disputes having become more legalistic in applying the letter of, but not necessarily the principle underlying, the tax law.[46]

---

43. Ernst & Young 2015, "Building the Balance: Cooperative Compliance in Practice" https://www.eycomstg.ey.com/Publication/vwLUAssets/EY-Building-the-balance-Cooperative-compliance-in-practice/$FILE/EY-Building-the-balance-Cooperative-compliance-in-practice.pdf.
44. Freedman 2015.
45. https://publications.parliament.uk/pa/cm201719/cmselect/cmtreasy/1914/191402.htm.
46. CBI (2018) In need of a reset https://www.cbi.org.uk/media/2326/2019-03-in-need-of-a-reset-hmrc-relationship-with-large-business.pdfU.K..

§14.08 PROGRAMME EVALUATION

HMRC has not formally evaluated its Co-operative Compliance programme, indeed it would be difficult to do so as many of the initiatives that comprise the programme are not confined to the large business segment. The model is, however, evaluated as part of the tax gap monitoring and measurement process. In addition, HMRC conducts customer surveys which provide insights into attitudes and opinions but no quantitative analysis of key indicators is publicly available in relation to the programme itself.

Oversight of HMRC's activities is facilitated by a number of institutional mechanisms. HMRC is a non-ministerial department such that Parliament cannot interfere with HMRC decision-making. Oversight of the department's activities is subject to oversight by the National Audit Office. In addition, the PAC is able to scrutinize HMRC's work, although some commentators suggest it oversteps its authority.[47]

Recently the Confederation of Business and Industry published a study suggesting that the relationship between HMRC and large businesses are in need of a reset.[48] The report draws on the views of members and makes a series of recommendations including greater clarity around how risk is evaluated by HMRC and rewards for positive "low-risk" behavior, support for CCMs by providing them with improved training and discretionary power and importantly, the development of performance metrics. The metrics recommended by the CBI are:

(a) Average time for enquiries to be resolved.
(b) Average response time to queries raised by business to be answered.
(c) Amount of tax at stake on open issues, and length of time those issues have been open.
(d) Feedback from annual business survey commenting on standard of key tenets of the Co-operative Compliance Framework: collaborative relationship; real-time working; commercial awareness by CCMs.
(e) Number of issues resolved before returns filed, and number of issues opened after returns filed.
(f) Aggregate value of tax paid associated with the issues resolved.
(g) Number of voluntary disclosures.
(h) Turnover of CCMs.
(i) Completion of handover packs.

§14.09 INTERNATIONAL COMPLIANCE ASSURANCE PROGRAMME

HMRC's historical collaboration with other tax authorities, for example through the Joint International Taskforce on Shared Intelligence and Collaboration, together with

47. For example Freedman 2016, "U.K. Institutions for Tax Governance: Reviewing Tax Settlements," British Tax Review, 1, 7-12.
48. CBI (2018) In need of a reset https://www.cbi.org.uk/media/2326/2019-03-in-need-of-a-reset-hmrc-relationship-with-large-business.pdf.

its position as a strong but flexible tax authority, makes participation in the ICAP a natural progression from unilateral Co-operative Compliance. ICAP has not received much publicity in the U.K. and it is difficult to assess how it is being received at present. A Business Tax Forum meeting in January 2019 between HMRC and industry representatives included a brief discussion of ICAP and the minutes disclose the following:[49]

> Participation has been very positive, and there has been evidence to show that it is effective in particular on addressing transfer pricing issues. The programme's pilot has been resource saving for tax administrations and large businesses. Members supported the work and were keen to get clarity on the outcome letters, for example whether legal certainty can be reached through the international programme. It was noted that although legal certainty was not given, outcome letters from ICAP have be (sic) used as evidence of compliance in other jurisdictions.

The voluntary participation in the ICAP may present problems for the U.K. in terms of equality of treatment which are not present in the general Co-operative Compliance model which is compulsory for all large businesses. The support of the OECD and participation by other countries will, of course, mitigate any such concerns.

§14.10 CONCLUSION

The U.K. approach to Co-operative Compliance is very much evolutionary and differs from other models in important respects. The application of the model to all large businesses falling within the purview of the Large Business Directorate means that there is no application and assessment process to determine which businesses gain entry to the programme. This also removes the concern about unequal treatment of taxpayers within the same population, even if questions remain about differing treatment of large business vis-à-vis small and mid-sized businesses.[50] The U.K. approach also reflects a balance of sound technical expertise and a realistic approach to the practicalities of compliance:[51]

> Reflecting on co-operative compliance as an always incomplete process, one of our interviewees notes:
>
> > over the years, the approach changed, but it didn't always change—it changed at different speeds in different areas and in different taxes. And it's something that you always have to keep focusing on. I don't think you can ever say that you've done co-operative compliance and that's it; you have to keep focusing. [U.K.29][52]

49. https://assets.publishing.service.gov.uk/government/uploads/system/uploads/attachment_data/file/820349/Business_Tax_Forum_minutes_10_January_2019.pdf.
50. *See also* Madjanska & Leigh Pemberton 2019, "Different Treatment, Same Outcome: Reconciling Co-operative Compliance with the Principle of Legal Equality," Journal of Tax Administration 5:1.
51. *See* De Widt & Oats 2019, "Co-operative Compliance: The U.K. Case—Playing the Long Game," FairTax Working Paper Series No 22 http://www.diva-portal.org/smash/record.jsf?pid = diva2%3A1279990&dswid = -5400.
52. *Ibid.*

The current position is that, following initial enthusiasm for collaboration in the period up to 2011, there has been a subsequent diminution of trust and goodwill. Most participants agree that there has been significant improvement in comparison with previous ways of working, e.g., prior to 2005. However, a number of features of the recent landscape in the U.K. have impacted on the model in negative ways. The ever-increasing range of anti-avoidance rules and processes in response to unprecedented publicity of large businesses tax planning strategies creating a highly politicized environment, coupled with a squeeze on HMRC resources, has put pressure on the Co-operative Compliance model.

CHAPTER 15

The U.S. Compliance Assurance Programme and Comparative Lessons

George Clarke & Joy Williamson

§15.01 INTRODUCTION

Tax uncertainty, along with the burden of trying to comply with frequently changing rules, is a persistent challenge in the United States (U.S.). Taxpayers and the Internal Revenue Service alike experience difficulties in interpreting and complying with the U.S.' complex tax laws, and both incur material costs in terms of resources, time, and money spent to ensure compliance. The extent of the ambiguity and room for disagreement in the Internal Revenue Code (IRC) and regulations issued thereunder can be seen in the significant number of tax cases that are brought to the courts each year.[1] This level of complexity and ambiguity results in taxpayers having uncertain positions, even if they incur significant costs to try and comply with the relevant rules and regulations. Taxpayers may also take more aggressive positions due to the uncertainty and ambiguity in the rules.

To help address increasing concerns about tax uncertainty and administrative burden, the Internal Revenue Service (IRS) established in 2005 the Compliance Assurance Process (CAP), a voluntary real-time audit programme for large business taxpayers.[2] The goal of CAP was to reduce the audit cycle timeframe and achieve voluntary compliance, while rewarding compliant taxpayer behavior.[3] In particular,

1. Forbes, *Tax Court IRS and Secret Law* (Dec. 8, 2017), https://www.forbes.com/sites/peterjreilly/2017/12/08/tax-court-irs-and-secret-law/#23901c3b2ba9 (explaining the U.S. Tax Court dockets approximately 30,000 cases each year).
2. IRM 4.51.8.2 (CAP Examinations), https://www.irs.gov/irm/part4/irm_04-051-008.
3. General Report of the IRS Advisory Council (Nov. 9, 2004), https://www.taxnotes.com/tax-notes-today-federal/tax-system-administration-issues/irsac-issues-annual-report-irs-divisions/2004/11/12/yq6k?highlight=%22compliance%20assurance%20process%22.

the IRS wanted to: (1) provide quicker resolution of issues and cases, along with prompt guidance to industry issues, (2) address emerging issues that could impact other taxpayers as well, (3) provide real-time feedback to transactions versus operate in catch-up mode, (4) resolve issues and provide certainty prior to tax return filing and allow for more concise financial reporting, (5) reward compliant behavior and reduce or eliminate need for post-filing examinations, and (6) allow for redeployment of IRS audit teams to non-compliant taxpayers.[4] As will be discussed below, CAP has evolved over time, with the IRS testing out different options in an attempt to satisfy the original goals of CAP. This Chapter provides an overview of CAP and how it has evolved, evaluates the overall effectiveness of CAP in reaching the aforementioned goals, and provides a comparison of CAP and the International Compliance Assurance Programme (ICAP), which is a voluntary programme similar to CAP, but designed to facilitate efficient taxpayer discussions with tax authorities from *multiple* countries through a unified process.

§15.02 CO-OPERATIVE COMPLIANCE IN THE U.S.: CAP

The IRS launched a CAP pilot programme in 2005[5] and made CAP permanent in 2011.[6] CAP is administered by the IRS' Large Business and International Division (LB&I), and as such, it is only open to businesses with at least USD 10 million in assets that also meet requirements around financial reporting, availability of records, current examination status, and history of cooperation with the IRS.[7] Indeed, when developing CAP, the IRS Advisory Council recommended the IRS leverage the increased reliance that could be placed on the financial statements of publicly traded companies subject to regulation by the U.S. Securities and Exchange Commission (SEC), as the new Sarbanes-Oxley legislation had implemented a strict regime of corporate governance that increased the reliability of reported financial statements.[8] Notably, this is similar to what many other countries are now doing as part of the implementation of ICAP, *viz.*, relying on financial statement audits as a means to ensure that entrants to ICAP have their tax positions properly vetted by a professional. Given the large degree of uncertainty in U.S. tax law, even when such audits are conducted, the level of certainty with respect to tax positions "signed off on" by financial statement auditors is still low.[9] That said, the financial accounting standards in the U.S. that require taxpayers to post

4. *Id.*
5. Ann. 2005-87, https://www.irs.gov/irb/2005-50_IRB#ANN-2005-87.
6. IR News Release 2011-32, https://www.irs.gov/pub/irs-news/ir-11-032.pdf.
7. In addition, beginning in tax year 2020, new applicants must be publicly-traded U.S. corporations. *See* IRS, *Statement of Interest for New CAP Applicants*, https://www.irs.gov/businesses/corporations/statement-of-interest-for-new-applicants-for-cap. *See* sub-section 2.03[A] below for further details on eligibility and suitability requirements.
8. General Report of the IRS Advisory Council (Nov. 9, 2004), https://www.taxnotes.com/tax-notes-today-federal/tax-system-administration-issues/irsac-issues-annual-report-irs-divisions/2004/11/12/yq6k?highlight=%22compliance%20assurance%20process%22.
9. *See*, https://www.irs.gov/pub/irs-utl/statements_on_standards_for_tax_services.pdf setting out the standards for various tax positions and confirming that a filed, undisclosed position need only meet the "realistic possibility of success" standard which is a 1/3 chance of being correct. The

a reserve for certain types of uncertain tax positions, along with the requirement for large taxpayers to disclose uncertain tax positions on their returns, may help the IRS better identify appropriate candidates for CAP.[10]

If accepted into CAP, taxpayers cooperate with the IRS to identify and resolve issues in real time before filing their returns.[11] Taxpayers that reach an agreement with the IRS on all material issues and file their returns consistently with these agreed-upon positions receive assurance in the form of a "no-change letter" closing the CAP examination and accepting the return as filed.[12] Any issues that cannot be resolved in this way are subject to the regular, post-filing IRS examination process.[13] By eliminating or reducing the role of traditional post-filing examinations, CAP aims to improve compliance, increase transparency, and provide tax certainty "sooner and with less administrative burden."[14] Participation in CAP is voluntary and can be terminated by the taxpayer at will or by the IRS if the taxpayer fails to meet its obligations.[15]

[A] CAP Phases

The 2005 CAP pilot consisted of a single phase, but later iterations have added phases to allow more flexibility in determining the appropriate level of IRS scrutiny. Currently, there are three main phases, with one newly introduced sub-phase called the bridge phase:

(1) Pre-CAP Phase. In this phase, taxpayers work with the IRS to close any ongoing examinations through the traditional post-filing audit process within an agreed-upon timeframe, with the goal of qualifying to enter the CAP phase.[16]

---

much higher "more likely than not" standard (which requires the taxpayer to believe it has a greater chance of winning an issue than the IRS) is not required for return filing positions.

10. *See* Financial Accounting Standards Board Financial Interpretation No. 48 (FIN 48) Implications—LB&I Field Examiners' Guide, https://www.irs.gov/businesses/corporations/fin-48-implications-lbi-field-examiners-guide. Indeed, larger taxpayers may be more likely to follow the "more likely than not" standard due to the FIN 48 requirement to record a full reserve for tax positions that do not meet the more likely than not standard. *See* 2018 Instructions for Schedule UTP, https://www.irs.gov/pub/irs-pdf/i1120utp.pdf. Corporations with assets in excess of USD 10 million must file Schedule UTP to report uncertain tax positions for which a reserve was taken or for which no reserve was taken because the company expects to litigate the issue.
11. Ann. 2005-87: https://www.irs.gov/irb/2005-50_IRB#ANN-2005-87.
12. IRM 4.51.8.5.28 (stating that "if the post-filing review indicates that all material disclosures were made in accordance with the CAP MOU and resolved, the IRS will issue a No-Change Letter concluding the examination of the taxpayer's books of account for purposes of IRC 7605(b).").
13. IRM 4.51.8.3(2).
14. IRM 4.51.8.2(3).
15. CAP FAQ at 9, https://www.irs.gov/businesses/corporations/compliance-assurance-process-cap-frequently-asked-questions-faqs.
16. CAP FAQ at 8, https://www.irs.gov/businesses/corporations/compliance-assurance-process-cap-frequently-asked-questions-faqs.

(2) CAP Phase. Taxpayers in this phase must make comprehensive, real-time disclosures of completed transactions, material items that occur during the year, and proposed tax positions with regard to these disclosures.[17]
(3) Compliance Maintenance Phase. Taxpayers selected for this phase continue to participate in CAP and are expected to exhibit the same level of cooperation and transparency, but will have more limited dealings with the IRS than they would in the CAP phase.[18]
(4) Compliance Management Bridge Phase. Taxpayers selected for this phase are considered low-risk, seasoned CAP participants who will essentially be subject to a one-year[19] hiatus from CAP.[20] For any year selected for this phase, taxpayers remain in CAP, but the IRS CAP team will not accept any disclosures, conduct any reviews, or provide any assurances.[21] Instead, if a taxpayer in bridge phase wants certainty on a particular issue, they must request a pre-filing agreement through ordinary, non-CAP channels.[22]

[B] Legal Framework for CAP

Like many countries surveyed for the Organisation for Economic Co-operation and Development's (OECD's) 2013 report, *Co-operative Compliance: A Framework*, the U.S. has not needed to change existing laws in order to formalize the approach taken with taxpayers under the CAP programme.[23] The IRS established CAP under its existing authority to administer the internal revenue laws, which includes very broad authority to conduct examinations.[24] Details of programme administration are set out in the Internal Revenue Manual (IRM), an internal IRS document that describes IRS operating procedures and processes and can be changed—within the bounds of the law—by the IRS at any time. The IRS makes the IRM available to the public, and also communicates changes through announcements published in the Internal Revenue Bulletin and guidance on the IRS website.

17. CAP FAQ at 9, https://www.irs.gov/businesses/corporations/compliance-assurance-process-cap-frequently-asked-questions-faqs.
18. 2019 CAP Memorandum of Understanding at 5, https://www.irs.gov/pub/irs-utl/2019_cap_memorandum_of_understanding_final.pdf, hereinafter "MOU."
19. Currently, a taxpayer cannot be in bridge phase for multiple consecutive years, so that a taxpayer selected for the bridge phase will be considered as a returning taxpayer when applying for CAP the next year. *See* CAP Recalibration Discussion Document at 9, https://www.irs.gov/pub/irs-utl/CAP_Recalibration.pdf.
20. IR-2018-174 ("As part of Compliance Maintenance, some taxpayers determined to be lowest risk may continue in the program without IRS review of a particular year"); CAP Recalibration Discussion Document at 9.
21. 2019 CAP MOU at 5.
22. CAP Recalibration Discussion Document at 9.
23. OECD, Co-operative Compliance: A Framework, 31 (2013), https://www.oecd.org/tax/co-operative-compliance-a-framework-9789264200852-en.htm.
24. 26 U.S. Code §7801; 26 U.S. Code §7803. 26 U.S. Code §6201 (authorizing IRS to make inquiries, determinations, and assessments of all taxes).

[C] CAP History

Throughout CAP's nearly fifteen-year history, the IRS has revised its view on how many taxpayers should be allowed to participate in CAP based on limited IRS resources and an evolving notion of what makes a taxpayer "suitable" to participate. The pilot programme, which ran from March 2005 to March 2011, was by invitation only with an inaugural class of seventeen. Over the course of the six-year pilot, there were 161 different taxpayers that participated in CAP. These taxpayers were among the largest in the nation, all with over USD 250 million in assets,[25] and were selected based on "industry leadership, industry diversity, working relationship with the IRS, lack of aggressive tax positions, no major litigation, and resource availability."[26]

In March 2011, the IRS declared the pilot a success, made CAP permanent, and opened it up to all applicants who met the eligibility criteria.[27] In addition, the IRS introduced two new phases that had modified eligibility requirements to expand access and free up resources: (i) the pre-CAP phase, and (ii) the compliance maintenance phase.[28] The pre-CAP phase created a pathway to CAP status for otherwise-eligible taxpayers willing to resolve their backlog of open returns.[29] If accepted into the pre-CAP phase, taxpayers work with the IRS to develop an action plan to close out existing examinations within a set time period.[30] The compliance maintenance phase is at the other end of the pipeline and is intended to free up resources by rewarding compliance with a lower level of review.[31] This structure continued for approximately five years before the IRS began re-thinking the efficacy of CAP and whether it was the best use of IRS resources.

In 2016, the IRS announced that it would not accept CAP applications for the 2017 tax year while it assessed whether or not the programme was "aligned with LB&I's strategic vision," citing limited resources and budget constraints.[32] The application freeze came as LB&I was rolling out a new campaign-based strategy, with one official emphasizing that the division would focus resources "on taxpayers that have those issues rather than just on the largest taxpayers across the country."[33] The potential discontinuance of CAP was met with consternation among taxpayers who felt their

25. Treasury Inspector General for Tax Administration, "The Compliance Assurance Process Has Received Favorable Feedback, but Additional Analysis of Its Costs and Benefits Is Needed," 16 (2013).
26. *Id.*, at 23; *See also* Jeremiah Coder, "The Future of the CAP Program," 65 Tax Prac. 235 (Mar. 29, 2010), https://www.taxnotes.com/taxpractice/compliance/future-cap-program/2010/03/29/1s434?.
27. IR-2011-32, https://www.irs.gov/pub/irs-news/ir-11-032.pdf.
28. *Id.*
29. IRM 4.51.8.
30. Trivedi & Elliott; IR-2011-32; IRM 4.51.8.4.
31. IRM 4.51.8.
32. Real-Time Audit Program Closed to New Participants, https://www.taxnotes.com/taxpractice/audits/real-time-audit-program-closed-new-participants/2016/09/12/1s9p5.
33. LB&I Campaigns Don't Reflect IRS's Top Priorities, Officials Say, https://www.taxnotes.com/tax-notes-today-federal/audits/lbi-campaigns-dont-reflect-irss-top-priorities-officials-say/2017/03/07/gf16 ("We are focusing our resources on taxpayers that have those issues rather than just on the largest taxpayers across the country").

investments would go to waste if CAP was discontinued.[34] It is also broadly reflective of an uncomfortable reality with respect to programmes like CAP (and ICAP): In a time of shrinking government resources, it is difficult to justify applying more resources to create and maintain a specialized programme for the most compliant taxpayers. Although CAP should *save* the IRS resources, despite its best efforts, the IRS has been unable to administer the programme in a way that does so. In the author's opinion, this is likely due to a continued trust deficit between the IRS and the taxpayer community that will need to be more broadly addressed in order for programmes like CAP to thrive.

Approximately two years later, in August 2018, the IRS announced that CAP would survive, but with substantive changes intended to better manage limited government resources, promote timely resolution of issues, and improve risk management by identifying key issues upfront.[35] In choosing to keep this programme, LB&I Commissioner Doug O'Donnell explained that "[a]fter extensive review, we believe this program continues to provide benefit for taxpayers and tax administration" as it "is intended to provide taxpayers and IRS certainty on treatment of certain tax issues even before the return is filed, while reducing the chance of potential disagreement and lengthy examinations."[36] This focus on certainty is critical as one of the major benefits of CAP for taxpayers is the clarity of the IRS' position that the programme provides compared to the normal return filing and auditing process. With U.S. tax law being so *uncertain*, programmes like CAP are sought out by taxpayers who value such certainty.

Under the new process, the IRS decided not to accept any new applications in 2019 and to subject 2020 applicants to narrower eligibility criteria, including a publicly-traded requirement, indicating the IRS may be going back full circle to the original recommendation that CAP leverage the benefits produced by Sarbanes-Oxley.[37] The IRS has also explained that existing CAP participants may be disqualified if they do not meet certain standards of transparency and cooperation, such as not adhering to information document response timeframes or providing incomplete responses, not engaging in meaningful or good faith issue resolution discussions, failing to disclose certain issues in a timely manner, or filing frequent claims or failing to resolve issues pre- and post-tax return filing.[38] A natural extension of some of these

34. Stephanie Cummings, "Taxpayers Concerned CAP Real-Time Audit Program Is in Jeopardy", https://www.taxnotes.com/tax-notes-today-federal/audits/taxpayers-concerned-cap-real-time-audit-program-jeopardy/2017/03/14/gf9c.
35. IR News Release 2018-174, https://www.irs.gov/newsroom/irs-announces-adjustments-to-the-compliance-assurance-process-cap-program; Eric Yauch, "Rumors of Compliance Assurance Program's Death Greatly Exaggerated," 2018 Tax Notes Today (TNT) 167-1 (8/28/2018), https://www.taxnotes.com/tax-notes-today-federal/compliance/rumors-compliance-assurance-programs-death-greatly-exaggerated/2018/08/28/28cwm.
36. IRS announces adjustments to the CAP programme (Aug. 27, 2018), https://www.irs.gov/newsroom/irs-announces-adjustments-to-the-compliance-assurance-process-cap-program.
37. IRS CAP Recalibration Discussion Document (Sep. 28, 2018), https://www.irs.gov/pub/irs-utl/CAP_Recalibration.pdf; Stephanie Cummings & Andrew Velarde, "CAP Eligibility Likely to Be Limited to Public Companies," 161 Tax Notes 103 (Oct. 1, 2018), https://www.taxnotes.com/tax-notes-federal/compliance/cap-eligibility-likely-be-limited-public-companies/2018/10/01/28gjg. *See* IRS, *Statement of Interest for New CAP Applicants*, https://www.irs.gov/businesses/corporations/statement-of-interest-for-new-applicants-for-cap.
38. CAP Recalibration Discussion Document at 6, https://www.irs.gov/pub/irs-utl/CAP_Recalibration.pdf.

requirements would be for accepted taxpayers to only take positions with a certain confidence level on their return (such as "more likely than not" rather than "realistic possibility of success") and/or agree to only challenge taxpayer unfavorable CAP determinations under certain circumstances.

The IRS also introduced the compliance maintenance bridge phase starting in 2019 as part of its efforts to recalibrate CAP and save resources in the face of declining LB&I staff. Since CAP began, the workforce of LB&I had declined by more than 25%, putting a strain on the IRS' ability to keep up with both CAP and traditional audits.[39] The IRS described the bridge phase as "recognition that compliance risk is very low and expending time by the IRS and taxpayer is not in the best interest of tax administration" and called it "the ultimate" and "a bit of a gold star."[40] However, some taxpayers and tax professionals are concerned that the bridge phase reintroduces uncertainty, since the IRS will not accept disclosures or provide assurance on tax returns for a year when a taxpayer is in the bridge phase. As explained by Daniel Rosen of Baker & McKenzie: "It's equivalent to being kicked out of CAP for the bridge year. . . Bridge year taxpayers don't get any certainty, so they're in the same positions as any corporate taxpayer."[41] Indeed, the Commissioner of the LB&I could not guarantee that a bridge year would not be audited, because of possible extenuating circumstances, but explained that "in general, that would be an exceptional case."[42] While this surely is true as a practical matter, the lack of any standards for determining when any such audit would be "exceptional" remains a concern to taxpayers.

In short, the 2018 changes show the IRS is considering whether its limited resources are best allocated to focusing on the nation's largest, most compliant taxpayers, or whether those strained resources should be devoted to higher-risk areas instead.[43] This struggle continues today. On September 25, 2019, Nikole Flax, Deputy Commissioner of LB&I, stated that, with respect to CAP, taxpayers "should expect to see additional changes going forward" as the IRS is "still struggling with what issues we

---

39. "IRS announces adjustments to the Compliance Assurance Process (CAP) program" (Aug. 27, 2018), https://www.irs.gov/newsroom/irs-announces-adjustments-to-the-compliance-assurance-process-cap-program.
40. CAP Recalibration Discussion Document at 2, https://www.irs.gov/pub/irs-utl/CAP_Recalibration.pdf; "IRS Tries to Assuage Uncertainty Concern in CAP Bridge Phase." 163 Tax Notes Federal 2047 (Jun. 24, 2019), https://www.taxnotes.com/tax-notes-federal/audits/irs-tries-assuage-uncertainty-concern-cap-bridge-phase.
41. "IRS's 2019 Change to Real-Time Audits Brings Back Tax Certainty." Bloomberg BNA Tax Management Weekly Report Nov. 19, 2018.
42. 163 Tax Notes Federal 2047. Further, the CAP Recalibration FAQ stated that some circumstances could require a bridge year to be opened. These include "(1) Any evidence of fraud, malfeasance, collusion, concealment or misrepresentation of a material fact; (2) Any new material issue not previously reviewed; (3) Any material change to a previously reviewed issue; (4) Any material issue that was reserved for or reported on Schedule UTP during the Bridge year; (5) Any material Campaign issue; (6) Any other circumstance where a failure to open an examination would be a serious administrative omission." CAP Recalibration FAQ at 43, https://www.irs.gov/businesses/corporations/mitt-and-other-cap-recalibration-frequently-asked-questions. Interestingly, issues reported on Schedule UTP are issues that do not rise to the level of "more likely than not."
43. 2019 CAP MOU at 5.

can actually accommodate in the program."[44] She also explained that it is "an open question of whether some transfer pricing issues are suitable for CAP" as some of those issues cannot be dealt with during the CAP timeframe, and indicated that for taxpayers with more complex structures, taxpayer behavior will be an important consideration in determining whether to accept the taxpayer into CAP.[45] As a general matter, intensely factual issues with large dollar impacts, such as transfer pricing, are very difficult to resolve in a situation where the two sides lack trust and the time to verify each other's positions. In order for such issues to be regularly resolved in a CAP context, these concerns will have to be addressed or, perhaps, side-stepped, by application of the advance pricing agreement or similar dispute resolution processes.

[D] Current CAP Requirements

Participation in the pre-CAP phase is subject to three eligibility requirements. First, applicants must have at least USD 10 million in assets,[46] with the result that in general, CAP participants are already in the group of taxpayers who would otherwise be under frequent audits by the IRS.[47] Second, starting in 2020, an applicant must be a U.S. publicly traded C-corporation[48] with reporting requirements under U.S. securities laws.[49] Third, applicants must not be under investigation by, or in litigation with, the IRS or other government agency that would limit the IRS' access to current corporate tax records.[50]

To move into the CAP phase, an applicant may only have one unfiled return (for the most recently ended tax year) and one open return (previously filed but still in examination).[51] For the 2020 year, the IRS will allow more open-year exceptions and provide a process to allow taxpayers who are currently under examination to apply for

44. Stephanie Cummings, "IRS Has No Set Number for Admitting New CAP Taxpayers," Tax Notes (Sep. 26, 2016), https://www.taxnotes.com/tax-notes-today-federal/audits/irs-has-no-set-number-admitting-new-cap-taxpayers/2019/09/26/29z9g. Currently, a previously closed return that has been reopened to process a claim, an LB&I Suspense, or a review by the national office or Joint Committee of Taxation do not count as open for purposes of applying to CAP. CAP Eligibility and Suitability Criteria, IRS, https://www.irs.gov/businesses/corporations/cap-eligibility-and-suitability-criteria.
45. *Id.*
46. IRM 4.51.8.5(2)(a).
47. Shamik Trivedi & Amy S. Elliott, "LB&I Expands, Makes Permanent CAP Real-Time Audit Program," 40 Ins. Tax rev. 705 (2011), https://www.taxnotes.com/insurance-expert/audits/lbi-expands-makes-permanent-cap-real-time-audit-program/2011/05/01/v586?.
48. A C-corporation is an entity whose profits are taxed separately from its owners. The rules governing the taxation of these types of entities are found under subchapter C of the Internal Revenue Code, thus giving the entity its name.
49. IR-2019-113; IRS, *Statement of Interest for New CAP Applicants*, https://www.irs.gov/businesses/corporations/statement-of-interest-for-new-applicants-for-cap. Previously, foreign and privately held companies could apply, subject to information requirements. IRM 4.51.8.5(2)(b).
50. IRM 4.51.8.5(2)(c).
51. IRM 4.51.8.5(2)(d).

CAP.[52] Finally, to be considered for the compliance maintenance phase, a taxpayer must have completed two CAP cycles through post-filing review.[53]

[1] Suitability for CAP

The 2018 recalibration stressed the concept of suitability, meaning that even if a taxpayer meets the eligibility requirements, its application may be rejected based on previous conduct interacting with the IRS.[54] In June 2019, Deputy Commissioner Nikole Flax of LB&I emphasized that because it is a cooperative programme, CAP represents a "higher bar" of engagement with the IRS, and companies should consider whether "the posture of the taxpayer is consistent with the spirit of the program."[55] In a recent statement, the deputy commissioner of LB&I said that it is still possible that some issues, such as transfer pricing, are deemed unsuitable for CAP because the "complex and opaque transactions" require more time and effort to examine.[56] However, it was noted that complex transactions would not completely rule out a taxpayer, because timely disclosures can allow the IRS to more efficiently use its resources, which is a key consideration.[57]

While framed as an innovation, the notion of suitability is already reflected in the memorandum of understanding (MOU) that governs the IRS-taxpayer relationship[58] and other existing IRS guidance. For example, the IRS decides whether or not to accept eligible taxpayers into the CAP phase by considering (1) the taxpayer's level of cooperation and transparency in prior CAP or pre-CAP years, (2) IRS and taxpayer resources, (3) whether the taxpayer had a majority ownership change, and (4) any material financial restatements.[59] Similarly, the IRS bases its decision to promote eligible CAP phase taxpayers to the compliance maintenance phases on factors including history of cooperation and transparency in prior dealings with the IRS and

52. Stephanie Cummings, "Expanded CAP Program Will Officially Open for Business," Tax Notes (Sep. 16, 2019), https://www.taxnotes.com/tax-notes-federal/audits/expanded-cap-program-will-officially-open-business/2019/09/16/29y33.
53. IRM 4.51.8.6(1).
54. CAP Recalibration Discussion Document at 6, https://www.irs.gov/pub/irs-utl/CAP_Recalibration.pdf. Disqualifying conduct includes (1) not adhering to information document request (IDR) response times or providing incomplete responses to IDRs, (2) not engaging in meaningful or good faith issue resolution discussions, (3) failing to thoroughly disclose a material item in a timely manner, (4) failing to disclose a tax shelter or listed transaction, (5) failing to disclose an investigation or litigation that limits IRS access to current corporate records, (6) frequently filing claims or failure to resolve issues in pre- and post-filing, and (7) not adhering to any other commitment in the relevant MOU.
55. "IRS Not Looking to Use CAP Info as Audit Trap, Official Says." 163 Tax Notes Federal 2048 (Jun. 24, 2019), https://www.taxnotes.com/tax-notes-federal/tax-system-administration/irs-not-looking-use-cap-info-audit-trap-official-says/2019/06/24/29mxx.
56. Stephanie Cummings, "IRS Has No Set Number for Admitting New CAP Taxpayers," Tax Notes (Sep. 26, 2016), https://www.taxnotes.com/tax-notes-today-federal/audits/irs-has-no-set-number-admitting-new-cap-taxpayers/2019/09/26/29z9g.
57. *Id.*
58. 2019 CAP MOU at 7 (listing taxpayer conduct that warrants termination from the CAP programme).
59. IRM 4.51.8.5(4).

quality of internal controls.[60] Furthermore, the IRS has always made clear that it may decline a CAP or pre-CAP application in its sole discretion, subject only to appeal to the Deputy Commissioner of LB&I, "when appropriate in the interest of sound tax administration or whenever warranted by the facts and circumstances of a particular case."[61] It is relevant to note though that this level of interaction and engagement—to be optimally successful—needs to be a two-way street. Taxpayers in CAP can be asked to be fully transparent, but the IRS should be responding in kind. In particular, the IRS should adopt a more proactive approach to making sure that CAP taxpayers have access to guidance on a real time basis that is well-thought-out, suitable, and properly applied to their facts. That would represent true engagement.

[2] Required CAP Application Information

Taxpayers applying or reapplying to CAP for the 2020 tax year witnessed another change to the application process: the IRS asked for considerably more information.[62] Previously, applicants had only to fill out a two-page application form,[63] but taxpayers applying to the recalibrated CAP programme must provide a Preliminary Issues List, a Material Inter-Company Transaction Template and Worldwide Tax Organization Chart to identify transfer pricing issues, a Research Credit Questionnaire, and a Tax Control Framework Questionnaire.[64] At least initially, the issues list is used for time management only and not as the basis of acceptance of decisions.[65] IRS officials have also assured taxpayers that the information submitted will not be used to target them for traditional audits.[66]

Historically, the IRS had not required applicants to describe their systems for managing tax risks, though having "good internal controls" has been and continues to be a factor the IRS considers when evaluating a taxpayer's eligibility for the compliance maintenance phase.[67] The change is part of the IRS' broader effort to "recalibrate" the

60. 2019 CAP MOU at 5; *see also* IRM 4.51.8.6(4).
61. IRM 4.51.8.4(6); IRM 4.51.8.5(6).
62. Nana Ama Sarfo, "LB&I Expanding Staffing and Use of Data Analytics," 93 Tax Notes Int'l 1151 (Mar. 18, 2019), https://www.taxnotes.com/tax-notes-today-international/corporate-taxation/lbi-expanding-staffing-and-use-data-analytics/2019/03/18/297c9.
63. Pre-2019 CAP and Pre-CAP Application Form, https://www.irs.gov/pub/irs-utl/cap_form_final.pdf.
64. 2020 statement of interest requirements, https://www.irs.gov/businesses/corporations/statement-of-interest-for-new-applicants-for-cap.
65. "CAP Eligibility Likely to Be Limited to Public Companies," 161 Tax Notes 103 (Oct. 1, 2018), https://www.taxnotes.com/tax-notes-federal/compliance/cap-eligibility-likely-be-limited-public-companies/2018/10/01/28gjg.
66. IRS Not Looking to Use CAP Info as Audit Trap, Official Says. 163 Tax Notes Federal 2048 (Jun. 24, 2019), https://www.taxnotes.com/tax-notes-federal/tax-system-administration/irs-not-looking-use-cap-info-audit-trap-official-says/2019/06/24/29mxx.
67. IRM 4.51.8.6(4); CAP FAQ at 5, https://www.irs.gov/businesses/corporations/compliance-assurance-process-cap-frequently-asked-questions-faqs. The IRS describes "good internal controls" as a proven process for disclosures that has worked unfailingly on prior CAP reviews. *Id.* Presumably, good internal controls are similar to those required under SEC regulations for publicly traded companies as the IRS Advisory Council recommended the IRS leverage the

CAP programme to better manage resources, including through improved risk management. As a first step, applicants for the tax year 2020 were required to answer a questionnaire describing their tax control framework, including:

(1) internal controls to ensure accuracy, completeness, and reliability of tax returns and disclosures;
(2) process for tax risk management, specifically the processes that are used to identify, monitor, prevent and manage risks arising from tax;
(3) process for assessing operational effectiveness of tax-related internal controls; and
(4) whether external auditors perform tests of the internal control framework for tax matters and if so, results of the testing and any deficiencies identified within the last three years.[68]

Taxpayers' responses to these questions will help to inform the IRS' tax control framework requirements for future CAP years.[69] The IRS has yet to announce whether it intends to use the information for other purposes, such as evaluating a taxpayer's suitability for the programme, determining which phase a returning CAP taxpayer should be in, or setting the level of review within a given phase.[70] Rules requiring a release of information relating to the tax control framework are already in place in other countries, such as the United Kingdom (U.K.). Some speculate that this requirement could result in the IRS investigating corporate governance more heavily in the future.[71] Whether this foreshadows something broader, such as a push to make tax compliance a corporate social responsibility (CSR) issue, is unclear. Such a push would require buy-in from taxpayers—and likely pressure from the investor community. However, viewed through the lens of CSR, having a sound tax control framework and being accepted into a more robust version of CAP or ICAP could seem to be a "badge of honor" which could provide benefits (both PR and otherwise) for both the taxpayer and the IRS.

[E] A Formalized Relationship: The MOU

The relationship between a participating taxpayer and the IRS is formalized in a uniform, non-negotiable MOU, which details each party's responsibilities under the

---

increased reliance that could be placed on the financial statements of publicly traded companies, which are subject to SEC regulation.

68. Tax Control Framework Questionnaire, https://www.irs.gov/businesses/corporations/tax-control-framework-questionnaire.
69. *Id.*
70. *Id.* ("This questionnaire will provide IRS with an understanding of your company's tax governance processes and the system of internal controls that ensure the accuracy and completeness of your federal income tax returns, information reporting, tax reporting data and other tax-related disclosures.").
71. Michael P. Dolan and Timothy J. McCormally, "IRS Extends CAP Program, Modifying Some Rules and Signaling More Significant Changes May Lie Ahead," KPMG (Sep. 10, 2018), https://home.kpmg/content/dam/kpmg/us/pdf/2019/09/tnf-cap-wnit-sep10-2018.pdf.

programme with respect to the tax year(s) specified in the document.[72] As the name suggests, the MOU is not a legally enforceable agreement, though it is "intended to govern the conduct of the CAP."[73] According to the IRS, the MOU "defines specific objectives for the CAP, sets parameters for the disclosure of information, describes the methods of communication, and serves as a statement of the parties' commitment to good-faith participation in the CAP."[74]

Taxpayers in the CAP or compliance maintenance phases execute a new CAP MOU every year as a condition of their acceptance or continuation in the programme.[75] The CAP MOU is effective immediately upon execution and remains in effect until all issues identified for that year (whether in the real-time audit stage or in a post-filing examination) are resolved, or until the CAP relationship is terminated.[76] In years when it is accepting new applications, the IRS publishes a separate Pre-CAP MOU, which taxpayers must execute upon being accepted into the pre-CAP phase.[77] The Pre-CAP MOU applies to all open tax years that are currently preventing the taxpayer from qualifying for the CAP phase.[78] Once executed, the Pre-CAP MOU remains in effect until the taxpayer is eligible for the CAP phase or until its Pre-CAP status is terminated.[79]

While both the CAP and Pre-CAP MOUs are standardized,[80] the generality of the terms provides some flexibility for the parties to tailor key parameters to the taxpayer's unique situation and risk profile. For example, the CAP MOU for the tax year 2019 listed certain issues, such as tax shelters, that are always in-scope and deems any issues covered under the existing mandatory disclosure scheme for uncertain tax positions to be per se material, but otherwise leaves it to the IRS and the taxpayer to jointly determine the scope of review, including materiality thresholds.[81] There is also room for the parties to adapt to changes in the taxpayer's circumstances by reconsidering materiality thresholds or reducing the level of review during a CAP year.[82]

[F] Review and Acceptance of Returns

Taxpayers in the CAP or compliance maintenance phases must provide the IRS with a post-filing representation letter within thirty days of filing their return, stating that all

72. CAP FAQ at 32, https://www.irs.gov/businesses/corporations/compliance-assurance-process-cap-frequently-asked-questions-faqs.
73. 2019 CAP MOU at 8.
74. IRM 4.51.8.5(5).
75. IRM 4.51.8.5(5); 2019 CAP MOU at 1.
76. 2019 CAP MOU at 1.
77. IRM 4.51.8.4(5).
78. 2015 Pre-CAP MOU at 1.
79. *Id.*
80. CAP FAQ at 32 ("Changes to the approved form Pre-CAP or CAP MOUs are not permitted. The only variable elements to the MOUs are TP name, EIN, and tax year(s). Additionally, supplements and/or addendums to the approved form MOUs are not allowed.").
81. 2019 CAP MOU at 2-4.
82. 2019 CAP MOU at 4-5.

material issues were disclosed and resolved and listing any exceptions.[83] Starting in 2019, this letter must be signed under penalty of perjury. If the IRS determines that the taxpayer has complied with the MOU and disclosed and resolved all material issues satisfactorily, the IRS will issue a "Full Acceptance Letter" confirming that it will accept the taxpayer's return if it is filed consistent with the resolutions agreed to in the pre-filing process, subject to its post-filing review. Otherwise, the IRS will issue a "Partial Acceptance Letter," confirming the same, but only with respect to satisfactorily resolved and disclosed issues.

The post-filing review consists of a joint meeting between the taxpayer and the IRS. Where a Full Acceptance Letter was issued, the IRS has set a sixty-day goal to confirm that all issues were reported in the agreed-upon manner. If issues were not properly reported and cannot be clarified or resolved, then those issues move to a traditional post-filing audit. The IRS will issue a No Change Letter if all issues were adequately resolved, which concludes the taxpayer's examination for that period.

[G] Relationship Management and Dispute Resolution

[1] Communication

Because the CAP programme involves frequent and close contact between the taxpayer and the IRS, it is crucial to maintain open channels of communication. To that end, the IRS assigns each CAP taxpayer an account coordinator, who serves as the "single point of contact for all federal tax matters."[84] Starting in the 2019 CAP year, the taxpayer must also designate an employee to serve as the primary point of contact for CAP review, so that there is "no communication barrier or filter between the IRS and the [t]axpayer."[85] The parties are expected to interact regularly as needed to exchange information and resolve issues, but there are no specific targets for how often they must meet. Higher-level members of the IRS team are not required to attend regular meetings except as needed. The IRS Territory Manager is expected to participate in the opening conference for new CAP taxpayers and at least one meeting per year thereafter. The highest-level member of the IRS team, the Director of Field Operations (DFO), is not required to attend meetings (except as needed), but is expected to communicate with each taxpayer at least twice in a given CAP cycle.

The IRS identified consistency in communication and expedited issue resolution as two goals of the recent CAP recalibration.[86] In February 2019, Deputy Commissioner Flax stated:

83. 2019 CAP MOU at 6. This letter is submitted separate from the tax return filing.
84. IRM 4.51.8.5(8); *See also* 2019 CAP MOU, https://www.irs.gov/pub/irs-utl/2019_cap_memorandum_of_understanding_final.pdf.
85. *Id.*
86. Nana Ama Sarfo, "LB&I Expanding Staffing and Use of Data Analytics," 93 Tax Notes Int'l 1151 (Mar. 18, 2019), https://www.taxnotes.com/tax-notes-today-international/corporate-taxation/lbi-expanding-staffing-and-use-data-analytics/2019/03/18/297c9.

> We had heard a number of examples where taxpayers or reps were hesitant to elevate issues because they didn't want to hurt the relationships they had with the teams, and we also heard from IRS teams that they felt that they were not supported when they attempted to raise issues through their management team. So we are trying to address both of those issues, as there are disagreements, or there's a view by one of us that we're not operating consistently with the spirit of the programme, either IRS or taxpayers, quickly.[87]

It is indeed appropriate to get this right. The main benefit to taxpayers of CAP is certainty. If the IRS is not viewed as investing the resources to get properly tailored, reasonable, and materially correct guidance to the CAP taxpayers, the programme will ultimately fail.

[2] Elevation & Dispute Resolution

In August 2018, the IRS announced a new ninety-day goal for issue resolution.[88] The 2019 CAP MOU specifies that once the taxpayer has fully disclosed an issue, which must be within ninety days of transaction being completed or having an impact on tax liability,[89] the IRS has ninety days to determine whether it agrees with the taxpayer's proposed tax treatment, unless an extension is requested and approved by the Territory Manager.[90] If, after ninety days or the approved extended period, the issue is still not resolved, the IRS may offer to resolve the issue through its Fast Track Settlement (FTS) process, and the taxpayer must agree to do so if offered.[91] If the parties are unable to reach an agreement through FTS, they may use any generally available issue resolution process, including IRS administrative appeals.[92]

The 2019 CAP MOU also provides new guidelines for elevating disagreements about issue identification. While the IRS has ultimate discretion in determining which issues are within scope of the pre-filing review, any disputes regarding which issues will be reviewed are elevated to the IRS Territory Manager. One specific addition to the 2019 CAP MOU hints at the type of communication problems the IRS is trying to solve with the recalibration: "If issues are added to the Issues List without consultation with the Taxpayer, the Taxpayer should elevate this situation to the Director of Field Operations ('DFO')."[93]

More generally, the parties are encouraged to meet to discuss and attempt to resolve any issues, including concerns about cooperation and transparency, and to document such meetings using the "Assessment of Cooperation and Transparency Form."[94] However, there is no formalized process for either party to elevate to a higher

87. *Id.*
88. IR 2018-174.
89. MOU at 2.
90. *Id.*
91. MOU at 2; Recalibration discussion document at 13 (noting that prior to the 2019 CAP year, Fast Track Settlement was encouraged, but not required).
92. MOU at 2.
93. *Id.*
94. MOU at 5.

level if they feel the relationship is not progressing satisfactorily, short of formal termination of CAP participation.

[3] Alternative Dispute Resolution

As reported by the Government Accountability Office (GAO), "CAP taxpayers retain the same appeal rights as non-CAP taxpayers if they disagree with IRS' audit findings,"[95] meaning that participants have access to the other avenues available for dispute resolution such as advance pricing agreements for transfer pricing issues, IRS administrative appeals, and FTSs. FTS, for example, allows the IRS and taxpayers to resolve disputes quickly, so long as the IRS has not issued a thirty-day letter. Should a taxpayer disagree with the CAP resolution options entirely, the case can be moved outside of CAP and under IRS administrative appeals. Under this option, an IRS Appeals Officer has jurisdiction and becomes the decision-maker of the case. This Appeals Officer has the ability to settle on a "hazards of litigation" basis,[96] which could be efficient for both the IRS and taxpayer. Under this view, an Appeals Officer may concede issues, in whole or in part, make mutual concession settlements, or split issue settlements.[97] If the taxpayer is unable to resolve the issue with IRS administrative appeals, it has the same litigation options as other taxpayers.

[H] Termination of CAP

Either the taxpayer or the IRS may terminate the CAP relationship by following procedures set forth in the MOU.[98] If a taxpayer fails to meet its obligations under the MOU, and the parties cannot resolve the matter informally, the IRS will issue a written notice of its concerns, followed by a termination letter if the failure is not remedied within thirty days.[99] Serious failures that will result in termination include not engaging in good faith issue resolution discussions, failing to disclose certain issues, and frequently filing claims or requesting appeals.[100] If a taxpayer is unsatisfied with CAP, the taxpayer may leave the programme voluntarily at any time by submitting a written request to withdraw, upon which the IRS will issue a termination letter.[101] If a taxpayer leaves or is terminated from the programme, the IRS may conduct a traditional post-filing examination of the taxpayer's return once it is filed, but there are no specific penalties for leaving CAP.[102] Prior to termination, the taxpayer and the IRS typically

---

95. Government Accountability Office (GAO) Report (GAO-13-662): "IRS Should Determine Whether Its Streamlined Corporate Audit Process Is Meeting Its Goals," https://www.gao.gov/assets/660/657092.pdf.
96. Treas. Reg. § 6.01.106(f)(2); *see*, e.g., IRM 8.6.4.1(2), 8.7.3.2.1(2).
97. I.R.M. 8.6.4.1.1; I.R.M. 8.6.4.1.2.
98. 2019 CAP MOU at 6-7.
99. *Id.*, at 6.
100. *Id.*, at 7.
101. *Id.*
102. CAP FAQ at 28.

proceed through the responsibilities and obligations outlined in the MOU in an attempt to resolve their differences and continue in CAP.[103]

[I] Evaluation of CAP

During the course of its almost fifteen-year history, the CAP programme has struggled to meet its goals of: (1) providing quicker resolution of issues and cases, (2) addressing emerging issues, (3) providing real-time feedback, (4) resolving issues and providing certainty prior to tax return filing and allowing for more concise financial reporting, (5) rewarding compliant behavior and reducing or eliminating the need for post-filing examinations, and (6) allowing for redeployment of IRS audit teams to non-compliant taxpayers. Indeed, the IRS expected to have significant savings in time spent by the IRS with respect to each tax year reviewed under CAP.[104]

The reality of CAP, however, is that while the IRS may spend less time auditing a particular CAP tax year than it would on a traditional audit, it allocates more resources to the review of that CAP year, thus generating no efficiencies through CAP.[105] Indeed, in 2013, the Treasury General of Tax Administration estimated that "the hourly revenue rate for CAP [was] approximately a third of the hourly rate examiners generated from traditional audits, $2,939 versus $8,448."[106] Academic analysis of CAP has similarly identified a lack of efficiency with the programme as CAP shifts the IRS' limited resources away from high-risk taxpayers where a greater focus could yield higher tax revenue and toward low-risk taxpayers.[107] This is because taxpayers who are more likely to apply to CAP are lower risk, with less aggressive tax positions.[108] More aggressive taxpayers are still audited, but through the traditional

103. CAP FAQ at 8, https://www.irs.gov/businesses/corporations/compliance-assurance-process-cap-frequently-asked-questions-faqs.
104. "Successes and Challenges on the Journey to Real-Time Tax Compliance: The U.S. Experience" at 6-9, https://ciatorg.sharepoint.com/:b:/s/cds/Ed04UBFRetNEnLtM0YJ1evIBKvxnckA5Wou5QBoVYF_XFw?e=sSSi6P.
105. *See* "Using Impact Evaluation to Examine Domestic and International Cooperative Compliance Programs," Tax Notes (Mar. 27, 2019), https://www.taxnotes.com/tax-notes-today-international/compliance/using-impact-evaluation-examine-domestic-and-international-cooperative-compliance-programs/2019/03/27/294kg?#294kg-0000040 (explaining that the Treasury General for Tax Administration found in an evaluation of CAP that while the length of the audit process for large businesses in CAP was reduced as compared to those under traditional audit, more resources were allocated to the CAP review, creating a less efficient and more expensive use of staff).
106. Report of Treasury Inspector General of Tax Administration: "The Compliance Assurance Process Has Received Favorable Feedback, but Additional Analysis of Its Costs and Benefits Is Needed," https://www.treasury.gov/tigta/auditreports/2013reports/201330021fr.pdf.
107. Paul J. Beck and Petro Lisowsky, "Tax Uncertainty and Voluntary Real-Time Tax Audits," 89(3) Accounting Rev. 867-901 (2014) (Nov. 13, 2013), https://ssrn.com/abstract=1761343.
108. In a 2013 study by Beck and Lisowsky, they examine the empirical relationship between participation in CAP and tax uncertainty disclosed in financial statements under FIN 48. The study separated firms into three groups based on FIN 48 reserve size: small, medium, and large. They found that the CAP participation rates are highest for firms in the middle group and the CAP firms in the middle group obtain the most significant reduction in their tax reserves. The average reduction in FIN 48 reserves for CAP participants was $16 million, which is about 16.5% of the tax reserve's beginning-period balance. The study interpreted the

audit process, rather than CAP. Further, because of the nature of CAP, it is possible that participation in the programme actually undermines the goals of the tax system as one study found that there is reduced accountability for the IRS regarding compliance because no information is available to show how much money is earned by using the process, unlike a traditional audit.[109]

A U.S. GAO assessment of CAP in 2013 found missing performance measures, nonexistent targets for goals, and incomplete data, making it essentially impossible for the IRS to evaluate whether the goals of CAP were being met.[110] For example, the IRS was not tracking data on resource savings that would be able to be invested in increase audit coverage in other areas, a key goal of CAP. Ultimately, the GAO recommended the IRS further "evaluate the process, develop measures and targets for the goals, consistently capture data to track goal progress, track resolution of tax issues and resource savings, develop a plan to expand Compliance Maintenance, and verify that audit staff understand attempts to clarify related guidance."[111] A follow-up GAO report in 2017 found that while the IRS had taken steps to compare the workload of CAP versus non-CAP team members, the IRS could still not show what this meant in terms of savings and did not have a plan for reinvesting the savings, if any.[112] While the introduction of the compliance maintenance bridge phase seems geared toward meeting one of CAP's goals (improving IRS resource allocation to higher risk taxpayers), it does so at the expense of other CAP goals, in particular, rewarding compliant behavior and providing taxpayers with certainty.

The goals of CAP have been compelling to taxpayers and widely praised; however, the feedback from CAP participants has been mixed. According to a 2010 IRS CAP satisfaction survey, 94% of taxpayers were satisfied with the programme, 89% had increased tax certainty for their organizations, and 82% were satisfied with issue

---

results to imply that the likelihood of participating in CAP is positively associated with tax uncertainty and negatively associated with tax aggressiveness. *Id.*

A second study focused on measuring the effectiveness of the CAP programme in taxpayer compliance. The study compared CAP firms with non-CAP firms and found that CAP firms have lower unrecognized tax benefits and higher foreign tax rates. They explain that this suggests CAP firms are less aggressive income shifters and likely have less intangible property offshore. They interpreted these results as some evidence that CAP firms are less tax aggressive, but the results were weak. "The Effect of CAP on Tax Aggressiveness," Article by Amy Dunbar and Andrew Duxbury of University of Connecticut, 2014; https://www.irs.gov/pub/irs-soi/14resconeffectcap.pdf.

109. Traditional audits have "extensive statistics" about the amounts earned while similar statistics are not available for CAP and practically will not be able to be produced because taxpayers and the IRS agree on the tax liability prior to the filing of the tax return. Therefore, the IRS has reduced accountability regarding the return from its compliance efforts. Leigh Osofsky, Some Realism About Responsive Tax Administration, https://repository.law.miami.edu/cgi/viewcontent.cgi?referer=https://www.google.com/&httpsredir=1&article=1097&context=fac_articles.

110. GAO Report (GAO-13-662): "IRS Should Determine Whether Its Streamlined Corporate Audit Process Is Meeting Its Goals," https://www.gao.gov/assets/660/657092.pdf.

111. *Id.*

112. GAO Report GAO-17-317: "Enforcement of Tax Laws" 2017 TNT 31-26, https://www.taxnotes.com/tax-notes-today-federal/compliance/enforcement-tax-laws-remains-high-risk-area-gao-says/2017/02/16/gdlj.

resolution and identification.[113] While these early results were promising, there have also been challenges with the programme. Since the programme is based on cooperation, rather than adversarial in nature, some IRS agents have been slower to adjust. A previous Commissioner of LB&I, Deborah Nolan, explained that there have been many instances where breakdowns in communication, disparate expectations, or misunderstandings about the process have negatively impacted CAP.[114] One CAP participant noted he has seen a "disturbing trend" of communication breakdown where CAP issues have been sent up to the National Office, where the issues are reviewed by people who are not heavily invested in the CAP objectives.[115] This type of activity slows down the process, increases the use of IRS resources, and lowers the likelihood of quick resolution of the issues.

Overall, for CAP to succeed in achieving its goals of providing taxpayers with certainty while allowing for better allocation of IRS resources, the IRS must be willing to provide certainty to certain taxpayers participating in CAP without putting them through the same type of extensive audit process that is applied to taxpayers in traditional audits. The current bridge phase, while freeing up IRS resources, does not achieve this goal because it provides no certainty to the taxpayers who are relegated to that status. As mentioned above, until the trust deficit between the IRS and (at least this group of) taxpayers is resolved, CAP will continue to be an "expensive option" from an IRS resource perspective. Fixing that trust deficit may require a combination of increased entry and compliance requirements, a serious focus on quality guidance, and a change in attitude toward the direction of viewing tax compliance as a CSR issue.

§15.03 RELATIONSHIP BETWEEN THE ICAP AND CAP

[A] The ICAP

The ICAP is a voluntary programme similar to CAP, but designed to facilitate efficient taxpayer discussions with tax authorities from *multiple* countries through a unified process.[116] The initial pilot included eight member countries of the Forum on Tax Administration: Australia, Canada, Italy, Japan, the Netherlands, Spain, the U.K., and the U.S.[117] Companies headquartered in the participating jurisdictions that have more than EUR 750 million of revenue can apply for the ICAP. Once accepted, the company must submit its County-by-Country reports and other tax information. The company then presents this information to the participating tax authorities, which must then

113. "Tension in IRS's CAP Program May Cause Growing Pains," https://www.taxnotes.com/tax-notes-federal/settlements-and-dispute-resolution/tension-irss-cap-program-may-cause-growing-pains/2011/01/24/qmfp.
114. *Id.*
115. *Id.*
116. Stephanie Soong Johnston, "Tax Chiefs Launch Pilot of Joint Risk Assessment Program," Tax Notes (Sep. 29, 2017), https://www.taxnotes.com/beps-expert/tax-system-administration/tax-chiefs-launch-pilot-joint-risk-assessment-program/2017/09/29/1wf6c.
117. OECD ICAP, OECD, https://www.oecd.org/tax/forum-on-tax-administration/international-compliance-assurance-programme.htm.

grant a collective risk assessment of the company that could possibly lead to an audit or not.

The programme was created to help reduce the audit caseloads of the participating countries, as several administrations realized that one conversation with all countries at once would be more efficient than each case proceeding through the mutual agreement procedure. The first pilot was set to run for twelve months and was to be judged based on the level of assurance companies and countries received and the efficiency of the process. While speaking at a transfer pricing conference, Irene Ros of Shell International B.V., confirmed that her company was participating in the ICAP and relayed that it was "a possibility to ultimately operate more efficiently."[118] Zahira Quattrocchi similarly discussed the ICAP experience she had when employed with Barilla, stating that having all relevant tax authorities at the table to see the risk assessment was "interesting" and "a very good initiative" that is "a big step forward."[119]

After the first pilot, the OECD advised that it would launch the ICAP 2.0, which retained some successful features of the first pilot, but also included improvements based on feedback from the pilot.[120] Of note, the ICAP 2.0 is expected to be more clear and flexible, depending on the risk assessment. Additionally, a new scoping stage was added to find the covered and excluded transactions, if necessary. An option for issue resolution was added to allow tax administrations to work with the company in order to resolve changes to keep the risk low. Finally, more tax administrations will be participating in the ICAP 2.0 to provide for greater certainty. The timeframe for a company to receive assurance is twenty-four-twenty-eight weeks from the receipt of the requested documents.

[B] Participation by the U.S.

The U.S. does not participate in any finalized multilateral co-operative compliance programmes at this time but is working toward this goal by participating in the ICAP pilot and now in the ICAP 2.0. While there are pros to participating in the ICAP process, such as stimulating constructive engagement amongst involved taxing authorities, challenges exist because of the multilateral context. Jennifer Best, Director of Treaty and Transfer Pricing Operations of LB&I, believes that difficulties could arise because of the different materiality thresholds of each country trying to determine what a common definition of each risk level should be.[121] The OECD responded by stating that

118. Stephanie Soong Johnston, "Participants Welcome Joint Tax Risk Assessment Pilot," Tax Notes (Apr. 13, 2018), https://www.taxnotes.com/beps-expert/transfer-pricing/participants-welcome-joint-tax-risk-assessment-pilot/2018/04/16/27z1r.
119. *Id.*
120. OECD ICAP, OECD, https://www.oecd.org/tax/forum-on-tax-administration/international-compliance-assurance-programme.htm.
121. Ryan Finley, "ICAP Participant Countries Working Toward Convergence." 92 Tax Notes Int'l 1232 (Dec. 17, 2018), https://www.taxnotes.com/tax-notes-international/competent-authority-matters/icap-participant-countries-working-toward-convergence/2018/12/17/28phk.

the risk and materiality issues are inherent and, as such, will not go away by avoiding the ICAP.[122] Instead, risk and materiality issues "actually get a lot more complicated" if a programme like the ICAP is not used.[123] Similarly, the Director General of the Canada Revenue Agency, Alexandra MacLean, stated that while participation in the ICAP has been labor-intensive, one of the programme's strengths is the pace; once companies provide information, assurance is given in less than a year.[124]

[C] Comparison of CAP and the ICAP

CAP and the ICAP are two separate programmes, but both work toward achieving similar goals of quickly reviewing a taxpayer's transactions and providing certainty, while reducing administrative burdens and resource constraint issues. Both programmes are voluntary and take approximately twelve months to complete, but the ICAP 2.0 is expected to decrease this timeline to close to six months. CAP focuses on providing certainty before the tax return is filed, by allowing the IRS to review and sign off on transactions before the return is filed, a process some have criticized as a "streamlined audit" versus a true compliance programme.[125] The ICAP, in contrast, is focused on providing a risk assessment with regard to tax issues, rather than providing assurance with respect to the correctness of any positions taken.

The programmes vary in the assessment of risk as well. CAP only grants certainty with regard to U.S. taxes (and typically no certainty with respect to U.S. transfer pricing issues), causing a multinational to need multiple programmes or risk assessments if greater tax certainty is desired. The ICAP, comparatively, evaluates all international tax issues and requires all involved taxing authorities to give a collective risk assessment of the company at the same time. As mentioned above, the varying risk appetites of each could cause debate and/or delay in the decision. However, this collective decision may give the company greater tax certainty at one time.

§15.04 CONCLUSION

In effect, both CAP and the ICAP strive to increase efficiency and tax certainty. Learnings from the CAP programme that can be applied to the ICAP include: (1) setting measurable goals that can be tracked in order to determine the success of the programme, (2) being mindful of resource allocations so that greater focus can be directed toward higher-risk areas, and (3) being willing to provide certainty in situations where taxpayers have demonstrated compliance and low risk in the past, without conducting a full review. An area where CAP has been more successful is in

122. *Id.*
123. *Id.*
124. *Id.*
125. "Using Impact Evaluation to Examine Domestic and International Cooperative Compliance Programs," Tax Notes (Mar. 27, 2019), https://www.taxnotes.com/tax-notes-today-international/compliance/using-impact-evaluation-examine-domestic-and-international-cooperative-compliance-programs/2019/03/27/294kg?#294kg-0000040.

encouraging transparency with taxpayers and creating an environment where taxpayers are willing to discuss the issues and engage with the IRS in an open manner. Indeed, while CAP has room to improve, companies are still applying to participate in CAP and consider acceptance into the programme as a sign of great compliance. Accordingly, the ICAP, like CAP, has the potential to be successful but must be managed carefully to ensure resources are being used appropriately and taxpayers are being adequately rewarded for their willingness to engage in compliance discussions.

CHAPTER 16

Preventing Double Taxation: Analysis of Recent Developments and ICAP 2.0*

Taco Wiertsema & Freek Braken

§16.01 INTRODUCTION

In order to prevent situations of double taxation, countries conclude tax treaties (hereinafter: "*Treaties*") in which they allocate taxation rights in respect of income and capital. If despite these Treaty provisions double taxation remains, as often occurs in respect of transfer pricing corrections, the Mutual Agreement Procedure (MAP) that is included in most Treaties provides for a fallback mechanism. Under the MAP, contracting states engage into a consultation process with each other with the aim to eliminate double taxation. The MAP statistics of the Organisation for Economic Co-operation and Development (OECD) and the EU Joint Transfer Pricing Forum (EUJTPF) show an exponential growth of the number of MAP cases reported by OECD Member States during 2006-2016 (i.e., from 2,352 to 7,190 cases). These statistics also show that transfer pricing disputes often result in double taxation and subsequently lead to MAPs. We expect that this exponential growth of the number of MAPs will increase in the coming years, specifically as a result of a further increase in transfer pricing disputes.[1]

* This contribution is to a certain extent based on a prior publication of the authors in Weekblad Fiscaal Recht (WFR 2019/134 of June 29, 2019). The opinions expressed and arguments employed herein reflect the authors' private views and not necessarily that of their employers.

1. The main reasons for this trend are (i) increased transparency for companies (i.e., as a result of country-by-country reporting, Master File and Local File transfer pricing documentation, exchange of rulings based on EU and OECD rules and the EU Mandatory Disclosure Directive) and (ii) the specific BEPS measures in the area of transfer pricing (BEPS Action 7 on permanent establishments and Actions 8-10 on risk allocation and intangibles). Transfer pricing disputes often occur when the "new concepts" derived from the BEPS action plans on transfer pricing are applied to years prior to the publication of these plans.

In this article we discuss recent developments in the elimination of double taxation in: (i) the European Union (EU) Dispute Resolution Directive ("*Directive*"), (ii) BEPS Action 14, and (iii) the Multilateral Instrument (MLI).[2] Further to that, we identify a number of existing areas of concern that impede companies[3] from applying an efficient process of preventing double taxation and we investigate the extent to which recent developments (will) remove these areas of concern.

We focus in particular on the prevention of double taxation through the MAP and, where relevant, on the subsequent arbitration procedure ("*Arbitration*"). Where relevant, we focus on the domestic (i.e., or "corresponding") side of a transaction for which a (foreign) transfer pricing correction is imposed.[4]

In addition to the recent developments with respect to dispute resolution, we consider the OECD's Pilot on the International Compliance Assurance Programme (ICAP 2.0) as a means of preventing disputes before they materialize.

The last paragraph of this chapter includes a summarizing overview of the impact of the recent developments on the areas of concern and provides suggestions for (any) remaining areas of concern.

§16.02 RECENT DEVELOPMENTS

[A] Introduction

In this section we set-out recent developments as reflected in the Directive, BEPS Action 14 and the MLI in the context of preventing double taxation through the MAP and (possibly) Arbitration. Before addressing recent developments in more detail, first we outline the process of the MAP as a means of prevention of double taxation.

[B] The Prevention of Double Taxation and the MAP

A (foreign) audit and the resulting (transfer pricing) corrections usually relate to one or more years in the past. Generally, at that point in time, the domestic company has already filed tax returns for the years that are under audit in the other jurisdiction and may also have paid the tax due for these years. The result of the correction is potential double taxation. The company can subsequently attempt to eliminate this double taxation by (i) initiating legal proceedings against initial correction (i.e., by the foreign

2. OECD (2015), *Making Dispute Resolution Mechanisms More Effective, Action 14: 2015 Final Report, OECD/G20 Base Erosion and Profit Shifting Project*, OECD Publishing, Paris; OECD, Multilateral Convention to Implement Tax Treaty Related Measures to Prevent BEPS; Directive (EU) 2017/1852, PbEU 2017, L 265/1-14.
3. In this chapter "company" and "taxpayer" are used interchangeably.
4. It follows from the statistics of the OECD and the EUJTPF that, particularly, transfer pricing disputes lead to double taxation and subsequently to MAPs. That is consistent with what we *see* in our daily practice.

related company under the domestic law of that jurisdiction, (ii) requesting domestic unilateral relief,[5] or (iii) initiating a MAP.

In the remainder of this chapter we focus solely on the MAP (and Arbitration) as a method to prevent double taxation. In many cases, the MAP offers companies the best chance of a favorable result. In practice, for example, we see that transfer pricing disputes are rarely litigated against, specifically as a result of the potential negative consequences of legal proceedings.[6]

Contracting states do not have a binding obligation under the MAP to reach a resolution and thereby to avoid double taxation. Because they are only required to "*endeavor to resolve*" a dispute, the MAP may merely result in the Competent Authorities (CA)[7] to "*agree to disagree*". A limited number of Treaties (and also the EU Arbitration Convention) includes an Arbitration clause in addition to the MAP. If the MAP is supplemented with mandatory and binding Arbitration, this will lead to an obligation for the contracting states to resolve the double taxation. Mandatory and binding Arbitration means that contracting states are required to (a) initiate the Arbitration stage after the expiry of the "resolution period" under MAP (i.e., CA usually have a two-year period to attempt to resolve double taxation) and subsequently (b) actually implement the outcome of the Arbitration stage.[8]

---

5. For "open years" (i.e., fiscal years for which no final tax assessment has been issued or for which objections can still be filed against such assessments) the company may file a revised tax return or file an objection against a tax assessment raised. For "closed years" (i.e., fiscal years for which the statute of limitation of objection against final assessments has lapsed) the company can submit a request for an ex officio (downward) corresponding adjustment of the assessment. In the Netherlands, such a request has to be made within a period of five years after the end of the year to which the tax assessment relates.
6. An important disadvantage of litigation is that, in the majority of EU Member States, any remaining double taxation, i.e., double taxation that remains because the domestic court has (partially) maintained the initial adjustment, cannot be resolved under the EU Arbitration Convention (or under a Treaty that provides for an arbitration provision in accordance with Art. 25, para. 5 of the OECD Model Convention). More specifically, in these jurisdictions access to Arbitration is legally blocked because domestic law does not allow competent authorities to deviate from prior judicial decisions. This is only different in the Netherlands, Germany, Finland, Sweden and the United Kingdom (*see* Taco Wiertsema, "European Union Council Directive on Double Taxation Dispute Resolution Mechanisms: Resolving Companies' Areas of Concern?," *Derivatives and Financial Instruments Issue*, 2017 (Volume 19), No. 5 (online publication: October 13, 2017), note 23. In addition, domestic legal proceedings against transfer pricing corrections may also result in negative spillover effects in other jurisdictions where the group is active. Even though judicial decisions are often published anonymously, in many transfer pricing disputes the name of the taxpayer / the group can be fairly easily distilled from the ruling. That may provide an open invitation to authorities in other jurisdictions in which the group operates to raise similar adjustments (e.g., if the dispute relates to core elements of the transfer pricing policy as applied by the group). Finally, in practice we see that companies, in areas other than their "core business," are generally unwilling to accept a slim chance of a big loss (i.e., these companies generally accept the adjustment and subsequently initiate an MAP).
7. *Competent Authority or Competent Authorities are the government body responsible for conducting the MAP process. In this article both are referred to as "CA."*
8. Certain Treaties may provide for "voluntary Arbitration," under which the process of Arbitration only commences at the request of one or both states. *See* for example Art. 25 para. 5 of the Treaty between the Netherlands and Poland.

[C] The Directive

The Council of the EU adopted the Directive on October 10, 2017. The aim of the Directive is to improve the existing dispute resolution mechanisms provided for in Treaties concluded between EU Member States and in the EU Arbitration Convention. The Directive has a wider scope compared to the EU Arbitration Convention.[9] Unlike the EU Arbitration Convention, whose scope is limited to disputes on transfer pricing and the allocation of profits to permanent establishments, the Directive offers taxpayers the possibility to apply the MAP, and Arbitration, to all disputes that lead to double taxation. Apart from its broader scope, the Directive's "foundations" are quite similar to the existing rules as included in the EU Arbitration Convention. For example, the Directive also provides for mandatory and binding Arbitration if the CA fail to reach a resolution for the double taxation within the two-year period of the MAP. The main benefit of the Directive, compared to existing mechanisms, is the inclusion of (i) clear (procedural) rules on the various stages of the elimination process (i.e., from unilateral relief to MAP and Arbitration) and (ii) mechanisms on the basis of which companies can force access to and progress of the process of the MAP and Arbitration stage before an independent Arbitration Commission[10] and (ultimately) domestic courts.[11] The Directive applies to requests to initiate a MAP (hereinafter "*Complaints*") filed from July 1, 2019 relating to taxable years beginning on or after January 1, 2018. The Directive had to be incorporated in the domestic laws of the EU Member States before July 1, 2019.

[D] BEPS Action 14

In BEPS Action 14, the OECD recognizes that the uncertainty for companies resulting from various anti-tax avoidance measures and the new views on the interpretation for the arm's length principle, as included in other BEPS action plans, needs to be balanced with more effective dispute resolution mechanisms. BEPS Action 14 contains a minimum standard for this purpose, supplemented with a number of best practices. Unfortunately, mandatory and binding Arbitration turned out to be "a bridge too far" for a large number of countries participating in the BEPS project. We subsequently focus on the following parts of the minimum standard of BEPS Action 14: (i) the peer monitoring mechanism and (ii) the MAP statistics reporting framework.

9. Compare Arts 1 and 4 of the EU Arbitration Convention with Art. 1 of the Directive.
10. The Arbitration Commission consists of a representative of each CA and three independent persons, or two representatives of each CA and five independent persons. The chairman is in any case an independent person.
11. For an extensive treatment of the Directive we also refer to: Taco Wiertsema, "European Union Council Directive on Double Taxation Dispute Resolution Mechanisms: Resolving Companies' Areas of Concern?," *Derivatives and Financial Instruments Issue*, 2017 (Volume 19), No. 5 (online publication: October 13, 2017), note 23.

[1] Peer Monitoring Mechanism

The peer monitoring mechanism (the "*Mechanism*") ensures that the countries, which have committed to the BEPS actions, monitor each other in respect of their compliance with the implementation of the minimum standard. For this purpose, the participating countries formed a Forum on Tax Administration (FTA), the MAP Forum (the "*Forum*"). The Forum firstly determined, in a "Peer Review Report," to what extent a country already complies with the minimum standard of BEPS Action 14. One year after the publication of this assessment, the participating countries are required to specify in a subsequent report (the "*Update Report*"), any further measures required to comply with the minimum standard. Other countries are then given the opportunity to comment on the Update Report and subsequent to that a "Peer Monitoring Report" is published by the Forum.

[2] MAP Statistics Reporting Framework

The OECD has collected MAP statistics from Member States and partner countries since 2006. However, these statistics were not (always) supplied (nor complete). In addition, countries used diverging definitions in respect of compiling the statistics. As a result, objectively comparing the statistics of the different countries proved to be quite difficult.[12] Due to BEPS Action 14, the MAP statistics reporting framework (the "*Reporting Framework*") now requires countries to commit to the minimum standard and to report comprehensive statistics to the Forum based on consistent definitions.

[E] The MLI

As part of the minimum standard of BEPS Action 14, the MLI implements a MAP provision in all covered treaties (i.e., Treaties that are brought under the scope of the MLI by both participating countries). This mandatory MAP provision of the MLI is almost identical to the MAP provision included in Article 25 of the OECD Model Convention. Although the minimum standard of BEPS Action 14 only includes the MAP as a mandatory provision, in the scope of BEPS Action 14, a leading group of twenty countries also endorsed mandatory and binding Arbitration.[13] This has resulted in the possibility for countries participating in the MLI to opt for mandatory and binding Arbitration in addition to the MAP.

Contrary to the mandatory and binding Arbitration provision as included in Article 25, paragraph 5 of the OECD Model Convention, the Arbitration section of the

12. OECD Center for Tax Policy and Administration, Improving the Resolution of Tax Treaty Disputes (Report adopted by the Committee on Fiscal Affairs on January 30, 2007), February 2007. *See* for example (i) the 2015 MAP statistics for Germany, which emphasize deviating from OECD terminology; and (ii) the MAP statistics of Italy that do not include the duration of MAPs.
13. These jurisdictions are Australia, Austria, Belgium, Canada, France, Germany, Ireland, Italy, Japan, Luxembourg, the Netherlands, New Zealand, Norway, Poland, Slovenia, Spain, Sweden, Switzerland, the United Kingdom and the United States.

MLI provides for extensive procedural provisions covering the Arbitration stage. This means that the Arbitration section of the MLI provides for standard procedural rules with regard to the establishment of the Arbitration Commission and the course of the Arbitration process. Furthermore, it is noted that under the MLI, the Arbitration section only applies if both participating countries explicitly "opt-in" and no reservations are made.

§16.03 IMPACT OF RECENT DEVELOPMENTS ON AREAS OF CONCERN

[A] Introduction

We identified a number of important areas of concern that in practice prevent companies from resolving double taxation through the MAP (and Arbitration). These areas of concern are (i) uncertainty about access to the MAP, (ii) uncertainty about the likelihood of reaching a resolution, (iii) the costs associated with the MAP, (iv) the influence of the MAP on the relationship with (local) tax authorities and (v) the blocking effect of domestic legal proceedings. These areas of concern are undesirable from the perspective of the company as well as from the perspective of the contracting states.[14]

In this section we first explain these areas of concern. We subsequently investigate to what extent the Directive, BEPS Action 14 and the MLI (can) remove the areas of concern.

[B] Access to MAPs

[1] Area of Concern

Whether or not the MAP will be initiated depends on the acceptance of the request by both CA. Companies are therefore uncertain whether or not a MAP will actually be initiated by the CA involved. For example, a MAP request can be rejected on the basis that there is (or likely will be) no double taxation, or if the request was submitted outside the (generally) three-year period. In specific situations, a request cannot be processed or it is suspended.[15]

Furthermore, we note that under Treaties that are in compliance with the OECD Model Convention and the EU Arbitration Convention, the initiation of the MAP depends on the CA of the country where the MAP request was filed to issue a formal decision not providing unilateral relief. It is noted in this respect that the OECD Model

14. For a company, double taxation represents an additional cost item that does not generate any incremental benefits. For contracting states, double taxation hinders economic growth. *See*: Commission Staff Working Document Accompanying the document Proposal for a Council Directive on Double Taxation Dispute Resolution Mechanisms in the European Union ("Commission Staff Working Document"), October 25, 2016, SWD (2016) 343 final, p. 5.
15. For example, if the company has not fulfilled its administrative obligations and this leads to a reversal of the burden of proof. Another example is the case where the company invokes a MAP under the EU Arbitration Convention, while a fine has been imposed for a serious offense.

Convention and the EU Arbitration Convention do not provide for a defined period during which the CA must render such a decision. In practice, countries appear to make use of this "loophole" (i.e., postponing the issue of a decision on unilateral relief) to effectively block access to the MAP.[16]

[2] The Directive

On the basis of the Directive, the CA must decide to accept or reject a Complaint (i.e., a request in the context of the Directive) within a six-month period after receipt thereof (i.e., in this respect the provision of unilateral relief by one of the CA is also deemed a decision rendered). However, fallback mechanisms will be triggered if (i) one of the CA rejects the Complaint, (ii) both CA reject the Complaint or (iii) one or both CA fail to render a decision within the six-month period.[17]

In the first situation, if one of the CA rejects the Complaint, the taxpayer can request the CA to set up an Arbitration Commission. The Arbitration Commission will then issue a binding opinion on the legality of the rejection of the Complaint. If the relevant CA fail to set up the Arbitration Commission within a period of 120 days after receiving the Complaint, the taxpayer can request the domestic court to set up the Arbitration Commission. If the Arbitration Commission accepts the Complaint and the CA subsequently fail to initiate the MAP within a period of sixty days after the decision of the Arbitration Commission, the Arbitration Commission will be entitled to independently resolve the dispute to which the Complaint relates.

In the second situation, if both CA reject the Complaint, the taxpayer has the right to request domestic courts of both countries to assess the legality of the Complaint. If both courts accept the Complaint, the CA are required to initiate the MAP. If either of both courts rejects the Complaint, the CA are obliged to have the Arbitration Commission rendering a decision on the Complaint. If the Arbitration Commission then accepts the Complaint, the CA must then initiate the MAP. If the CA fail to do so, the Arbitration Commission will also have the right to resolve the dispute itself.

In the third situation, if one or both CA fail to render a decision on the Complaint, the Directive determines that the Complaint is deemed to have been accepted. This means that the MAP has to be initiated when both CA fail to render a decision on the Complaint or if the other CA has accepted the Complaint. If alternatively the other CA has rejected the Complaint, the Arbitration Commission must be set up to decide on the Complaint. If the Arbitration Commission accepts the Complaint, the CA are obliged to initiate the MAP. Also, for this third situation, if the CA fail to initiate the MAP, the Arbitration Commission will resolve the dispute itself.

---

16. H.M. Pit, "Commission Initiative to Improve Dispute Settlement Mechanisms within the European Union: The EU Arbitration Convention (90/436)," European Taxation, 2016 (Volume 56), No. 11, section 4.3.2.2.
17. The Directive offers the CA three situations in which a Complaint can be rejected: (i) if the information required for the Complaint has not been provided (in full) or has not been provided in time, (ii) in the absence of a dispute, or (iii) if the Complaint was not submitted within the three-year period.

Companies will be able to enforce access to the MAP as a result of the clear deadlines and fallback mechanisms included in the Directive. The Directive further allows companies the possibility to have the domestic court of the other state assess the legality of a Complaint. This effectively allows for guaranteed access to the MAP if the Complaint is objectively justified. The Directive will therefore have a positive impact on the ability of companies to enforce access to the MAP.

[3] The MLI

Unfortunately, the MLI does not remove the areas of concern with respect to access to the MAP. However, indirectly, Part IV of the MLI (i.e., the adjustments to the definitions of the permanent establishment) may have contributed to improve access to the MAP. It is noted in this respect that authorities often disagree on the existence of a (dependent agent) permanent establishment (e.g., if they apply a formal or economical interpretation of the condition "authority to conclude contracts" under Article 5(5) of the OECD Model Convention). Without agreement on the existence of a permanent establishment, double taxation cannot be resolved.

By accepting the reduced permanent establishment thresholds included in the MLI (in particular in the case of commissionaire arrangements), countries could prevent disagreement with their Treaty partners in the presence of a (dependent agent) permanent establishment. This allows them, subsequently, on the basis of the MAP, to focus on reaching a resolution with the other country on the (often limited) additional business profits to be attributed to such a (dependent agent) permanent establishment. In other words, checking the "MLI box" can provide "home jurisdictions" with increased effectiveness when preventing double taxation that results from permanent establishments being recognized by foreign tax authorities.

[4] BEPS Action 14

Unfortunately, the minimum standard of BEPS Action 14 does not require participating countries to provide a legal basis to enforce access to the MAP in domestic courts. However, we expect that the increased transparency resulting from the publication of the Peer Review Reports (i.e., for the "process" of the MAP) and the Reporting Framework (for the "output" of the MAP) will incentivize countries to improve their administrative procedures for the MAP. We also expect that increased transparency will lead to a reduction in the number of rejections of justified Complaints.

[C] Resolution for Double Taxation

[1] Area of Concern

Under the MAP, CA are only required to "endeavor to resolve" double taxation. If, however, the relevant Treaty provides for a MAP with (mandatory and binding) Arbitration, CA have an obligation to actually resolve double taxation. When the CA fail to reach a resolution under the MAP, usually within a two-year period, the matter will be submitted to an Arbitration Commission. This Arbitration Commission will then render a binding opinion. In practice, however, Arbitration does not always offer a company a hard guarantee that double taxation will actually be resolved. For example, the absence of procedural rules in a Treaty may result in arbitrators not being appointed and, consequently, Arbitration cannot take place. In addition, some Treaties render access to Arbitration dependent on a request from (one or both) CA.

The EU Arbitration Convention, which in principle requires mandatory and binding Arbitration, in practice also does not provide for a hard guarantee that double taxation will be resolved. It is noted in this respect that the EU Arbitration Convention does not provide for a (fixed) timeline for setting up the Arbitration Commission required for the Arbitration procedure. By not rendering a decision on the Arbitration Commission (or by postponing that decision), EU Member States are able to effectively block the Arbitration stage.[18]

[2] The Directive

After the start of the MAP, the CA have a two-year period under the Directive to reach a resolution on the dispute.[19] If the CA do not reach a resolution within this term, they have to inform the taxpayer thereof. Subsequently, the taxpayer has the right to request the CA to set up an Arbitration Commission.[20] If the CA fail to set up the Arbitration Commission within the required term, the taxpayer has the right to request the domestic court to set up the Arbitration Commission. The Directive also contains clear rules for the selection of members of the Arbitration Commission and the operating rules of procedure. After its establishment, the Arbitration Commission will advise on the dispute within six months.[21] The CA subsequently have a "reconsideration period" of another six months in which they may attempt to reach a (different) resolution on the dispute themselves. If they fail to do so, the advice of the Arbitration Commission will become binding to the CA and also to the company (i.e., if it accepts the advice and

18. Statistics from the EUJTPF provide indications that these situations actually occur. For example, Germany and Italy have dozens of MAP cases that qualify for Arbitration, while only a handful of Arbitration procedures were actually conducted under the EU Arbitration Convention. As regards Germany, it has failed for some reason to submit more than half of eligible disputes to Arbitration (i.e., disputes that have not been resolved in MAP with in the resolution period of (generally) two years).
19. Subject to argumentation from one or both CA, this period can be extended by one year. However, if a solution can be reached, but not all elements of the dispute can be settled within the two-year period, the company will arguably note have an objection to the extension of the MAP term by one year. This is because the alternative (i.e., Arbitration) will extend the full period of the dispute resolution process with at least one and a half years.
20. It is remarkable that the Directive does not provide for a clear term within which the CA must notify the taxpayer that they did not reach a resolution, specifically because the "CA notification" forms the stepping stone for the Arbitration stage (i.e., the company to request the CA to set up the Arbitration Commission).
21. The Arbitration Commission has the possibility to extend this period by three months if the nature of the dispute so justifies.

waives any legal proceedings under domestic law).[22] Subsequently, the taxation of the countries involved in the dispute has to be adjusted in accordance with the "advice" (or rather, the decision) of the Arbitration Commission or the alternative decision of the CA. Such adjustments have to be processed regardless of relevant domestic law time constraints. If the decision or the alternative resolution is not implemented, the taxpayer has the right to enforce implementation of the decision before the domestic courts.

The above justifies the expectation that the Directive will remove the concerns of companies in respect of CA failing to reach a resolution for a dispute. After all, the Directive contains clear procedures and rules for initiating and completing the Arbitration procedure. Furthermore, companies have the possibility to enforce access to Arbitration and have a hard guarantee that the decision reached by the Arbitration Commission, if accepted by the company, will actually be implemented (i.e., by means of access to the domestic courts if the CA fail to do so). We expect that the Directive's hard resolution guarantee will incentivize countries, specifically in transfer pricing disputes, to complete the MAP stage with a resolution that eliminates the double taxation. After all, if CA fail to reach a resolution under the MAP stage, unlike other mechanisms (i.e., the EU Arbitration Convention or Treaties) the Directive will ultimately allow another party than the CA to render a final decision.

[3] BEPS Action 14 and the MLI

Mandatory and binding Arbitration is not part of the minimum standard of BEPS Action 14 and is therefore not a required provision of the MLI. If the participating countries have opted in to mandatory and binding Arbitration, this will only take effect provided that both participating countries did not make any reservations on the Arbitration provision.[23] The MLI will therefore result only in mandatory and binding Arbitration in a fairly limited number of Treaties. BEPS Action 14 and the MLI will therefore only have a limited positive impact on resolving double taxation through mandatory and binding Arbitration.[24]

22. It appears that the six months "reconsideration period," during which CA have possibility to conclude an agreement which deviates from the Arbitrations Commission's advice, was only included in the Directive to allow countries to proclaim that they maintain a (theoretical) degree of sovereignty in respect to domestic tax law. From a practical point of view, it seems very unlikely that after the opinion of the Arbitration Commission (which logically leads to a "winner" and a "loser" in respect to the dispute), CA involved will be able to reach a different resolution.
23. Almost all countries that opted for mandatory and binding Arbitration have made reservations with regard to the application of the Arbitration. These reservations range from timing limitations to limitation on the nature of disputes that are eligible for Arbitration (*see* positions regarding Art. 28 para. 2 part a, and Art. 36 para. 2 MLI).
24. Moreover, it is remarkable that no fixed period has been included in the MLI during which the Arbitration Commission has to provide its opinion on a dispute. In the explanatory notes to the MLI (Explanatory Statement to the Multilateral Convention To Implementation Tax Treaty Related measures To Prevent Base Erosion And Profit Shifting, para. 230) it is only noted, in this context, that the proper functioning of the Arbitration process requires the CA to reach a resolution on the procedural details of the Arbitration process (i.e., including the time limit for

[D] Costs and Interest-Asymmetry

[1] Area of Concern

The process of a MAP generally results in high costs. These costs may include the time spent by the taxpayer in relation to the preparation of the Complaint and the substantiation of the taxpayer's position in respect to the dispute. These costs may also relate to advice from external specialists. It is furthermore noted in this respect that it is quite difficult to make a sound estimate, in advance, of all (direct and indirect) costs involved with the procedure. Furthermore, requests for additional information during the consultation stage or long procedures can also lead to unforeseen high costs.

The expected high costs and the uncertainty about the total costs of the procedure can lead companies to simply decide to accept the double taxation (i.e., and therefore refraining from starting a MAP). We expect that specifically smaller companies will more often decide to refrain from starting a MAP, because such companies will generally face lower adjustments. In practice, we recognize that, due to budget constraints, some companies decide to file quite brief MAP requests and thereby primarily rely on the CA for additional fact finding and the substantiation of a proposed resolution of the dispute. Although we realize that such an approach will allow the taxpayer to reduce the (immediate) direct costs of the procedure, one may question whether such an approach will ultimately lead to an efficient resolution of the double taxation. In practice, we see that "one pager-requests" often lead to additional questions being raised by CA, quite lengthy procedures and therefore to overall costs in excess of the costs that would have been incurred in relation to a proper (and therefore more elaborate) MAP request.[25] In our experience a proper MAP request at least includes the following elements: (i) an overview of all relevant facts (i.e., including those facts that have not been brought up in the course of the audit phase), (ii) a clear description of the dispute, (iii) a summary of the views of both tax authorities in respect to the dispute, and (iv) a detailed analysis of the dispute from the position of the taxpayer together with one or more potential solutions.

In addition to the direct costs of the procedure, the company involved may also incur substantial indirect costs resulting from a different treatment, by the countries involved, of interest on tax over the amount of double tax. Such "interest-asymmetry" occurs if the country imposing the initial correction also charges interest on the amount of additional tax, while the other country does not refund interest on an amount of cash tax paid as a result of the corresponding (downward) adjustment. If double taxation is ultimately resolved without dealing with "interest-asymmetry," a taxpayer will still be faced with a (potentially) substantial amount of additional costs. Given the, on average, quite lengthy discussions in MAPs (i.e., recent OECD data indicates that

---

the judgement on the dispute). Given the optional nature of the Arbitration section of the MLI, we expect for countries that have opted-in to apply a benevolent and proactive attitude when adopting these procedural rules.

25. We are thinking here of a Complaint that at least includes the following elements: an overview of all (known and unknown) relevant facts, a summary of the views of both authorities, an analysis of the dispute by the company and one or more potential solutions.

transfer pricing MAPs take on average thirty-three months to resolve), the amount of double interest costs may even approximate the amount of the double taxation. Although this issue is generally acknowledged (e.g., in BEPS Action 14 which contains a "best practice" to this end), few countries actually provide solutions for interest on tax (and penalties) in their domestic tax law or MAP guidance.

[2] Directive, BEPS Action 14 and the MLI

Unfortunately, neither the Directive nor the minimum standard of BEPS Action 14 and the MLI recognize the (often) high costs associated with initiating a MAP and potential (double) taxation interest charges.[26] These measures primarily aim at removing the more formal barriers in the MAP process. In our opinion, this issue is particularly important because the overall costs associated with the MAP are expected to increase further in the future. This will specifically be the case where taxpayers need (under the Directive) to enforce access to the MAP and/or Arbitration before domestic courts. On top of that, in case of interest-asymmetry, increased durations of proceedings may also lead to substantial double interest on tax-charges.

[E] Relationship with the Tax Authorities

[1] Area of Concern

Anecdotal evidence indicates that companies, from specifically Southern Europe, fear the potential negative impact of filing a Complaint. In these countries, a Complaint submitted by the taxpayer results in a significant increase in the likelihood of a tax audit being initiated.[27] This type of situation is more likely to occur in jurisdictions where CA in charge with resolving MAPs are required to obtain approval from tax administration staff that imposed the initial corrections underlying the disputes.

[2] Directive, BEPS Action 14 and the MLI

The (justified) fear of "additional" audits and (possible) additional corrections may incentivize local companies to refrain from resolving double taxation through the MAP. These (potentially) negative effects of the MAP are only recognized in BEPS Action 14.[28] For example, the minimum standard of BEPS Action 14 requires for CA to be independently authorized to resolve MAPs (i.e., not requiring approval from tax officials involved with the initial correction). This measure reduces the likelihood of

26. BEPS Action 14 does include a "best practice" which means that the MAP policy of countries should address the consideration of interest and fines in the MAP. This "best practice" does not provide any guidance on how countries should do this and, moreover, is not part of the minimum standard.
27. *See also* Comments Received on Public Discussion Draft—BEPS Action 14 Make Dispute Resolution Mechanisms More Effective, January 19, 2015, pp. 113 and 374.
28. *Section 2.3 of the minimum standard.*

disputes leading to a (recurrence of the) conflict with the local tax officials. In our experience opposite situations also occur. Companies will be more easily inclined to opt for the MAP if they maintain a good working relationship with the tax officials. These companies expect that the co-operative and transparent working relationship of the past increases their chances of resolving double taxation through the MAP.

[F] Blocking Effect of Domestic Legal Proceedings

[1] Area of Concern

The majority of EU Member States' domestic laws contains (constitutional) provisions that prevent the CA from resolving double taxation through Arbitration in case of a previously rendered domestic judicial decision. EU Member States that do allow CA the possibility to deviate are the Netherlands, Germany, Finland, Sweden and the United Kingdom.[29] For the EU Member States that do not allow deviations, the EU Arbitration Convention, as well as Treaties with mandatory and binding Arbitration concluded by these countries, include provisions that block access to Arbitration if a domestic court has already rendered a decision on the correction. If a decision has been rendered, the CA of the country that made the initial correction may still enter into the MAP. However, because the procedure can no longer lead to Arbitration, the involvement of said CA may be limited to providing an additional explanation of a court decision and can only result in a "agree to disagree" with the other CA. In case a (foreign) court decision has been rendered, the taxpayer may still request a unilateral corresponding adjustment. However, double taxation will not be resolved if the domestic tax authorities have a different view on the dispute or if the request for an adjustment was submitted outside of the statute of limitations.

[2] Directive, BEPS Action 14 and the MLI

The Directive, the minimum standard of BEPS Action 14 and the MLI include references to the negative impact of domestic legal proceedings on MAP and Arbitration. However, these measures do not provide solutions for situations in which a taxpayer is faced with blocked access to Arbitration due to prior domestic legal proceedings.[30] This would realistically require an adaptation of the domestic (constitutional) law and it therefore does not seem to fit within the framework of the Directive, BEPS Action 14 and the MLI. After all, these developments are mainly aimed at improving the MAP procedures (in Treaties) and the related policy. In practice,

29. Taco Wiertsema, "European Union Council Directive on Double Taxation Dispute Resolution Mechanisms: Resolving Companies' Areas of Concern?," *Derivatives and Financial Instruments Issue*, 2017 (Volume 19), No. 5 (online publication: October 13, 2017), note 24.
30. BEPS Action 14 includes a "best practice" that suggests that countries clarify the relationship between national procedures and the MAP in their MAP policies. However, no substantive policy or legislative amendment is suggested in this area. Moreover, the "best practices" are not part of the minimum standard.

taxpayers are well advised in case of adjustments to thoroughly analyze the various mechanisms available for avoiding double taxation and possible negative consequences of the order in which these options are pursued (i.e., where CA cannot deviate from prior domestic legal proceedings, companies are well advised to first attempt to resolve double taxation through a MAP and Arbitration and to postpone domestic legal proceedings). If a resolution reached in the scope of a MAP or Arbitration is not accepted by the company, domestic legal proceedings can still be pursued as a fallback scenario.

§16.04 ICAP 2.0

Further to the concerns and developments with respect to dispute resolution, we would like to point out the OECD's Pilot on the ICAP, which focuses on avoiding disputes from materializing (i.e., rather than solving them afterward).

At the OECD's FTA meeting, held in Santiago, Chile in March 2019, FTA members recognized the importance of improving dispute prevention and dispute resolution mechanisms. To that end, FTA members also announced a second pilot of the ICAP 2.0. It is anticipated for the ICAP 2.0 to reduce the resource burden on both multinational enterprises (MNEs) and tax authorities and to reduce the number of disputes requiring resolution through the MAP.

The ICAP 2.0 is a voluntary risk assessment and assurance program designed to facilitate open and co-operative multilateral engagements between participating MNEs and tax authorities in jurisdictions where the MNEs have business activities. Although the ICAP does not provide for hard legal certainty as regards MNEs' direct tax liability in participating countries, it does allow for a certain level of comfort and assurance where participating tax authorities assess an MNE's covered risk in their jurisdictions to be "low."[31]

Main benefits vis-à-vis the first program are that the ICAP 2.0 provides for (i) medium-risk MNEs to participate (i.e., contrary to only "low"-risk MNEs in the first program); (ii) other categories of risk (e.g., hybrid mismatch arrangements, withholding taxes and treaty benefits, etc.) in addition to only transfer pricing and permanent establishment risks that were included in the initial program and (iii), in our view most importantly, "issue resolution" to be included in the risk assessment stage.

The "issue resolution" measure included in the ICAP 2.0 will allow participating tax authorities to work together with an MNE, to identify any changes that are currently needed to allow these authorities to conclude that one or more of the covered risks are low risk (i.e., this allows MNEs to change the present facts and thereby prevent disputes from materializing rather than resolving the negative consequences of the disputes, i.e., double taxation, afterward through the MAP).

31. The first ICAP pilot programme was launched in January 2018 with eight MNEs and FTA member jurisdictions participating. ICAP 2.0 will see ten additional tax administrations participating (and perhaps the same number of MNEs).

§16.05 SUMMARY AND RECOMMENDATIONS

[A] Summary

In this chapter we have discussed the MAP and subsequently Arbitration as means to prevent double taxation. The areas of concern identified and our analysis of the impact of the Directive, BEPS Action 14 and the MLI on these areas of concern are summarized in the overview below:

Area of Concern/Development	*Directive*	*BEPS Action 14*	*MLI*
Access	Predominantly positive	Positive	None
	- Enforceable access and clear procedural rules. - Potentially long start-up phase if access to MAP has to be enforced.	- Increased transparency (Monitoring Mechanism and Framework) creates (political) pressure to review requests on content only.	- MAP provision in line with OECD Model Convention.
Resolution	Predominantly positive	Limitedly positive	Limitedly positive
	- Resolution guarantee through enforceable Arbitration. - Potentially long procedures if access to Arbitration has to be enforced.	- No relevant impact on Arbitration (i.e., only commitment from a limited number of countries). - Increased transparency (Monitoring Mechanism and Framework) is expected to encourage countries to resolve MAPs (in time).	- Mandatory Arbitration and procedural rules, but positive effect may be limited through reservations made by countries that opted in.
Costs and interest-asymmetry	None/Negative	None	None
	- Enforcing MAP access may lead to additional procedures and therefore to additional (interest) costs.		

Area of Concern/Development	*Directive*	*BEPS Action 14*	*MLI*
Tax authority relationship	None	None	None
Blocking effect of domestic legal proceedings	None	None	None

[B] Recommendations

The Directive and the MLI provide for additional mechanisms to resolve double taxation and these new mechanisms allow for some of the areas of concern to be resolved. However, we also conclude that following the recent developments, some areas of concern remain to be obstacles for effective resolution of double taxation. We therefore invite policy makers at the OECD, the CA as well as tax authorities to consider the following suggestions that target remaining areas of concern.

Unilateral adjustments

A judgement in legal proceedings against a (foreign) adjustment can lead to (i) double taxation (partially) being maintained and (ii) access to Arbitration being blocked (i.e., when the CA of the foreign country in the scope of Arbitration cannot deviate from such a judgement). For these situations, policy makers can explore the possibility for the CA to waive the statute of limitations with respect to a request for a unilateral (downward) adjustment (i.e., due to the length of legal procedures, the statute of limitations for unilateral (downward) adjustment will often have lapsed). Naturally, such waiver could be subject to the foreign court ruling being in line with the domestic view in respect to the correction.

Prevention of interest-asymmetry

Transfer pricing disputes generally deal with distribution of "consolidated profit" between the countries involved, rather than the level of "consolidated profit." In these cases, double interest charges (due to tax interest-asymmetry) can be avoided by suspending the calculation of interest on tax in both countries under the condition that the taxpayer contributes into an interest-bearing blocked account the amount of tax on the "consolidated profit" (after deduction of tax already paid). Upon reaching a resolution in the MAP, the countries involved will be entitled to their corresponding part of funds on the blocked account including interest.

ICAP 2.0

Irrespective of the (perceived) benefits of the ICAP 2.0, the level of transparency required from MNEs participating in the program also increases the risk of tax authorities having different views on covered risks (e.g., diverging view on the application of the arm's length principle to transactions involving intangibles). This may very well result in one or more covered risks being identified that the participating tax authorities subsequently fail to resolve within the ICAP 2.0's issue resolution stage. In view of this real risk, we would welcome OECD officials and participating authorities to explore the possibility of accepting a request for MAP at the moment that the participating authorities recognize insurmountably different views on any covered risks identified during the ICAP's risk assessment stage (i.e., at that point in time one may consider that there is a likelihood of double taxation and therefore the possibility for a taxpayer to request the CA to initiate MAP). Participating authorities may also consider to directly allow the dispute to be resolved under Arbitration if they consider it likely that their diverging views will not be resolved during the two-year MAP period.

CHAPTER 17

Concluding Remarks and Observations

Ronald Russo

§17.01 INTRODUCTION

In this book, as well as at the congress, we have looked at the workings of the International Compliance Assurance Programme (ICAP) and Co-operative Compliance. ICAP can in some ways be viewed as a form of international Co-operative Compliance, but with some differences. The most important difference is that only tax risks with an 'international and cross-border' connection are covered, whereas Co-operative Compliance:

(i) usually also applies to tax issues of a purely domestic nature;
(ii) is usually applicable to more taxes than just corporate income tax; and
(iii) covers a broader range of tax related issues.

Practically, however, the main tax risks in an international setting are generally related to transfer prices, both from the perspective of the taxpayer and of the tax authorities. In this respect, the original focus of ICAP on transfer pricing is understandable.

As mentioned in Chapter 1, there are some points that can be seen as characteristic of Co-operative Compliance and the reporters for the various jurisdictions have reported on these points in their respective chapters, if and when applicable. In this final chapter we will look at some of the findings in the reports on these selected topics:

- Working in the present and real-time consulting procedures.
- Possibility of agreeing to disagree.
- Potential requirement of a formal instrument.
- Compulsory Tax Control Framework (TCF).
- Relevance of corporate tax strategies.
- Evaluation of existing (national) Co-operative Compliance schemes.

§17.02 WORKING IN THE PRESENT AND REAL-TIME CONSULTING PROCEDURES

One element of Co-operative Compliance that is usually classed as an advantage by all parties involved is that it focuses on the present rather than the past. This involves the TCF (making sure that the input and the process are correct and therefore the output is acceptable), but also the possibility for company and tax administration to confer on possible differences of opinion before or when they arise. Germany and Austria have (legal) tools for this: *zeitnahe Betriebsprüfungen* (Germany) and *begleitende Kontrolle* (Austria). In other jurisdictions these possibilities are also there, but not always so clearly defined. In Italy the system of *interpello* is applied, but strangely enough outside a Co-operative Compliance framework, with the implication that it could render Co-operative Compliance superfluous. Australia has the Annual Compliance Agreements and pre-lodgment compliance reviews, Spain has its Rule UNE (*see* 13.0.2.B). On the other hand, Japan only has informal (i.e., not formally regulated) advance consultations and administrative circulars. In the Netherlands, the desire to work in the present has been laid down in an administrative regulation, but not in the law.

The image is therefore mixed if looked at from the perspective of technical implementation, but in general, working in the present seems to be an integral part of Co-operative Compliance once it has been implemented.

§17.03 AGREE TO DISAGREE

The possibility of agreeing to disagree seems to be formally possible in all jurisdictions, because the normal rules for litigation are not limited by the Co-operative Compliance programmes. No comprehensive regulations seem to be in place in case a company wants to opt into a programme, but the tax administration does not accept this. The same seems true when a tax administration wants to end a company's participation in a programme against the company's wish. Sometimes an administrative procedure is in place for these situations, but not a formal procedure with the right to take the matter to a (tax) court. In general, tax administrations seem to prefer regulating possible problems in this regard without litigation.

§17.04 FORMAL INSTRUMENT REQUIRED?

Jurisdictions have tackled this issue very differently. Some jurisdictions develop a system of Co-operative Compliance within the existing discretionary powers of the tax administration and need no new legislation, such as the Netherlands and the United Kingdom (UK), where Co-operative Compliance is not legally regulated but based on a tax administration policy (and in the case of the Netherlands formalized in a covenant). In Norway and the United States, there is no formal instrument (such as a covenant) at all, but Co-operative Compliance has taken the form of an administrative programme in which a company can elect to participate. In the UK, no formal instrument is required as all large companies are assessed under the programme. Poland has a legally regulated arrangement that requires an individual agreement, whereas Australia has the system of reportable tax position schedules and streamlined assurance reviews. These examples show that all variations are possible. ICAP has explicitly taken the form of a programme that companies may voluntarily enter, without a formal covenant or other requirement. It will be interesting to see whether, and if so, how this will influence the various jurisdictions.

§17.05 COMPULSORY TCF

In all jurisdictions covered, some form of control of the company's tax position is required as a fundament to the co-operation between the company and the tax administration. Another matter is whether - and if so, to what extent - a tax administration should provide guidance on how to build a TCF. Some jurisdictions do provide some guidance, but usually on a highly abstract level. The new Polish system (effective as of 1 January 2020) seems to be the most far-reaching, with published guidelines, normative requirements regarding the TCF's effectiveness and a mandatory independent audit of the tax function. Such an audit is also mandatory in the Austrian system. It will be interesting to see whether this formal requirement will lead to formal or informal regulations, or some other form of guidance, on this point.

§17.06 TAX STRATEGIES

As with the TCF, the tax strategy of a company is usually relevant for the Co-operative Compliance programmes. In the UK, publication of the strategy is mandatory for large corporates (although this requirement is not formally connected to Co-operative Compliance), but in other jurisdictions the strategies are very relevant as well, sometimes with a direct link to corporate governance regulations (Spain[1] and Canada). In the Netherlands, having a tax strategy was not a requirement for participating in the Horizontal Monitoring scheme on the assumption that the company was transparent in its communications with the tax authorities, but in the current re-development of the national Co-operative Compliance policy the presence of a tax strategy does play an important part.

§17.07 EVALUATION OF EXISTING CO-OPERATIVE COMPLIANCE SCHEMES

Some jurisdictions seem more active than others in evaluating the achievements of their Co-operative Compliance regimes. Notably the UK, Australia, Austria and the Netherlands have reported on such evaluations and these reports are often used to change or refine the applicable regime. As such, these reports can play an important

1. As related in the chapter about Spain (Chapter 13, section §13.03[A] of that contribution), the Board of Directors of a Spanish company must determine a tax strategy and establish a monitoring process.

role, possibly also for other jurisdictions. The impact of the reports would in our opinion be greater if the actual research is performed by an independent party and not the tax administration itself (which is now usually the case).

§17.08 FINAL REMARKS

There are many other aspects that could also be mentioned in this chapter. There is the aspect of the size of the company: usually the programme is just open for large multinational companies, but there is also a tendency to have programmes for smaller companies (e.g., in the Netherlands, Austria and Poland). Another facet is the degree to which a jurisdiction's tax authority communicates transparently about its participation in ICAP: in some jurisdictions there is basically silence on this point (for instance, in Japan, Canada and Australia). These and many other interesting details that are provided in the chapters in this book merit further comparative research.

Index

D

E

M

N

Q

R

S

U

EUCOTAX Series on European Taxation

(1) Peter HJ Essers, Guido JME de Bont & Eric CCM Kemmeren (eds), *The Compatibility of Anti-Abuse Provisions in Tax Treaties with EC Law,* 1998 (ISBN 90-411-9678-1).

(2) Gerard TK Meussen (ed.), *The Principle of Equality in European Taxation,* 1999 (ISBN 90-411-9693-5).

(3) Michael Lang (ed.), *Tax Treaty Interpretation,* 2001 (ISBN 90-411-9857-1).

(4) Pasquale Pistone, *The Impact of Community Law on Tax Treaties: Issues and Solutions,* 2002 (ISBN 90-411-9860-1).

(5) René Offermanns, *The Entrepreneurship Concept in a European Comparative Tax Law Perspective,* 2002 (ISBN 90-411-9887-3).

(6) Michael Lang & Mario Züger, *Settlement of Disputes in Tax Treaty Law,* 2002 (ISBN 90-411-9904-7).

(7) Carlo Pinto, *Tax Competition and EU Law,* 2003 (ISBN 90-411-9913-6).

(8) Michael Lang, Hans-Jörgen Aigner, Ulrich Scheuerle & Markus *Stefaner, CFC Legislation, Tax Treaties and EC Law,* 2004 (ISBN 90-411-2284-2).

(9) Mattias Dahlberg, *Direct Taxation in Relation to the Freedom of Establishment and the Free Movement of Capital,* 2005 (ISBN 90-411-2363-6).

(10) Michael Lang, Judith Herdin & Ines Hofbauer, *WTO and Direct Taxation,* 2005 (ISBN 90-411-2371-7).

(11) Dennis Weber, *Tax Avoidance and the EC Tray Freedoms: A Study of the Limitations under European Law for the Prevention of Tax Avoidance,* 2005 (ISBN 90-411-2402-0).

(12) Félix Alberto Vega Borrego, *Limitations on Benefits Clauses on Double Taxation Conventions,* 2005 (ISBN 90-411-2370-9).

(13) Michael Lang, Josef Schuch & Claus Staringer, *ECJ-Recent Developments in Direct Taxation,* 2006 (ISBN 90-411-2509-4).

(14) Reuven S. Avi-Yonah, James R. Hines Jr. & Michael Lang, *Comparative Fiscal Federalism. Comparing the European Court of Justice and the US Supreme Court's Tax Jurisprudence,* 2007 (ISBN 978-90-411-2552-1).

(15) Christiana HJI Panayi, *Double Taxation, Tax Treaties, Treaty-Shopping and the European Community,* 2007 (ISBN 978-90-411-2658-0).

(16) Dennis Weber, *The Influence of European Law on Direct Taxation: Recent and Future Developments,* 2007 (ISBN 978-90-411-2667-2).

(17) Michael Lang & Pasquale Pistone, *The EU and Third Countries: Direct Taxation,* 2007 (ISBN 978-90-411-2665-8).

(18) Oskar Henkow, *Financial Activities in European VAT: A Theoretical and Legal Research of the European VAT System and Preferred Treatment of Financial Activities,* 2007 (ISBN 978-90-411-2703-7).

(19) Michael Lang (ed.), *Tax Compliance Costs for Companies in an Enlarged European Community,* 2008 (ISBN 978-90-411-2666-5).

(20) Michael Lang (ed.), *Source versus Residence. Problems Arising from the Allocation of Taxing Rights in Tax Treaty Law and Possible Alternatives*, 2008 (ISBN 978-90-411-2763-1).
(21) Ioanna Mitroyanni, *Integration Approaches to Group Taxation in the European Internal Market*, 2008 (ISBN 978-90-411-2779-2).
(22) Rolf Eicke, *Tax Planning with Holding Companies. Repatriation of US Profits from Europe:Concepts, Strategies, Structures*, 2008 (ISBN978-90-411-2794-5).
(23) Peter Essers et al. (ed.), *The Influence of IAS/IFRS on the CCCTB, Tax Accounting, Disclosure and Corporate Law Accounting Concepts: 'A Clash of Cultures'*, 2008 (ISBN 978-90-411-2819-5).
(24) Tonny Schenk-Geers, *International Exchange of Information and the Protection of Taxpayers*, 2009 (ISBN 978-90-411-3142-3).
(25) Raymond Adema, *UCITS and Taxation: Towards Harmonization of the Taxation of UCITS*, 2009 (ISBN 978-90-411-2839-3).
(26) Michael Lang, Jianwen Liu & Gongliang Tang (eds), *Europe–China Tax Treaties*, 2010 (ISBN 978-90-411-3216-1).
(27) Michael Lang, Pasquale Pistone, Josef Schuch & Claus Staringer (eds), *Procedural Rules in Tax Law in the Context of European Union and Domestic Law*, 2010 (ISBN 978-90-411-3376-2).
(28) Sjaak J.J.M. Jansen, *Fiscal Sovereignty of the Member States in an Internal Market: Past and Future*, 2011 (ISBN 978-90-411-3403-5).
(29) Dennis Weber & Bruno da Silva, *From Marks & Spencer to X Holding: The Future of Cross-Border Group Taxation*, 2011 (ISBN 978-90-411-3399-1).
(30) Claus Bohn Jespersen, *Intermediation of Insurance and Financial Services in European VAT*, 2011 (ISBN 978-90-411-3732-6).
(31) Sabine Heidenbauer, *Charity Crossing Borders: The Fundamental Freedoms' Influence on Charity and Donor Taxation in Europe*, 2011 (ISBN 978-90-411-3813-2).
(32) Michael Lang, et al., *The Future of Indirect Taxation: Recent Trends in VAT and GST Systems around the World*, 2012 (ISBN 978-90-411-3797-5).
(33) Harm van den Broek, *Cross-Border Mergers within the EU: Proposals to Remove the Remaining Tax Obstacles*, 2012 (ISBN 978-90-411-3824-8).
(34) Michael Lang, et al. (eds), *Tax Treaty Case Law around the Globe – 2011*, 2012 (ISBN 978-90-411-3876-7).
(35) Dennis Weber (ed.), *CCCTB: Selected Issues*, 2012 (ISBN 978-90-411-3872-9).
(36) Daniël Smit, *EU Freedoms, Non-EU Countries and Company Taxation*, 2012 (ISBN 978-90-411-4041-8).
(37) Rita de la Feria, *VAT Exemptions: Consequences and Design Alternatives*, 2013 (ISBN 978-90-411-3276-5).
(38) Karin Simader, *Withholding Taxes and the Fundamental Freedoms*, 2013 (ISBN 978-90-411-4842-1).
(39) Madeleine Merkx, *Establishments in European VAT*, 2013 (ISBN 978-90-411-4554-3).
(40) Carla De Pietro, *Tax Treaty Override*, 2014 (ISBN 978-90-411-5406-4).

(41) G.K. Fibbe & A.J.A. Stevens (eds), *Hybrid Entities and the EU Direct Tax Directives*, 2015 (ISBN 978-90-411-5942-7).
(42) Gerard Staats, *Personal Pensions in the EU*, 2015 (ISBN 978-90-411-5953-3).
(43) Michael Lang & Ine Lejeune (eds), *VAT/GST in a Global Digital Economy*, 2015 (ISBN 978-90-411-5952-6).
(44) Massimo Basilavecchia, Lorenzo del Federico & Pietro Mastellone (eds), *Tax Implications of Environmental Disasters and Pollution*, 2015 (ISBN 978-90-411-5611-2).
(45) Cristina Trenta, *Rethinking EU VAT for P2P Distribution*, 2015 (ISBN 978-90-411-6137-6).
(46) Marie Lamensch, Edoardo Traversa & Servaas van Thiel (eds), *Value Added Tax and the Digital Economy: The 2015 EU Rules and Broader Issues*, 2016 (ISBN 978-90-411-6612-8).
(47) Raffaele Petruzzi, *Transfer Pricing Aspects of Intra-Group Financing*, 2016 (ISBN 978-90-411-6732-3).
(48) Mario Grandinetti (ed.), *Corporate Tax Base in the Light of the IAS/IFRS and EU Directive 2013/34: A Comparative Approach*, 2016 (ISBN 978-90-411-6745-3).
(49) Bruno da Silva, *The Impact of Tax Treaties and EU Law on Group Taxation Regimes*, 2016 (ISBN 978-90-411-6905-1).
(50) Michael Lang, Alfred Storck & Raffaele Petruzzi (eds), *Transfer Pricing in a Post-BEPS World*, 2016 (ISBN 978-90-411-6710-1).
(51) Marta Papis-Almansa, *Insurance in European VAT: Current and Preferred Treatment in the Light of the New Zealand and Australian GST Systems*, 2017 (ISBN 978-90-411-8360-6).
(52) Wolfgang Speckhahn, *Real Estate Investment Trusts In Europe: Europeanising Tax Regimes*, 2017 (ISBN 978-90-411-8360-6).
(53) Frank J.G. Nellen, *Information Asymmetries in EU VAT*, 2017 (ISBN 978-90-411-8837-3).
(54) Erik Ros, *EU Citizenship and Direct Taxation*, 2017 (ISBN 978-90-411-8584-6).
(55) Werner Haslehner, Georg Kofler & Alexander Rust (eds), *EU Tax Law and Policy in the 21st Century*, 2017 (ISBN 978-90-411-8815-1).
(56) Claudia Sanò, *National Legal Presumptions and European Tax Law*, 2018 (ISBN 978-90-411-6613-5).
(57) Christoph Marchgraber, *Double (Non-)Taxation and EU Law*, 2018 (ISBN 978-90-411-9410-7).
(58) Dennis Weber & Jan van de Streek (eds), *The EU Common Consolidated Corporate Tax Base: Critical Analysis*, 2018 (ISBN 978-90-411-9233-2).
(59) Werner Haslehner (ed.), *Investment Fund Taxation: Domestic Law, EU Law, and Double Taxation Treaties*, 2018 (ISBN 978-90-411-9669-9).
(60) Jérôme Monsenego, *Selectivity in State Aid Law and the Methods for the Allocation of the Corporate Tax Base*, 2018 (ISBN 978-90-411-9413-8).
(61) José Manuel Almudí Cid, Jorge A. Ferreras Gutiérrez & Pablo A. Hernández González-Barreda (eds), *Combating Tax Avoidance in the EU: Harmonization and Cooperation in Direct Taxation*, 2019 (ISBN 978-94-035-0154-3).

(62) Werner Haslehner, Georg Kofler & Alexander Rust (eds), *Time and Tax: Issues in International, EU, and Constitutional Law*, 2019 (ISBN 978-94-035-0354-7).
(63) Nathalie Wittock, *Sales Promotion Techniques and VAT in the EU*, 2019 (ISBN 978-94-035-0861-0).
(64) Carla De Pietro (ed.), *New Perspectives on Fiscal State Aid: Legitimacy and Effectiveness of Fiscal State Aid Control*, 2019 (ISBN 978-94-035-1415-4).
(65) Giorgio Beretta, *European VAT and the Sharing Economy*, 2019 (ISBN 978-94-035-1435-2).
(66) Claudio Cipollini, *Special Tax Zones and EU Law: Theory, Implementations, and Future Challenges*, 2020 (ISBN 978-94-035-1885-5).
(67) Gianluigi Bizioli, Mario Grandinetti, Leopoldo Parada, Giuseppe Vanz & Alessandro Vicini Ronchetti (eds), *Corporate Taxation, Group Debt Funding and Base Erosion: New Perspectives on the EU Anti-Tax Avoidance Directive*, 2020 (ISBN 978-94-035-1170-2).
(68) Ronald Hein & Ronald Russo (eds), *Co-operative Compliance and the OECD's International Compliance Assurance Programme*, 2020 (ISBN 978-94-035-1951-7).

www.ingramcontent.com/pod-product-compliance
Ingram Content Group UK Ltd.
Pitfield, Milton Keynes, MK11 3LW, UK
UKHW020240290926
15470UKWH00002B/655

9 789403 519517